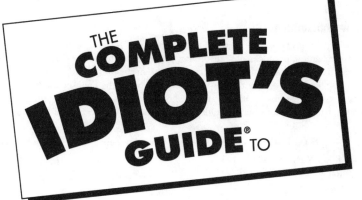

THE COMPLETE **IDIOT'S** GUIDE® TO

MBA Basics

Second Edition

by Tom Gorman

ALPHA

A Pearson Education Company

For marketing and publicity, please call: 317-581-3722

The publisher offers discounts on this book when ordered in quantity for bulk purchases and special sales.

For sales within the United States, please contact: Corporate and Government Sales, 1-800-382-3419 or corpsales@pearsontechgroup.com

Outside the United States, please contact: International Sales, 317-581-3793 or international@pearsontechgroup.com

Publisher: *Marie Butler-Knight*
Product Manager: *Phil Kitchel*
Managing Editor: *Jennifer Chisholm*
Senior Acquisitions Editor: *Renee Wilmeth*
Development Editor: *Jennifer Moore*
Production Editor: *Katherin Bidwell*
Copy Editor: *Amy Borrelli*
Illustrator: *Chris Eliopoulos*
Cover/Book Designer: *Trina Wurst*
Indexer: *Heather McNeill*
Layout/Proofreading: *Mary Hunt, Ayanna Lacey*

Contents at a Glance

Part 1: **Managing People**   1

1 The Meaning of Management   3
Why a business needs managers and how the profession developed.

2 The Seven Skills of Management   13
What managers do and why they do it.

3 The Moving Parts of a Business   27
How the various functions in a company fit together.

4 Leading the Charge   41
How leaders get extraordinary results from ordinary people.

5 The Nuts and Bolts of Managing People and Teams   51
Hiring, firing, improving performance, and heading a team.

Part 2: **Making Decisions About Resources and Operations**   63

6 Essential Economics   65
How the economy—and the business cycle—affect your company.

7 Going by the Numbers: Economic Indicators   81
Growing your business in good times and bad.

8 Getting Down to Business: Operations Management   91
Important guidelines for running any business.

9 Decisions, Decisions: Analytical Tools and Some Statistics   103
Sophisticated decision making made simple.

10 Budget Basics   125
How managers use budgets in making decisions.

Part 3: **Managing Money, Accounting, and Finance**   139

11 Meet Your Balance Sheet   141
Assets, liabilities, owners' equity, and how they work together.

12 Making a Statement: Income and Cash Flow   155
Understanding income statements and cash flow statements.

13 Digging Deeper: Financial Analysis 167
Analyzing the financial statements to see what's going on in your company—or another company.

14 Look at the Books: Accounting Systems 183
Understanding key principles and calculations in accounting.

15 Making Investment Decisions 199
Analyzing business opportunities the professional way.

16 Ups and Downs: The Financial Markets 215
Understanding stocks, bonds, and options.

Part 4: Managing Marketing for Maximum Sales 233

17 Ready, Aim, Sell 235
How marketing and sales create a customer-focused business.

18 Who Are Your Customers, Anyway? 249
Using market research to understand your customers and to target new markets.

19 The Five Ps of Marketing 263
Using product, positioning, price, place, and promotion to create a winning marketing strategy.

20 You Can Understand Advertising
(and That's a Promise!) 275
How to use advertising and public relations to build brands and motivate buyers.

21 Selling to Customers and Keeping Them Happy 287
Managing your sales force and customer service.

22 Product Development: Pioneers at Work 299
How to stay at the forefront of your market with new products that people want.

Part 5: Steering the Business into the Future 309

23 Charting a Course with Strategic Planning 311
How to develop and implement a strategic plan.

24 Information, Please 327
Why information and computers have become crucial, and what to do about it.

25 Mind Your Ps and Qs: Productivity and Quality 343
How your company can deliver more—and better—
products to customers.

26 Growing Oaks from Acorns: Entrepreneurship
and Small-Business Management 361
Managing start-up ventures and small businesses.

27 Doing Well by Doing Good: Business Law and Ethics 375
Understanding—and meeting—the ethical obligations of a
business to society.

Index 391

Contents

Part 1: Managing People   **1**

1 The Meaning of Management   **3**

What Makes a Good Manager? 4

The Professional Manager 5

The Six Business Principles Every Manager Must Know 7

  Value: What Customers Pay For...*8*

  Let's Get Organized...*8*

  Competitive Advantage: The Winner's Edge...............................*9*

  Control Means Never Having to Say You Lost It *10*

  Profitability: You Gotta Have It *10*

  Practicing Ethical Practices..*11*

Remember the Essential Six 12

2 The Seven Skills of Management   **13**

Proper Planning Prevents Poor Performance 14

Goal Setting: Where To? 15

A Professional Decision-Making Process 17

Delegate All You Can 19

Support Your People 22

Communication: Important Beyond Words.............................23

Controlling to Plan 25

3 The Moving Parts of a Business   **27**

Forms of Business Organization 28

The Parts of a Business 30

Finance Controls the Money 30

Accounting Counts the Money...31

Operations Makes What the Company Sells 32

Marketing Sells to Groups 33

Sales Brings in the Money..34

Information Systems Keep Everyone Informed.......................35

Support Functions Do the Rest 36

Above All: The Board of Directors...37

Putting It All Together: The Org Chart 38

4   Leading the Charge   41

Style or Skills? Role or Position? 42

Leadership Skills 43

Lay a Firm Foundation: Building Trust *43*

Think Big: Share a Vision *45*

Over Here: Focus People on the Right Tasks *46*

Who Does What? Creating Accountability *47*

Get This Straight: Maintain Alignment................................*48*

How Am I Doing? Coaching and Mentoring *48*

Leadership Lessons of Life 50

5   The Nuts and Bolts of Managing People and Teams   51

What Does Human Resources Do? 52

Hiring the Right Person for the Job...53

Interviewing Candidates...*54*

Checking References *55*

Extending the Offer *55*

Getting New Employees Oriented...*55*

Dealing With Problem Employees..56

Take Performance Appraisals Seriously *57*

When It's Time to Go: Firing an Employee............................*58*

Take Your Time 59

Team, Team, Teams 59

Pros and Cons of Teams *60*

Managing Teams *61*

Part 2:   Making Decisions About Resources and Operations   63

6   Essential Economics   65

Our National Economy: As Easy as C + I + G............................66

Imports and Exports: Easy Come, Easy Go *67*

Can Exports Move an Economy? *68*

Growth Is Good..69

GDP: It's All Connected 70

What Goes Up, Must Come Down *70*

Tracking the Business Cycle *71*

Booms and Busts...*71*

The Government's Role 73

What Does the Government Want? *73*

The Inflation-Unemployment Trade-Off................................*74*

Economic Policy 75
Fiscal Policy: Taxing and Spending.................................75
Monetary Policy: Money Makes the World Go Round.............76
The Role of the Fed 77
Moving Rates to Get Things Moving 78
Buy! Sell!...79
When the Fed Talks ... .79

7 Going by the Numbers: Economic Indicators   81

What Are the Key Indicators? 82
The Biggest Indicator: Economic Growth Rate 83
Buying Power: Prices and Inflation 84
The Cost of Money: Interest Rates 84
Out of Work: Unemployment...85
Safety and Security: Consumer Confidence 86
Settling Down: Housing Starts and Sales......................86
Shop 'Til You Drop: Retail Sales and New Car Sales 87
More, More, More: Productivity Growth 88
Watching Wall Street: The Stock Market 88
Index of Leading Indicators 89
What to Watch for When You Watch 89

8 Getting Down to Business: Operations Management   91

Managing Your Resources...92
Cost-Benefit Analysis: What's It Worth? 93
What About Social Costs and Benefits? 94
Too Much of a Good Thing: The Law of Diminishing
Returns...95
Counting Costs: Fixed and Variable Costs 97
Size Matters: Economies of Scale 98
Come Together, Go Apart: Centralization and
Decentralization..99
How Much Centralization Is Good? 100
You'll See These Concepts, If You Look 101

9 Decisions, Decisions: Analytical Tools and Some Statistics   103

The Manager's Toolbox..104
Break-Even Analysis 104
Finding the Break-Even Point 105
Crossover Analysis..107

Planning and Scheduling Tools 108
  The Critical Path to Project Management *108*
  Getting the Picture *109*
  Getting PERT *110*
Decision Trees: More Visual Aids 111
Statistics for Business Decisions 113
Frequency Distributions 114
  Displaying Distributions *115*
Measures of Central Tendency 116
  The Mean *117*
  Weighted Average *117*
  The Median *119*
  The Mode *120*
Measures of Variability 120
  The Range *120*
  The Standard Deviation from the Mean *121*
Use as Many as You Can 123

10 Budget Basics   125
What Are Budgets and Why Do You Need Them? 125
Types of Budgets 126
Sales Budgets and Variance Reports 127
  A Sample Sales Budget and Variance Report *127*
  How to Read a Sales Variance Report *128*
  Year-Over-Year Variances *129*
Expense Budgets and Variance Reports 129
  How to Read an Expense Variance Report *130*
Explaining Budget Variances 131
Cost Control 133
  Radical Surgery *134*
Take Credit Management Seriously 135
  The Credit-Approval Process *135*
  When Things Go Wrong, Collections Gets Tough *136*
  Getting Very Serious *136*
Stay on Top of Your Finances 137

Part 3: Managing Money, Accounting, and Finance   139

11 Meet Your Balance Sheet   141
Assets, Liabilities, and Owners' Equity: You Need 'Em All 142
Meet the Balance Sheet 143

A Sample Balance Sheet 144
A Tour of the Assets...146
    Cash *146*
    Marketable Securities...*146*
    Accounts Receivable and Bad Debt *147*
    Inventories *148*
    Property, Plant, and Equipment *148*
    Land *149*
    Prepayments and Deferred Charges *149*
    Intangibles *150*
The Major Liabilities..150
    Accounts Payable *150*
    Notes Payable..*150*
    Accrued Expenses Payable......................................*151*
    Federal Income and Other Taxes Payable *151*
    Current Portion of Long-Term Debt......................*151*
    Long-Term Debt *152*
Owner's Equity 152
    Stock *152*
    Preferred Stock..*153*
    Common Stock *153*
    Additional Paid-in Capital *153*
    Retained Earnings *154*

12 Making a Statement: Income and Cash Flow   155

Introducing the Income Statement............................156
A Tour Through the Income Statement......................157
    Sales *158*
    Cost of Goods Sold *158*
    Gross Income *158*
    Selling, General, and Administrative Expense (SG&A) *159*
    Depreciation Expense *159*
    Operating Income...*159*
    Other Expenses *160*
    Interest Expense *160*
    Other Income *160*
    Income Before Taxes *161*
    Provision for Income Taxes *161*
    Net Income (Loss)..*161*

Get Insights into Income 162
How Are Your Employees Doing? 162
The Cash Flow Statement...163
   Easy Come, Easy Go: Cash Flow...............................*163*
   A Sample Cash Flow Statement *164*
   Getting Reconciled *165*

13   Digging Deeper: Financial Analysis   167

Let's Get Analytical: Financial Ratios 168
Liquidity Ratios 168
   Working Capital *168*
   Current Ratio *169*
   Quick Ratio *170*
   Accounts Receivable Turnover *171*
   Collection Period *172*
   Inventory Turnover *173*
   Days' Sales on Hand *173*
Solvency Ratios 174
   Debt-to-Equity Ratio *174*
   Debt Ratio *175*
   Times Interest Earned *175*
Profitability Ratios...177
   Gross Margin *177*
   Operating Margin *178*
   Net Margin *179*
   Asset Turnover *179*
   Return on Assets..*180*
   Return on Investment...*181*
Keep Your Pencils—and Eyes—Sharp 181

14   Look at the Books: Accounting Systems   183

The Major Ledgers 183
The Double-Entry System 184
   What About the Financial Statements? *186*
   The Accountant's Opinion...*186*
Accounting Treatment of Assets 187
Accounting for Inventory 188
   FIFO and LIFO *189*
   FIFO Effects *190*
   LIFO Effects *190*
   Which Method Should You Use?................................*191*

Accounting for Depreciation 192
   Straight-Line Depreciation...*193*
   Double Declining Balance...*193*
   Sum of the Years' Digits...*195*
   Comparing the Three Methods of Depreciation *195*
   Matching Depreciation to Productive Life.................*196*
Number Games 197

15 Making Investment Decisions   **199**
Time Is Money 199
   A Present Value Table *200*
Major Business Investment Decisions.......................................201
   Investment in Plant and Equipment................................*202*
   Acquisition of a Company *202*
   GIGO, Once Again *203*
Three Ways to Analyze Investments 204
Net Present Value 204
   Calculating NPV *204*
   Seeing the Time Value of Money.......................................*206*
Internal Rate of Return 206
   Figuring the Internal Rate of Return *207*
Payback Period 208
Pick a Rate, but Not Just Any Rate 209
   Using the Opportunity Cost *210*
   Using the Cost of Capital *210*
   What's the Cost of Equity? *212*
   Calculate the Cost of Capital..*212*
   Beyond the Numbers...*213*
The Lease-Versus-Buy Decision...213

16 Ups and Downs: The Financial Markets   **215**
What Are the Financial Markets? 216
   The Players in the Market *216*
   Why Companies Sell—and Investors Buy—Stock *217*
   The Price/Earnings Ratio...*218*
Bulls, Bears, Bubbles, and Crashes 219
Information and the Market 220
Types of Investors and Traders 222
Options: Puts and Calls...223
   Calls *224*
   Puts...*225*

Fundamental Analysis vs. Technical Analysis 226
Corporate Bonds: Big IOUs 227
Commercial Paper 228
Government Securities 228
Other Government Securities 229
How Bond Prices Fluctuate *230*
The Risk/Return Tradeoff..231
Other Financial Markets and Investment Vehicles 231

Part 4: Managing Marketing for Maximum Sales   **233**

17 Ready, Aim, Sell   **235**

Marketing, Sales—What's the Difference?.............................236
Commercial vs. Consumer Sales...237
Marketing Strategy Basics 238
Sales Tactics, Summarized..238
Translating Sales Goals into Marketing Plans 239
Increase Your Prices *239*
Sell More Existing Products to Current Customers *240*
Sell New Products to Current Customers *240*
Sell Existing Products to New Customers *240*
Sell New Products to New Customers *241*
Product Differentiation 242
Improved Performance *242*
Improved Appearance *243*
Improved Image *243*
Marketing Basics 243
Who Drives Your Company? *243*
The Product Adoption Curve *245*
The Product Life Cycle..*246*

18 Who Are Your Customers, Anyway?   **249**

What Is a Market?..249
Divide and Conquer: Market-Segmentation Strategies............250
Why Do Market Research?...251
Who Needs Market Research? 252
The Two Types of Market Research....................................253
Creating a Market-Research Study.....................................253
Define Your Goal *254*
Design the Study *254*

Develop the Questionnaire 256
Do's and Don'ts of Questionnaire Design 258
Fielding the Questionnaire 259
Analysis and Presentation of Results 260
Powerful Presentations Pack a Punch.........................261

19   The Five Ps of Marketing   263

The Marketing Mix Made Easy 264
Product Is Paramount 265
Pricing Problems 267
Pricing Strategies...267
Mix Pricing Strategies 269
Packaging Presents Your Products 270
A Proper Place Produces Profits.................................271
Promotion Boosts Purchases 273
Proper Positioning Prevents Poor Performance 273

20   You Can Understand Advertising (and That's a Promise!)   275

What Is Advertising and What Does It Do? 276
Components of Advertising...277
Ad Messages: Say What? 277
Hot Copy 278
Money: Your Advertising Budget 280
Media: Who's Watching? 281
Consider the Demographics 282
Other Media Characteristics 283
Promotional Tools 284
Public Relations Programs 285

21   Selling to Customers and Keeping Them Happy   287

Types of Sales...288
The Sales Process 288
Prospecting: On the Hunt...289
Problem Solving and Presenting: Show and Ask 290
Persuasion: Overcoming Objections 290
Organizing a Sales Force..292
Sales-Force Size: When Is Bigger Better? 292
Sales-Force Alignment: Three Choices 292
Compensating and Motivating Your Sales Force 294
Supporting a Sales Force 296

Customer Service...297
A Few Words on Sales Training 297

22 Product Development: Pioneers at Work **299**

The Value of Cross-Functional Teams 300
The Product-Development Process 300
Step One: Get a Good Idea...301
   Listen to Your Customers *301*
   Ask Your Salespeople..*301*
   Watch Your Competitors *302*
Step Two: Test the Concept 302
Step Three: Design the Prototype and Product 303
Step Four: Test the Product 304
Step Five: Do a Market Test 304
Step Six: Launch the Product 305
Know When to Stop 305
Extending Your Line 306
What About R&D? 307

Part 5: Steering the Business into the Future **309**

23 Charting a Course with Strategic Planning **311**

What Is Strategic Planning? 312
Define the Company's Goals...312
   Define Your Business Broadly *313*
   How Will You Know You've Arrived?...........................*313*
   Consider the Sales-Growth Strategies *313*
Analyze the Company's Environment...............................313
   Customers and Prospects *314*
   Competitors *314*
   Suppliers *315*
   Regulatory and Social Change *315*
   Economic Trends..*315*
   Add It Up *316*
Consider the Company's Resources 317
   Profitability and Growth *318*
   People Are the Company...*319*
   Productive Capacity *320*
   Other Resources *320*
   Add It Up Again *320*
   What's SWOT?..*322*

Identify Actions 323
Implement the Steps 324
Strategic-Planning Guidelines 325
   Set a Time Frame *325*
   Get Everyone Involved *325*
   Who Needs a Plan? *326*

24   Information, Please   327

Why Information Has Become a Strategic Resource 328
The Intelligence Pyramid 329
Using Information to Gain Competitive Advantage 330
   Financial Information: Where's the Money? *330*
   Marketing Information: What Do Customers Want? *330*
Information Flows 331
Securing Corporate Knowledge 333
Exploiting Corporate Knowledge 335
   Apply Corporate Knowledge to New Products *335*
   Apply Corporate Knowledge to Your Processes *335*
   Use Templates to Stop Reinventing the Wheel *336*
   Leverage Your Information *336*
   Be Your Own Best Competitor *337*
The Role of IS 337
The Promise of E-Commerce 339

25   Mind Your Ps and Qs: Productivity and Quality   343

What Is Productivity? 344
Measuring Productivity 344
   Calculating Worker Productivity *344*
   Calculating Machine Productivity *345*
More, More! Faster, Faster! 345
Boosting Employee Skills and Motivation 346
   Paying for Production *346*
   What's the Motivation? *347*
Improving Equipment 348
Improve the Processes 349
What Is Quality, Anyway? 351
Quality Assurance 351
How to Control Quality 352
Developing Quality Standards 353
   What About Zero Defects? *353*
   What Are Quality Standards? *354*

Applying Quality Standards 354
Creating a Corporate "Culture of Quality" 355
Tools for Quality Control 356
  Supplier Programs *356*
  Quality Circles...*357*
  Control Charts..*357*
  Best Practices and Benchmarking *358*
The Challenge of Global Competition 359

26 Growing Oaks from Acorns: Entrepreneurship and Small Business Management   361

Big Plans 362
  Outline for a Business Plan *362*
  Describe the Business, Products, and Services........................*363*
  Analyze the Market *364*
  Marketing and Sales Strategy *364*
  Introduce the Management Team *365*
  Describe the Operation *365*
  Analyze the Financial Needs and Potential Returns *366*
  Keep It Short and Substantive *366*
Finding Financing 367
Managing Growth 368
  Financing Growth *370*
  The IPO *371*
Buying a Business...371
Corporate Ventures 373
Entrepreneur Away 374

27 Doing Well by Doing Good: Business Law and Ethics   375

Society, Business, and the Law 376
Business Law 376
  Antitrust *377*
  Consumer Protection *377*
  Product Liability *378*
  Bankruptcy *379*
  Business Organization *379*
  Contracts *379*
  Real Estate and Insurance *380*
  Employment..*380*
  Intellectual Property *380*

Securities Regulation *380*
Uniform Commercial Code..*381*
Taxation *382*
Rules and Regulations 382
What Does This Mean to Managers?............................382
About Business Ethics 383
Hot Legal and Ethical Topics 385
Governing the Corporation 387
Act with Integrity..388

Index   **391**

Foreword

A good MBA program changes the way you think. It gives you the foundation you need to make good business decisions. When you combine that knowledge with decisive action, you have the recipe for business success.

The Complete Idiot's Guide to MBA Basics presents the business essentials that you would get from attending an MBA program, but without the tests or high tuition. MBA essentials are included in these pages, but it's still up to you, the reader, to put that information to work in a way that is right for your particular business circumstances. Quite often when I am hired to consult with business people, I apply the MBA-type principles that are presented in this book. You can, too, if you are willing to learn, assimilate, and then apply what you learn.

I use both *The Complete Idiot's Guide to MBA Basics* and my own book, *The Complete Idiot's Guide to Starting Your Own Business*, as textbooks for a series of university level entrepreneurship classes that I teach here in the Chicago area. I find that the business fundamentals presented by Tom Gorman combined with the applied approach of my own book provides students—mostly aspiring entrepreneurs—with what they need to make it in the business world. This book can be your instructor, and your workplace can be your lab. And if you work for a larger company and want a better understanding of its internal operations, this book is a great place to obtain that understanding.

The first edition of *The Complete Idiot's Guide to MBA Basics* did a great job of presenting the financial, economic, operational, and marketing essentials that every business manager should know by heart. This new edition adds practical details to personnel management, the realities and vagaries of financial markets (an essential topic to those seeking funding or working for publicly held companies), and a primer on entrepreneurship, a particularly important subject in today's environment of corporate downsizing and restructuring.

Another aspect of this revised edition that readers will find appealing is the use of case studies to illustrate important points, added material on international and e-business, and the overall special emphasis on ethics as a business necessity. If every business was run using the principles outlined in this book, fewer business managers would find themselves on the short end of a financial audit or ethical inquiry.

Spelling MBA is easy. Thinking like one is a lot tougher. Reshape your business thinking by grabbing a cup of hot coffee, putting on a little Mozart, and reading this book. Tom Gorman has provided the information. It's now up to you to learn it and then put it to good use.

—Ed Paulson

President, Technology and Communications, Inc.

www.edpaulson.com

Author of *The Complete Idiot's Guide to Starting Your Own Business*

Introduction

M-B-A. These three letters spell success in business, and for good reason. Now, in reality, just having a Master of Business Administration degree does not make anyone a master of business administration. That takes years of on-the-job experience. But the course of study that leads to an MBA prepares you extremely well for a business career.

How? By giving you several things that (until now) have been hard to get elsewhere.

First, an MBA gives you the key principles of how to manage a business. A business can be managed either by the "seat of the pants" or professionally, and business school teaches you the professional way. Professional management calls for setting goals that motivate people, allocating resources to activities that move the company toward those goals, monitoring progress, and making any necessary adjustments. These principles, and others taught in an MBA program, usually lead to success.

Second, an MBA gives you exposure (at least classroom exposure) to the departments—the functions—that you'll find in most businesses. These include management and operations, finance and accounting, and sales and marketing. You learn about the roles these functions play in a business and how to get these areas to work together. All of this prepares you to deal effectively with the various people working in a company.

Third, an MBA program gives you sophisticated ways of approaching business problems. It gives you methods, which often involve simple calculations or diagrams, so you can clearly see the parts of the problem, develop potential solutions, choose the best course of action, and present your case to others in a winning way.

Finally, MBAs know the language of business. Like any profession, business has its own lingo and special terms. While at times some MBAs seem to get a kick out of throwing these words around for the heck of it (or to confuse the uninitiated), the fact is that most management, financial, and marketing terms refer to important business concepts. If you understand the words, you understand the concepts. If you understand the concepts, you can apply them in your business.

The Complete Idiot's Guide to MBA Basics, Second Edition, will give you all of these advantages—an overview of business, an understanding of the various functions, a set of analytical tools, and knowledge of the language of business just like an MBA program would.

Well, it's not exactly the same thing. For one thing, this book costs a tiny fraction of the price of even one course at a business school. For another, it cuts right to the core of each item it covers. In the tradition of *The Complete Idiot's Guide* series, this book makes the material clear and applies it to the kinds of situations that you'll run into on the job. It also leaves out what you don't need: the heavy detail that most MBAs either forget or never use.

Why a second edition of *The Complete Idiot's Guide to MBA Basics?* Haven't the subjects covered in an MBA program remained the same over the past several years?

Most have, particularly in areas such as accounting, financial analysis, and marketing. But even those areas needed to be updated given various business developments.

Moreover, MBA programs keep pace with the times. Many B-schools now offer courses in leadership and in entrepreneurship. You'll find new chapters on these topics in the second edition (Chapters 4 and 26, respectively), as well as a new chapter on the financial markets and securities (Chapter 16), new coverage of teams (in Chapter 5), e-commerce and the Internet (in Chapter 24), and managing a business with integrity (in Chapter 27). Also, I've addressed an oversight in the first edition by explaining basic concepts in statistics (in Chapter 9).

This book amounts to a "mini-MBA" and it will prepare you to manage a business of any size, even a start-up.

If you work (or plan to work) for a large company, the knowledge and skills that you'll get from this book will prepare you to compete and succeed. In fact, a management position in a large company typically demands an understanding of these business concepts.

If you manage (or start) a small company, it will run much more smoothly and be far more competitive if you allocate your resources properly; understand budgeting, finance, and accounting; and use sophisticated sales and marketing techniques.

Having earned my MBA over 20 years ago at New York University, I have benefited as a corporate manager, small businessman, and citizen. Most of all, the broad business knowledge, the grounding in finance and marketing, and the decision-making tools I gained in B-school have enabled me to be comfortable and effective in any business situation. That's the major benefit I want you to get from this book.

Here's the approach I'll take:

Part 1, "Managing People," shows you ways of getting things done through other people. It also covers leadership and shows how it differs from management.

Part 2, "Making Decisions About Resources and Operations," covers the workings of both economics and operations and the principles that determine how a country or a company wins or loses the money game. In this part, you will learn about the business cycle of recession and recovery and discover sophisticated decision-making techniques that will help you succeed in any environment.

Part 3, "Managing Money, Accounting, and Finance," takes you into the world of accounting systems and financial statements. Here you will learn how a company keeps track of sales, expenses, and profits, and how it makes budgeting and investment decisions. This part also examines the financial markets and the major securities bought and sold on those markets.

Part 4, "Managing Marketing for Maximum Sales," shows how companies learn about their customers' needs, develop products and services to meet those needs, and use marketing strategy to focus on the customer and outsell the competition.

Part 5, "Steering the Business into the Future," deals with strategic planning, which is the major tool for managing longer-term aspects of the business, and with ways to increase productivity, improve quality, and manage information. This part also covers managers' legal and ethical responsibilities as well as entrepreneurship. It closes with strategies and tips for managing your career in today's environment.

Extras

In addition to the text, throughout the book you'll find the following signposts that highlight information I want to be sure you catch.

MBA Lingo

These sidebars give you definitions of words and business concepts that might not be familiar to you.

MBA Mastery

Read these hints to find out how to boost your—and your company's—performance to higher levels with insider tips and lessons from the current best practices in business.

Case in Point

These boxes provide real-life examples that illustrate and expand on the material.

MBA Alert

Here you'll find examples of how to deal with problems you'll face on the job.

Acknowledgments

Many thanks to everyone who helped to make this book possible: For assistance on the second edition, I'd like to thank Renee Wilmeth, senior acquisitions editor, Kathy Bidwell, production editor, Jennifer Moore, development editor, and Amy Borrelli, copy
editor. My thanks also goes to the original editorial team of Jennifer Perillo, Lynn Northrup, and Kristi Hart. Thanks also to Mike Snell, my agent; Ron Yeaple, technical editor (and author of *The Success Principle*); my wife, Phyllis and my sons, Danny and Matt; my professors and instructors at New York University's Stern School of Business; and all of my past employers, employees, and customers.

Special Thanks to the Technical Reviewer

The Complete Idiot's Guide to MBA Basics, Second Edition, was reviewed by an expert who double-checked the accuracy of what you'll learn here, to help us ensure that this book gives you everything you need to know about the basic contents of an MBA program. Special thanks are extended to Ron Yeaple.

Trademarks

All terms mentioned in this book that are known to be or are suspected of being trademarks or service marks have been appropriately capitalized. Alpha Books and Pearson Education, Inc., cannot attest to the accuracy of this information. Use of a term in this book should not be regarded as affecting the validity of any trademark or service mark.

Part 1

Managing People

Management has been defined as "the art and science of getting things done through other people." Of course, there are other areas of management. These include making decisions about plant and equipment and managing the organization's money and investments.

However, most managers find managing people to be the most challenging aspect of the job. Those who succeed at it understand their role in a business and know a bit about organizational structure. They practice certain managerial and leadership skills and use proven procedures for hiring the right people and guiding them toward their goals.

These areas of management are all covered in Part 1 because most of what a manager gets done, gets done through others.

Chapter 1

The Meaning of Management

In This Chapter

- A (very) brief history of management
- A manager's responsibility and role
- The "Essential Six" principles every manager must know

Imagine an army with no general, a team with no coach, or a nation with no government. How could the army beat the enemy? How could the team win games? How could the nation avoid complete anarchy?

They couldn't. And an organization can't succeed without a manager. Managers make sure that an organization stays, well … organized. Organizing and directing the work of others is the work of the manager. People need organization and direction if they are to work effectively, and managers provide that.

Management is generally defined as the art and science of getting things done through others. This definition emphasizes that a *manager* plans and guides the work of other people. Some (cynical) individuals think that this means managers don't have any work to do themselves. As you'll learn in this book (if you don't already know it), managers have an awful lot of work to do.

Organizing and directing the work of others is known as administration. In a business it is called business administration. (In a hospital, it is called health-care administration. In a government agency, it is called public administration.) Thus, *business administration* means managing a business, and an *MBA—master of business administration—* degree prepares a person to manage a business. In an MBA program, which is a graduate school program, you learn about the structure, parts, and purpose of a business, and about the tools you need in order to manage the business. These tools include budgets and financial statements as well as methods of analyzing business decisions.

This chapter will introduce you to management by touching on the development and role of management and by covering the key principles of managing any business.

MBA Lingo

Management is the art and science of getting things done through others, generally by organizing and directing their activities on the job. A **manager** is therefore someone who defines, plans, guides, assists, and assesses the work of others, usually people for whom the manager is responsible in an organization.

Business administration means organizing and directing the activities of a business. An **MBA**, or master of business administration, degree is a postgraduate degree from a university with a business school (or B-school, for short) that teaches management. Essentially, the program covers the structure and purpose of a business and its various functions, and the tools needed to manage these functions—just as this book does.

What Makes a Good Manager?

As in politics or sports, some people seem more naturally suited to being managers than others. In our society, people often believe that men and women with a certain personality or appearance are best qualified to be managers. However, often it doesn't work that way. Management isn't about personality or appearance. I've known many managers with the so-called right image who were "empty suits."

It takes dedication to avoid being an "empty suit" or someone who enjoys being a manager but shirks the actual work of a manager. And it *is* work. A manager must think ahead several moves; planning is central to good management. A manager must deal skillfully with people, giving positive feedback for solid performance, helping those with performance problems, and, occasionally, terminating those who cannot improve their performance. Managers must keep financial considerations, as well as customer service, front and center because a business exists to make money by serving a customer need.

Nonetheless, despite these "musts" some managers try to avoid stepping up to the real work of managing. Some managers fail to plan realistically, don't develop their interpersonal skills, and lose sight of financial considerations and customer needs. Such managers not only make it tough for their employees, superiors, and customers, they also give all managers a bad name. They give people the idea that a manager is someone "paid to do nothing" or who "watches while we work." Managers who are worthy of the name take their responsibilities and roles seriously.

A manager has an area of responsibility, that is, an activity or a function that he or she is responsible for running. A financial manager is responsible for some area of finance. In sales, an account manager is responsible for a set of accounts. A departmental manager or branch manager is responsible for a specific department or branch.

A manager's role is to run his or her function properly. It may be as large as the entire company, as is the case for the CEO (chief executive officer). It may be as small as the mail room. Whatever the area of responsibility, management represents the sum of a set of tasks. Being a manager comes down to doing these tasks well and consistently. Before we look at these tasks, let's view the role of the manager in historical context.

The Professional Manager

How can "being the boss" be a profession? A profession has its own principles, tasks, and standards, and it requires a course of study. (Think of the traditional professions: medicine, law, engineering, architecture, and accounting.) Does management share any of these characteristics?

The answer is yes, and it has been for most of this century. When factories became large and complex enough to demand skills beyond those of a simple owner-boss, management grew out of economics and engineering to become a distinct discipline.

The need to apply concepts from economics and engineering became apparent as businesses grew beyond relatively small, simple craft operations and farms into larger, more complex operations capable of higher production. Economics enabled managers to analyze ways to drive costs down and produce the most money. Engineering helped managers think of ways to best handle the physical (as opposed to financial) aspects of production. These include decisions regarding the layout of the factory, methods for dividing job functions, and ways to handle and distribute finished products.

The need for professional management arose when larger factories and the new machines of the Industrial Revolution were adopted. A mere "boss" in the sense of someone who basically just told others what do to was not equal to the demands of managing such operations. Therefore, the professional manager stepped up to the task.

MBA Lingo _____

Scientific management applies scientific tools (such as research, analysis, and objectivity) to business to improve productivity. A **time-and-motion study** breaks work down into subtasks to discover how long each task takes. The goal is to understand the job and improve the way it is done in order to improve efficiency.

MBA Lingo _____

An **efficiency expert** is an outdated term for someone who uses scientific management principles to improve business processes. Today this work usually falls to management consultants, who work either as hired independent professionals or as employees within the company (as internal consultants).

In the early 1900s, the professional status of management got a big boost from the concept of *scientific management*. Frederick Taylor was "The Father of Scientific Management." (It's on his gravestone.) Taylor believed that managers could improve the productivity of factory workers if they understood workers' tasks and then properly planned each task for each worker.

"Taylorism," as scientific management came to be called, led to legions of *efficiency experts* doing *time-and-motion studies* in organizations. These studies led to the redesign of factory work. Some experts credit Taylorism with helping the U.S. win the Allied victory in World War II. U.S. factories were able to quickly gear up production of arms, ammunition, vehicles, airplanes, uniforms, equipment, and other materials needed for the war effort, and to establish and maintain high levels of quality while doing so. This was largely thanks to modern management methods, many of which were introduced by Taylor or others who extended his work.

The professional standing of management was enhanced when management associations and business education flourished in the first half of the 1900s. Of course, graduate schools offering MBA degrees also boosted management as a profession.

Today, the quest for better management practices continues with as much intensity as ever—with more intensity than in many eras, in fact. Business now occurs on a more international scale than in the past, so competition is tougher than ever. Customers around the world become more sophisticated and demanding with each passing year. Technology creates (and destroys) companies and even entire industries more quickly than ever. So managers face challenges as great or greater than they did in any other time.

Despite the essential role that managers play in business, you will occasionally hear about companies laying off managers. You may read stories about economic uncertainty, rapid change, and new technological demands making life tough for managers. There is some truth to these stories. However, three facts remain unchanged:

♦ Business will always need managers because no business can manage itself.

♦ Economic and competitive conditions will always present challenges (a business must always do better no matter how well it's doing).

♦ Those who understand the job of the professional manager and dedicate themselves to doing it well will always have a business to manage and will be prepared to deal with the challenges.

Case in Point

Professional management principles made the U.S. auto industry a productivity machine. Ford Motor Company's assembly line, in which a car moves along a conveyor belt so workers can perform individual tasks in a certain sequence, grew directly out of scientific management. By scientifically studying work and identifying each task needed to complete a larger task, such as assembling the motor or body, Ford focused each worker on performing a few tasks as the car traveled along the assembly line. Critics argued that workers lost their sense of craftsmanship by being limited to "tightening bolt number 47." While there's some truth to the charge, the assembly line produced cars so efficiently that it became the standard operating system for most manufacturing industries, as well as the entire auto industry.

The professional manager, like any other professional, understands certain principles, performs certain tasks, and upholds certain standards. These elements are what makes a manager a professional.

The Six Business Principles Every Manager Must Know

The following six concepts are central to business and are the reasons that business needs managers:

♦ Value for customers

♦ Organization

♦ Competitive advantage

♦ Control

♦ Profitability

♦ Ethical practices

I'll describe each concept in more detail over the following pages.

Value: What Customers Pay For

A business exists to create value of some kind. It takes raw materials or activities and increases their value in some way, transforming them into products or services that customers will buy. Value is what customers pay for. Customers buy things that they value.

For example, McDonald's creates value by setting up places where people can eat inexpensively away from home. The company builds restaurants, hires cooks and counterpeople, buys food, and prepares meals. The customers value the convenience of location (you don't have to go home to eat), the speed of service (it's not called "fast food" for nothing), and the tastiness of the meals (most people like hamburgers, chicken, soft drinks, and fries).

A business—and its managers—must create value for customers. This can be done in almost limitless ways because human desires are limitless. But a single business cannot serve limitless desires. Instead, it must create a specific kind of value in a specific way. In other words, management must decide what the business will do, and then organize itself accordingly.

Let's Get Organized

An organization must have goals and the resources (human, material, and financial) to meet those goals. It must keep track of what it does and how well it does it. Each department has to perform its function properly. Employees must be assigned specific tasks that move the outfit toward its goals.

Management is responsible for keeping the company organized. The employees— human resources—and all other resources of the business, such as equipment, floor space, and money, must also be organized.

Managers achieve organization by means of *structure*. The overall structure can be represented in an organization chart like the one you'll see in Chapter 3. But managers have other structures for achieving organization. For example, the company's financial structure organizes the way it handles money. The sales force can be structured into sales teams by geography, by products, or both.

Companies achieve organization in various ways. Some take a highly structured, almost military approach, with strict hierarchies, sharply defined duties, and formal protocol. Other outfits take a more informal approach, which allows people greater leeway and creates a more unstructured environment.

The nature of the business can determine how structured or unstructured a company will be. For example, smaller firms (those with fewer than 50 employees) tend to be less structured than large ones. Companies in heavy manufacturing are usually more structured than those in creative fields, such as advertising or entertainment.

Regardless of how tightly or loosely structured a company is, managers must keep it organized. Even a highly structured company will become disorganized if management fails to manage properly. And even a very loosely structured company will be organized as long as management does its job.

> **MBA Lingo**
>
> **Structure** refers to the way a company or department is organized. A company's structure includes elements such as the corporate hierarchy, the number and kinds of departments, number of locations, and the scope of operations (for example, domestic or international).

Competitive Advantage: The Winner's Edge

To succeed in a particular market, a company must do something better than other companies in that business. Doing something better creates a competitive advantage. That "something" may be only one aspect of the product or service, as long as customers value it highly. For example, a company can gain a competitive advantage by offering the widest selection of products. Or rock-bottom prices. Or high quality. Or great service. But it can't do all of those things.

Managers decide what basis the company will compete on, and they must be quite clear about this. For example, despite advertising claims, no company can really provide both the highest quality and the lowest price, at least not for long. (It can offer the highest quality in a certain price range, but not at the lowest price.) So management must decide whether it wants to compete on quality or on price. Or on service. Or on convenience of location. Then it has to manage the company so that it does compete on that basis by delivering that advantage to customers.

By this, I mean that a company must consistently present a certain advantage to its customers. John's Bargain Stores does not pretend to be Bergdorf Goodman, and vice versa. John's competes on price and pulls in bargain hunters.

> **Case in Point**
>
> In the late 1970s, the Cadillac division of General Motors introduced a relatively low-priced, "sporty" Cadillac called the Cimarron. The product failed miserably. Why? Because it departed from what had always been Cadillac's competitive advantage: big, plush, luxury cars with status-symbol appeal. This is a good example of a company that temporarily forgot the source of its competitive advantage.

Bergdorf's competes on quality and service and attracts customers motivated by those considerations, rather than price concerns. If John's displayed designer clothing and $400 fountain pens, customers would laugh. If Bergdorf's carried no-name clothing and Bic pens, customers would turn up their noses.

Customers who can afford high quality will buy from the high-quality company; those who want low prices will buy from the low-price company. Customers can figure this out. But sometimes managers cannot.

Control Means Never Having to Say You Lost It

After management decides how to create value, organize the business, and establish a competitive advantage, it must control the outfit. This does not mean ruling with an iron fist (although some managers believe it does). Rather, it means that everyone must know the company's goals and be assigned tasks that will move everyone toward those goals.

Controls ensure that the right manager knows what's going on at all times. These controls are based mostly on information. For example, every company needs financial controls. Managers have budgets so they can control their department's spending. They receive regular information about the amount their department has spent and what it was spent on. Financial controls ensure that the company spends what it needs to spend—no more, no less—to do business and meet its goals.

A business is made up of many processes, so "process control" is something you may hear about. A manufacturing process, a hiring process, and a purchasing process all require controls. In these examples, the controls ensure, respectively, that product quality is maintained, that the right people are hired at the right time, and that the right materials are purchased at a reasonable price.

Controls, and the information that supports them, enable managers to manage.

Profitability: You Gotta Have It

A business is set up to make money. As you will see in Part 3, the money a business earns can be measured in various ways. But no matter how it is measured, a business has to make money—earn a profit—on its operations.

If, during a certain period of time, a business takes in more money for its products than it spends making those products, it makes a profit for that period. If not, it has a loss for the period. Losses cannot continue for long or the company will go *bankrupt*.

The most basic goal of management is to make money for the business owners. Regardless of how well they do anything else, managers who lose money for the owners will not keep their jobs for long. Whatever else a business does, its overall goal must be profitability.

Practicing Ethical Practices

In 2002, a series of business scandals came to dominate the news. Senior managers at Arthur Andersen, WorldCom, Adelphia Communications, and Imclone Systems faced criminal charges brought by the U.S. Justice Department. Executives at AOL, Computer Associates, Enron, Global Crossing, and Qwest were under criminal investigation. The charges involved securities fraud, *insider trading* and other illegal transactions, and obstruction of justice as well as improper accounting procedures.

MBA Lingo

A company may go **bankrupt** when it is continually unable to pay its bills for an extended time. After a company declares bankruptcy, it goes through a legal process either to reorganize itself so it can become profitable, or to close down completely.

As a result of these and other cases, investors came to distrust the sales and profit figures that many companies were issuing because of so-called aggressive accounting practices, which are described in Chapter 14.

Today's competitiveness and the drive for profits have been blamed for an upswing in bad behavior in business. However, dishonesty and greed have been around as long as business itself—longer, in fact. Although the vast majority of businesspeople are honest, managers in particular must engage in and tolerate only completely ethical practices.

This is true for three reasons: First, managers, especially senior managers, hold a position of trust as stewards of the company for the stockholders, employees, customers, and community. Second, managers have the most opportunity to enrich themselves at the expense of the stockholders, employees, customers, and community. Third, managers set the standard for the entire company. If they are fudging their numbers, how can they expect honest numbers from their subordinates?

MBA Lingo

Insider trading occurs when a manager, employee, or other person "inside" a company uses information not known to the public to profit from a purchase or sale of the company's stock.

Chapter 27 more fully covers the role of ethics and integrity in business. Yet it is worth noting here that integrity has always been a fundamental principle of business, if for no other reason than the lack of it destroys companies.

Remember the Essential Six

Remember the six concepts summarized in this chapter. Think of them as the "Essential Six" because they underlie everything a manager does. That is, all the activities of management have one collective aim: to make these concepts real for the company and its employees and customers.

The essential six are guiding principles, as opposed to skills. Skills, which you will learn about in the next chapter, enable managers to make sure that these principles are realized at the day-to-day level in the business.

The Least You Need to Know

- Managers must monitor the "Essential Six" business principles: value for customers, organization, competitive advantage, control, profitability, and ethical practices.

- A business—and its managers—must create a specific kind of value for customers.

- Management is responsible for keeping the company organized.

- Managers decide what basis the company will compete on.

- Managers are responsible for control. They must know the company's goals and assign tasks that will move everyone toward those goals.

- The most basic goal of management is to make money for the business owners.

- Managers must hold themselves to the highest ethical standards.

The Seven Skills of Management

In This Chapter

- ◆ The importance of proper planning
- ◆ How to develop your decision-making skills
- ◆ The secrets of effective delegation
- ◆ How to communicate with your employees effectively

Management skills and tasks all have one purpose: to help you get things done through others. Management theories and fads come and go. Most of the theories (and even some of the fads) have something useful to say about management. But the skills and tasks we examine in this chapter have always been, and always will be, essential to managing others. They are how a manager should spend his or her time.

The seven main skills and tasks of management are as follows:

- ◆ Planning
- ◆ Goal setting
- ◆ Decision making

- Delegation
- Support
- Communication
- Controlling to plan

In this chapter, I'll show you how to use each of these skills to get things done.

Proper Planning Prevents Poor Performance

The Five-P Rule—Proper Planning Prevents Poor Performance—represents the starting point in management. A manager must have a plan. The pervasive need for planning underlies the many kinds of plans you'll find in large outfits: strategic plans, financial plans, marketing plans, and production plans, to name a few. (I'll talk about these plans in more detail in later chapters.)

The need for planning is equally important, although more often ignored, at smaller companies. The lack of a plan leads to reactive, seat-of-the-pants management, which you find more often in small firms. We examine business planning (and management) for small companies in Chapter 26.

A plan must be in writing. At times you may hear people say, "I have a plan. It's right here in my head," as they tap their noggin with a forefinger. They don't have a plan. They have an idea. An idea can be in one's head. A plan must be on paper.

Planning incorporates many of the other six managerial tasks discussed later in this chapter. Goal setting and decision making are integral to planning. A plan must consider delegation—who will do what—and, of course, a plan must be communicated to others. Controlling to plan, which is a follow-up to monitor progress, assumes that you have a plan in the first place.

MBA Mastery

Planning is not just for companies and departments. As an individual, you need daily, weekly, monthly, and yearly plans for your success. A long-term study of college graduates revealed that the major determinant of their level of professional success was whether or not they had written plans for themselves.

There are various plans in business, but they all share the goal of creating order and discipline. A plan does this by enabling you to bring the future into the present. This lets you imagine a certain future and then take steps to create that future. Those who dislike planning often cite the unpredictability of the future as the reason for not planning. Yet despite the murkiness of the future (or perhaps because of it), planning—thinking about the future, getting resources in place, making certain moves, and developing *contingency plans*—has proven its worth.

Most plans share these elements:

- ◆ A goal and a measure of the distance from the goal

- ◆ An assessment of the environment

- ◆ An assessment of the company's strengths, weaknesses, opportunities, and threats

- ◆ An assessment of existing and needed resources

- ◆ A series of tasks that will move the company toward the goal

- ◆ A mechanism for measuring progress

MBA Lingo _____

A **contingency plan** is a Plan B or a backup plan you can adopt if Plan A fails or conditions change.

I'll show you these steps in detail in Chapter 23, which concerns strategic planning (that is, planning for the entire company). At this point, you need only understand that planning is essential to progress.

Goal Setting: Where To?

I've always liked the saying, "Ready! Fire! Aim!", which humorously describes so many business situations where things go wrong. You have to have an aim, an objective, or a goal, before you act. Equally important, it has to be the right goal.

Goals can be stated in a variety of ways:

- ◆ *Business goal:* To be the world's largest exporter of automobiles to Canada by the year 2010.

- ◆ *Financial goal:* To increase our net profit to 8 percent of sales next year.

- ◆ *Marketing goal:* To increase our share of the soft-drink market by 1 percentage point in each of the next three years.

- ◆ *Individual goal:* To be head of the marketing department within five years.

Each of the examples above exhibits the three characteristics of a good goal. Each one is

- ◆ Specific

- ◆ Measurable

- ◆ Time-limited

A *specific* goal goes beyond shooting to be "the biggest," "the best," "the highest quality," or some other nice-sounding adjective. It is sharper and expressed more precisely. Even the size-related goal—to be "the largest exporter of autos to Canada"—is specific (and measurable).

A goal must be *measurable* so you can know whether or not you achieved it. Whenever possible, devise goals expressed in numbers; that is, in dollars, percentages, or a numerical increase or decrease. (Some goals cannot be measured numerically but they can still be clear, as in the case of "to be head of the marketing department.")

A *time-limited* goal has a deadline. Personally, I don't consider a goal to be a goal unless it has a deadline. A deadline motivates those who must reach the goal. It creates urgency and energy. Deadlines are also important because most plans specify that certain tasks must be completed by certain dates. These interim deadlines, often called milestones, help you measure progress toward the goal well before the final deadline.

Case in Point

In the 1990s, many companies, including some large, well-established ones, invested heavily in websites without having a real goal. During this time, I heard a vice president at a major company tell his managers, "The CEO says we've got to do something on the web." When one of the managers asked, "What's the goal?" The VP said, "He didn't talk about that."

While establishing a website just to have a "presence" on the web is not necessarily bad, the companies with the most successful websites had specific goals for them. For instance, Fidelity Investments had the goal of creating an online channel that could serve their clients at a lower cost and with greater convenience than the telephone, fax, or mail. FedEx had the goal of giving customers a real-time capability for tracing their letters and parcels. Companies with fuzzier goals often found themselves spending large amounts of money but wound up with sites with little utility or value.

Problems arise once a company launches an endeavor without a well-defined goal. In badly defined web-based projects, companies didn't know which human, technological, and financial resources they needed. Many spent way too much for way too little. They didn't weigh the effect on current and prospective customers, nor did they define measures of success (beyond the number of "hits" or unrealistic revenue projections). As a result, many web-based efforts were declared a failure. But without a clear goal, how could management declare even that with any accuracy?

These three characteristics add up to the one characteristic that any useful goal must have—clarity. The "Ready! Fire! Aim!" approach comes from having a fuzzy goal as often as it does from having no goal.

Goals should be the right size—meaning big enough to inspire people, but small enough to be achievable. Tiny goals won't inspire anyone, but big goals capture the imagination. Big goals create a sense of mission, and a sense of mission creates motivation. Motivation calls forth people's energy and commitment.

Keep in mind, though, that even large goals must be basically achievable or employees will see them as manipulative or just plain silly. A company that sets unattainable goals sets itself up for failure.

MBA Mastery

A manager has to keep his or her people aware of company goals. This means breaking big goals into smaller ones that (1) relate to the employee's day-to-day job, and (2) can be completed in a relatively short time. To motivate your people, give them tasks related to the overall goal and short-term deadlines for completing them.

The right-size goal will depend on your business. For a fast-growing company in a new industry, it might make sense to try to grow sales volume at 25 or even 50 percent a year. For a company in a mature industry, growth at perhaps the rate of the industry's growth plus a few percentage points might make sense. One way to target ambitious goals for sales and profit growth is to pick a solid competitor and try to match or exceed their growth rate.

Be aware, however, that no goal can be permanent. According to *Fortune* magazine, in 2000, when the 1990s technology boom was well into old age, the CEO of Cisco Systems was still projecting 50 percent annual growth in sales. He held to this goal even as customers were going bankrupt and suppliers were forecasting lower demand. When the economy or the business environment changes, goals must often change to reflect new realities.

A Professional Decision-Making Process

You've probably heard managers referred to as "decision makers." A good manager is exactly that. There are, however, managers who dislike decision making, which is sad since it's a key part of their job.

Most managers who "pass the buck" are afraid of being wrong. They see any mistake as major failure. Usually they either lack confidence (or backbone, if you prefer), or they work for superiors who can't tolerate failure.

However, some people simply don't know how to go about making a good decision. They lack a framework for decision making. So here is a six-step process for making business decisions (and personal ones, for that matter) in a rational way:

1. *Define the problem.* Most decisions relate to a problem or can be framed as a problem. This means that making the right decision depends on first defining the problem correctly. If your sales are falling, the problem could be low quality, high prices, poor performance by the sales force, or new competition. Each problem would call for a different solution. So start by asking: "What's the problem?" Answering that question may require exploration.

2. *Gather information.* Good business decisions are based on good information. Once you define the problem, gather all relevant facts. This often requires research, such as studying competitors, talking with suppliers, searching an electronic database, or hiring a consultant to dig up facts. However you go about it, get the facts.

3. *Analyze the information.* Having information is not enough, because different people can draw different conclusions from the same facts. Therefore, you may need to apply analytical tools to the facts. These tools, formal ways of analyzing information, often involve making calculations or setting up charts showing the connections between facts. You may even have a *decision-support system.* However you go about it, analysis helps you understand the facts and what they mean. (You will learn about ways of analyzing information in Part 2.)

MBA Lingo _____

A **decision-support system** is a formal means of helping people make decisions. Usually these systems, which are often computerized, help in the analysis phase of the process. A decision-support system may consist of guidelines in a policy manual (for example, for employee discipline cases) or checklists (such as the ones bank employees use when making lending decisions) or computerized models that help forecast future business conditions. As the name indicates, these systems support, rather than replace, the decision maker.

---

4. *Develop options.* When you have a decision to make, you need to have choices. For example, to increase sales in the face of new competition, you could improve quality or cut prices. You could hire more salespeople or pay your current salespeople differently. Options like these give you a basis of comparison—and a choice. With options to choose from, you have a better chance of finding a real solution instead of doing what seemed like a good idea at the time. There may be instances in which you have only one option, but they should be rare if you openly consider all possible solutions.

5. *Choose and use the best option.* Now comes the moment of truth. You must decide. If you followed the first four steps, you will probably make a good decision. But be sure that you do make a decision. Avoid "analysis paralysis"—that is, analyzing a problem forever instead of acting. Decision makers make decisions.

6. *Monitor the outcome.* You usually cannot just make a decision and then forget about it (much as you might like to). Generally, the only way to know whether your decision solved the problem is to follow up afterward. If your solution worked, great. If not, you may need to take corrective action, try another option, or even reexamine the problem to make sure you defined it correctly, got all the facts, and analyzed them properly.

MBA Mastery

If you like to decide based on feelings rather than facts, this decision-making process will be especially useful for you. Look at the six steps as a supplement or an alternative to going with your gut. Either way, use it. Business-people value facts. They like dealing with people who are comfortable with facts. This process will help you to avoid a reputation for being in denial or shooting from the hip. What's more, it generally yields better decisions.

With experience, this six-step process can become second nature. For small decisions you need not launch a major fact-finding effort. You may need to make one phone call. Nor will you always need a long list of options. Two may be enough. But even when you're making day-to-day decisions in a fast-paced environment, this process will help you. And major decisions always require information, analysis, and clear thinking about options.

In various forms, this framework for decision making has stood the test of time. The process promotes rational business decisions that can be explained to others. (Meaning that even if you mess up, you'll at least be able to tell your boss what you were thinking at the time.)

Delegate All You Can

Delegation is the act of assigning tasks to subordinates for them to perform. This is actually how a manager gets things done through others. The assignment may be verbal or written, long- or short-term, phrased as a request (usually) or as an order (less often). Assigning tasks to others and ensuring that they perform them properly is essential to any manager's job.

Effective delegation goes well beyond merely telling people what to do. Good delegation calls for knowledge of the underlying principles: responsibility, accountability, and authority.

Responsibility means that every manager and employee has a specific function or activity to perform as their job. This is called their *area of responsibility*. The CEO is ultimately responsible for the entire company. He or she has a *big* area of responsibility. But the CEO delegates the actual work to everyone else in the company through the *chain of command*.

> **MBA Lingo**
>
> An **area of responsibility** refers to the scope of someone's job. This generally includes a set of functions (such as matters relating to finance or marketing), tasks (such as preparing budgets or advertising programs), goals (such as accuracy and timeliness or increased sales), and subordinates, if people report to you.

The principle of responsibility implies that a manager must respect the chain of command by delegating work only to people in his or her area and by not going over the head of the manager above or below him or her.

Accountability ensures that everyone in the organization answers to someone else. Everyone is held accountable for performing his or her responsibilities. The CEO is accountable to the board of directors (who represent the owners of the business) and everyone else in the organization reports, directly or indirectly, to the CEO.

> **MBA Lingo**
>
> The **chain of command** refers to the system by which directives come from above and are transmitted downward in an orderly manner through layers of management. **Delegation** means passing responsibility for performing a task along to a subordinate, that is, to someone who reports to you, the manager.

Authority means that someone has been empowered to do a job. If you have a budget, you have budgetary authority. If you can hire someone, you have hiring authority.

Essentially your *responsibility* is what you usually think of as your job. You are held accountable for doing your job by the manager above you. The organization, through the manager above you, gives you the authority necessary to do your job.

Ignoring these principles causes real trouble …

♦ When managers ignore the chain of command. When Bob, who manages Sue, goes over Sue's head and tells Leo, who reports to Sue, what do to, Bob undermines Sue's authority.

♦ When a manager holds a subordinate accountable for completing a task without extending the authority necessary to complete it, that subordinate has been placed in an untenable position. For instance, if Mary holds Jim accountable for expenses on a project when she did not give him authority over spending, she's treating Jim unfairly.

MBA Lingo

Responsibility refers to the work that a member of an organization is supposed to do and the standards for that work to be considered properly accomplished. **Authority** is the power to do something. The company gives the president of the company the power to run the organization, and he or she shares out that power to other managers lower in the organization. **Accountability** refers to the fact that people with certain responsibilities are held to account for performing them. Their superior will make certain that these responsibilities are properly handled.

◆ When someone is given two managers to report to, when someone is not given clear job responsibilities, or when a manager leaves the company and no one tells his or her people who they now report to, the outfit can't run properly.

Sadly, anyone who has been in business for several years has seen most of these things occur. Good delegation—orderly, sensible, consistent delegation—requires effort.

Everyone should have clear job responsibilities, be held accountable for them, and have enough authority to carry them out. Everyone should report to one, and only one, superior. Everyone should understand and respect the chain of command. When someone in the chain leaves, people should be informed about what happens next.

Here are proven guidelines for effective delegation:

◆ Carefully consider the task and its deadline and importance. Weigh the employee's strengths and weaknesses. Try to give your people a mix of assignments so they can capitalize on their strengths and overcome their weaknesses.

◆ When you give someone an assignment, be very clear about the results you expect and when you expect them. Clarify the assignment in a memo. If you give the assignment verbally, be sure to double-check that the employee understands your expectations.

MBA Mastery

Effective delegation comes naturally to very few managers. It is a skill most of us must learn. As with most of the skills in this chapter, you can learn a lot by watching good role models. Delegating is easily observed. When you find people who are good at it, watch closely. Imitate them. Ask them for pointers.

◆ To the extent possible, let the person who is doing the work decide how to do it.

◆ Understand that even though someone may not do a job exactly as you would, it can still be done to a high standard. If the work is not up to your standards, have the employee do it correctly rather than correct it for him. That way he'll learn your standards.

◆ Delegate all of the responsibilities that you can and delegate them to the lowest level of employee who can accomplish them. Don't withhold responsibility *or* authority from your people.

◆ Understand that you are delegating the work and the authority needed to get it done, but you cannot actually delegate your accountability. If something goes wrong, you as the manager of that area are ultimately accountable. Blaming your subordinates is extremely bad form.

Support Your People

A manager's work doesn't end with effective delegation. In fact, the toughest work lies ahead. A big part of getting things done through others is supporting those others.

Why is support necessary? What kind works best?

MBA Alert

Ignoring employee complaints can create financial and legal exposure for your firm. A manager I know ignored complaints from a worker, who claimed she had wrist problems from doing a heavy amount of word processing. The outfit wound up paying for the woman's wrist surgery and time off, plus compensatory damages to keep her from pursuing the matter in court.

Employees need support because barriers usually stand between them and the desired result. These barriers exist inside the company in the form of bureaucracy and limited resources, and outside the company in the form of competition and customer resistance.

Employees also need support because they're human. They need correction, pointers, encouragement, and humor, particularly when the going gets tough; for example, on a big push to meet a tight deadline or during a series of layoffs.

The best way to support your employees is to remove barriers to their success, help them improve their performance, and treat them fairly. Here are some ways to do these things:

◆ Be an effective advocate for your employees with your superiors and the rest of the company. Lobby for their interests. Be loyal to them. Try as hard as you can to get them the resources—the equipment, staffing, money, and time—they need to do their jobs well.

♦ Take your employees' concerns and complaints seriously. The "stop whining" approach will get you only so far, and it can backfire horribly when employees have legitimate concerns.

♦ If your employees need correction, do it in private. When they deserve praise, give it in public.

♦ Keep your employees aware of how their efforts support the company's goals and benefit the entire outfit.

♦ Help your employees develop and advance. Most people want increased responsibilities, advancement, and a chance to gain new skills. I've found this to be true even of employees who pretend otherwise. Give everyone ample opportunity to prove themselves—and allow for failures now and then.

♦ Don't play favorites. This should go without saying, but you are human and you are going to like some employees more than others. If you don't treat people with equal fairness, you will create serious morale problems.

Supporting your employees involves leadership, which is covered in Chapter 4. Leadership and support are the opposite of what I call "wave-of-the-wand" management, which I've seen some managers try. They act as if they can merely assign a job and it will magically get done. Often these managers seem shocked or upset when it doesn't work out that way.

Think of management as a contact sport, which brings us to the next task.

Communication: Important Beyond Words

Communication skills consistently top the list of desired qualities in a manager. This includes written and oral communication. Business demands that you communicate clearly, accurately, honestly, and persuasively. Several techniques encourage effective communication in business. (Here, I'm going to focus on oral communication. See my previous book, *The Complete Idiot's Almanac of Business Letters and Memos* for more information on written communication.)

Listening skills are the starting point in good communication. So few people are used to someone who actually listens to them, with full attention and without interrupting, that the technique can be downright disarming. It's tempting, even natural, to use the time when someone is talking to think about your response or whether you agree.

Instead, try to listen with the goal of understanding the other person. Over time, that understanding forms a bond between two people. Not listening undermines that bond. People know whether or not someone is really listening to them. (You do, don't you?)

Whether you are talking or listening, be aware that the message sent may not be the one received. That's because each of us has his or her own *frame of reference* through which we filter what we say and hear.

MBA Lingo _____

A person's **frame of reference** is the set of facts, ideas, and concerns that make up that person's viewpoint. For example, the word *charge* means different things to a foot soldier, a retail clerk, and a defense attorney, due to their different frames of reference.

In American culture, businesspeople generally get the best results by speaking directly, rather than indirectly, and in concrete, rather than abstract, language. That way your message has the best chance of fitting your listener's frame of reference. In some other cultures, however, people tend to be less direct and less informal than in the United States. Being too direct or informal on the job can alienate people. With business becoming more international with each passing year, every manager must be acutely aware of cultural differences and to allow for them when communicating.

However, it pays to be precise when managing others so that they know what you expect. Here are some examples of both vague and precise language for some common business situations. The statements are from a manager to a subordinate, and in general the more precise ones will get better results.

Too Vague	More Precise
"I'd like you to complete this project quickly."	"I'd like you to complete this project by noon this Friday."
"Please get in touch with somebody about that."	"Please call Jim in Marketing about those missing pages."
"I can't talk now. Please catch me later."	"I'm sorry I'm too busy to talk now. Please call back after four, or tomorrow morning."
"You've been arriving late to meetings a lot recently."	"I've noticed that you arrived late to our last three staff meetings. Is anything wrong?"
"I believe your performance is dropping off."	"Your analysis of our markets left out some key points, and you seemed poorly prepared for last Tuesday's meeting."
"You've been doing good work lately."	"Thanks for your good work on the Acme project and for staying late last Monday."

Much of the on-the-job communication between managers and subordinates aims to guide and assist the subordinate in getting his or her tasks accomplished on time and up to standards. Vague, imprecise language leaves room for misunderstanding regarding what is expected and when it is expected. However, being a manager and speaking precisely does not mean that you should issue orders or "boss people around." The best communicators view their subordinates and, for that matter, their superiors, as colleagues focused on the same thing: getting the job done well.

Finally, be sure to share information with your employees to the greatest extent possible. Most employees resent it when they're not "in the loop." While you cannot usually tell every employee everything you know and cannot compromise others' privacy, you should keep your people informed about anything that directly affects them.

Don't practice "mushroom management," which says, "keep them in the dark and feed them fertilizer."

MBA Mastery

Cultivate an objective attitude toward people on the job. Think of them as you would fellow players on a team. The key is to work well together on your common goals. If you become friends, great. But it's more important to respect one another and work well together. Of course, truly thorny performance problems do arise. I discuss ways to address them in Chapter 5.

Controlling to Plan

There's a wonderful saying in business: "Plan your work and work your plan." In other words, have a plan and use it. This is more formally known as controlling to plan, which means managing your resources—your people, time, equipment, and money—as planned in order to reach the goal. A good plan will help you every step of the way toward a goal.

A plan is not a document to write and then throw into your drawer and forget. It's a road map, to be consulted as you move forward. Sometimes you'll need to change what you're doing or speed things up in order to keep to the plan. Other times you may find that the plan, rather than your activities, needs to be adjusted. That's fine. But to adjust your plan, you have to have a plan—and refer to it regularly.

Over time, success in business, as in any endeavor, comes from diligent, daily execution of the basics. In management "the basics" are the six managerial tasks of planning, goal setting, decision making, delegating, supporting, communicating, and controlling to plan. Master these, and you will be a master of business administration.

The Least You Need to Know

- ◆ Management begins with planning and goal setting, and ends with controlling to plan. You must have a goal and a plan for reaching it, and use the plan to move toward the goal.

- ◆ Try to use a process for decision making, rather than operating by the seat of your pants. Start by defining the problem, then gather related facts, analyze them properly, develop alternative courses of action, and choose the best one. Then follow up to see if it was the best choice.

- ◆ Good delegation is the only way to get things done through others. Pick the right person for a task, then let them do the job. Delegate all that you can and delegate it to the lowest level at which it will be properly done.

- ◆ Support your employees in the organization and remove barriers to their success.

Chapter 3

The Moving Parts of a Business

In This Chapter

- The major departments of a business
- How finance and accounting control and track money
- How marketing and sales sell products and services
- The role of management information systems
- How support functions serve the rest of the business
- Understanding the org chart and company hierarchy

What is the purpose of a business? Stated in the most basic possible way, a business sells a product (anything from widgets to pizza pies to automobiles) or delivers a service (sending packages, making loans, or catering parties) and—if things are working properly—makes a profit. All businesses use some combination of labor, equipment, and materials to produce products or services.

A business of any substantial size has to be divided into departments, each with its own job to do. For example, one department may oversee the company finances, another may handle marketing, and still another may handle sales. The job of the manager is to run his or her department so that it makes its contribution to the entire company. This chapter will introduce you to the different parts of a business and the role managers play in running them. In this chapter, you'll also examine the basic forms in which a business can be organized.

Note that in this chapter I will be dealing with businesses large enough to warrant having different functions and departments. This includes many small businesses, some with as few as 10 or 20 employees right up to those with 50 to 100 (still considered small businesses by most banks and larger companies), and on up to giant enterprises.

Forms of Business Organization

A business may be organized in four basic ways: proprietorship, partnership, corporation, or limited liability company.

A proprietorship (also known as a sole proprietorship) is a business owned by an individual. That person, the proprietor, has the right to the profits generated by the business and is personally responsible for its debts. Most small businesses are organized as proprietorships, and any self-employed individual is essentially a proprietor. Although there is no legal limit on how large a proprietorship may become, most large businesses are organized as partnerships or corporations, so that multiple owners have a share in the profits. A proprietorship cannot use the designation "company" or "incorporated" in its name; only a corporation can use those terms.

A partnership is a business owned by two or more individuals, who enter into a formal agreement to contribute their funds and other resources to the business and to share its profits. A limited partner (sometimes called a "silent partner") contributes money to the business, but does not make management decisions or participate actively in the business. A general partner contributes money, makes management decisions, and participates actively in the business. Many consulting firms and most professionals services firms, including large accounting, law, and architectural firms, are organized as partnerships.

General partners are personally liable for the financial obligations of the business. However, the liability of limited partners is limited to the amount of their investment (hence the name limited partner). Also, a decision or action by a general partner binds all of the partners to that decision or action.

A corporation is a legal structure in which the owners are not personally liable for the financial obligations of the business. They can lose only the money they invest in the corporation. That investment occurs when they contribute money to fund the start-up of the business or, later, when they buy stock in the company. A share of stock represents a share in the ownership of the company.

Although the owners are not personally liable for its obligations, a corporation is often referred to as a "legal person." This means that the corporation has some of the characteristics of a person. For instance, it can own property, initiate lawsuits, and be the object of lawsuits.

A corporation is usually chartered by a state and can raise capital in the public financial markets (as discussed in Chapter 16). It is the only form of business permitted to use the terms *Inc.*, *Incorporated*, or *Company* to identify itself. (However, in everyday discussions, *company* can refer to any sizable business.) Although most people think of large, publicly held companies when they hear the term, a corporation need not be large. In fact, many privately held corporations are as small or smaller than a proprietorship or partnership.

Limited liability for the owners and access to the financial markets are two major advantages of the corporate form of organization. Two others are that an owner can sell part or all of his or her stake in the business simply by selling his or her stock, and that the business exists apart from the owners and thus can easily be passed on to future owners.

A limited liability company (not corporation) is a relatively new form of business organization that's becoming quite popular. A limited liability company, or LLC, provides some of the benefits of both partnerships and corporations. As in a partnership, the company pays no tax itself. Instead, the earnings flow through to the owners, who are taxed at their personal tax rates. This does away with the "double taxation" that occurs when a corporation pays its income tax and then the owners pay personal income taxes when the earnings are distributed to them as dividends. (Dividends are discussed in Part 3.)

Owners of an LLC are granted the limited liability that owners of a corporation enjoy. LLC owners are not personally responsible for the debts of the company, nor are they liable for debts arising from law suits. In addition, an LLC is much easier to administer because there are no requirements to hold quarterly meetings of the owners and to keep minutes of the meetings, as there are for corporations.

MBA Mastery

In a publicly held corporation, shares of stock are sold to and owned by investors in the general public rather than only by the managers of the company and people they know. In a privately held—also known as closely held—corporation, the stock is owned by the managers of the company or people they know and is not offered for sale to the general public.

LLCs have been permitted in all 50 states since 1988, and a federal law authorizing them is in the works. Although the state laws vary, essentially they all allow the owners—who are called members, rather than partners or shareholders—to agree among themselves on how the company will be operated. That contract will then be upheld in court.

Note that an LLC cannot issue stock or bonds in the public markets. They can raise money from private investors and lenders and, because of the limited liability, they can do so more easily than proprietorships and partnerships. Many professional services firms have chosen to organize (or reorganize) themselves as LLCs during the past 10 years.

Most of the discussion of the parts of a business in this chapter refers to corporations. However, a business organized in any of these four ways will have most of these functions in some form or other.

The Parts of a Business

Numerous activities must take place for a company to successfully create, sell, and profit from its products or services, and each activity is handled by a specific department. Each department has to be well managed for the company to succeed.

Let's take a closer look at each of the departments most large companies have and what they do.

Finance Controls the Money

A business generates a flow of money. Money flows into, out of, and through each department in the company. The *finance department* (or, more simply, finance) makes sure that the company has the money it needs in order to operate. This includes the money to buy or lease property (such as office space) and equipment, purchase raw materials, and pay employees. Finance also ensures that the company continually has good investment opportunities and the money to pursue them.

Finance helps the other departments in the company prepare their *budgets* and consolidates them into one company budget. Finance works with senior management to set the company's sales and profit goals for the following year and designs controls to keep the firm's finances in order.

> **MBA Lingo**
>
> The **finance department** is responsible for controlling the funds that come into and go out of a company. The tools for control include financial and investment plans, sales and expense budgets, records supplied by the accounting department, and procedures regarding who can sign and cash checks for the company.

In a large company, finance includes the treasury function, which manages the company's cash and deals with banks. Many of the people in finance and the treasury are financial analysts, professionals who deal in budgets and investments and generate financial reports for the managers of other departments.

MBA Lingo

A **budget** is a set of estimates for sales or expenses, or both, for a specific period of time. These estimates represent limits or targets, and are thus key financial controls. In most businesses, every department has its own budget. Within those departments, individual projects may have budgets. One of a manager's main responsibilities is *making budget*, that is, hitting his or her sales targets or keeping expenditures for his or her department or project within budget.

Accounting Counts the Money

The *accounting* department works closely with finance, mainly by tracking the flow of money the company generates. For example, within accounting you'll find an *accounts receivable* department that tracks the money that the company is owed and paid. *Accounts payable* tracks expenditures and authorizes checks to be cut so the company can pay its bills to suppliers. The *payroll* department ensures that employees get paid.

MBA Lingo

The **accounting** department keeps the company's financial records by tracking sales, expenses, and receipts and disbursements of cash. Accounting also calculates the taxes that the company owes. The **accounts receivable** department tracks money that is owed to the company for sales made on credit. The **accounts payable** department makes sure that the company pays its bills to suppliers. The **payroll** department tracks employee wages and salaries.

Accounting also usually includes the *credit department*, which decides how much *credit* (also called trade credit) the company will extend to a customer. If you've ever groaned over a Visa bill, you are already familiar with the concept of credit. Customers (which may include other companies) with good payment records can buy thousands or even hundreds of thousands of dollars worth of goods on credit, meaning they are given an extended amount of time in which to pay the bill. This is done in

MBA Lingo

A company may extend **credit** (or trade credit) to a customer with a good payment record, which allows the customer a certain extended period of time—usually 30 days—to pay the bill. Customers who are denied credit usually must pay **COD** (cash on delivery). Credit decisions are made by the company's **credit department.**

most businesses that sell expensive goods (say, pricey automobiles) or services (extensive consulting work) because it makes it easy for customers to buy, and thus easier for the company to make sales.

Customers or companies that do not have good payment records must buy *COD*, meaning cash on delivery.

Finally, accounting includes the *tax department*, which calculates the company's taxes and manages the timing of its federal, state, local, and foreign tax payments.

The accounting department is staffed mainly by accountants, logically enough. Accountants are trained in accounting practices and accounting and tax law. Since the practices and regulations are complex and change often, and because substantial amounts of money are at stake, these professionals spend a lot of time keeping up-to-date on practices and regulations. In most accounting departments, accountants are dedicated to a certain area, such as accounts receivable, accounts payable, tax, and so on, and can move among these jobs to enrich their careers. Finally, a company's accountants work with any outside accounting firms that the company uses. (I talk about the accounting function in more detail in Part 3.)

Operations Makes What the Company Sells

In a *manufacturing company* (one that produces goods, such as widgets, rather than one that sells services, such as loans), *operations* includes the factory where the company makes its products. It also includes departments such as shipping and receiving, where the company ships products to its customers and receives materials from its suppliers. The purchasing department buys the company's materials and supplies. Operations is often called the production function.

MBA Lingo

In a very large company, the **tax department** calculates the company's federal, state, and local taxes, as well as taxes on any foreign operations, and works to find ways of minimizing the company's taxes.

In a *service organization* (one that sells services, such as a bank or a brokerage firm), operations includes the employees who serve the customers and the places where they work. For example, in a bank, operations would include the branch locations.

Operations also includes back-office functions in a service organization—that is, activities that the customers don't see but that relate to customer transactions. Let's take the bank example again. You may have no idea what happens when you write someone a check. In fact, once the bank gets it, that check travels through a series of steps before it is eventually deposited into someone else's account and deducted from yours. Those check-processing functions would be an example of a back-office function.

The managers and employees in operations are directly responsible for employee productivity (how many widgets an employee can make in an hour), cost control (how much it costs to assemble a widget), and quality (assuring the correct form and function of the finished widget).

In most companies, people who work in operations are those who do what most of us think of as the actual work of the company. In a manufacturing out-fit, they are the production workers and their managers. In a service firm, they usually work directly with customers to deliver the service. Most people in operations are hourly employees as opposed to salaried managers.

MBA Lingo

A **manufacturing company** produces a product from raw materials or parts and components made by another manufacturer, or both, and sells it. A **service organization** delivers a service such as meals (restaurants), insurance and banking services (financial services), haircuts or massages (personal services), transportation (bus lines and trucking companies), or hotel accommodations (hospitality services), among many others. In any company, the term **operations** refers to the area that actually creates and delivers the product or service.

Marketing Sells to Groups

It's useful to think of marketing as selling to groups of people or businesses (as opposed to selling, which is done one-on-one). The *marketing department* works to get the story of the company's products and services out to customers and potential customers, known as *prospects*. Marketing does this through advertising, promotions, direct mail, special events, and other ways of creating awareness (I'll cover these terms in more detail in Part 4). Marketing's key job is to help the salespeople sell.

MBA Lingo

The **marketing department** prepares strategies, plans, programs, and messages that get the word of a company's products and services—and the benefits they deliver—out to customers and potential customers. **Prospects** are potential customers of a company.

MBA Lingo

Market research conducts surveys among a company's customers and prospects to learn about their attitudes and buying behavior. **Product development** conceives, plans, designs, and develops new products and services for the company to sell. In firms that sell complex products, such as chemicals or medical instruments, R&D has scientists and engineers who work on new products.

The marketing function often includes *market research*, which studies customers and prospects to learn about their needs, motivations, and buying behavior (for example, the age and educational level of the average widget buyer). Marketing can also include *product development*, which devises new ways of serving customer needs (for example, a faster, more powerful widget), and public relations (or corporate communications), which prepares written material on the company and its products.

People in marketing either are specialists in a certain area within marketing or are marketing generalists. Specialists tend to work in market research, product development, public relations, direct mail, telemarketing, or writing product literature or other company literature. Specialists typically work for large companies with large marketing departments. Generalists tend to do a bit of everything (but usually not with the sophistication of a specialist in the area) and can work for either large or small companies.

Case in Point

Some companies are famous for a specific functional area that performs particularly well. Proctor & Gamble, the largest advertiser in the United States and the maker of Tide detergent, Crisco shortening, Comet cleanser, and Zest soap, is legendary for its marketing capabilities. Southwest Airlines and Disney have reputations for operations that deliver first-rate customer service. General Electric has long excelled at finance, and indeed now owns substantial financial services businesses.

In today's competitive environment, marketing can make or break a company. A firm can have a wonderful product, but unless it spreads the word, gets shelf space, prices its products properly, and induces customers to buy, the company won't generate sales and profits.

Sales Brings in the Money

The *sales department* includes the men and women who sell the company's products or services. Salespeople may work on the telephone, in person, or both. They may sell to distributors or retailers who resell the product. They may sell directly to customers. They may sell to individuals or to businesses, to one-time buyers or to *national accounts* (a major account with a nationwide business). However, wherever and whatever they sell, salespeople bring in the money.

In most companies, the sales force is the most critical part of the business. Salespeople persuade customers to actually pull out their wallets and checkbooks and pay for a product or service, which is not an easy thing to do.

In many companies, the sales function includes *customer service*, which works with customers after the sale is made. Customer service ensures that customers are truly satisfied with what they've bought, and helps with any problems that arise after the sale.

Many companies think of themselves as sales-driven. These outfits have a sales force that aggressively presents products to customers, does all it can to please customers, and thinks creatively and competitively about ways to make every potential sale. For all its technology, IBM has always been famous for its sales force, which views selling for IBM as a mission.

MBA Lingo

The **sales department** includes the men and women who sell the company's products or services. In most companies, a **national account** is a major account with a nationwide business. For example, Sears is a national account for the power-tool maker Black & Decker.

MBA Lingo

After a sale is made, **customer service** works with the company's customers to maintain a link between the company and the customer and to answer customer questions, resolve complaints and, for some products, provide instructions for proper use and maintenance.

Sales departments are staffed mostly by salespeople, people who work to find new prospects and to turn them into customers. Customer service personnel usually work on the phone with the company's customers and may be headed for sales jobs or use the experience to move into marketing.

I'll discuss sales in more detail in Part 4.

Information Systems Keeps Everyone Informed

The *information systems* function, or *IS*, runs the company's computer systems. Computers have become so essential to running a business that the importance of this department has increased more than that of any other in the past 20 years. No longer

MBA Lingo

The **information systems,** or **IS,** function defines the company's requirements for computers, software, and related items; purchases, installs, programs, and maintains them; and uses the system to provide reports to managers throughout the company.

does senior management view IS, which used to be called *data processing*, as a backwater remote from the company's "real business." IS is now integral to most businesses, especially large service businesses.

IS deals with the purchase, programming, maintenance, and security of the company's computers. Recently, companies have focused on using information for competitive advantage, as opposed to just tracking things. (Competitive advantage was covered in detail in Chapter 1.) As the value of information has increased, so has the value, and status, of IS.

For example, for years the airlines issued tickets to their customers and tracked where the flights originated and ended. They also knew the mileage between those two points. However, in 1979 American Airlines introduced Frequent Flyer Miles. This program, the first of its kind, used the power of computerized record keeping—data processing—to turn some very dull information into a very exciting marketing tool. This tool gave American Airlines an advantage over competitors for several years (that is, until they all copied it).

Information systems is mainly staffed by computer systems analysts and software programmers. Systems analysts work to define and meet the company's hardware needs, while programmers work on the software needs. Programmers usually specialize in one or a few programming languages.

Support Functions Do the Rest

Any other area of a company not already discussed (aside from the board of directors) can be called a *support function*. The key support functions in a large company include

- Human resources
- Legal department
- Investor relations
- Facilities management

The *legal department*, staffed mostly by attorneys, ensures that the company remains in compliance with laws and government regulations. Legal, as it is usually called, also deals with lawsuits, whether they are brought by the company or against the company. The legal department is also known as house counsel (as opposed to outside counsel, which refers to an independent law firm). Most large companies will use independent counsel for more complex legal situations.

Human resources (usually referred to as HR) works with managers in other departments to attract, hire, retain, and train employees. Because this department works closely with managers throughout the company, you'll examine human resources in detail in Chapter 5.

Investor relations will, in many companies, be part of marketing or corporate communications or report directly to senior management. Investor relations communicates with the company's shareholders, the owners of the company, and organizes the annual meeting of shareholders. (Investor relations exists only in publicly held corporations.)

Facilities management (or the facilities department) may be part of operations, particularly in a service company. Facilities deals with real estate matters and the maintenance and upkeep of the company's buildings. For example, facilities maintains the heating, air conditioning, and other systems in buildings. Related functions which may be part of facilities include telecommunications, which runs the telephone system, and security, which prevents crime on the company's premises.

MBA Lingo _____

Support functions basically support all of the other departments that are making something, selling something, or dealing with money. One support function is the **legal department** (also known as house counsel), which consists of attorneys employed by the company to handle its legal affairs.

MBA Lingo _____

The **human resources** department (also known as HR) works with the managers of other departments to attract, hire, retain, and train employees and to ensure that the company is in compliance with government employment regulations. Human resources also sees that employee benefit programs are in place.

Above All: The Board of Directors

The board of directors is not considered a department or a functional area in the sense that marketing and finance are functions. However, the board of directors, often simply called the board, serves an important function.

A board consists of the CEO, who is typically also the chairman of the board, and usually other senior executives of the corporation. These are the inside directors. The outside directors are chosen from other businesses, academe, and the community to bring a broad, objective, external viewpoint to the company.

The directors are elected by the corporation's stockholders (who are its owners), usually at the shareholders' annual meeting, and are paid for their work as directors. The board represents the interests of the owners, and oversees the management of the company and advises management on matters of policy. This oversight and policy function is known broadly as corporate governance.

Unless the chief executive officer owns all the stock of the company, he or she reports to the owners (and, through ownership of stock, may also be an owner). The CEO reports to the owners through the board of directors. As the owners' representatives, the board of directors has as serious duty. They hire and fire the CEO and advise the CEO on filling the other key senior management positions. They set broad policies, exercise corporate governance, and represent the interests of the community and the larger society as well as those of the owners. For example, directors—particularly outside directors—advise management on the effect that certain policies and decisions may have on the larger community and society.

The board is not responsible for day-to-day operating decisions. The company's CEO and other senior managers are responsible for those. This, however, is where responsibilities can become unclear, because broad policies and matters of corporate governance are played out in day-to-day operations. If the board, for example, insists on honest accounting practices, what is their responsibility if the senior sales manager for European operations, who works in Frankfurt, overstates the company's European revenues by $12 million?

MBA Mastery

Smart senior managers want directors who will truly advise them and review major decisions. That way, management has other eyes (and brains) assisting them in the difficult task of managing the enterprise.

Unfortunately, boards have traditionally had a cozy relationship with management. They are often simply friends of management, routinely elected by the shareholders, and told only what management wants them to know. This situation is slowly changing as directors realize that they may be liable for decisions made by management, and that those decisions are not always right.

There is no easy answer. Technically, they are responsible, and so is the CEO, the corporation's senior sales manager, and any other managers on the chain of command between the board and the senior sales manager for Europe. In practice a strong board that insists on full and detailed accounting reports from the CEO (and reads them) stands the best chance of creating an environment that discourages dishonest accounting and catches and terminates those who practice it.

Members of lax boards may say that there is no way they can know about every decision that occurs in their company. However, lax boards are the very kind that encourage improper and illegal behavior. In that sense, if a board is lax and gives management a free hand, it has not really fulfilled its responsibility to the shareholders and to society.

Putting It All Together: The Org Chart

The following chart, an organization chart or org chart, shows how the departments I've just discussed would be organized in many companies.

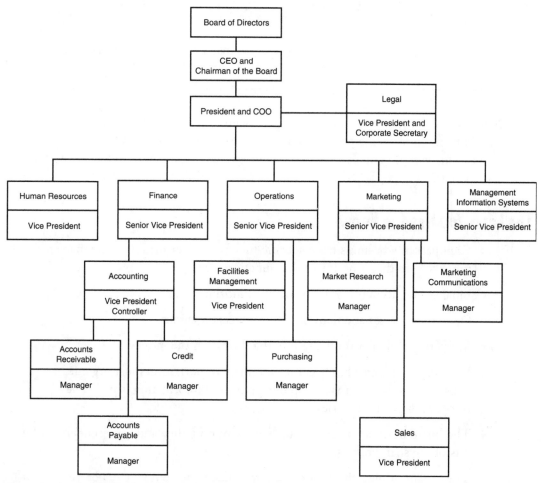

Organizational chart (or "org chart") for a large company.

As you can see, every department ultimately reports to the chief executive officer (CEO), usually the chairman of the board or the president. In a corporation, the CEO reports to the board of directors. In most companies, the titles of CEO and chairman of the board are both held by one person who has ultimate responsibility for the company, whereas the president and chief operating officer (COO), also usually one person, oversees day-to-day operations.

MBA Lingo

On an organization chart, **reporting lines** refer to the relationships between employees and their managers, and between managers and more senior managers. A direct line links a manager with his or her immediate, primary boss. In some outfits a dotted line in the org chart indicates a secondary, less formal reporting arrangement in addition to the primary one. For example, Accounting could report directly to the chief executive officer (CEO) but have a dotted line to the chief financial officer (CFO).

Note that each division is run by managers, who in turn report to vice presidents, who in turn report to the president and chief operating officer (COO). This organization chart is representative because *reporting lines* in companies follow fairly standard patterns.

The Least You Need to Know

- ◆ Each part of a business has a specific function to perform. It is the manager's job to make sure that it performs that function well.

- ◆ Finance and accounting control and count the money.

- ◆ Operations makes and delivers the products or services.

- ◆ Marketing and sales do the selling that brings in the money.

- ◆ Information systems has become extremely important in most organizations. This reflects the fact that computer-generated information is now a key resource in most industries.

- ◆ The board of directors advises management on policy and represents the interests of the shareholders.

- ◆ The organizational chart, or org chart, reflects the company structure.

Chapter 4

Leading the Charge

In This Chapter

- ◆ The difference between a manager and a leader
- ◆ Leadership skills that really work
- ◆ All about coaching and mentoring

Until recently, leadership wasn't covered as a subject in MBA programs. But leadership has become essential in business because many companies now employ mainly well-educated people engaged in knowledge work. This kind of work demands motivation, creativity, and flexibility, and you cannot simply ask (let alone order) people to be motivated, creative, and flexible.

Leadership has also come to the fore because most companies have moved away from so-called command-and-control management. They realize that while a "traditional" manager directs people to do what they should do, a leader gets people to do what they should do—and more—with less direction and greater efficiency.

Management and leadership are different, but related. A manager's job is more defined than a leader's. Management skills, such as planning and delegation, are concrete compared with leadership skills, which are more abstract. A leader relies more heavily on influence, inspiration, and collaboration than on directives, policies, and procedures. Yet the two sets of skills overlap.

Management skills and leadership skills work together to boost the effectiveness of both managers and employees. For example, the management skill of goal setting is related to the leadership skill of sharing a vision. If a leader can share a compelling vision of what the organization could accomplish *and* can set goals and define tasks that move people toward that vision, everyone will achieve more.

Not every leader is a good manager, nor is every manager a good leader. But the best executives have mastered both management and leadership skills. Therefore, this chapter focuses on various styles of leadership.

Style or Skills? Role or Position?

For many people the word *leader* conjures a mental image of a famous leader, a George Washington or Winston Churchill. For some people these famous leaders, and portrayals of leaders in popular culture, create the idea that leadership requires a confident, charismatic personal style. While confidence and charisma won't hurt a leader, they don't make someone a leader.

The term *leadership style* actually refers to the way in which a leader interacts with his or her followers. We'll examine leadership styles later in this chapter. However, please know that becoming a leader does not mean mimicking leaders portrayed in popular culture. Extremes of behavior seen in leaders in the movies and on television—the Mafia don's icy calm or the newspaper editor's bluster—simply don't work in real life, particularly if you don't happen to be naturally calm or blustery.

Yet effective leaders *are* playing a role. They know that, although they must be themselves, playing a leadership role in an organization demands certain things of them. It demands that they practice certain skills and interact in ways that meet people's expectations of leadership behavior.

For example, people expect a leader to hold him- or herself accountable and to hold them accountable for doing their jobs. If a leader fails at some aspect of her job but won't admit it, she will not be seen as an effective leader. Similarly, if an employee fails to do his job and the leader promotes him to a job with even more responsibility, she will not be seen as effective. Instead, the leader will undermine her employees' morale and motivation.

Leadership depends on sending strong, consistent messages—through words and actions—that demonstrate that the leader cares deeply about the organization and its people and purpose. This kind of caring is almost impossible to fake, because people watch leaders closely and judge them constantly. They will tolerate foibles and even failure (up to a point). But they will not bestow the mantle of leadership, which is theirs to bestow, on a manager who is lazy, unfair, inconsistent, unsupportive, or otherwise uncaring about the organization and its people and purpose.

So, although leadership does not depend on personality, it does depend on the person.

People need leaders. That is why in a leadership vacuum—for instance, in a badly managed department—the group will often recognize an unofficial leader. An unofficial leader doesn't officially head the group, yet people look to him or her for information, guidance, and decisions. Why? Because people trust him or her. A leader has people's trust, and therefore building trust is the first among the leadership skills we will examine.

MBA Mastery

One good way to think about the difference between a leader and a manager is that leader is a role while manager is a position. You can be promoted to a management position, but you must earn and grow into a leadership role.

Leadership Skills

Effective leaders motivate people to adopt the organization's purpose as their own and to do their best to fulfill that purpose. They inspire people to achieve more than they ever thought they could. They generate loyalty to the organization and get people to work together rather than against one another.

How do effective leaders do these things? Essentially, they

- ◆ Build trust.
- ◆ Share a vision.
- ◆ Focus people on the right tasks.
- ◆ Create accountability.
- ◆ Maintain alignment.
- ◆ Coach and mentor.

These skills are more complex and more difficult to learn than management skills. Yet they *are* skills, and that means that you can learn them, practice them, and use them.

Lay a Firm Foundation: Building Trust

Trust is the foundation of the relationship between leader and follower (as it is in every human relationship). Therefore, effective leaders consciously build trust between themselves and their people.

They build trust by considering the good of all *stakeholders* when making decisions. They do not allow one stakeholder or group of stakeholders to benefit at the expense of another. Leaders also build trust by using their power properly. As noted in Chapter 1, leaders are the stewards of the organization and are in a position to enrich themselves at the expense of others. If they do, they destroy trust.

MBA Lingo

A **stakeholder** has a tangible interest in an organization or project. Stakeholders benefit if the enterprise succeeds and incur losses if it fails. In a company, typical stakeholders include employees, customers, suppliers, investors, lenders, and the community.

Effective leaders build trust by fostering collaboration. Some managers believe that internal competition strengthens a company. Giving a department some competition can work—for example, General Motors allowed its production managers to purchase parts from outside the company if GM parts were inferior. But pitting people within a company against one another or allowing "turf battles" undermines trust in the leader and within the company.

Why is trust so important?

Business is among the most collaborative of human endeavors. To collaborate well, people must trust one another. They will share information openly, contribute their best effort, and support one another only when they trust one another. It is management's job to create that trust. Fair, principled behavior is the only way to create it.

Case in Point

The energy-trading firm Enron unraveled in late 2001 as accounting practices designed to hide its losses came to light. The companies' stakeholders, including its retirees and the citizens of Houston, the city where Enron is headquartered, suffered serious financial losses. The failure of its accounting firm, Arthur Andersen, to disclose Enron's true condition undermined trust in the entire system of financial reporting in U.S. companies. That trust was further undermined as improper accounting practices at other companies were discovered in 2002.

Trusting someone is not the same as liking them. Trust is based on respect and expectations, not on personal affection. Members of a football or basketball team do not have to like one another. But they have to trust one another on the field or court if they are to win games. Similarly, leaders do not need to be liked by all stakeholders, nor does he or she have to like all of them. But a leader and those whom he or she would lead must trust one another or there can be no leadership.

Think Big: Share a Vision

The term *vision* has been misused and maligned over the past 10 years or so. President George H. W. Bush derided "the vision thing." Lou Gerstner, when he took the helm as CEO of IBM, announced that he had no "vision" and only wanted to get things done.

However, effective leaders usually have a vision of what they want the organization to stand for and achieve. When they share that vision with their stakeholders, everyone knows what he or she holds a stake in. (Arguably, even leaders who say they have no "vision" are sharing a vision, which is, "We don't envision—we act!") A vision is broader than a goal. It articulates the underlying values and sets the context in which goals are selected and pursued.

Case in Point

Not every business vision succeeds. AOL Time Warner envisioned an entertainment company in which magazines, books, television, movies, and the Internet all worked together to support and reinforce one another. As of this writing, it has not succeeded. The reason may be that it was focused on the company and the supposed synergy the various divisions could generate, rather than on the customer.

Dell Computers began with a more customer-focused vision that also benefited the company. Michael Dell's innovation was to sell and ship computers assembled to the customers' specifications and directly to the customers. This not only enabled Dell to give customers exactly what they wanted; it also let the company eliminate retailers and their share of the profits.

The best leaders are students of human nature. They know that people want more from their work than a paycheck. They understand that people want a sense of purpose, that they want to be given a mission they can believe in.

These leaders also understand the business reasons for creating a shared vision. People with a vision will work harder and longer and with a greater sense of achievement than they ever would for just a paycheck. But they need to be doing the work that the company exists to accomplish. Therefore, although it incorporates values, the vision must be a business vision. It

MBA Mastery

Don't be afraid to envision something revolutionary for your business and its customers. A vision goes well beyond "making a profit" or "increasing market share." Those things are important, of course, but they often are achieved most spectacularly when a leader envisions a breakthrough to a new level of technical innovation, product quality, or customer service.

must be rooted in the reasons for the organization's existence. And it must include the customer, because a company exists to serve its customers.

Creating a shared vision calls for two-way communication. Many people don't adopt a leader's vision immediately. They need to ask questions, grasp the underlying values, interpret the vision, and see their role in achieving it. Smart leaders allow this process to occur. They realize it is the way that some people make the vision their own.

Over Here: Focus People on the Right Tasks

As managers, leaders must get things done through others. This means focusing people's attention on the most important tasks. Those are the tasks that will move the organization toward fulfillment of its vision and achievement of its goals. Effective leaders first identify the key tasks that will create the results they want to achieve. Then, through training, coaching, and incentives, they get people to perform these few tasks to the very best of their ability.

This leadership skill overlaps with the management skill of delegating, but even here leaders do things differently. They accept the fact that a company cannot do everything well. With this in mind, they consciously decide what the organization will do well, and get people focused on those tasks *and not on other tasks*.

The typical manager lacks the laserlike focus on the few key tasks that leaders develop and impart to the troops. The manager lacks this focus not because he can't identify the key tasks, but because he can't keep himself and his people focused on them as intensely as the leader can.

Effective leaders do not distract people with a flavor-of-the-month activity. Yes, if costs must be cut, they will get people to focus on cutting costs. If customer service slips, they will have people focus on improving customer service. However, the basic tasks that people in a given position must perform remain few in number and consistent in character.

In leadership literature, these tasks are often referred to as *core competencies*. Core competencies are the things that the company does extremely well to create value for the customer. For instance, in Disney's film entertainment division, business animation is a core competency. Disney has a history of making excellent animated films, does them extremely well, has created brands around animated characters—most famously Mickey Mouse—and attracts talented animators and technicians.

MBA Lingo

A **core competency** is a task, activity, or skill that a company does extremely well and that adds value for customers.

Case in Point

MBNA, the world's largest independent credit card company, has become so efficient at marketing cards, making credit decisions, and servicing customers that other banks now turn those tasks over to MBNA. The other banks keep their names on their MasterCard or Visa, but pay MBNA to do the operational tasks, which are MBNA's core competencies. In handling so many other types of banking business, those other banks cannot match MBNA's efficiency or profitability in credit cards.

Who Does What? Creating Accountability

As we learned in Chapter 3, a corporation's owners entrust management to organize human and other resources to do certain things for customers and to make a profit doing them.

The owners hold the board of directors accountable, the board holds the CEO accountable, the CEO holds his or her senior managers accountable, the senior managers hold their managers accountable, and those managers hold their employees accountable for accomplishing certain things profitably.

Accountability is often the "missing link" in the management process. It is difficult, even unpleasant, to hold people accountable. They make excuses and cite reasons beyond their control. Or they admit that they screwed up but can't explain how they will prevent it from happening again. Or they hide their failures so that they cannot be held accountable in the first place.

MBA Mastery

Hold people accountable for achieving results *ethically*. When people feel they must achieve a result no matter what, they will find a way to achieve it no matter what. Many things aside from the result—such as building trust and staying out of jail—also matter.

Effective leaders hold people accountable by allowing for mistakes and failures and realizing that they are part of the process, particularly when people are pursuing difficult goals. That way, people will admit their mistakes and failures and accept accountability. Effective leaders also have developed the ego strength to confront people about their failures and the skill to help them improve.

Finally, effective leaders hold themselves accountable for the things they say they will do and deliver. A leader undermines his credibility and trust if he doesn't hold himself to the same level of accountability as he holds his people.

Get This Straight: Maintain Alignment

A leader must ensure that the organization's resources are aligned with its vision and goals. Alignment means that "everyone is driving in the same direction."

On an operational level, alignment refers to consistency in strategy, structure, and resource allocation. For instance, if a company decides on a strategy of growth through new-product development, it must put structures in place that support the strategy and allocate resources to implementing it.

On an interpersonal level, alignment means that the leader's actions are congruent with his or her words. When a leader says one thing and does another, people stop trusting management and become cynical. For instance, when senior management announces a cost-cutting effort and then continues to fly first-class, they are throwing the organization out of alignment.

Organizational alignment demands that strategy, structure, resources, beliefs, words, actions, and goals all line up logically and fairly. If the CEO says. "People are our greatest asset," but allows (or encourages) high employee turnover, the company will go out of alignment. If he or she states that growth in sales will come from new products and then cuts the new-product development budget, there will be lack of alignment.

Consistency and congruence generate organizational alignment. The messages from management and the commitment of resources must be aligned with one another and with the company's goals and strategies. Effective leaders work hard to achieve this alignment, even to the point of firing people who cannot align themselves with the company's goals and strategy. These leaders know that an organization that's out of alignment will soon wind up in the ditch.

MBA Alert

Every member of management must be aligned in the messages they send to employees. It's fine for managers to hash out among themselves the message that they want to send to people. But once the message has been defined, every manager must accept it and communicate it clearly throughout the organization.

Case in Point

Certain companies have executive compensation plans that continue to reward senior managers lavishly even when profits plummet and employees are laid off. This throws the company way out of alignment (and undermines trust and accountability).

How Am I Doing? Coaching and Mentoring

A true leader must also be a coach and mentor. Coaching and mentoring bring all the other leadership skills down to the person-to-person level. That is, coaching and mentoring are means by which a leader can build trust, share his or her vision, focus people on the right tasks, create accountability, and maintain alignment.

What's the difference between coaching and mentoring?

In general, coaching helps a person do his current job better, while mentoring prepares him for his next job. Coaching helps people achieve results they are now accountable for achieving. Mentoring enhances a person's *promotability* to greater responsibility.

MBA Lingo

Promotability refers to a person's readiness to assume greater responsibility within the organization. Factors that determine promotability include management and leadership skills, past and current performance, ability to collaborate, and knowledge of the organization as a whole.

Coaching essentially means giving people feedback on their performance in a specific area. The word *feedback* is both accurate and useful here, although *critique* might also describe the process. Feedback is less judgmental than criticism, and that's what coaching should be. In business, a superior's comments about a subordinate's performance are often conveyed and perceived in negative ways. In sports, however, the coach assumes that the athlete wants to perform well and gives him information on what is working and not working in terms of his fundamentals, form, play, and approach to the game. Meanwhile, the athlete understands that coach is commenting on his performance and not on him as a person.

A good leader offers feedback in the same spirit. She offers information—potentially helpful observations and advice on performance. She comments on what the employee is doing well and on what he could improve.

Coaching should occur both informally—for instance, after a meeting or presentation—and formally in scheduled sessions. Without a formal program, many managers fail to practice these skills often enough with all of their people.

Comments should be specific. Saying, "You're doing a great job," isn't going to be as useful as saying, "You presented that material with all the right facts at the management meeting last week."

Coaching also involves setting goals for improvement in specific skills, developing a plan for improvement, and following up to ensure progress.

Mentoring involves similar types of communication. However, a mentor is often a level or two above the subordinate, while a coach coaches the people who report directly to him. A mentor exposes the subordinate to other functional areas of the company, explains how higher-level decisions are made, and helps the subordinate manage his career at the company. A mentor will tell the subordinate where in the company he should think about working and what skills he should develop to get into that area.

Coaching and mentoring enable leaders to develop the organization's talent pool while showing people that the company cares about their development. Coaching and mentoring help a company keep good people. Also, the communication involved encourages people on both sides of the relationship to invest more of themselves in the organization.

Leadership Lessons of Life

The greatest management fallacy is to believe that employees will do things because they are told to do them. Executives who believe this will often ask questions like, "Why aren't people cutting costs? Didn't they read the memo we sent them last month?"

Most people will work hard in pursuit of their company's goals. But they must believe that the work and the goals are worthwhile. The company's leaders—the senior managers and everyone else in a management position—must instill those beliefs in their people.

The only way to accomplish this is to build an organization that holds to high product and service standards and treats all stakeholders fairly. Leadership skills won't work in the absence of high standards and fairness to all stakeholders. With those elements in place, leaders still have challenging roles to play. Yet with diligent practice of leadership skills and consciousness of their leadership styles, they can reach their business goals while enriching the lives of everyone their organizations touch.

The Least You Need to Know

◆ The basic leadership skills include building trust, sharing a vision, focusing people on the right tasks, creating accountability, maintaining alignment, and coaching and mentoring.

◆ Leadership skills complement, and to some degree overlap, management skills. However, manager is a position you can be promoted to, but leader is a role you must grow into.

◆ Coaching, which helps an employee improve current performance, and mentoring, which prepares an employee for promotion, are leadership skills most managers must be encouraged to practice.

The Nuts and Bolts of Managing People and Teams

In This Chapter

- ◆ The role of human resources

- ◆ Hiring and firing employees

- ◆ Dealing with difficult employees

- ◆ Types of teams and how to manage a team

In Chapter 2, we examined the everyday activities of management, such as planning, setting goals, and delegating. In Chapter 4, we learned about the fundamentals of leadership, such as building trust and sharing a vision. To be successful in their own right, managers must also be able to guide their people to success. I call skills required to do this the nuts and bolts of management, but they could also be called the administrative side of managing people: hiring, firing, conducting performance appraisals, and working with difficult employees.

Fortunately, these nuts and bolts aren't things you'll have to do everyday, because most sizable companies have a human resources function, or more simply HR, to help managers deal with them. HR professionals also take care of a lot of other nuts and bolts, so that managers are free to manage their day-to-day operations. These other administrative matters include setting policies and pay scales, ensuring company compliance with employment regulations, assisting in employee growth and development, promoting diversity in the organization, and negotiating with health insurance firms and other providers of employee benefits.

In this chapter, I'll explain how human resources does its job and how HR can help you do your job. If your company is too small to have an HR department, this chapter will brief you about the "nuts and bolts" issues that every manager must understand and occasionally address. This chapter also covers managing teams, an activity that has grown in importance over the past several years.

What Does Human Resources Do?

HR helps managers to hire, orient, and train employees and establishes guidelines for employee compensation, performance appraisals, and disciplinary action. HR also helps a company comply with laws regarding employment discrimination and workplace safety. In companies with *unionized workers*, HR helps managers deal with the union's work rules.

> **MBA Lingo**
>
> **Unionized workers** are employees who have banded together to engage in collective, instead of individual, bargaining with management. The union negotiates a contract with management that applies to the workers, once the workers approve it.

Other key HR activities include the following:

- ◆ Recruitment
- ◆ Compensation analysis
- ◆ Benefits administration
- ◆ Training and development
- ◆ General employee administration

Let's cover each of these briefly.

> **MBA Lingo**
>
> **Recruiters** are responsible for filling open positions in the company. Most companies have recruiters on staff in the HR department. Recruiters also work in independent companies set up to fill open positions in their client companies, usually at the executive levels—hence the name executive recruiters.

Recruiters develop a pool of candidates to fill open positions in the company. To do this, they place ads in newspapers, work with employment agencies, and visit college campuses. They also screen candidates before they're sent to the hiring manager. (And, yes, HR is where those maddening individuals read and file—or throw out—all those resumés from people who want a job at the company.)

Compensation analysts define job functions and qualifications and write *job descriptions* for each position in the company. (A job description is an official definition of the responsibilities of a position.) They then decide what level of *compensation*, that is, wages or salary plus benefits, should go to people in that job. The wage or salary is usually defined as a range; for example, $33,000 to $38,000.

Compensation analysts also set policies regarding how often someone in the job should be considered for a raise.

Benefits administrators work with suppliers of health, retirement, and other benefit plans to see that employees have and receive benefits.

Training and development professionals bring in outside training firms and develop in-house courses to ensure that all employees are trained for their jobs and prepared for advancement.

General employee administrators handle employee communications, charitable efforts (such as blood drives), and employee grievances. In large companies, they may put out a newsletter or other regular publications. They also set policies regarding things such as smoking, office parties, and compliance with safety regulations.

Although the HR staff is there to answer virtually any question you may have about managing employees, its advice is particularly valuable when you are

- Hiring new employees.
- Dealing with problem employees.

> **MBA Lingo**
>
> A **job description** is an official definition of the responsibilities of a position. Every job in a company should have a job description, and every employee should have a copy of his or her job description. As a manager, you need copies of the job descriptions of everyone on your staff.

> **MBA Lingo**
>
> **Compensation** refers to an employee's pay plus his or her bonus (if any) plus the value of any benefits, such as company-paid health or life insurance. Total compensation refers to the value of all pay, bonuses, benefits, and what are known as perquisites, such as a company car or company-paid club membership.

Let's look at each of these issues in more detail.

Hiring the Right Person for the Job

In a large company, HR will usually be involved in the hiring process. This is for your convenience and the company's protection, and it saves money.

MBA Lingo

An **employment agency** is a firm that other companies use to fill jobs. An **executive search firm** (or executive recruiter or headhunter) identifies, meets, and screens potential candidates, whether or not they are seeking a new job. When a position becomes available, the recruiter may then recommend a candidate.

MBA Mastery

My best advice on hiring: Get strength in numbers. *Always* interview more than one candidate for a job and *always* have more than one person in your shop interview the candidates.

For example, if you need an *employment agency*, HR knows reliable ones and can negotiate the best fees. The same applies to *executive search firms* and help-wanted advertising. HR also keeps some resumés on file, and a look through them might uncover a solid candidate still interested in joining the company.

Human resources ensures that the company stays within legal and regulatory guidelines governing employment. For example, a company cannot discriminate in hiring on the basis of ethnic background, gender, or age. Companies of a certain size must accommodate the handicapped. The manager of every department cannot be an expert on employment law, so the HR function has this expertise.

Interviewing Candidates

Interviewing job applicants calls for more preparation and effort than many managers devote to the process. Many job interviews are almost perfunctory, with the real agenda of assessing "chemistry." Unfortunately, chemistry alone isn't a good indicator of how well a candidate can actually do the job.

Before the interview, prepare questions in writing and be sure to get answers to them. After greeting the applicant and putting her at ease, gear your questions to the two major issues: *Can* this person do the job? *Will* this person do the job?

To get at the first issue—can she do the job?—ask questions related to the candidate's education, work experience, and (key point) past performance. Ask for specifics about her role and her accomplishments at past employers.

The second issue—will she do the job?—relates more to the candidate's character, motivation, and genuine interests. Probe deeply about what she liked and disliked about past positions and why she moved on. What seems to excite her? How does she see herself and others? How fully does she answer your questions? When you probe in a certain area, does she change the subject?

Finally, be aware that there are questions you cannot legally ask a job candidate. These include questions about health, religious and ethnic background, marital status, family plans, and age. Your HR department can give you a better picture of what you can and can't legally ask. Rule of thumb: Don't ask any question that does not directly relate to the candidate's ability to do the job.

Checking References

Check references yourself, if possible. Otherwise, be sure HR does. If you check them, tell the person you've been referred to that this is an extremely important hire and that you need an honest perspective on the candidate.

It's not easy to get objective answers, but try. Many companies are wary about being sued by former employees if they give out negative information. Some will only verify that the person was employed there. However, you should still try to get an objective, useful reference from a former boss.

Extending the Offer

After you've interviewed what you consider to be enough candidates (I like to see five to eight for a professional position), you'll be ready to extend an offer.

Company protocol usually dictates how an offer is extended. Some outfits believe the offer should come from HR, while others believe the hiring manager should extend it. The latter may be warmer, but the former provides "distance" between the hiring manager and the candidate if negotiations ensue. If HR can act as a buffer, why not let them? Whoever does it, generally an offer is extended by phone and followed up with a verifying letter.

MBA Mastery

When you ask a question, wait for the answer. Don't attempt to answer the question for the candidate or "lead" the candidate to make a particular response. If the answer is incomplete, wait for more. If you don't get more, prompt with a phrase like, "Can you be more specific?" or "In what sense?" or "Why is that?" The human tendency may be to let the interviewee "off the hook." Don't.

MBA Alert

A lukewarm or poor reference should raise a red flag, but not necessarily end the candidate's chances. Personal animosity can fuel a poor reference, so ask for specific details about the employee's performance. If the specifics sound believable, beware. If instead you get vague negatives or descriptions of personality traits rather than specific behaviors, the poor reference may be "just personal."

Getting New Employees Oriented

After the candidate becomes an employee, HR provides materials that help him or her understand company policy, structure, benefits, and ethics. These materials include policy manuals, benefits handbooks, and so on. HR may also have worthwhile videos on the company.

Part of your responsibility as a manager is to develop your employees. This includes arranging for the training they need as well as any they might request that is both relevant to their job and in the budget. If you have people reporting to you, you should have some money (even if it's just $500–$1,000 a year) budgeted for training. Or your area may have a share of a larger departmental or central HR budget for training and development. Employees interested in training or in furthering their education should be encouraged to pursue it.

Dealing With Problem Employees

No one, and I mean no one, likes dealing with a problem employee, one who is performing poorly, slacking off, displaying personality problems, or undermining the outfit. Because no one enjoys the task, many managers try to "work around" problem employees, rather than deal with them. As a manager, you owe it to your organization and to your good employees to hold problem employees accountable and, when necessary, fire them.

I'm defining a problem employee as one who is not performing or is disruptive, but who you cannot or should not fire immediately. Few offenses warrant immediate firing. Most large companies limit these offenses to proven or admitted dishonesty (beyond stealing pencils), threatening language, violent behavior, on-the-job drinking or drug use, and gross *insubordination* (refusal to follow a reasonable request from a superior).

At most companies virtually all other offenses (poor attitude, attendance, or job performance) require a formal termination process to give the employee time to improve. Note, however, that in most companies, the employee's first 90 days on the job are officially a probationary period during which the employee can be terminated immediately.

Large companies require managers to build a case before terminating a problem employee, partly out of fairness and partly because no company wants a *wrongful termination* suit on its hands. The HR department

> **MBA Lingo**
>
> **Insubordination** is an employee's direct refusal to follow a reasonable, direct, job-related request from his or her superior. Repeated or vigorous refusal amounts to gross insubordination.

> **MBA Lingo**
>
> **Wrongful termination** is firing someone based on age, gender, race, or religion. Another example would be firing a woman because she became pregnant or firing someone because he or she got a divorce. These are not legal because there are laws against discriminating against workers on that basis. Valid reasons for terminating an employee are those relating to job performance.

assists the manager during this termination process, while also giving an ear to the problem employee.

The termination process gives the employee an opportunity to improve his performance or else be terminated. Typically an employee receives written notice of his failure to perform to the standards of the job. The notice mentions the specific areas in which his performance falls short, such as attendance or the quality of his work, and specific goals that the employee must achieve, such as perfect attendance or only two defects per one hundred pieces of product.

It also usually mentions a time frame, usually 30 or 60 days, during which that improvement must be achieved. The notice is usually worded so that improvement must "be maintained thereafter" so that the employee does not improve temporarily just to keep his job, and then fall off again.

Some problem employees do pull themselves together, but that's not the way to bet. Many simply refuse to change their behavior even after verbal warnings. By the time problem employees are given a formal written warning and are placed on probation, they are, in my experience, usually on the way out.

Case in Point

Some firms drag out the termination process unnecessarily. I've seen two cases in which employees (one mine, one another manager's) with disordered personalities were kept on the job for months because the managers were not permitted to terminate. One of these employees ultimately had to be escorted from the building by security after "losing it." Lobby hard for termination in such situations. Helping inefficient employees move on to the next stage of their lives is the best thing for them, as well as the fairest thing for the individual's fellow employees.

HR can provide good advice on the legal and procedural aspects of termination. For example, when you write someone up, HR will help you focus on behavioral issues rather than personality conflicts. HR can also help you deal with the emotional dimensions of the situation, both yours and the employee's.

The best way to avoid problem employees is to hire carefully and do regular performance appraisals.

Take Performance Appraisals Seriously

Most companies require managers to give each of their employees a formal, annual, written performance appraisal. Unfortunately, not all managers follow through. But every manager should, because first, employees deserve a periodic written record of where they stand, and second, appraisals document the employee's performance for future managers.

The HR department (and your superior) will have the necessary forms and advice on how to go about writing and administering performance appraisals.

<table>
<tr><td>

Case in Point

A survey several years ago revealed that in the average company, over 50 percent of employees rate their job performance in the top 10 percent of the outfit's employees. This is a practical, as well as a mathematical, impossibility. Quite possibly, overly positive performance appraisals contribute to this situation.

</td></tr>
</table>

The most common mistakes (aside from not doing appraisals regularly) is rating people too highly given their actual performance and not giving them a clear program for improvement. I'm not encouraging negative performance appraisals, but balanced ones. I have seen perfect employees—exactly two in 20 years. Most of us (myself included) have strengths *and* weaknesses, and you must document both in the appraisal.

If a poorly performing employee is due for his or her annual appraisal, use it as an opportunity to document the poor performance and give him or her an action plan and 30 or 60 days to improve.

When It's Time to Go: Firing an Employee

Once an employee has been given a real chance to improve and has failed, she should be terminated quickly. (Of course, you will have input from HR as well as your supervisor before you actually terminate an employee.) The following are general guidelines that I have found useful:

♦ Meet with the employee in a conference room or an office other than yours or hers. That way you are both on "neutral territory" and the new environment signals to the employee that the process has moved to a new and final stage.

♦ Give the person formal, verbal notice of termination and a brief, blandly worded letter that states that "the company will no longer require your services."

♦ Don't apologize. You can say you're "sorry that things did not work out" if you like. But it isn't your place to make a true apology.

♦ Deliver the news yourself, but have someone from HR at the termination. That way you have a witness to this final conversation (or confrontation), as well as someone to back you up.

♦ Ask the terminated employee to leave the premises when the conversation is through. If you prefer, you may give the employee until the end of the day, but the sooner she leaves, the better.

Don't be shocked if the employee threatens you with a lawsuit. When I hear that, I say, "You have to proceed in the way that's best for you," and nothing else. Many companies forestall legal action by providing (often absurdly generous) *severance pay* to terminated employees. Senior managers may receive this as part of their employment contract. But by no means does every fired employee get severance pay.

When severance pay is given to a fired employee, he or she usually signs a letter agreeing not to sue and accepting the payment as full settlement. Often these employees are "allowed to resign" instead of being fired.

MBA Lingo

Severance pay is a final payment made by the company to an employee who is being terminated or laid off. The company makes this payment partly out of fairness to the employee, to "tide her over" during the period of unemployment presumably ahead, and partly to assuage any hard feelings the employee may have.

Take Your Time

Although terminating employees is often taxing, fortunately, it is not an everyday task. However, when you take over a department, you may well find that one or two people will either have to improve their performance radically or be asked to leave. Just don't make any snap judgments or try to move too quickly. It takes at least six months to a year to build or significantly improve a department. It takes time to size up people's performance, communicate your standards, and bring employees up to those levels or replace them.

When you take over an existing function, unless it's a disaster, resist any gung-ho urges you may feel. Get to know your people—and let them get to know you—before trying to make radical changes. Use a consultative leadership style until you know who's who and what's what. Then, if or when you do start directing and delegating, you will be positioned to direct and delegate with more knowledge and credibility.

Team, Team, Teams

Although the traditional departments, such as finance, marketing, and production, can accomplish most tasks, at times a company needs a small, specialized work group—a team—to address a specific situation.

MBA Lingo

A **task force** is a temporary work group under one leader formed to accomplish a well-defined, often urgent, project and then disband.

Situations best addressed by teams include crises (such as disaster recovery); tasks that demand the expertise of several functions (such as product development); and complex, short-term projects (such as changing the company's structure).

MBA Alert

Some companies call almost any department or area a team. This is meant to promote teamwork. It may even be accurate. After all, a department is a group of people working toward a common goal. And, someday, they won't be working together. However, true teams are specialized groups with a specific mission to accomplish within a certain time. Referring to standing departments as teams may cloud the meaning of the term and reduce the impact that true teams can have on the organization.

The most common tasks involve fact-finding, developing recommendations, and implementing a course of action, or some combination of the three.

A fact-finding team conducts research and gathers information—for instance, on the causes of employee turnover. That same team or another one may then develop recommendations, such as policies and procedures to reduce employee turnover. Then a team may be needed to implement the recommended course of action, perhaps by training managers in policies and procedures to reduce turnover.

Cross-functional teams, which have become quite popular in recent years, comprise members from various functions, such as sales, marketing, finance, and production, or perhaps various geographic locations across the company. Not every function in a company must be represented. But every area that can truly contribute should be represented.

Pros and Cons of Teams

The advantages of teams stem from their nature. Small work groups often can accomplish a task faster than a traditional department because they are small, focused on a specific task, and less tied up in "red tape." Teams work especially well when the expertise of several functions is required or when multiple functions will be affected by a decision or course of action. Having the contribution and buy-in of those functions (on a cross-functional team) will heighten the chances of success.

A team appointed by senior management has the authority to get things done where "business as usual" would be slow or ineffective. In fact, the very act of forming a task force to deal with a problem often signals to the organization a serious commitment to fixing it.

So, teams can tap the right people, move quickly, bring disparate functions together, generate buy-in, and solve problems.

Yet teams have some disadvantages. They pull high performers off their regular jobs. If a team places additional demands on an employee, he or she won't be able to devote as much time and energy to his or her regular job.

Teams are also tricky to manage. Sometimes they are not given a well-defined goal and enough authority to achieve the goal. Even teams with a goal can get derailed if a strong personality takes over the team and clouds its aims or skews the results of its work. Teams have limited time to get up and running and to demonstrate effectiveness. Therefore, they must be disciplined and task-oriented. This means that even when members don't know one another well, they must quickly develop trust and start collaborating effectively. Representatives of a team must also act with diplomacy as they navigate the organization or they will alienate others (who were not asked to join the team).

MBA Alert

Scrutinize requests to join teams, particularly if you work for a large company. If you have the option of not participating, you may want to consider gracefully declining if the costs to you or your department would outweigh the benefits of your participation. (But don't alienate senior management or create the impression that you're not a team player.)

Also be wary of task forces formed to make it appear as if management is solving a problem it has no intention of addressing. The people on that type of team are at best wasting their time and at worst being set up for failure.

Managing Teams

Most businesspeople like "teams" but hate "committees." They believe that teams get things done and committees do nothing. Worse, a committee is apt to come up with a complex, unworkable solution to a problem. (You've probably heard the saying: "A camel is a horse put together by a committee.")

How do you keep your team from turning into a committee? By considering the following questions and guidelines:

- *What must the team accomplish?* Decide at the outset whether the team is gathering information, making recommendations, implementing a course of action, or some combination of these tasks. Define the scope of the team's project carefully.

- *Is a team really necessary in this situation?* Sometimes one or two people can get more done in less time. Or perhaps hiring a consulting firm would be more effective.

MBA Mastery

A team should be composed of people at similar management levels. If one member is far senior to the others, he or she may alter the group dynamics for the worse, for instance by suppressing contributions, even unknowingly. It is the rare executive who can say to subordinates, "I am just another member of this team," and be believed.

◆ *Who should be on the team?* Include only the people that the team really needs. Stakeholders who can't contribute but who will be affected, for example, should be kept informed and asked for input, but they should not be on the team.

◆ *How are we going to accomplish our goals?* At the outset, the team must define its tasks, who will complete them, at what cost, and by when. Each member must have a role, tasks, deliverables, and deadlines.

◆ *Who is leading the team?* A team should have a leader. Although the leader can think of him- or herself as a facilitator, someone must guide the team's efforts and be accountable for its results.

A team leader must build trust, share a vision, focus on the right tasks, create accountability, maintain alignment, and coach and mentor the team members. In other words, a team leader must employ leadership skills.

The Least You Need to Know

◆ To build or improve a department, you must get to know your employees, communicate your expectations and standards to them, and guide them to that level of performance.

◆ Hiring carefully and with the input of human resources, another interviewer, and former employers of the candidate will help you avoid problems later.

◆ Problem employees must be handled through a procedure designed to be fair to them and to the organization.

◆ Teams may be formed for fact-finding, to make recommendations, or to implement a course of action.

◆ Forming a team does not guarantee that an effort will succeed. Indeed, the team must be formed for the right reasons and be properly constructed and well managed in order to succeed.

Part 2

Making Decisions About Resources and Operations

Much of a manager's work comes down to making decisions. Most of these decisions have to do with how the company's resources are allocated to various operations. These decisions can range from small ones, such as should a restaurant schedule two cooks or three for Thursday evening, to large ones, such as should a natural gas company build a pipeline across Canada.

Management decisions occur in the context of the larger economy, which affects virtually every business. Therefore, Part 2 begins by explaining how our economy operates and how to how to read economic indicators so you know where you are in the business cycle. You will also learn methods for analyzing business situations, methods that help you make the best decision in a given situation. Finally, you'll learn how to read a budget and make decisions that help you stay within a budget.

Chapter 6

Essential Economics

In This Chapter

- ◆ The structure of the economy
- ◆ Understanding GNP and GDP
- ◆ The causes of recessions and recoveries
- ◆ The effects of inflation and unemployment
- ◆ The difference between fiscal policy and monetary policy

The national economy is the total of all of the financial transactions that go on in the nation. This includes everything: a kid buying candy with the quarter in his sweaty hand, one megacorporation acquiring another in an international transaction, the government opening (or closing) a military base. An economy includes every exchange of money that takes place in a city, state, nation, or region.

Business decisions—and those of consumers and the government—affect the economy. They are also, as you will see, affected by the economy. That's why businesspeople follow the economic news. They want to understand the context in which they are making decisions to hire or lay off employees, build or sell a factory, or spend more or less on advertising.

This chapter gives you an overview of the economy and a summary of economic concepts you should know. More important, it will help you understand the economic news and the effect the economy has on your business. That way you will understand the "big picture" when you make a decision as a manager (or as a consumer or citizen). You may notice that this chapter uses the U.S. economy as a specific example from time to time. Please understand that these economic concepts are universal and apply to all countries.

Our National Economy: As Easy as C + I + G

Because an economy is the total of all financial transactions in an area, you can measure the size of an area's economy by adding up the transactions. The dollar value of all goods and services produced in a country, for example, is measured by the *gross domestic product*, or GDP. GDP measures the size of a national economy.

MBA Lingo

Gross domestic product, or GDP, is the total value of all goods and services produced within a nation's borders, including those produced by foreign-owned companies in that nation. (In contrast, gross national product includes the value of all goods and services produced by a nation's companies, even when those companies and facilities are located outside the country.) Most economists now usually use GDP, rather than GNP, to measure a nation's economy.

Here is the formula for GDP:

$$GDP = C + I + G + (Ex - Im)$$

The parts of this formula are simple:

C = total household consumption (essentially, spending by consumers)

I = total investment (spending by businesses)

G = total spending by government (federal, state, and local)

(Ex – Im) = net exports (exports minus imports)

The U.S. economy is now about $10 *trillion*. That means that the United States produces $10,000,000,000,000 worth of goods and services within its borders *every year*. The U.S. economy is the world's largest national economy.

If you look at the GDP formula, you'll see that if any one component increases, then the total GDP increases. For example:

- If consumer spending grows—if people buy more clothing and cars and homes—then the economy grows.

- If business investment grows—if companies invest in buildings and equipment and hire new workers—then the economy grows.

- If government spending grows—if money is poured into space programs and roads and police forces—then the economy grows.

By the same token, if any one component of the GDP decreases, then the total GDP decreases.

We'll look at the dynamics of the economy in a bit, but first let's examine exports and imports.

Imports and Exports: Easy Come, Easy Go

When a country *exports* goods, it sells them to a foreign market, that is, to consumers, businesses, or governments in another country. Those exports bring money into the country, and that increases the GDP. However, when a country *imports* goods, it buys them from foreign producers. The money spent on imports leaves the economy, and the GDP decreases.

The term *net exports* assumes that exports are greater than imports. If a nation exports, say, $100 billion dollars' worth of goods and imports $80 billion, it has net exports of $20 billion. That amount gets added to the country's GDP. Net exports can be negative, in which case they are subtracted from the GDP.

Conceivably, net exports could be zero, with exports equal to imports.

If net exports are positive, the nation has a positive balance of trade. If they are negative, the nation has a negative trade balance. Virtually every nation in the world wants its economy to be bigger rather than smaller, and to be growing (we'll see why in a minute). That means that no nation wants a negative trade balance.

MBA Lingo

Exports are goods shipped *out of* the country in which they are made to be consumed in another nation. **Imports** are goods shipped *into* the country that will consume them. The goods were made by the exporting nation. One country's exports are another country's imports. **Net exports** are a nation's total exports minus total imports during a certain period—for example, a calendar year.

Because no nation wants a negative trade balance, some countries try to protect their own markets. This policy, called (logically enough) *protectionism*, uses barriers to keep out imports. These barriers include high *tariffs* (taxes or surcharges on imported goods) and strict rules about what products can be imported.

MBA Lingo

Protectionism refers to government policies designed to restrict imports from coming into the nation. A **tariff**, also called a duty, is a tax on imports as they come into the country. **Free trade** means international trade that is unrestricted by tariffs or other forms of protectionism.

Despite some nations' attempts at protectionism, *free trade*—trade unencumbered by barriers—has been the dominant trend for most countries for most of this century. Economists usually favor free trade because it tends to give consumers the greatest choice of products at the lowest prices. That occurs because some nations are better at producing certain products than others.

Recognizing the benefits of unencumbered trade, a number of countries have formed *free-trade zones*. In the mid-1990s, Canada, the United States, and Mexico created the North American Free Trade Agreement (NAFTA), which is one such zone. Even before NAFTA, several countries in Southeast Asia formed the Association of Southeastern Asian Nations (ASEAN), another free-trade zone. More recently, the European Union (EU) eliminated barriers to trade among most western European countries, with the remaining few countries not participating slated to join the union soon. The EU has also taken the revolutionary step of adopting a single currency, called the euro.

MBA Lingo

In a **free-trade zone**, the member nations eliminate most barriers to trade, such as tariffs, complex documentation, and needless product standards. They also often agree to freer cross-border movement of workers and capital, which has been the case in the European Union.

Despite occasional fits of protectionism (even in the United States, where President Bush recently raised tariffs on imported steel), the world has been moving toward freer trade.

Can Exports Move an Economy?

In most economies, exports and imports are less important in the business cycle than the other three sectors (consumer, business, and government). But there are exceptions.

Suppose a nation that exports a lot of oil experiences a sudden fall-off in foreign demand for its oil. That nation could quickly skid into recession. Similarly, if that nation saw a sudden surge in demand for its oil, it could well move into recovery. (I'll talk more about recession and recovery later in this chapter.)

An economy that depends heavily on exports, particularly a single export, can be quite vulnerable to recession. An economy like that lives and dies by trade policy—and by its major export, whatever it is.

Case in Point

A nation's balance of trade is calculated for a country in relation to the rest of the world, and in relation to other individual nations. It can even be calculated for a specific industry.

For example, the U.S. usually has a negative balance of trade with the rest of the world. That means the U.S. imports more than it exports.

The U.S. also has a negative balance of trade with Japan. The U.S. imports more from Japan than it exports to Japan. However, the U.S. exports more fruits, grain, and vegetables to Japan than it imports from Japan. So the U.S. has a positive agricultural trade balance with Japan.

Growth Is Good

What's the importance of economics? Why should anyone care about this stuff? What does it have to do with anyone's job or business?

Plenty!

An economy is a dynamic system for supplying people's wants and needs. Like any dynamic system, it doesn't stand still. It is either growing or contracting.

If the economy is growing, that's good. It's good for two reasons: First, in most economies the population is growing and new people have needs that must be met. If the population gets larger, the economy has to get larger to meet those needs.

Second, even if the population were not growing, people always want and need more goods and services. They want a rising *standard of living*. Only an economy that grows most of the time can give people a rising standard of living.

MBA Lingo

The **standard of living** is the total quality of life supplied by an economy. It includes the availability and quality of jobs, housing, food, education, transportation, sanitation, recreation, and health care in a city, state, nation, or region.

GDP: It's All Connected

There's an important aspect of the GDP formula that we haven't discussed: The elements are all interconnected.

When the state police buys cars from Ford Motor company, it increases G, government spending. When Ford pays its advertising agency, it increases I, investment or business spending. When a copywriter at that ad agency goes out and buys a bottle of French champagne, she increases C, household consumption. When her wine merchant buys more champagne from his distributor in France, he increases Im, imports. If he has excess inventory of California Chardonnay that he sells to a merchant in Canada, he increases Ex, exports. And so on.

> **MBA Lingo**
>
> The **business cycle** is the recurring pattern of expansions and contractions in an economy. The expansions are also called **recoveries** and the contractions are also called **recessions.** Officially, a recession is two consecutive quarters of contraction—that is, GDP growth of less than zero.

Conversely, if the state closes down an agency, it reduces G. Those ex-workers without paychecks will then decrease their spending; for example, they'll postpone buying a new Ford, thus reducing C. When Ford sees its business decrease, it will cancel factory expansion plans, thus reducing I, investment. And so on.

In an economy, everything—every activity, transaction, person, and organization—is directly or indirectly connected. An economy expands or contracts as a result of millions of separate decisions to buy or invest, or not to buy or invest. Similarly, when the economy expands or contracts, everyone is affected. That is why everyone is concerned about the economy's expansions and contractions, or the *business cycle*.

What Goes Up, Must Come Down

The business cycle exists because of fluctuations in demand. (Demand here is just another word for spending.) C + I + G + (Ex – Im) represents total demand. Household consumption is consumer demand. Business spending is investment demand. Government spending is government demand. Exports represent foreign demand for a country's goods. Imports represent domestic demand for foreign goods.

Fluctuations in demand tend to be unpredictable in both their timing and intensity. Some economists spend their lives trying to predict recessions and recoveries, but as a group their record is fairly poor. The one thing they, and we, do know is that a recession always follows a recovery, and a recovery always follows a recession. We just don't know when and with what strength. The business cycle never stops.

Tracking the Business Cycle

Here's what happens in a typical business cycle. During a recovery, things steam along nicely. Consumers are buying, which means that spending, or demand, is increasing. In the GDP formula, C increases.

To meet this increased demand, industry expands its productive capacity. Businesses lease new space and buy new equipment and hire new workers so they can expand their capacity and increase production. This increases I, investment. During a recovery, most businesses want to "make hay while the sun shines," so they expand vigorously.

As long as consumers keep buying and businesses keep investing, the recovery continues and everything is fine. The business cycle stays on an upswing. GDP growth continues.

Yet, inevitably, demand eventually decreases. This can occur because consumers get to a point where they have enough new cars, clothes, and homes, and therefore cut back on spending. Or businesses may reach a point where they have enough computers, factories, and workers to produce what their customers need, and so they cut back on investment. Or some event, such as a war, can cause consumers or business, or both, to hunker down, cut spending, and start saving.

When this happens, a downward cycle begins. If consumers reduce their spending, businesses will lay off workers and stop investing in plants and equipment. If businesses lay off workers, consumers will have less money and will reduce their spending. When consumers or businesses (or both) reduce their spending, the economy stops growing. If they reduce their spending by enough for long enough, the result is a recession.

Yet eventually, consumers decide they need new cars, clothes, and homes and start spending again. When they do, economic recovery begins and businesses must start investing to meet this new demand and the upward cycle begins again.

> **MBA Mastery**
>
> As a manager, you should understand how economic cycles can affect your business. For example, if you sell goods or services to consumers, you may get stuck with excess inventory when consumer spending slows because demand fell off and you didn't see it coming.

Booms and Busts

When consumers and businesses increase or decrease demand gradually, the cycle of recession and recovery will be relatively smooth (although not painless for the consumers and businesses affected). However, exaggerated responses by consumers or businesses can create a cycle of booms and busts.

A boom occurs when demand increases sharply over a sustained period. A large, broad-based upswing in demand can create a booming economy. Or a boom can be more specific. For example, a nationwide housing boom may be driven by a dramatic increase of adults in the population who are ready to become homeowners. More specifically still, a housing boom can occur in a rapidly growing city, as occurred in Las Vegas in the late 1980s through most of the 1990s.

In general, an economic boom means good times for most people. However, if a boom continues long enough and vigorously enough it can generate overexpansion by business or an increase in prices, known as inflation (which I discuss later in this chapter). If businesses overexpand, they wind up with too much productive capacity and too many employees for the existing level of demand. When that happens, they must cut their costs by cutting back on purchases of materials and equipment and decreasing the number of employees through layoffs. When employees are laid off, they cut back their spending, too. If businesses and employees cut back their spending sharply enough for long enough a recession begins. If economic conditions become bad enough, the result can be bust. (Bust is a slang term, rather than a technical term used by economists, that people use to describe a boom that ends abruptly.) Officially, a recession is defined as two consecutive quarters of contraction (or "negative growth" as economists say).

Economists call a deep, prolonged contraction a depression. A depression is characterized by rising unemployment, falling incomes, falling prices, excess inventories and productive capacity, lack of confidence, and a generally low level of business activity. Fortunately, depressions are very rare. The Great Depression of the 1930s was the only one to occur in the United States and Europe in the past century, but it had worldwide repercussions.

In the United States, economic expansions last far longer than recessions. For instance, the most recent prolonged expansion officially started in March 1991 and ended in March 2001, and thus lasted exactly 10 years. The recession that preceded that expansion officially lasted a mere eight months. In fact, since the end of World War II, the longest recession, in 1973 and 1974, lasted 16 months.

Starting in March, 2001, the U.S. economy experienced three quarters of slightly negative growth. A contraction of –1.6 percent (at an annualized rate) in the second quarter of 2001 was the worst of it, although March alone was bad enough to turn growth for the entire first quarter of 2001 negative. However, the recovery that began in the fourth quarter of 2001 has been uneven. Growth was 2.75 percent in the fourth quarter of 2001, shot up to 5 percent in the first quarter of 2002, but drifted down to 1.3 percent in the second quarter of 2002.

Rather than a good, steady expansion, the U.S. economy is moving unevenly, posing the risk of a "double dip" recession. In a double dip recession, growth resumes for two or more quarters, but after that the economy contracts for at least two quarters. This occurs when demand resumes, but then falls off again.

Also, this most recent recovery has been uneven, with some sectors of the economy, being hit harder than others.

The Government's Role

I've described the business cycle in terms of consumer and business behavior. But what about the government?

The government has only two sources for the money it spends: taxes or debt.

Most of the government's spending money comes from taxes on—guess who?— consumers and businesses. During a recession, consumer and business spending, and thus consumer and business *income*, decrease. Since federal (and many state) taxes are based on income, tax receipts also decrease. Similarly, during a recovery, consumer and business spending, and thus income, increase, and so do tax receipts.

> **MBA Lingo**
>
> **Income** equals spending. Because the economy is interconnected, what one person or business spends, another collects as income. Total spending, total income, and GDP are essentially the same thing.

Now all of this is what happens if the government does nothing to try to affect the business cycle. But in fact, the government plays an active role in most modern economies, including ours. Let's spend some time examining that role.

What Does the Government Want?

Essentially, the government wants order in the economy. The government wants a sound currency, low unemployment, and sustained economic growth.

More specifically, the government wants a currency with minimal *inflation* (rapid price increases that erode the value of the dollar). It wants low unemployment, as close to 4 percent as possible—it can't go much lower. And it wants sustained growth, at a long-term average of about 3 percent a year, which is about what's possible without inflation getting out of hand, given historical levels of productivity.

MBA Lingo

Inflation refers to price increases that erode the value of currency. These increases can occur gradually or rapidly. If prices rise gradually, consumers can adjust their spending habits and their incomes have time to rise in response. Rapid inflation—also called hyperinflation—can destabilize an economy, because people cannot depend on the buying power of the currency. Rational lending, borrowing, international trade, and planning of purchases become impossible. People lose the value of their savings and their faith in the currency and, if it goes on long enough, in the government that oversees that currency.

As for the unemployment rate, 4 percent is generally recognized as the lower limit because some small portion of the work force will always be officially out of work because they are between jobs. Most of the people between jobs have just been fired or laid off and have not yet found another job. Or they were fired or laid off and are still counted as unemployed, although they are not really looking for work and want to take some time off.

The Inflation-Unemployment Trade-Off

Since the economy is a dynamic system, it can go out of whack. It is often growing too slowly to provide full employment or too fast to keep inflation low. Indeed, that is the traditional trade-off in managing the economy: You either get low inflation and high unemployment or high unemployment and low inflation.

Here's why.

An economy is said to be "overheating" when the increased demand in a recovery pushes up the price of everything. This is inflation, defined as too many dollars (too much demand) chasing too few goods. When demand outstrips capacity, consumers "bid up" the price of goods. Also, businesses know they can charge higher prices when demand is high.

MBA Alert

Some economists believe that increased productivity in the U.S. economy has done away with the traditional trade-off between inflation and unemployment. Indeed, during the 1990s recovery, inflation remained quite low—about 2 percent or less per year—even as unemployment approached the rock-bottom rate of 4 percent. Other economists argue that the inflation-unemployment trade-off may still exist because the 1990s were an unusual period of unsustainable productivity growth.

However, the bright side of this is that unemployment is low because businesses have hired all those workers to handle the new capacity that's been added. So in a recovery, and especially in an overheated economy, there are inflationary pressures—but there is also low unemployment.

The economy is said to be "cooling," that is, going into recession, when demand falls. When demand falls, of course, you don't have too many dollars chasing too few goods. Instead you have unsold goods, because demand for them has decreased. So inflationary pressure, that upward pressure on prices, goes away.

The dark side to this is that jobs go away, too. Why have workers making things when demand for those things is falling? So there is low inflation—but high unemployment.

So ultimately what the government, and the rest of us, want is a happy medium. We want steady jobs and steady prices. But since an economy is dynamic, it keeps going out of whack. Government economic policy aims to keep it in whack.

Economic Policy

In the United States, the government plays a big role in the economy because the federal government alone represents over $2 trillion in spending. There's a lot of demand there to be managed. When you add in state and local governments, the total government component amounts to more than one quarter of the U.S. economy.

However, we're concerned only about the federal government. While states and cities have their economies to manage, only the federal government can affect the whole economy. It does this through *economic policy*.

MBA Lingo

Economic policy is the means by which the federal government stimulates or reigns in economic growth. There are two kinds of economic policy: **fiscal policy** and **monetary policy**. Fiscal policy is the use of government spending and taxation to affect the economy. (The term **fiscal** refers to budgetary matters.) Monetary policy refers to measures aimed at affecting the amount of money in the economy. Governments use both fiscal and monetary policy to keep their economies growing. But these do represent two different schools of economic thought, and each school has its extremists.

Fiscal Policy: Taxing and Spending

Since there are two sides to the government budget—taxes and spending—the government has four tools of fiscal policy. It can raise or lower spending and it can raise or lower taxes.

If the government raises spending, it will heat up the economy. Why? Because it will increase G in C + I + G. It will increase demand. It will contribute to GDP growth. It is putting money in the accounts of businesses and the pockets of consumers. Using an increase in government spending to ignite a recovery is called *fiscal stimulus*.

Incidentally, this is true whether the government uses money from taxes or borrows the money by issuing debt. If the government spends more than it collects in taxes, it is *deficit spending*. It has been a common practice ever since the British economist Maynard Keynes (pronounced *canes*) theorized in the 1920s that governments could help economies out of recessions by deficit spending. Economists who believe in using fiscal policy to stimulate the economy are called Keynesians.

If the government sees the economy overheating and inflation heading upward, it can cool things off by doing the opposite. If the government cuts or postpones its spending, it decreases demand and that will ripple through the economy.

Taxes have similar effects. If the government wants to stimulate a lackluster economy, it can cut taxes instead of increasing spending. This leaves more money in the hands of consumers and businesses, and that money tends to get spent. If, on the other hand, the government raises taxes, it takes money away from consumers and businesses. This will cool off the economy.

Monetary Policy: Money Makes the World Go Round

An economy runs on money. The amount of money available therefore plays a role in the size of the economy. Monetary policy enables the government to affect the money supply and therefore the growth rate of the economy.

Economists who believe in monetary policy are called monetarists. They oppose the Keynesians and fiscal policy because they believe the money supply has more affect on economic growth than the federal budget does. The economist Milton Friedman has been a major force in this movement, which favors slow, steady growth in the money supply. (In practice, governments use a combination of fiscal and monetary policy to try to keep the economy stable and growing. However, schools of economic thought and many economists strongly prefer either fiscal or monetary policy.)

A monetarist looks at GDP through the following formula:

GDP = money supply × velocity

GDP here is the same GDP that results from C + I + G + (Ex − Im). But it is determined differently, by the money supply—the amount of currency in circulation plus deposits in savings and checking accounts—multiplied by its velocity. *Velocity* is the number of times the money supply circulates through (or "turns over" in) the economy. Picture each piece of currency in an economy, including the money in savings and checking accounts at banks. The average number of times the total stock of currency changes hands is velocity.

MBA Lingo

The **velocity** of money is the number of times the total money supply changes hands, or circulates through an economy. If you divide GDP by the money supply, the number you get is the velocity of money.

For simplicity, let's say that the U.S. money supply is $1 trillion and that the $1 trillion circulates through the economy ten times a year. Since $1 trillion times 10 is $10 trillion, GDP would equal $10 trillion.

There are some complexities with this concept. Velocity can be difficult to measure accurately. Also, velocity can change. For example, some experts believe that aggressive *corporate cash management* (through which companies attempt to slow down the payment of bills and speed up the collection of debts) has increased the velocity of money in the past 30 years.

The Role of the Fed

The Federal Reserve, or "the Fed," controls the U.S. money supply. The Federal Reserve System is the U.S. central bank. Think of a nation's central bank as a "bank for banks." The Fed replaces old currency with new currency, guarantees bank deposits, and governs the banking system.

The Fed affects the economy in three major ways:

- ◆ By moving interest rates

- ◆ By selling and buying government securities

- ◆ By talking about the economy

Let's take a closer look at each of these.

Moving Rates to Get Things Moving

Since *interest rates* are "the price of money," the Fed can stimulate a sluggish economy by lowering interest rates. If interest rates decrease, that makes for easier credit. The lower the rate, the easier it is to repay the loan. Consumers and businesses see the low rates and take out loans, start spending, increase demand, and start an upswing.

MBA Lingo

Interest rates are simply prices that borrowers pay for money in different circumstances. Although money is always the same (a thousand dollars is a thousand dollars), its price—that is, the interest rate—depends on who's borrowing the money. The greater the risk that the borrower will not be able to repay the money, the higher the interest rate. Interest rates also depend on the supply of money, which the Fed controls, and on the demand for money by consumers, businesses, and governments.

On the other hand, the Fed can raise interest rates in order to cool off an overheating economy. If the Fed sees inflation moving up, it is very likely to do this. (As the guardians of the currency, central bankers *hate* inflation.) When the Fed moves rates upward, money becomes more expensive, so consumer and businesses borrow less, spending slows and demand decreases.

Because it hates inflation, the Fed likes to raise rates at the first sign of it. Thus the Fed is often accused of "removing the punch bowl when the party gets going." In a way, though, that's its job.

The Fed also sets the rate for short-term loans that banks make to one another (the *federal funds rate*) and the rate at which the Fed makes loans to banks (the *discount rate*). Although these are the only rates that the Fed directly controls, they tend to drive other *interest rates*.

Case in Point

Economists are currently pondering several questions, which may or may not be resolved by the time you read this: With interest rates already at historic lows, can monetary policy get the economy moving again? Will the Bush tax cuts stimulate spending? Will interest rates rise and choke off investment when the government borrows to finance the deficits that lay ahead? Will the stock market return to its 1990s levels? If not, will consumers keep spending? And, most notably, when will strong growth return?

Buy! Sell!

The Fed also controls sales and purchases of *government securities* (government debt), and can use this to affect the money supply.

When the Fed wants to cool the economy, it sells securities and that takes money out of circulation. Think about it: If businesses and consumers buy government bonds, they have the bonds and the government has their money. Less money is in circulation, so there will be less spending, less economic growth, and a cooler economy.

When the Fed wants to heat up the economy, it buys government securities. This puts money back into the hands of businesses and consumers and thus back into circulation. Money in circulation means more spending and an economy on the upswing.

> **MBA Lingo**
>
> The **federal funds rate** (commonly called the fed funds rate) is the interest rate that banks charge one another on overnight loans. (Federal funds themselves are funds that commercial banks deposit with the federal reserve to meet certain legal requirements.) The **discount rate** is the interest rate that the Federal Reserve charges on loans that it makes to member banks.

Although people watch interest closely, purchases and sales of securities are equally important to the Fed in managing the money supply. These sales are done at the direction of the Federal Open Market Committee by the Securities Department at the Federal Reserve Bank of New York. (That bank, by the way, is one of 12 Federal Reserve Banks that oversee the U.S. banking system.)

When the Fed Talks ...

The Fed, or more accurately, the chairman of the Federal Reserve, also talks to the business community. Indeed, the business community is so focused on the pronouncements of current Fed Chairman Alan Greenspan that people joke about it. You'll often hear things like, "If Alan Greenspan sneezes, the economy catches cold," and so on.

This talking function of the Fed is called "moral suasion." The Fed, in other words, directs statements at banks, consumers, and businesses to get them to "do the right thing" with regard to the economy.

If you want to join the ranks of serious "Fed-watchers," be sure to review the Fed chairman's periodic testimony before Congress. These comments are reported and analyzed in newspapers and the full text of the testimony is available at www.fmcenter.org. Also, watch for changes and trends in the Fed funds rate and the discount rate. For example, an increase in the Fed funds rate after a series of rate cuts means that the Fed thinks the economy may be overheating. Conversely, a decrease in the Fed funds rate means that the Fed wants to stimulate the economy.

However, keep two things in mind. First, the Fed's action may or may not have the intended effect. Second, the Fed may be wrong. Many economists and businesspeople feel that the Fed kept interest rates too low for too long during the 1990s expansion. Whether they felt this way before the expansion ended is another story. However, if they are right, the Fed contributed to the overexpansion by keeping the price of money too low.

Case in Point

While people hear the Fed chairman, do they actually listen to him? In December 1996, Mr. Greenspan stated that "irrational exuberance" on the part of investors in stocks could harm the economy. The comment was widely reported, and "irrational exuberance" even became popular catchwords. Yet investors continued to bid up stock prices well into the year 2000. Months later Greenspan backed off this comment, but by then the market momentum had already been established.

The Least You Need to Know

- ◆ The economy is the environment—the climate—in which business operates.

- ◆ In a recession, spending and demand decrease, making the economic climate more difficult. In a recovery, spending and demand increase, making it easier.

- ◆ Gross domestic product, or GDP, is the value of all goods and services produced within a nation. Four sectors comprise the total economy: consumer spending, business investment, government spending, and net exports (exports minus imports).

- ◆ The federal government uses fiscal policy to stimulate or cool off the economy by adjusting taxes and spending.

- ◆ Monetary policy uses interest rates, purchases, and sales of government securities, along with moral suasion, to heat or cool the economy. Monetary policy is controlled by the Federal Reserve Board.

Chapter 7

Going by the Numbers: Economic Indicators

In This Chapter

- ◆ Where to find economic indicators
- ◆ The single most important economic indicator
- ◆ What housing starts mean to businesses
- ◆ How to view economic trends

In the previous chapter, you learned the basics of economic theory: the concepts of recessions and recoveries, of inflation and unemployment, and the effects of fiscal and monetary policy on the business cycle. All of these influences have a strong impact on business—and on your business.

Managers steer their companies through the economic waters much the way a captain steers a ship on the ocean. The waters are sometimes calm, sometimes rough. A squall can pop up out of nowhere, and a full-blown storm can do damage. But you can also see some smooth sailing.

Just as sea captains navigate by reading their charts and buoys and getting regular weather reports, managers steer their businesses by reading economic signals, what economists call indicators. These indicators help us to know where the economy is and where it might be headed. Then, as a manager, you can make the right moves, gearing up for recoveries and cutting back for recessions.

In this chapter, I'll show you how to analyze and understand the key economic indicators and their importance.

What Are the Key Indicators?

How can we understand what's happening in the economy? Economists use *economic data* to track, forecast, and analyze economies and industries.

From the various economic data issued by the government agencies and other institutions, economists have found that certain statistics point to the current or future state of the economy. These data, called *economic indicators* because they indicate the state of the economy, can help you as a business person steer your company through periods of economic change.

Where can you find economic data? You'll find data presented with solid analysis in the business press, particularly in *The Wall Street Journal*, the nation's daily business newspaper. The economic and business coverage in *The New York Times* and many other newspapers has improved a lot in the past decade as well. A number of business magazines, especially *Business Week*, also provide solid economic news.

Several sites on the World Wide Web, particularly those of the U.S. Department of Commerce (www.doc.gov) and the economic consulting firm DRI/WEFA (www.driwefa.com), provide economic data online.

In the following pages, we'll examine these key economic indicators:

- Economic growth rate
- Prices and inflation
- Interest rates
- Unemployment
- Consumer confidence
- Housing starts and sales
- Retail sales and new car sales
- Productivity growth
- Stock market
- Index of leading indicators

MBA Lingo

Economic indicators are key statistics and pieces of economic data that show the current and sometimes the future direction of the economy. **Economic data** includes actual and estimated counts of transactions and items (for example, on income, prices, employment, auto sales, and interest rates). In the United States, these data are collected by government agencies, such as the Bureau of Economic Analysis (BEA), and by state agencies.

The Biggest Indicator: Economic Growth Rate

Economic growth rate is the major indicator to watch: It's the rate at which the economy as a whole, as measured by GDP, is growing. You'll recall that in Chapter 6, I defined GDP as the total economy. It's measured by adding the following: total spending by consumers, total investment by businesses, total spending by the government, and net exports (exports minus imports).

This number is reported every month. Unfortunately, it is then later revised as the Bureau of Economic Analysis collects more data. The difference between the originally reported estimate and the final revision can be as high as 1 to 2 percentage points. This is on a number with a long-term average of 3 percent.

Look for deviations from that 3 percent baseline as well as the trend over time. The most important element is the trend. If economic growth is slowing down over a period of months or quarters, there is a good chance that conditions will become more difficult for many businesses. If you see your business slowing down, it is generally a good idea to monitor your customers' behavior—and your sales trends—closely and perhaps adjust your hiring, buying, and production plans downward. Don't panic, but do be especially careful during a slowdown.

MBA Lingo

The **economic growth rate** measures how much bigger (or smaller) an economy is in one period compared with the same period a year ago. The economic growth of a city, state, province, or nation can be measured. The growth of national economies is the most widely followed.

If economic growth is speeding up, consumers tend to spend more freely. They feel secure in their jobs and are more willing to spend and to use credit to finance purchases. When you see an economic expansion coming, be ready to gear up your production. You may have to hire more people and even expand your facilities.

You still need to watch your sales closely to see if your business is sharing in the good times. Avoid overexpanding and adding too many people on staff or adding too much new office space or equipment. Just like bad economic times, good ones don't last forever.

Case in Point
In the 1990s, many businesses overexpanded, particularly those in high-technology and telecommunications. As a result, there is now too much capacity in those industries, and high-tech and telecom must wait until demand gears up again. For some companies, that kind of wait can be long enough and unprofitable enough to put them out of business. In general, however, in the past 15 years companies have become much better at adjusting to the ups and downs of the economy, particularly in their ability to control inventories and to lay off workers when necessary.

Buying Power: Prices and Inflation

As noted in Chapter 6, inflation refers to an overall increase in the price of goods and services when demand exceeds supply. Some inflation usually accompanies rapid economic growth.

However, inflation also represents a decrease in the buying power of the currency. If a suit that costs $100 this year costs $200 next year, for example, the value of the dollar has decreased. In times of inflation, prices rise more quickly than wages, so the buying power of consumers decreases.

High inflation is considered bad because it undermines confidence in the currency and can generate disorder. U.S. monetary policy aims to minimize inflation—that is, to keep the inflation rate near zero.

The main indicators of inflation are the Consumer Price Index (CPI) and the Producer Price Index (PPI). The CPI measures the price of various goods and services consumers purchase. The PPI measures the price of materials that businesses purchase. When these indexes are reported, the year-earlier numbers are also usually given, so you will know whether inflation is up or down. Because inflation is news, the media will report whether the indexes are up or down.

The Cost of Money: Interest Rates

As I discussed in Chapter 6, an interest rate is the price of money. Low interest rates make money—in the form of credit—available to consumers and businesses. Low interest rates generate demand because "easy money" prompts people to borrow and then buy.

Key interest rates to watch are the federal funds rate and the discount rate because the Federal Reserve can directly affect the federal funds rate and sets the discount rate. As you learned in Chapter 6, if the Fed raises rates, it is trying to slow down growth. If it lowers rates, it is trying to stimulate growth. Rather than over-react to an increase or decrease, look for a pattern in increases and decreases over several months or quarters.

The other key rate to watch is the *prime rate*, which is the interest rate large banks charge to their best business customers. This rate is set by banks, not by the Fed. Again, watch the trend in the prime rate to get a general idea of where interest rates are headed.

MBA Lingo

The **prime rate,** often simply called "the prime," is the rate on loans that a bank charges its most creditworthy corporate customers. The prime rate is traditionally set by several major New York City banks.

MBA Mastery

If interest rates are rising, it can be a good time to get a mortgage or loan if you need one. Borrowing money will only get more expensive if rates are headed upward. If interest rates fall, you will be able to refinance the loan at lower rates.

Out of Work: Unemployment

The unemployment rate measures the percentage of people in the work force who are out of work. Some controversy surrounds this rate, mostly because the definition of "work force" is unclear. If a person has stopped looking for work, he or she is no longer considered in the work force. Therefore, many long-term unemployed people are not included in the rate. Some experts believe that the rate as currently calculated in the United States understates unemployment.

Nonetheless, an unemployment rate from 4 to 7 percent is considered very good in the United States, or in a single state or city. Anything over 8 percent is considered high.

While low unemployment is certainly good, it puts pressure on businesses to increase their wages (and thus one of their biggest costs). Low unemployment indicates a "tight labor market" and enables workers to demand higher wages because they cannot be so easily replaced. Higher unemployment allows businesses to hold the line when workers demand higher wages because the workers know they may not be able to find new jobs easily.

Unemployment often persists after an economic recovery begins because businesses can be slow to rehire workers. Managers want to be sure that the recovery is underway, and (let's face it) the longer they hold off rehiring workers, the longer they hold off increasing their payrolls. This can make for a so-called "jobless recovery," one in which unemployment persists for a few quarters into the expansion.

Speaking of jobs, the media regularly report the number of new jobs created in the economy in the past month or quarter. Listen for the "net" number of new jobs, meaning the number of new jobs less the number of jobs lost. Continuing job creation indicates a growing economy.

Safety and Security: Consumer Confidence

Both the University of Michigan and the Conference Board (a business-supported source of information located in New York City) issue their own indexes of *consumer confidence*. These indexes gauge consumer psychology by asking a sample of consumers whether they expect to be better or worse off in the upcoming months, whether they feel secure in their jobs, and similar questions.

MBA Lingo

Consumer confidence is a measure of how consumers feel about the economy and about their prospects in the current and future economy.

The University of Michigan index includes a survey of buying plans, which indicate how many consumers are planning a major purchase such as a heavy appliance or a car in the next six months to a year.

Many economists and businesspeople watch indexes of consumer confidence because they see them as early warning signs of the future path of the economy. High or increasing confidence means continued or coming recovery, while low or falling confidence means the opposite.

Note, however, that consumer confidence can be affected by developments not directly related to the economy that trigger emotions such as fear or enthusiasm. The financial accounting scandals in late 2001 and 2002 certainly took a toll on consumers' (not to mention investors') confidence, even though many economists kept citing the strong fundamentals and positive economic signs at the time.

Settling Down: Housing Starts and Sales

Housing trends are important not just because buying a house, apartment, or condominium represents a major purchase. It represents a chain of major purchases. A house or condo needs furniture, carpeting, draperies, appliances, electronic equipment, and, often, the services of painters, plasterers, or landscapers. (As you sign all those mortgage papers, be happy to do your part to boost our economy!)

Housing starts and *housing sales* indicate the strength of the economy. Increasing or high levels of starts and sales indicate a robust economy, while decreasing or low levels of starts indicate a weak economy. People build and buy homes when they expect the economy to remain strong enough to provide them with jobs and incomes to pay the mortgage. Housing starts and sales at the local or state level are an excellent indicator of the health of the local or state economy.

In general, the more housing activity there is in a nation, state, or city, the better for the economy.

Finally, the trend in home prices indicates the demand for housing in an area, as well as the general desirability of that area as a place to live. High or increasing prices indicate high demand. To a degree, this reflects the strength of the economy and availability of jobs in the area.

MBA Lingo

Housing starts are the number of houses on which construction started in a specific area during a certain period. These are a sign of things to come, since it takes three to six months for those houses to enter the inventory of homes to be sold.

Housing sales, which are usually broken into sales of new and existing homes, are another indicator of economic health.

Shop 'Til You Drop: Retail Sales and New Car Sales

Strong retail sales and new car sales indicate economic vitality and high consumer income. Watch for changes in the trend, that is, for a strengthening or weakening of retail or auto sales.

When retail sales are strengthening, it is important to be able to meet consumer demand. Many businesses find that they must expand their operation by adding sales space or equipment or increasing the size of the sales or production staffs. It may also be possible to raise prices when sales are strong because demand is strong enough to support higher prices.

Weakening retail sales signal a time for many businesses to pull back. If customer demand is about to decrease, it is generally a good idea to trim production and to avoid building up inventories. If your sales decrease, you don't want to be stuck with unsaleable goods. Also, if you overexpanded your operation during the good times, you may find that you have to lay off some workers or stop leasing as much space and equipment as you needed during the economic expansion.

More, More, More: Productivity Growth

Productivity growth has become a widely followed indicator, mainly because a new higher level of productivity may be responsible for a new, higher level of U.S. economic performance.

Productivity itself is measured as output per hour worked in the economy. Essentially, it means total output divided by the number of hours worked (agricultural work is not included in the formula). If output rises but the number of hours that employees worked decreases, remains the same, or increases at a lower rate than output does, then productivity is growing.

MBA Mastery

Economic statistics mean business. For instance, if productivity were to rise at an average of 2.5 percent rather than 1.5 percent annually over the next 20 years, it would add an additional $3 trillion to U.S. GDP.

As noted in Chapter 6, many economists and managers believe that more efficient business practices and advances in technology have increased employees' productivity. In fact, productivity growth surged in the late 1990s, accelerating to 2.5 percent a year after averaging 1.5 percent from 1973 to 1995. As a rule of thumb, growth over 2 percent is considered very good.

Watching Wall Street: The Stock Market

The stock market is a favorite economic indicator, but few people are completely certain what it is an indicator of, aside from general business and consumer confidence. It is more of a psychological barometer than an actual economic indicator, because although stock prices are strongly related to corporate earnings, market emotion can also move prices.

MBA Lingo

A **lagging** indicator points to an economic development—a recovery or recession—that has already occurred. A **leading** indicator points to a development that lies ahead.

The Dow Jones Industrial Average is based upon 30 New York Stock Exchange–listed stocks taken to be representative of the market as a whole. This is probably the most widely followed indicator, but the S&P 500, a group of 500 stocks monitored by the financial information firm Standard & Poor's, is more representative because it's based on a much larger sample than the Dow.

In general, a high or rising stock market indicates a recovery is in progress; a falling market indicates recession. But because it takes awhile for investors to react to economic developments, the stock market can usually be viewed as a *lagging*, rather than a *leading*, indicator.

Index of Leading Indicators

A number of organizations periodically release an index of leading indicators. The most authoritative are those from the Bureau of Economic Analysis and from the Conference Board. While the accuracy and, more to the point, timing of the forecasts implied by the index are debated in economic circles, it is worth it for a manager to note whether the index is moving up or down over one or more quarters.

The components of indexes include (among a few other indicators): average weekly hours worked in manufacturing, average weekly initial claims for unemployment insurance, new orders for consumer goods and materials, orders for plant and equipment, building permits for housing units, stock prices, and growth of the money supply.

As you can see, economists rival sports fans in their obsession with statistics. But as a manager, you need to track only the indicators that you see as relevant to your business and to have a good idea of where we are in the business cycle.

> **MBA Mastery**
>
> Whether you think the economy will improve or you think it will worsen, sooner or later you're going to be right—thanks to the never-ending business cycle.

What to Watch for When You Watch

As I've emphasized throughout this chapter, watch for trends in economic data. By this, I mean both the trend over the past few reports of each indicator and *year-over-year* comparisons. (These comparisons compare the data for the most current period with the data for the same period last year.) Watching trends and year-earlier comparisons will enable you to place the data in context.

Don't react to every change in an indicator. But don't wait forever to start adjusting or to incorporate a change in the economy into your planning. If you've been operating in a recovery (or a recession) for a while, you could adopt a mind-set geared to that climate and be caught off guard by a change.

Learn to understand the economy's effect on your business. Over years of observation, you'll get a feel for this. Some businesses, such as finance companies (nonbank lenders of money), collection agencies, and used-car dealers, do well in recessions. Many others, including restaurants, travel agencies, and other businesses that sell highly discretionary (nonessential) items, can get hurt in a severe downturn. If you see a recession coming, prepare for it.

Also learn about the effect of the national economy on your region. Regional differences can be significant. While no city, state, or region is recession-proof or prone to depression, some have proven more resilient or vulnerable to downturns than others. For example, in the recession following the 1990s boom, the high-technology area of Silicon Valley saw a sharp downturn.

Finally, here's a rule of thumb: Mixed signals often herald change. If all the indicators point upward toward recovery, we are in a recovery and will probably stay there for a while. And if all the signals are pointing downward toward recession, we are probably in one. But if some signals point up and some point down, a change from the current situation, whatever it is, is more likely.

The Least You Need to Know

- Economic indicators can often tell you about the general direction of the economy, but how your specific business will be affected can only be determined by you over time.

- The economic growth rate represents the most important and (aside from the Dow Jones Industrial Average) most widely reported indicator. If growth is about 3 percent or more, the economy is generally considered healthy.

- Housing starts and sales are a particularly good indicator of future economic growth because when people buy houses, they then need to buy furniture and other goods to stock up the house.

- The important thing to watch in any economic indicator is the trend over several periods. That can tell you much more about the economy's direction than one or two readings of an indicator.

Chapter 8

Getting Down to Business: Operations Management

In This Chapter

♦ The secrets of resource management

♦ Performing a cost-benefit analysis

♦ The law of diminishing returns

♦ The difference between fixed and variable costs

♦ Understanding economies of scale

♦ Centralization versus decentralization

Managing a business operation calls for making dozens of decisions a day, some of them small, some large, some of them routine, and some extraordinary. For certain kinds of decisions—particularly those relating to the operations and resources of the business—analytical tools like the ones in this chapter will help you make the best decision.

Here is an example of what I mean.

Picture two people, each running a separate business. One is a trained manager, the other is not and operates by the seat of his pants. They are each going to face dozens of similar decisions every day: A supplier will call and ask how much he should deliver next week. The evening-shift supervisor will want to know if she should add another person to her team because it's getting busy after 7 P.M. A machine will break down and it may have to be replaced or repaired, depending on which is more economical. Each of the businesses may need to add capacity, but the boss must decide how much to add.

The trained manager will have ways of looking at these decisions that are unavailable to the guy who goes by his gut. He will have a way of thinking about these situations that is more systematic and organized than the approaches the other fellow uses. The trained manager has this more sophisticated view of business situations because he understands key concepts in operations management.

The concepts we'll examine in this chapter can make the difference between guesswork and a good decision.

Managing Your Resources

Many business decisions come down to figuring out how to allocate your resources. Your resources include money, labor, materials, or buildings and equipment. Every business operates with limited resources—a finite amount of money, labor, materials, and buildings—so the savvy manager must decide the best use of the resources he or she has.

Here are some tough calls a manager may have to make when it comes to allocating resources:

◆ How much money should a company invest in developing a new product?

◆ What is the best size for a business? How much staff and physical space is needed?

◆ How does a manager determine the best buys on expensive equipment (for example, computer networks, industrial ovens, or tractors)?

◆ When should a store open and close for business?

◆ How much time should a project take, and how should it be done?

◆ Given two or more potential locations to expand a business, which one should a company choose?

How do managers answer these questions? Since resources are limited, managers must put them where they will do the most good—that is, where they will earn the highest *return*, or profit.

Certain key concepts help managers determine the best ways to use resources to maximize returns. These concepts are

- Cost-benefit analysis.

- The law of diminishing returns.

- Fixed costs and variable costs.

- Economies of scale.

- Centralization and decentralization.

I'll cover each of these concepts over the following pages.

> **MBA Lingo**
>
> **Return**, in this context, is the amount of profit that the company earns. This can be expressed as a percentage. For example, if the owners have a total of $10 million invested in the company and the company has profits of $1 million for the year, then the return on investment is $1 million, or 10 percent.

Cost-Benefit Analysis: What's It Worth?

Everything in business—an item, a campaign, an employee, an operation—has a cost associated with it. This cost is almost always measurable in dollars. Most things that have a cost also have an associated benefit. This benefit is usually (but not always) a return measurable in dollars.

You'll often hear a businessperson say, "You've got to spend money to make money." However, not every expenditure earns money. Among those that do, some earn more than others. Therefore, before spending money, most businesspeople do a *cost-benefit analysis*. There are various tools for conducting cost-benefit analysis, and you'll see some of them, such as break-even analysis and crossover analysis, in Chapter 9.

For now, let's consider a small neighborhood copy shop. Like the owner of any business that serves the public, the guy running the copy shop has to figure out his hours of operation. He might consider several factors; for instance, the hours of his nearest competitor and the convenience of his largest customers. But his major concern is the cost versus the benefit of opening an hour earlier or closing an hour later.

Let's say he long ago figured out that he has to open the shop at 7 A.M., because that's when people who are headed to work and school stop off on their way. However, he's been closing at 11 P.M. only because the previous owner did. He isn't sure the evening hours are worth it.

> **MBA Lingo**
>
> **Cost-benefit analysis** is a way of measuring the benefits expected from a decision, measuring the costs expected to be incurred in the decision, and then see if the benefits exceed the costs. If they do, then the analysis is in favor of going ahead with the planned course of action.

After sitting down with sales data from the past three months, he has the information he needs for a cost-benefit analysis. He knows the cost of staying open that last hour, and he knows the average amount of money he makes in that last hour.

He's figured out that it costs him $23.00 to stay open from 10 to 11 p.m. This includes the cost of electricity for the lights and equipment, the cost of heat, and the assistant manager's salary. If he closes at 10, he saves all this money.

In terms of the benefit, he's figured out the profit on the volume he does in that last hour. He makes an average profit of $5^{1}/_{2}$¢ a copy (this is based just on the cost of making the copy; it doesn't count the costs of electricity, heat, and labor). He makes an average of 460 copies in that last hour. Thus, he makes an average of $25.30 (460 copies times .055¢ per copy) in that last hour of operation. That's the "benefit."

MBA Lingo

The **net benefit** is the benefit after deducting (or "netting out") the costs.

MBA Mastery

Some people find it odd that a business or office manager will try to scrape a few cents off on some small items (coffee, pens, office supplies) that the firm buys regularly. But in a high-volume operation, pennies add up. Cost control lowers costs, and by lowering costs you automatically increase the benefit.

Now the big question is: Does the benefit outweigh the cost?

In this case it does. If you take the benefit of $25.30 and subtract the cost of $23.00, you get $2.30. (This is also known as the *net benefit*—the benefit after deducting or "netting out" the costs.) So on a pure cost-benefit basis, it is worth it to keep the copy shop open that last hour.

Of course, other considerations may enter into the decision. For instance, if the assistant manager wants to start going home earlier or if late-evening crime is rising, the owner may decide that it's just not worth it to stay open the extra hour for $2.30. But on a pure cost-benefit basis, it *is* worth it.

There are various ways of doing cost-benefit analysis. There are even various ways of placing a dollar value on the costs and benefits. We will explore some of them in this book. The key element at this point, however, is that a manager looks at most situations in terms of costs and benefits.

What About Social Costs and Benefits?

Over the past 25 years, people have become more aware of the social costs and benefits generated by a business. Social costs are costs that are not directly borne by the company. Social benefits are positive effects that do not directly benefit the company.

Environmental pollution is a social cost. The larger community bears the costs of pollution generated by manufacturing processes or inefficient vehicles. These costs take the form of illness, increased health-care costs, inconvenience to people confined to their homes on bad air days, and so on. The costs also include the expense of cleaning up a river or toxic waste site.

The trend has been for society, in the form of local, state, and federal legislation and the courts, to make social costs explicit and make businesses bear or defray those costs. This happens through legislation—for example, the establishment of the federal Superfund, which is financed by companies that contribute to environmental pollution to pay for the cleanup of specific sites. It also happens through liability lawsuits, such as those brought against tobacco companies by people with lung disease.

Social costs can, however, be difficult to assess and address in some cases. For instance, many communities have seen increased automobile traffic as a result of companies moving from cities to suburban office campuses. While public hearings on the matter are often held, little has been done to assess these costs and bill companies for them.

In part that's because businesses also generate social benefits. They do so by creating jobs, paying taxes, and purchasing goods and services in a community or state. They also provide the social benefits of a minimum wage and reduced discrimination (although some companies have been forced to do so by law).

Chapter 27 deals with the relationship between business and society as well as business ethics. Social costs and benefits are mentioned here because it is useful to consider the potential for them as part of a cost-benefit analysis.

Case in Point

Often a business will do things not justified on a pure cost-benefit basis. These include encouraging employees to do volunteer work, sponsoring a local little league team, or even keeping a long-term, newly disabled employee on the payroll until retirement.

The company does these things out of decency or good citizenship. However, many managers believe these actions also create a positive corporate image and that this benefit can translate to increased sales.

Too Much of a Good Thing: The Law of Diminishing Returns

The *law of diminishing returns* basically says you *can* have too much of a good thing. In other words, if you keep adding more resources to your company's existing resources, you will at first see an added return. But after awhile, you'll see a falloff in the added return the resource brings.

MBA Lingo

The **law of diminishing returns** states that the marginal return—that is, the added return—produced by any resource will decrease with each additional unit of that resource that is added.

For example, let's say our copy shop owner decides to advertise his business, something he's never done before. He wants to place ads in local newspapers and on the radio. The following chart shows what happens. At first, his sales increase rapidly as people hear about his shop and stop in for copies. Then, sales continue to increase, but each additional day or week of advertising will produce more sales at a reduced or diminished rate. Hence the idea of diminishing returns. In other words, there is a limit on how many dollars of new sales that additional advertising will add.

Diminishing returns are inevitable.

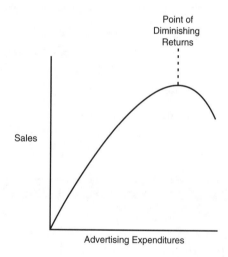

The law of diminishing returns pops up constantly. For example, in most situations requiring workers, you will get more work done, or get it done faster, with each worker that you add. However, eventually each added worker will be able to add less and less additional production (unless you add more of another resource, such as machinery).

Estimating when returns will diminish can be tricky. There are no commonly used formulas or rules of thumb, because when the "law" will kick in depends upon the situation. For example, a logging operation selectively clearing a forest can keep adding new workers, and at first each added worker will be able to cut down more trees per day.

But at some point the added worker is not going to be able to cut the same number of trees. There may be so many workers that they get in one another's way or the trucks may not be able to haul away the logs fast enough for them to be able to work, or some other factor will limit their productivity. In a sense, the only way to figure out when this will occur is by balancing your resources—for example, two loggers per saw, ten loggers per truck—or through experience, or both.

Counting Costs: Fixed and Variable Costs

Most businesses have both *fixed costs* and *variable costs*. Fixed costs are those that remain the same regardless of the amount of product the company makes and sells. For the copy shop, for example, the mortgage on the building and the cost of insurance are fixed. Some, but not all fixed costs, are considered overhead (costs not directly associated with production or sales).

Variable costs, on the other hand, change with the company's production and sales volume. For the copy shop, variable costs include the compensation of the copy clerks and the cost of copy paper and ink. One reason layoffs are common in troubled companies (and during recessions) is that in most firms, labor represents the largest variable cost. (If the copy shop hits a drastic downturn in business, some of the clerks may be fired in order to save the owner money on their salaries.)

There's a saying in business: In the long run, all costs are variable. This means that over a long enough period the company can eliminate even a fixed cost; for example, the company can sell its factory or equipment. This is true, but the long run can be very long indeed, so it's wise to think of fixed costs as being fixed.

Some businesses, particularly in manufacturing, have inherently high fixed costs. Oil refining, automobile manufacturing, and printing are

MBA Lingo

Fixed costs are those that remain the same regardless of the amount of product the company makes and sells; for example, the rent on office space, the cost of insurance, and the cost of managerial salaries are fixed. **Variable costs** change with the company's production and sales volume. Variable costs include the compensation of the sales force and production workers, the cost of materials, and delivery costs.

MBA Alert

Try to keep fixed costs as low as possible, particularly in a new or small business. If sales decrease because of a recession or new competition, you can cut your variable costs and fight back—for example, by selling harder. But if you're stuck with high fixed costs when sales decrease, your business can get killed.

good examples. Other businesses, particularly service businesses, tend to have a high proportion of variable costs. Delivery services, temp agencies, and law firms fall into this category. Keep in mind, however, that almost every business has a mix of fixed and variable costs.

Size Matters: Economies of Scale

Economies of scale explain why many things are "cheaper by the dozen." Economies of scale make *volume discounts* possible because the average cost of making a unit of product decreases with each additional one you make.

Economies of scale occur as volume increases because fixed costs are spread out over more pieces, or units, of product. Each added unit absorbs a bit more of the fixed costs, and that lowers the amount of fixed costs that all the previous units must absorb. Thus, the average cost per unit falls. This occurs even though variable costs remain pretty much the same on each unit.

MBA Lingo

A **volume discount** occurs when you pay less per item the more you buy. Businesses give volume discounts in order to increase their sales. They take a lower profit on each item in order to make a greater total profit.

Let's go back to the copy shop example. Let's say the owner has a high-volume copier that cost $10,000 per year to lease. Let's also say that the variable costs, for paper and toner and so on, are 2¢ a copy.

Look at the difference in cost per copy at two levels of volume: 500,000 copies and 1,000,000 copies over the course of five years.

	500,000 Copies/Yr	1,000,000 Copies/Yr
Total variable costs (paper, toner)	$10,000	$20,000
Total fixed costs (annual copier lease)	10,000	10,000
Total cost of copies	20,000	30,000
Cost per copy	$0.04	$0.03

As you can see, although the fixed costs (the annual lease cost of the copier) and variable costs (the 2¢ cost per copy) are the same, the total cost per copy is lower at the higher volume.

Economies of scale mean that the more a company does something—that is, the greater the scale of its operation—the more economically it can do it. This can give a company a competitive advantage.

MBA Lingo

Economies of scale refer to the lower costs that occur with higher production volumes. The cost per unit of manufacturing an item generally decreases, the more of them that an operation makes.

Consider this: In the copier example, the company that makes a million copies in a year could charge customers an average of 8¢ a copy and still make a profit of 5¢ a copy. The company doing half a million copies a year would have to charge customers 9¢ a copy in order to make a nickel a copy. The company with the higher volume could thus charge a lower price than the one with the lower volume. This could enable that company to pull in even more business, and boost volume further.

Case in Point

Many people decry the big commercial chains that dominate many businesses, but these megacompanies have been thriving for years. Long ago, chain businesses began to dominate markets like general retailing (Sears and Wal-Mart) and fast food (Pizza Hut and McDonald's). More recently they've gone into, yes, photocopying (Sir Speedy, Kinko's).

Economies of scale often enable these operations to underprice local, single-site operators and ultimately make it impossible for the single-site shops to compete on price. They typically compete on selection and services.

Economies of scale are also the reason behind many corporate mergers. (A merger occurs when two companies combine their operations.) Most mergers consolidate certain functions to lower the costs of doing business. For example, the merged company does not need two accounting functions or two human resources departments. So they combine them into one (or just eliminate one) and then spread the fixed costs of the consolidated department over the larger, merged operation.

Come Together, Go Apart: Centralization and Decentralization

Centralization and its opposite, decentralization, drive many business decisions. *Centralization* is an attempt to combine functions or operations. You centralize various functions by putting them together into one function. Often you seek economies of scale or some other form of efficiency.

Think of it this way: McDonald's is a huge franchise with thousands of separate restaurants all over the world. McDonald's could have each restaurant buy its own food, paper goods, and so on. However, by buying food and paper goods from one supplier—that is, by using a centralized purchasing function— McDonald's can give greater volume to suppliers and get volume discounts. Likewise, a magazine publisher such as Condé Nast, which puts out *Vogue*, *House & Garden*, and *Vanity Fair*, among others, can get better deals on paper and ink with centralized purchasing.

MBA Lingo

Centralization means placing a function or decision, such as buying office supplies, hiring workers, or pricing products in one area for the entire company. This yields more control and more standardized results or decisions.

MBA Lingo

Decentralization means allowing individual business units—for example, offices in various cities or countries—to handle functions and decisions independently. A middle ground is for headquarters to issue guidelines within which individual units can make their own decisions.

If you have all your buying done from one central function in the company, that increased scale gets you volume discounts. However, there are other reasons to centralize an operation. A major one is control. A centralized function, for purchasing or hiring, for example, provides greater control over costs or salaries than letting a bunch of smaller units make their own decisions. Centralization can also bring greater control over the quality of materials purchased or the qualifications of people hired.

The central function, whatever it is, should not meddle in decisions that it has decided to leave to the operating managers. It should either take care of those decisions completely for the smaller units or issue guidelines and let the operating managers make decisions within those guidelines. For example, purchasing can either deal with suppliers so individual operating managers don't have to, or it can issue a list of approved suppliers, supplies, and prices and let the operating managers decide how much of what they need and when.

How Much Centralization Is Good?

Managers repeatedly wonder how much centralization is good. As often occurs, where you stand depends on where you sit. Senior managers like centralization because it gives them greater control. Managers lower in the ranks prefer *decentralization* because they can make more decisions. They often feel positioned to make the best decisions because they're closer to customers and employees than "some guy back at headquarters." Plus, they need the authority to do their jobs.

A company has to balance the urges to centralize and decentralize. If decision-making authority is too centralized, people feel like automatons. They feel they're not trusted to think. But if decision-making is too decentralized, there's a danger of lost control, particularly financial and quality control.

You'll See These Concepts, If You Look

The five key concepts discussed in this chapter come up often in business. Even when managers do not discuss them or refer to them directly, these notions underlie many business decisions.

A manager often makes decisions almost subconsciously based on one of these concepts. She may know that adding another worker would not be worth it, without actually thinking about diminishing returns or cost-benefit. Or she may squeeze more workers into the same space because she knows she can't buy a new facility and increase her fixed costs yet. A manager doesn't have to talk about economies of scale to understand volume discounts or group life insurance.

Nonetheless, understanding these business basics will help you know what's really at work in business decisions. They will also help you use the analytical tools we examine in the next chapter.

The Least You Need to Know

- ◆ A conscious or subconscious cost-benefit analysis underlies almost every decision a manager makes.

- ◆ Given societal trends, managers must consider the social costs (and benefits) of a decision, for business reasons as well as for ethical reasons.

- ◆ Every business faces both fixed and variable costs. Fixed costs do not change with the amount you produce and sell, but variable costs do.

- ◆ Economies of scale occur when a business produces high volume, which enables it to drive down the cost per unit. Economies of scale are the reason many large operations and chain stores are so successful.

- ◆ Be aware that the law of diminishing returns affects almost all new ventures or campaigns. When you first do something, you get a relatively high return, but over time, the return decreases.

Chapter 9

Decisions, Decisions: Analytical Tools and Some Statistics

In This Chapter

- ◆ The importance of break-even analysis
- ◆ Performing a crossover analysis
- ◆ Using planning and scheduling tools
- ◆ Making a decision tree
- ◆ Understanding basic business statistics

Having seen the concepts that can help you look at business situations like a pro, it's time to get hold of some tools that can help you in these situations. These analytical tools, as they are called, are structured ways of examining business situations and making managerial decisions. These tools all have one purpose—to help you make better decisions more easily.

Some of these tools, such as break-even analysis and crossover analysis, enable you to compare two or more choices in a standard manner. Others, such as planning and scheduling tools and decision trees, enable you to get the various parts of a complex problem "on the table" so you can see what you are dealing with. These tools are not a substitute for managerial decision making. Instead, they are designed to help managers in that process, and generally these tools do what they are designed to do.

This chapter also introduces you to basic business statistics. A course in statistics is required in most MBA programs because many managerial decisions in marketing, production, and finance are based on statistical information.

The Manager's Toolbox

Analytical tools have one purpose—to help you make better business decisions. The four tools we consider in this chapter are:

- Break-even analysis

- Crossover analysis

- Planning and scheduling tools

- Decision trees

These tools apply to a wide variety of businesses and situations.

Break-Even Analysis

The break-even point for a product or service is the point at which the sales revenue equals the production costs. It is expressed in the number of units sold. Simply put, it is the point where you start making money.

The importance of a break-even analysis is that when you are planning to offer a new product or service, you need to know how many sales you have to make to begin making a profit. Break-even analysis shows you that number of sales.

Calculate the break-even point with the following formula:

$$\text{Break-even units} = \frac{\text{Fixed Costs}}{(\text{Selling Price} - \text{Variable Cost per Unit})}$$

Note that to use this formula, you need to know both the fixed and variable costs of making the product or delivering the service (see Chapter 8).

Finding the Break-Even Point

Let's go back to the copy shop example used in Chapter 8. Remember, the shop uses a copy machine leased for $10,000 (which represents a fixed cost) and that paper, ink, and so on cost 2¢ a copy (which represents a variable cost). Let's say that the average copy sells for 8¢.

Plugging these figures into the formula gives us:

Break-even units = $10,000 ÷ ($0.08 – 0.02)

or

Break-even units = $10,000 ÷ $0.06

or

Break-even = 166,667 units

Another way of saying this is that the machine "pays for itself" after about 167,000 copies.

Break-even analysis helps in this decision because the manager can think about the volume he can expect to do in some period of time. Also, plugging other values into the formula shows what might happen in other circumstances.

For example, if the shop owner can lease a machine with total fixed costs of $5,000 per year, or 50 percent of $10,000, the break-even point will also fall by 50 percent, to about 83,000 units.

Break-even = $5,000 ÷ $0.06

or

Break-even = 83,333 units

Alternatively, if the outfit can raise the average price of a copy to 10¢, it can decrease the break-even point below 167,000 units even with fixed costs of $10,000.

Break-even units = $10,000 ÷ ($0.10 – 0.02)

or

Break-even units = $10,000 ÷ $0.08

or

Break-even = 125,000 units

You could also figure out the result of both raising the price to 10¢ a copy *and* lowering fixed costs to $5,000 (which lowers the break-even point to 62,500 units).

Break-even analysis is frequently used to make decisions about major purchases, investments, and leases involving plants and equipment. You consider the variables involved—aspects such as lease price, selling price, and variable costs—and then compare these from one machine to another. Of course, you must also consider the machine itself, the volume it can handle, copy quality, and reliability. But financial aspects like the ones considered in break-even analysis are key to any decision.

> **MBA Mastery**
>
> When you do break-even analysis, be sure to consider *all* fixed and variable costs. I've simplified the examples in this chapter for the sake of clarity. But you will sometimes have to dig for all the information you need in order to factor every cost into the analysis.

You can plot the break-even point on a chart that will help you visualize the break-even point, as well as the costs and profits, at various sales volumes.

This chart doesn't precisely reveal costs and profits, but it does portray the relation between them at various volumes.

The break-even point.

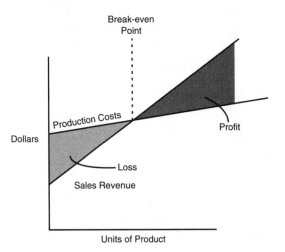

The chart also implies that anything that you do to shift the break-even point to the left—for instance, lowering your fixed or variable costs or raising your price—will get you into profits sooner. Conversely, anything that shifts the break-even point to the right will delay your profits.

Crossover Analysis

As a manager, you will at times face the option of buying one of two comparable pieces of equipment. Usually each will have its own set of fixed and variable costs. The question is: Which machine should you buy?

Suppose you are still the copy shop owner from our example in Chapter 8 and you can buy one of two copiers. Machine 1 has fixed costs of $10,000 and variable costs of 2¢ a copy. Machine 2 has fixed costs of $5,000 and variable costs of 4¢ a copy.

MBA Lingo

Crossover analysis
enables you to identify the point where you should switch from one product or service to another one that delivers similar general benefits but has different fixed and variable costs.

Which machine you will buy depends mostly on the volume of copies you expect to do. So the first thing to do is figure out the crossover point—that is, the unit volume at which the cost of the two machines is equal. *Crossover analysis* will identify that point.

Here's the formula:

Crossover units = (Machine 2's fixed costs – Machine 1's fixed costs) ÷ (Machine 1's variable costs – Machine 2's variable costs)

Crossover units = (5,000 – 10,000) ÷ (.02 – .04)

Crossover units = (–$5,000) ÷ (–.02)

Crossover units = 250,000 copies

At 250,000 copies (per year), the total cost of each of the two machines is equal.

Above and below that volume, one machine is preferable to the other. Which one?

To find out, calculate the cost of each machine at a unit volume just below the crossover point and just above that point.

For instance, at 240,000 copies the cost of each machine is as follows:

Machine 1   (240,000 × $0.02) + $10,000 = $14,800

Machine 2   (240,000 × $0.04) + $5,000 = $14,600

These two calculations tell us that Machine 2 is the cheaper one, at 240,000 copies.

At 260,000 units the cost of each machine is as follows:

| Machine 1 | $(260{,}000 \times \$0.02) + \$10{,}000 = \$15{,}200$ |
| Machine 2 | $(260{,}000 \times \$0.04) + \$5{,}000 = \$15{,}400$ |

These two calculations tell us that Machine 1 is the cheaper one, at 260,000 copies.

So we see that Machine 2—the one with the lower fixed costs—will be preferable below the crossover point, and Machine 1 will be preferable above that volume.

Again, which machine should the copy shop owner buy? It depends on the volume he expects. If the volume will be above 250,000 units, he should purchase Machine 1. If the volume will be lower, he should purchase Machine 2.

This, of course, assumes that he can forecast the volume with some accuracy. Also, as with break-even analysis, these calculations ignore any differences in copy quality, speed, reliability, and so forth.

Planning and Scheduling Tools

Project management—planning, launching, and controlling a project—requires special tools, ones somewhat different from those needed when managing an ongoing operation. A project has a beginning, a middle, and an end. The project manager must plan and coordinate numerous activities, and keep them on track so that the project achieves its goal, on time and on budget. In the following sections I'll show you how you can best manage projects.

The Critical Path to Project Management

The Critical Path Method, or CPM, is a visual tool that will help you plan and control the tasks and activities in a project. The Critical Path Method was developed by the chemical giant DuPont in the late 1950s for managing large projects, such as the construction of huge production facilities.

Let's say you are planning to open a restaurant and have identified the following major tasks as the key ones in the project:

Task Code	Task Description	Predecessors	Time (Weeks)
A	Find location	none	6
B	Negotiate lease	A	2
C	Do renovations	A, B	8

Task Code	Task Description	Predecessors	Time (Weeks)
D	Hire chef	none	8
E	Purchase fixtures	A, B	2
F	Plan menu	D	2
G	Hire and train crew	D, F	8
H	Install and test fixtures	A, B, F	4
I	Conduct a dry run	All	1
	Total time		41

Notice that in addition to identifying the tasks, you must put them in order. You must identify predecessor tasks, that is, tasks that must be completed before others can begin. You must estimate the time each task will consume.

Notice also that the nine tasks in our restaurant example are not exhaustive. For simplicity I've left out advertising, food purchasing, and so on.

Getting the Picture

The first step in CPM analysis is to chart the tasks visually in order to see the relationships among them.

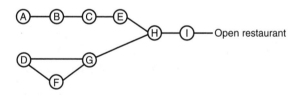

Once you see the relationships, you realize that you can do certain tasks concurrently. In this example, you might think of the project as having two tracks: a "Facilities Track" and a "Food Track." The Facilities Track (Tasks A, B, C, and E) involves getting the restaurant space ready. The Food Track (Tasks D, F, and G) involves hiring the chef and crew and getting the menu squared away.

CPM helps you see how to "collapse" the project and get it finished in less elapsed time than the total project will require. Here's how to set it up with estimated times included:

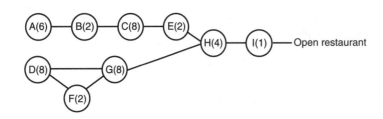

The longest path through the project is called the *critical path*. In our example, that path extends from point A to point I, and it will take a total of 23 weeks. This means that the total elapsed time of the project will be 23 weeks, even though the total project time is 41 weeks. That's because the Facilities Track will take 18 weeks, but the 16-week Food Track can be completed concurrently.

> **MBA Mastery**
>
> If you'd like to explore project management software, you can find planning tools such as Critical Path Management in project-planning software packages such as Microsoft Project.

Note that the Food Track itself can be collapsed from 18 weeks to 16 weeks by planning the menu with the chef while also hiring the crew. This does not improve the total elapsed time, but there is no reason not to get whatever you can done in the most efficient way possible. After all, in business, Murphy's Law is always in operation.

Getting PERT

PERT, which stands for *Program Evaluation and Review Technique*, resembles Critical Path Management. PERT was developed by the U.S. Navy and the Lockheed Corporation for the Polaris missile system project in the late 1950s.

> **MBA Lingo**
>
> **Program Evaluation and Review Technique,** or **PERT**, is a project management system that allows you to make an optimistic, pessimistic, and "best guess" estimate of the time it will take to complete a project. This system then lets you incorporate these three estimates into a unified analysis.

The major difference between PERT and CPM is that PERT enables you to make an optimistic, pessimistic, and "best guess" estimate of the time it will take to complete each task and the entire project. Then you calculate a weighted average by assigning a value of 1 to the pessimistic and optimistic estimates, and a value of 4 to the best guess. Then you plug the values into the following formula:

Estimated time = (Optimistic × 1) + (Best Guess × 4) + (Pessimistic × 1) ÷ 6

(You divide by 6 because 1 + 4 + 1 = 6, and you are calculating a weighted average of the time estimates.)

Let's say the best guess estimate of a task's duration is 10 weeks, the pessimistic estimate is 14 weeks, and the optimistic estimate is 8 weeks. The PERT formula would calculate the estimated time as follows:

Estimated time = 8 + (10 × 4) + 14 × 6

Estimated time = 62 × 6

Estimated time = 10.3 weeks

I am showing you a simplified version of PERT. The actual system can incorporate very sophisticated statistical techniques.

For your planning purposes, the real value of PERT is the idea of coming up with the optimistic and pessimistic estimates, and then seeing which way any deviation from the best guess would be likely to go. In this case, since 10.3 is greater than 10, the likelihood is that if you vary from the best guess, it is likely to be in the pessimistic direction.

In my own version of PERT, I figure pessimistic estimates for the large tasks that I can't directly control. When telling senior management about a project, I give them only the pessimistic estimates for these tasks (and thus the project) and pretend they're best guesses.

On a product-development project with a major company, I brought the project in eight weeks late from the best guess (due to "programming problems" beyond my control). But it was only two weeks late from the pessimistic estimate, which was the only one I gave management. And I had *doubled* the programming time estimate that Management Information Systems had given me!

Decision Trees: More Visual Aids

A *decision tree* is another visual tool to help you in decision making. Like PERT, a decision tree includes the element of probability by allowing three estimates.

Let's say that our copy shop owner has an opportunity to expand to the west side of his own city or into the next city. He also, of course, could choose not to expand at all.

He estimates his profits over the next five years at each of the two locations to be:

Estimate	West Side	Next City
Optimistic	$6 million	$5 million
Best Guess	3 million	4 million
Pessimistic	2 million	2 million

For both locations, he has a 60 percent likelihood that the best guess will occur, and a 20 percent likelihood that either the optimistic or pessimistic estimate will occur.

Therefore the decision tree would look like this:

A single decision tree.

		Expected Profit	Expected Value
	Optimistic 20%	$6 million	$ 1.2 million
West Side	Best Guess 60%	$3 million	$ 1.8 million
	Pessimistic 20%	$2 million	$ .4 million
			$ 3.4 million
	Optimistic 20%	$5 million	$ 1.0 million
Next City	Best Guess 60%	$4 million	$ 2.4 million
	Pessimistic 20%	$2 million	$ .4 million
			$ 3.8 million
Do Nothing			0.0

The decision tree lets you visually consider choices and risk. Putting probabilities on the estimates forces you to think carefully about what might really happen. When viewing an opportunity, it's easy for many of us to get carried away with optimism, so it's good to incorporate a pessimistic estimate into the analysis. The decision tree is one way of doing that.

MBA Lingo

A **decision tree** enables you to graphically illustrate potential decisions (or "scenarios") and the potential outcomes of these decisions. Essentially, this is a visual aid to decision making that incorporates probabilities.

So, back to our example. What should our copy shop owner do?

If he were to make his choice strictly on the basis of the decision tree, he should choose the alternative with the highest "expected value." In our example, that means he would choose to expand into the next city. The expected value of that choice is $3.8 million dollars, while that of expanding to the west side is $3.4 million.

In actual practice, of course, he would use the decision tree as simply one more tool in his analysis. And that is what I hope you would do.

Statistics for Business Decisions

The term *statistics* refers both to numerical data and to the discipline of analyzing numerical data. When data are analyzed, they can help you make decisions.

However, statistics can also be misused and misunderstood. This occurs when managers pick and choose data that supports only their own point of view or slant an analysis to prove their point. As a manager, you must know when this is happening and know the right questions to ask so you can see the whole picture. You must also know how to conduct honest analysis of honest numbers, so you don't fool anyone, including yourself. This knowledge comes with an understanding of basic statistics.

For example, suppose a company conducted a survey of 50 former customers to learn why they took their business elsewhere. If the survey was well constructed and the responses were properly analyzed, the company's managers would know why those customers left.

More important, they could infer that other former customers probably left for similar reasons. Then—and this is the reason for the whole project—management could decide which changes they needed to make in order to keep customers happy. (We will look at the elements of good surveys in Chapter 18.)

Statistical analysis is used in science, health care, public policy, and many other fields. In business, it is used most often in marketing, finance, economics, and quality control.

Key concepts in statistics include:

- Frequency distributions
- Measures of central tendency
- Measures of dispersion

Let's examine each of these concepts.

Frequency Distributions

A frequency distribution tells you how many times (that is, how frequently) a certain value occurs in an array of values. For example, here is a frequency distribution of the weight of 100 dressed chickens, to the nearest quarter pound, being shipped by a commercial poultry farm:

Weight	Quantity
3.00	3
3.25	8
3.50	10
3.75	16
4.00	28
4.25	15
4.50	11
4.75	6
5.00	3

This frequency distribution tells us how many chickens were in each weight bracket. It shows the frequency of each weight (for instance, 16 chickens weighed 3.75 pounds) and shows how the frequencies were distributed.

Frequency distributions can also compile *classes* of *values*, expressed in ranges. The following is a frequency distribution for the amount spent per customer in a four-hour period in a supermarket:

Amount Spent	Number of Customers
Less than $20	18
$20–$39.99	18
$40.00–$59.99	44
$60.00–$79.99	23
$80.00–$99.99	11
$100 and over	33

Classes are very useful for grouping values so they are more manageable and easier to analyze, as shown by the six classes in the preceding table of customers expenditures.

Displaying Distributions

It is often useful in business to display this kind of information in charts. The most commonly used are bar charts, histograms, and line charts. Charts are constantly used in business meetings and presentations to summarize and communicate numerical data.

A bar chart is useful for comparing values to one another. The chart below depicts the weights of the chickens in the frequency distribution example:

MBA Lingo

A **value,** also called an observation, is a single, numerical instance of whatever is being measured. A **class** groups values into a range so they can be more easily handled and understood.

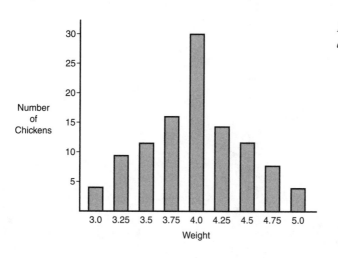

Bar chart: weight of dressed chickens.

Histograms are like bar charts except that they depict classes of values rather than a single value. Following is a histogram of the amounts spent per shopper in the previous supermarket example.

A line chart is best for showing the relationship between two types of data—for example, time and sales. The following line chart shows a company's annual sales for the years 1995 through 2002.

Histogram: amount spent by
supermarket customers.

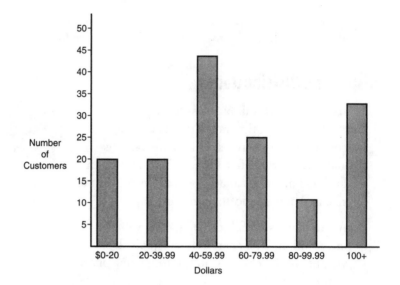

Line chart: annuals sales
1995–2002.

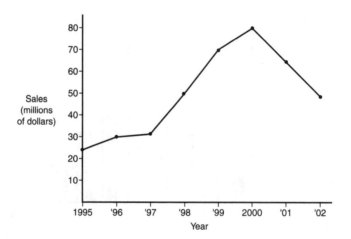

Measures of Central Tendency

Measures of central tendency attempt to capture a set of values in a single statistic. The term *central tendency* means that the values tend to cluster around a central value. In any given situation, the values may or may not tend to cluster around a central value. But the measures of central tendency can still be calculated and compared. As you will see, in comparing them you can learn a bit about how much the values tend to cluster.

The three key measures of central tendency are the mean, the median, and the mode.

The Mean

The mean is just a fancy word for the average. It is calculated by adding up each value and dividing by the number of values. For example, here are the hourly salaries of five consultants on a project:

Joe	$32
Helen	40
Jim	29
Stan	46
Lee	58
Total	$205

To calculate the mean, you add up the values and divide by the number of consultants:

In this case the mean hourly salary would be $41 ($205 ÷ 5).

Weighted Average

The weighted average accounts for the frequency of a value in a distribution. For instance, the weighted average of the 100 chickens in the previous example would be calculated as follows

$3.00 \times 3 =$	9.00
$3.25 \times 8 =$	26.00
$3.50 \times 10 =$	35.00
$3.75 \times 16 =$	60.00
$4.00 \times 28 =$	112.00
$4.25 \times 15 =$	63.75
$4.50 \times 11 =$	49.50
$4.75 \times 6 =$	28.50
$5.00 \times 3 =$	15.00

$$398.75 \div 100 = 3.9875$$

For practical purposes, the weighted average of the chickens can be rounded to 4 pounds.

The weighted average finds wide application in business. For instance, take our five consultants and put them on a project. Management estimates that it will take a total of 315 man-hours to complete the project, but each consultant will work a different number of hours on it. If you wanted to know the average hourly salary the consulting firm (not the client) will be paying the consultants on the project, you would use the weighted average.

Consultant	Hourly Wage	×	Estimated Total Hours on Project	=	Total Wages
Joe	$32		90		$2,880
Helen	40		55		2,200
Jim	29		115		3,335
Stan	46		35		1,610
Lee	58		20		1,160
			315		$11,185

The weighted average hourly salary on the project would be $35.50 ($11,185 ÷ 315).

Here the weighted average accounts for employees at different wage levels spending different amounts of time on the project. How could this information help the managers of the consulting firm make a decision?

Case in Point

Most service firms, including consulting and legal practices, bill out their professional employees at some multiple of their hourly salaries. For most firms, that multiple is about four or five. In our example, we have a 315-hour project with a weighted average hourly salary of $35.50. Thus, using the multiples of four and five, the price charged to the client for this project should range from $44,730 ($35.50 × 315 × 4) to $55,912 ($35.50 × 315 × 5).

First, in quoting a price to the client for the project, the managers of the consulting firm need to know two things: the number of hours the job will take and their cost per hour. The weighted average of the salaries of the consultants on the project is the cost per hour.

Second, the weighted average will help the managers adjust the human resources dedicated to the project before or during the project. In other words, if they add a consultant to the project who makes more than $35.50 per hour, they'll raise the hourly cost of the project. But if they add a consultant making less than $35.50, they'll lower their costs. If they raise their costs, they reduce the project's profitability. If they lower their costs, they increase the profitability.

Note that putting the lowest-paid employees on a client project is not always the best way to cut your costs. For some tasks, highly paid employees are more efficient and can complete the job in less time (and get it right the first time).

The Median

The median is the value in the center of an array. An array is an arrangement of values in their numerical order, either from highest to lowest (descending order) or from lowest to highest (ascending order). For example, if we arrange the hourly salaries of our five consultants in descending order, we find that $40, Helen's salary, falls in the center. That $40 is the median.

Lee	$58
Stan	46
Helen	40
Joe	32
Jim	29

In other words, half the values in an array fall above the median and half fall below the median. For instance, in an array of 15 values the median will be the eighth value. Seven values will be above the eighth one and seven values will be below it.

The median will be an actual value only when there is an odd number of values in the array. If the array has an even number of values, for instance six, the median position must be calculated by adding one to the number of values in the array and dividing the result by two.

For example, the median position in an array of six values would be 3.5 ([6 + 1] ÷ 2).

If the median position is 3.5, what is the median value? It is the average of the third and the fourth value in the array (because 3.5 falls between the third and fourth values). Let's add a sixth consultant—Diane, who is a junior partner earning $95 an hour—to our team of five in the preceding example and calculate the median.

Diane	$95
Lee	58
Stan	46
Helen	40
Joe	32
Jim	29

The median position is 3.5 in this array of six values. The third and fourth values are $46 and $40. So the calculated median is $43 ([40 + 46] ÷ 2).

MBA Mastery

You will hear the median mentioned often in the business news. The median price of a home and median income are two statistics often quoted. The median is used in these instances so that a relatively small number of expensive homes or well-paid people don't result in a misleading measure of central tendency.

This means that half the salaries are above $43 and half are below $43, which you can see by looking at the array.

Note that compared with the mean, the median is less affected by extreme values (known as outlying values) in an array. The mean of the six salaries, thanks to Diane, is $50 ($300 [the total of all six salaries] ÷ 6). But four people out of the six are earning under $50 per hour, and two of them, Joe and Jim, are earning well below that amount. Thus, in this case the median would be the better measure of central tendency.

The Mode

The mode is merely the observation in a data set that occurs most often. For example, in our example of the weights of the chickens, the mode equals 4 pounds because it occurs most often (28 chickens weigh 4 pounds).

Not every set of data will have a mode. If no one value occurs more often than the others, there will be no mode.

In practice, the mean, median, and mode are best viewed in the context of a measure of variability.

Measures of Variability

Two measures of variability are used most often in business. Here variability refers to how much the values vary around the measure of central tendency. One measure of variability—the range—is quite simple. The other—the standard deviation from the mean—is rather complex, but it's presented simply here.

The Range

The range is represented by two values: the lowest in the array and the highest in the array. If possible, always consider the range along with one or two measures of central tendency. For example, let's look at the hourly salary ranges of our two groups of consultants, along with the mean and median for each group.

Case A (five consultants): range = $29–$58

mean = $41

median = $40

Case B (six consultants): range = $29–$95

mean = $50

(calculated) median = $43

In Case A, the range is more tightly distributed around the mean and the median. At $41 and $40, the mean and the median are almost identical and they both fall almost at the halfway mark between $29 and $58, which is $43.5).

In Case B, the range is more widely distributed around the mean and the median. At $50 and $43, the mean and the median differ significantly. The mean is higher than the median, which means that an outlying value is pulling it up. That value, of course, is Diane's $95 per-hour salary, as the range indicates.

Thus we see that measures of central tendency and variability are best viewed together. Of course, it's not really necessary when you have only five or six values to keep track of, which are used here to keep things simple. However, in business these kinds of statistics can represent hundreds or thousands of values, and you need good measures to summarize that much information.

MBA Alert

As Mark Twain famously said, there are lies, damn lies, and statistics. It's also been said that statistics will tell you that a man with one foot in a bucket of freezing water and the other in a bucket of steaming water will, on average, be comfortable. Clearly, we must view statistics critically and understand exactly what they are—and aren't—saying.

The Standard Deviation from the Mean

The standard deviation from the mean is just what it sounds like: a standard measure of how far the values in a set deviate from the mean. The underlying idea behind the standard deviation from the mean is the central limit theorem.

Stick with me here. The central limit theorem states that the mean of a sample drawn from a larger population will approach a normal distribution as the size of the sample becomes larger. In fact, a sample as small as 30 will begin to approach a normal distribution. What, you may be asking, is a normal distribution?

This is a normal distribution:

A normal distribution ("bell curve").

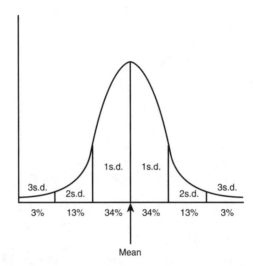

A normal distribution is one in which the values are distributed as follows:

- 34 percent fall within one standard deviation above the mean

- 34 percent fall within one standard deviation below the mean

- 13 percent fall between one and two standard deviations above the mean

- 13 percent fall between one and two standard deviations below the mean

- 3 percent fall beyond two standard deviations above the mean

- 3 percent fall beyond two standard deviations below the mean

The standard deviation is an amount calculated from the values in the sample. You can find the formula in any introductory book on statistics. But everyone who calculates standard deviations does so with software or a calculator.

The standard deviation from the mean for our 100 chickens would be about 6 ounces. (Take my word for it.) You may recall that the mean weight was 4 pounds. Thus the farmer can say with some certainty that 68 percent of the dressed chickens he ships weigh 4 pounds, plus or minus 6 ounces. He can also say that 94 percent of the dressed chickens weigh 4 pounds, plus or minus 12 ounces. Only 3 percent weigh 3 pounds and 3 percent weigh 5 pounds.

Think of what this means for quality control. For instance, the farmer may not want to ship any birds weighing 3 pounds or less. That means that those underweight chickens must be identified (before they are killed) and permitted to grow a bit heavier. The farmer will need a procedure for identifying these birds—or he will have to discard 3 percent of his chickens, which he certainly wouldn't want to do.

Here's what you need to know about the standard deviation and the normal distribution:

♦ The normal distribution applies to many characteristics found in nature, such as the weight of chickens, the width of rose petals, and inches of daily rainfall in a region. That is, when you calculate the mean and the standard deviation from the mean for the weights or widths or inches of rainfall, 34 percent of the values will be within one standard deviation above the mean, 13 percent will be between one and two standard deviations above the mean, and so on.

♦ By definition, 68 percent of observations will fall within one standard deviation above or below the mean, and 94 percent will fall within two standard deviations above or below the mean.

♦ This implies that the top or bottom 3 percent in any given sample or population are quite exceptional—exceptionally wealthy or poor, short or tall, likely to be watching television or unlikely to be watching it.

♦ The normal distribution has predictive value. For instance, the farmer knows that if he weighs a randomly chosen dressed bird there is a 68 percent chance that it will weigh 4 pounds plus or minus 6 ounces. Therefore, if he pulled a sample of, say, 30 chickens and found that most of them weighed about $3^{1}/_{2}$ pounds, he would want to check the bird-feed situation. After all, there's only a 13 percent chance that a bird will weigh that amount.

Statistics underlie many management decisions, which often depend on the validity of information and the probability of an outcome. Moreover, statistics are often bandied about in meetings and the media. Therefore, a grounding in basic statistics will help you develop better information and make better decisions—and keep you from getting snowed in meetings or by the media.

Use as Many as You Can

In this chapter, I've given you some MBA-style analytical tools. There are many more of these tools, but these are the most useful of the bunch.

These tools are here to give you an edge. So use all of the tools that you can, because the risk of making a wrong decision is often greater than you think.

Remember, though, that analytical tools and statistics are not magical. They are only ways to develop information and communicate about plans and decisions. In almost all situations, you have to decide based on what the tools and statistics tell you *and* on other considerations that they simply cannot incorporate into the analysis.

The Least You Need to Know

- Analytical tools are structured ways of examining business situations, and they help you make better decisions more easily.

- Break-even analysis tells you how many units of something you must sell in order to start making a profit.

- Crossover analysis helps you decide which of two competing prices of equipment you should buy or lease, depending on the amount of use the machine will get.

- Visual tools, such as the critical path method and decision trees, can help you "see" solutions because they help you see the parts of the problem and your choices.

- Statistical information underlies many business decisions, and the better a manager understands that information, the better his or her decisions will be.

Chapter 10

Budget Basics

In This Chapter

- ◆ Understanding budgets and variance reports
- ◆ The importance of staying on budget
- ◆ How to cut costs quickly
- ◆ The basics of credit management

Nearly every business decision must be considered in light of what it does to the budget. The budget itself is the result of management decisions regarding priorities, trade-offs, and the needs of the business. Future decisions that depart from those reflected in the budget must be made carefully and with sound justification. Also, problems may arise when a department deviates from its budget. In these situations, a manager has to understand budgets, variances from the budget, and cost control.

This chapter shows you how to understand a sales or expense budget and variance report. It also covers key steps in cost control and the basics of credit management.

What Are Budgets and Why Do You Need Them?

A budget is a financial plan and a means of control. There are three ways in which a budget serves these planning and control functions.

First, the budget helps management allocate the company's resources. As you know from Chapter 8, some of a senior manager's key decisions concern resource allocation.

MBA Lingo _____

The **budgeting process** occurs annually and creates the budget for the coming year. A **variance** is any deviation from the number originally planned for an item in the budget.

Those resources are represented by expenses. In the *budgeting process*, management decides how much to spend on which resources.

Then they "work up the numbers" by adjusting last year's budgets upward or downward in light of the current economy, the goals for the year ahead, and the needs of the departments and the company. This is a balancing act in which nobody gets everything they want, but (hopefully) everyone gets what they need.

Second, managers at most levels have some budget authority. This authority may be given in various ways. One way is to allow managers to spend whatever amounts they feel are right as long as they don't exceed their budget for that item. Another way is to give a manager "signing authority," which lets him or her authorize individual payments up to a certain amount, such as $500, $1,000, $5,000, or more.

For control, most companies combine the two, allowing a manager to authorize payments up to a certain amount but requiring him or her to stay within an overall budget.

Third, if a manager feels it is necessary to exceed his or her signing authority or budget, he or she must get additional authorization to do so. This means that the manager above him or her must authorize the payment or the budget overrun.

Types of Budgets

MBA Lingo _____

Capital is another term for plant and equipment. Money budgeted or spent on plant and equipment is called a *capital expenditure*, and a capital budget guides managers making capital expenditures. (And, yes, the word *capital* also means money to finance a business.)

A sizable business will have two broad categories of budgets: a capital budget and an operating budget. A capital budget governs significant expenditures on plant and equipment. This productive equipment will last for more than a year and therefore represents a long-term investment. These types of expenditures are often referred to as *capital* expenditures.

In contrast, an operating budget covers the company's normal day-to-day operations and expenditures. The operating budget typically includes wages and salaries, materials and supplies, rent or lease payments, and so on.

Other types of budgets include budgets for special projects, meaning efforts that are neither capital expenditures nor part of normal operations. For instance, a business that must defend itself in a major lawsuit would allocate money to a legal defense budget. You will also hear about budgets that are actually subsets of the capital budget, such as the construction budget, or of the operating budget, such as the advertising budget or the travel budget.

However, there are two essential types of operating budgets: sales budgets and expense budgets, and our examination of budgets will focus on them. The sales budget sets forth the amount of revenue the sales force is committed to bringing in. Expense budgets apply to all areas that incur expenses (including the sales department).

Unfortunately, as often happens with plans, budgets do not always work out as originally foreseen. In other words, there is often a *variance* from the budget.

Sales Budgets and Variance Reports

In most companies, the sales budget represents a motivational tool, as well as a planning tool. During the budgeting process, the CEO goes to the sales manager and says something like, "Jim, we're looking to grow the bottom line by 15 percent next year. Can we count on you folks in sales to increase the top line by that amount?"

Now if Jim says no, he's not being a team player. But if he just says "Sure!" without really thinking about it, he's committing his people to growing sales by 15 percent. That might make sense sometimes, but other times it would be professional suicide.

So while management always wants sales to increase, there are many reasons why an increase can be hard to achieve. These include competitive products, good salespeople leaving for better jobs, and new taxes or regulations that hurt your product. So there is some back and forth about the sales budget before management and sales agree on the numbers. Even then, variances will occur.

A Sample Sales Budget and Variance Report

Here is an example of a sales budget and variance report, usually just called a variance report. Incidentally, in these budgets and variance reports, a slash (/) means "or," since it gives this variance as both an amount and a percentage.

Acme Corporation–Office Products Division

Sales Budget Versus Actual, Six Months Ended June 30 (in Thousands of Dollars)

	June Actual	June Budget	June Variance $/%	YTD Actual	YTD Budget	YTD Variance $/%
Northeast	180	240	(60/25%)	1,530	1,800	(270/15%)
Southeast	160	160	0/0	1,140	1,200	(60/5%)
Central	180	200	(20/10%)	1,110	1,500	(390/26%)
West	220	200	20/10%	1,620	1,500	120/8%
Total	740	800	(60/7.5%)	5,400	6,000	(600/10%)

This variance report, like most, shows the actual sales achieved, the budgeted amounts, and the variances from budget—the difference between the actual and budgeted amounts. The numbers in the variance columns show both the dollar amount and the percentage of the deviation—upward, or in parentheses, downward—from budget.

As the table shows, Acme Corporation breaks down its sales budget by four major sales regions. Except in the Western region, things aren't going well for Acme so far this year.

How to Read a Sales Variance Report

When reviewing variance reports, carefully read the column headers and *line items* so you know what you're looking at. You want to know who's "ahead of budget" (the regions exceeding their budgeted sales), who's "behind budget" (those not reaching their budgeted figure), and who's "on budget" (those meeting their figure).

Most variance reports show the most recent period—the week, month, or quarter—and the year to date. This sample is a monthly report, but many companies use weekly sales variance reports. Managers receive these reports so they can know where they are and improve areas that are behind budget.

Looking first at total sales in the fictitious sample variance report, you see that Acme's sales are off (meaning behind or below budget) 7.5 percent for the month of June and 10 percent for the year so far.

Turning to the individual regions, we see that the Southeast is doing fairly well: In June, they were on budget. For the year, they're behind 5 percent.

MBA Lingo

A **line item** is an item with its own line in the budget; that is, its own row on the ledger paper or spreadsheet. In this example, each sales region has its own line.

Acme would probably see the Southeast as a region that can "make budget" if they push hard for the rest of the year. The West is in good shape, running 10 percent ahead of budget for the month and 8 percent ahead for the year.

CAUTION

MBA Alert _____

When you "miss budget"—that is, bring in sales below budget or costs above budget—you must have two things ready for your superior: reasons for the variance and a plan for improvement. By reasons, I do not mean excuses, but rather a clear, honest analysis of what's wrong. By a plan, I do not mean vague promises that "we'll try harder," but rather a realistic program to address what's wrong. No good manager will settle for less. Nor should you settle for less from your people—or from yourself.

The problems are in the Northeast and Central regions. The Northeast had a terrible June, missing budget by $60,000 or 25 percent. For the year, they're 15 percent behind budget, which is bad, particularly when you consider that the Northeast is the largest region—budgeted for 30 percent of Acme's January-through-June sales.

The Central region is an even bigger problem. June was bad enough, at 10 percent below budget, but the year-to-date is a disaster. The Central region is $390,000, or 26 percent, behind budget for the year so far. And they are budgeted for 25 percent of total sales, so this is bad news.

Year-Over-Year Variances

To save space, I have not shown year-over-year variances in this report. But they are important. Year-over-year variances show the actual values this year versus the actual values for the same period last year.

Year-over-year comparisons can be valuable if the budgets were unrealistic in the first place. If so, you may have a reasonable defense, particularly if you are doing better than last year, but worse than the budget.

Any time you have budget responsibility, you want to know how you are doing against the budget *and* against last year's figures.

Expense Budgets and Variance Reports

Virtually all operating expenses go into expense budgets. The company expense budget is broken down into departmental budgets. Departmental expense budgets are prepared by the department managers with the financial staff during the budgeting process.

The following is an expense budget for a production department. (To keep this simple, I haven't shown the June figures as I did for the sales budget. Instead I've shown just the year-to-date numbers through June.)

Acme Corporation—Office Products Division

Production Budget and Variance Report, Six Months Ended June 30 (in Thousands)

	Year-to-Date Actual	Prorated Budget	Variance $/%
Salaries & Wages	$1,150	$1,200	(50/4%)
Benefits	500	500	0
Materials	1,200	1,300	(100/8%)
Supplies	140	150	(10/7%)
Maintenance	70	80	(10/13%)
Transportation & Freight	420	500	(80/16%)
Training & Development	5	20	(15/75%)
Consulting Services	30	50	(20/40%)
Computer Leases	340	340	0/0
Utilities	140	150	(10/7%)
Depreciation	200	200	0/0
Miscellaneous	5	10	(15/75%)
Overhead Allocation	300	300	0/0
Total Production Expense	**4,500**	**4,800**	**(300/6%)**

This budget shows the expenses incurred so far this year and the prorated expenses for the first six months. These prorated expenses are just the annual amount budgeted for each line item divided by two to get the six-month figure.

How to Read an Expense Variance Report

This production budget tracks the expenses incurred in manufacturing Acme Corporation's line of office products. As we saw in Chapter 8, many production expenses are variable expenses that will fluctuate with the level of sales. Others are fixed costs. In Acme's case, fixed costs include computer leases and depreciation. But most of the costs here are variable.

For example, wages, particularly those of production workers as opposed to management, vary with production. When sales are slow there will be no overtime and no new hires. There may even be layoffs. Materials costs vary quite directly with sales. If sales are slow, then production slows down, and purchases of materials (and supplies) also slow down. If fewer products are being produced, fewer will be shipped, and therefore transportation and freight will decrease.

So if sales are behind budget, as they are in Acme's case, you should be reducing production activity, and thus production expenses. This is what Acme did. Year-to-date sales are 10 percent behind budget, and production costs are also below budget—but by 6, rather than 10, percent. This may indicate that Acme's managers should be cutting back production even more.

As with the sales variance report, people talk in terms of running "behind budget" or, more often, "under budget" or "over budget," for the month or the year. They also talk about the run rate, which is the amount they'll spend for the year if they keep spending at the rate so far for the year. In other words, for Acme Corporation, the run rate for the whole production budget is $9 million ($4.5 million × 2; the $4.5 million is what they've spent in the first six months, as shown in the preceding table).

Explaining Budget Variances

Budget variances are rarely self-explanatory. Therefore, the manager accountable for meeting a sales or expense budget must identify the causes of any significant variances. Then, within the scope of her authority, she must do whatever she can to eliminate those causes.

The reasons for shortfalls in sales are among the most difficult to identify and address. Assuming that the sales budget was realistic and achievable, variances can usually be traced to one or more of the following factors:

♦ Competitors with better prices, products, service, warranties, advertising, or promotions

♦ Market *saturation*

♦ Loss of major accounts or high-performing salespeople (which still leaves the reason for the loss to be identified)

♦ Misallocated marketing and sales resources

♦ Inadequate training or support of salespeople

MBA Lingo

The market for a product is **saturated** when virtually all potential buyers have already purchased all they want or need of the product.

- Poor post-sale customer service and support

- Low morale among sales or customer service employees (again, why is morale poor?)

Identifying the correct factors is essential. For instance, if sales are being lost to a new competitor with a cheaper, more effective product, the sales manager cannot do much about that. However, the people in R&D or product development may be able to. Note, too, that if morale is poor or sales resources are being misallocated, the sales manager himself may be the reason for the variance. He may require coaching, additional training, or replacement. (Part 4 examines the entire subject of sales and marketing.)

Variances in the expense budget often can be identified and addressed more readily. In general, either the price or the usage of the resource has increased to levels beyond the budgeted amounts. So first, the manager must identify which of these factors is at work, keeping in mind that at times both can contribute to a variance.

If the price of materials or supplies has risen, it may be necessary to negotiate a better deal with the vendor. Admittedly, this may be difficult since you probably tried to resist the price increase in the first place. A search for a new vendor often turns up a better price, particularly if you haven't done any recent comparison shopping. Soliciting competitive bids for major purchases is always a good practice.

If the variance stems from higher-than-budgeted usage of a resource, first determine whether its usage varies with the volume of sales, production, or some other factor. For example, a department paying heavy overtime wages usually does so because of extraordinary demands on the staff. On the other hand, if the overtime was necessary to handle the normal workload, then either the budget was unrealistic or the department is understaffed.

MBA Lingo

Bundling a product with other products is a way of creating a system or a total solution for a customer, and thus increase the product's appeal. For example, most personal computer manufacturers bundle software with their computers, saving the customer the trouble of having to purchase the software separately (and increasing their profit on the sale).

In all cases, it's wise to identify short-term solutions and, whenever possible, long-term solutions to a budget variance. For example, it may take a year or two to deal with a competitor that has introduced a new and better product. That would be the long-term solution (provided it is worth pursuing). The short-term solution may be cutting your prices or *bundling* the product with other products of yours (or another company's) to create an appealing package that the competition cannot match.

In a sense, budgets are like flight plans. As conditions change and new information becomes available, a manager must respond, just as a pilot would respond to changes in weather or schedule.

Cost Control

At times, managers face a situation in which cost control extends beyond a few budget items. During an economic downturn or a sustained slide in sales, across-the-board cost cutting may be necessary.

For most companies, labor represents a significant, readily controlled cost. You can control labor costs by *not* doing certain things. You can not hire new employees, not replace workers who leave (a tactic called attrition), and not approve overtime. You can also reduce employees' hours or lay off workers.

How layoffs are handled can make the difference between a momentary dip in morale and the devastation of employees' spirits. Management must communicate honestly with employees and make the case for the layoff. Provided the managers are not gutting the company out of executive greed, employees can understand the financial realities that lead to a layoff. Whether business is down or costs are up, or both, the reasons for the layoff, and the expected benefit to the company, must be described clearly. No company can guarantee lifetime employment in times of change, and today most people recognize that.

Nonetheless, some companies are slow to adjust to decreasing sales. Many wait until the last quarter of the fiscal year before they get serious about cost control. This is unfortunate because it is more orderly and less painful to control costs throughout the year.

Case in Point

I have worked for several companies that put a hiring freeze in place for the last quarter of almost every year. A hiring freeze can either allow no new employees to be hired or allow only replacements of employees who leave their jobs. A hiring freeze is often accompanied by a freeze on salary increases and promotions.

These outfits did this because they were slow to react to underbudget sales (or overbudget expenses) earlier in the year. At times, they kept hoping for a "Big September" that never materialized. Consistent control earlier in the year would have been much less disruptive.

If you need to cut costs in your business or department, consider cuts in your travel and entertainment, long distance telephone, new equipment, and publications budgets.

You might also consider refinancing debt if interest rates have fallen below what you're currently paying.

These are piecemeal measures, but the pieces can add up. Yet sometimes you need to reduce costs drastically.

Radical Surgery

The decision to close down an operation is among the toughest a manager will face. People's livelihoods are at stake and management's competence can be questioned. However, if a department, production unit, product line, or sales office consistently fails to contribute to income, it's best to shut it down or sell it.

How long a money-losing operation should be allowed to continue in business is purely a matter of judgment. However, decisions to close an operation are often made too late. Management keeps hoping things will improve. They know people in the money-losing unit are trying. But when the writing is on the wall and there's no clear path to growth and profitability, the best decision for the whole company is to end the operation.

MBA Mastery

Often companies claim they can't account separately for product lines or operations because certain costs are shared. In those cases accounting *must* develop a way of allocating shared costs to the individual products or operations. Even if their system isn't perfect, if it is at least consistent it will yield useful information over time.

Money-losing operations are a tremendous drag on a company. They suck up time, energy, and money and deliver little in return. They divert resources from successful operations. You owe it to everyone—the shareholders, the employees in the winning units, and even to the employees in the losing units (since they have no future)—to close operations that should be closed.

All of this assumes that you have the information that will tell you what is and isn't profitable. Some companies use accounting systems that combine operations in ways that make it hard to tell what's making money and what isn't.

As is the case in conducting a layoff, in closing down an operation honest communication with the affected employees is essential. Management should explain why the unit must be closed and, if it is to be sold, tell employees as much as they can about the future of the firm under the new owners. Yes, some employees may become resentful or even confrontational, and that is why so many managers shy away from honest communication about these matters. However, managers owe their employees an explanation of why their place of business is being shut down or sold.

Take Credit Management Seriously

Good credit management can cut costs, boost income, and free up cash. The key to good credit management is to decide what your credit policy will be and then implement it consistently.

Credit policy should not be too tight or too loose. If it's too tight, the company will lose sales because *credit analysts* will be turning away customers or not approving them for all they would buy—and pay for—on credit. Overly aggressive *collectors* can alienate good customers in temporary trouble.

If credit policy is too loose, the company will have difficulty collecting its money or, worse yet, excessive bad-debt expense. Customers who don't pay their bills are useless.

There's a natural tension in credit policy. Resolving it means deciding how much bad-debt expense you can accept as a cost of doing business and how quickly you want to collect your money from customers. This must be discovered over time, as you gain experience with your customers.

The Credit-Approval Process

The credit-approval process requires more information and analysis as the requested *credit line* (amount a customer can buy on credit) increases.

Many companies automatically approve any order under some amount, such as $250. For orders between this "automatic approval" figure and the next level (for example, $1,500), they would ask the customer to complete a form and provide credit references, and they would order a *credit report*.

Beyond that next-level amount, credit will request financial statements of a company or

MBA Lingo

Credit analysts decide how much trade credit customers should be extended. **Collectors,** or collection clerks, contact past-due accounts with the aim of getting them to pay up.

MBA Lingo

A **credit line** is the amount of credit a customer is approved for by a company or bank. It's the total amount the customer can have outstanding with the outfit at any time.

MBA Lingo

A **credit report** is a record of how a company (or individual) pays bills from other companies. The largest source of credit reports on businesses in the United States is Dun & Bradstreet Business Information Services, Murray Hill, NJ, 908-665-5000.

client requesting credit and analyze them for creditworthiness—their ability and willingness to pay their bills.

When Things Go Wrong, Collections Gets Tough

If a company is paying slowly, use aggressive collection efforts, particularly if the amount owed is large. By aggressive, I do not mean threatening to sue the company or even (necessarily) cutting off their credit. I'm instead suggesting that you get in touch, by phone, as soon as they are 30 days past due and ask (nicely) when you'll get paid.

Doing this has several benefits:

♦ Collection letters—letters "reminding" the customer to pay and then asking for payment in increasingly demanding tones—are more easily ignored than phone calls. (But use them, too, along with calls.)

♦ Personal contact creates personal relationships. Most people find it hard to not pay people they know.

♦ If you get promises to pay that turn out to be hollow, then you know the debtor is either in trouble or defrauding you. In either case, it's time to limit your *exposure* (amount of money they owe you). Do not sell them any more goods on credit until they pay, or at least start to pay, what they already owe you.

MBA Lingo

Exposure is the amount of money owed to you on trade credit or for borrowed money. A business person will say, "Our exposure on this account is $100,000."

Try to work something out with slow payers, but unless you see them headed for bankruptcy, don't accept some lower amount as "full payment" of what is owed to you. Work out a payment schedule that will ultimately pay off the debt, even if it takes awhile.

Getting Very Serious

There is a time when aggressive collection means threatening to refer the account to a collection agency or attorney. Don't do this until the situation is hopeless. After two or three threats, refer the account.

Collection agencies are in the business of collecting past-due accounts. Generally they charge one third of the money they collect, and if they collect nothing, you pay nothing. They use aggressive letters, phone calls, and threats of legal action; some may even visit the account in person.

A collection attorney will threaten to sue the account for the money owed, plus their fee and court costs—then follow through on that threat. However, even if the attorney wins a *judgment* (court order) against the company, it must still be paid. If the company had money enough to pay the judgment, they probably would have paid the bill long ago.

Uncollectable debts are a sad aspect of business. Credit is one area where an ounce of prevention is truly worth a pound of cure.

> **MBA Lingo**
>
> A **judgment** is a court order for a company or person to pay a sum of money to a company or person. Judgments are shown on credit reports as either satisfied or not satisfied, meaning paid or not paid.

Stay on Top of Your Finances

Financial management, even for a large business, is not brain surgery. The math and management are simple, but the decisions underlying the numbers are difficult due to competing demands on resources.

The budget process, cost control, and tension between the sales and credit departments are all examples of the competing demands that characterize finance. But having a plan—a budget—and meeting that budget is the essential first step. Everything else flows from that.

With a budget in hand you must then do all you can to grow sales (we'll look at how in Part 4 of this book) and to make sure that as much of every sales dollar as possible makes it to the bottom line. Speaking of dollars, we have a lot more to examine on that subject, which we take up in Part 3.

The Least You Need to Know

- A budget is the most basic financial planning and control tool. Every department that makes sales or spends money needs a budget. Every manager with a budget needs to know how his department is doing in relation to that budget.

- Budgets must be fair and achievable if they are to be useful in the long run.

- Investigate budget variances and address the short- and long-term causes of the largest variances.

- To control costs effectively, look for significant expenses you can reduce, such as labor costs or a department or operation that's not earning its keep. Also scrutinize travel, entertainment, and telephone expenses as well as new equipment purchases, publications, and consulting.

◆ Whenever interest rates decrease, look into refinancing any outstanding debt that has a fixed rate.

◆ Good credit management repays itself. Be sure to call slow-paying accounts as soon as they're past due.

Part 3

Managing Money, Accounting, and Finance

Some people find accounting confusing and finance frustrating, but I'm not sure why. It can't be the arithmetic, because if you can add, subtract, multiply, and divide—or use a calculator—then you can deal with the numbers in everything from basic budgets to major investments.

Of course, if the numbers don't give you trouble, then the words might. If you find terms like "depreciation," "present value," and "shareholders' equity" mysterious, don't worry. They're just words. And they have straightforward meanings, once they've been explained.

This part of the book explains all that and more, including how money flows through a company, where it comes from, and where it goes. It also shows you how to read financial statements, and once you can do that, you're on your way to real "business literacy."

Meet Your Balance Sheet

In This Chapter

◆ The importance of financial statements

◆ Assets and liabilities: how money flows through a business

◆ A tour through the balance-sheet accounts

Money constantly flows through a company, and someone has to keep track of it. That's why God made accountants. Someone also has to make sure the company makes decisions that make money. That's where financial managers come in.

Accountants and financial managers have special ways of analyzing the health and growth of a company. They mainly use numbers, and they present these numbers in financial statements. Financial statements are the most important way you can understand and analyze a company. As a manager, you must understand these statements in order to know how your budgets, transactions, and decisions affect the company.

This chapter introduces the first of three main financial statements—the balance sheet.

Assets, Liabilities, and Owners' Equity: You Need 'Em All

To understand the balance sheet, you must first understand how money moves in and out of a company. Every transaction that a company conducts represents either an inflow or outflow of cash. Most inflows of cash come from sales, but some come from loans or from the sale of stock. Most outflows of cash are created by expenses. When the company purchases materials, pays its employees, or pays interest on a loan, it has paid an expense.

In general, every single thing the company owns can be classified as an *asset*. The furniture, the inventory, the equipment, the building, even the cash in the bank and in the petty-cash drawer—all are assets. Assets have one thing in common: They are there to generate cash (unless they *are* cash, and even then, the cash should be in-vested). If an asset can't generate cash somehow, it doesn't belong on *the books*—the records kept by the bookkeeper or accounting staff.

> **MBA Lingo**
>
> **Assets** refer to everything the company owns: the furniture, the inventory, the equipment, the building, even the cash in the bank are all assets. A **liability** is an amount of money owed by the company to an organization or individual. Most liabilities are owed to the company's suppliers, creditors, and the government (in the form of taxes).

Assets also include accounts receivable—money owed the company by customers who have purchased goods or services on credit. I'll explain accounts receivable in more detail later in the chapter.

A *liability* is an amount of money owed by the company to an organization or individual. Liabilities must be paid on or before some specific date and for a specific reason. Most liabilities are owed to the company's suppliers and creditors. One common exception is taxes payable, which are, of course, owed to the government.

Liabilities arise from transactions that took place in the past. For instance, if someone sent you a keg of nails, they also sent you an invoice that you probably have 30 days to pay. That invoice is a liability.

> **MBA Lingo**
>
> **Owners' equity** is the amount left for the company's owners after the liabilities are subtracted from the assets. Assets minus liabilities equals owners' equity. Owners' equity is also called **net worth**.

Owners' equity is the amount left for the company's owners after the liabilities are subtracted from the assets. Put another way:

Assets – Liabilities = Owners' Equity

This simply means that the shareholders *own* the assets and *owe* the liabilities. After you subtract what is owed from what is owned, you have the actual stake the owners have in the company, and the actual value of the company. Owners' equity is also called *net worth*.

Meet the Balance Sheet

The *balance sheet* shows assets, liabilities, and owners' equity at a certain time, usually at the end of a quarter or *fiscal year* (the year that the company uses for budgeting and financial reporting).

The formula for the balance sheet is:

Assets = Liabilities + Owners' Equity

You'll notice that this version of the formula is a bit different from the calculation for owners' equity. This version expresses three things:

◆ The balance sheet presents assets on the left-hand side of the statement and liabilities and owners' equity on the right-hand side. (For reasons of space or format, some balance sheets present assets on the top and liabilities and owners' equity below, but the concept remains the same: Assets = Liabilities + Owners' Equity.)

◆ The balance sheet must balance. Assets *must* equal liabilities plus owners' equity.

◆ Assets are financed by liabilities and owners' equity. Liabilities and equity exist to finance assets. Assets exist to generate cash to pay off the liabilities, with enough left over to give the owners a profit.

> **MBA Lingo**
>
> The **balance sheet** shows assets, liabilities, and owners' equity at a certain time, usually at the end of a quarter or fiscal year. A **fiscal year** is the year that the company uses for budgeting and financial reporting. Most U.S. companies (about 70 percent) are on a calendar year fiscal year—that is, their fiscal year is from January 1 through December 31. Other companies use fiscal years geared to their particular season.

This is how the money flows through a business. Owners invest money in the company and suppliers extend it credit. That creates owners' equity and liabilities. Management uses that money to buy assets. Assets generate cash that flows back to the right-hand side of the balance sheet to pay off the liabilities, with money left over for the owners (which is profit or income).

The balance sheet is usually described as a snapshot of a company. That is true, because it is a picture of the company's accounts at a certain date. But the snapshot idea leads some people to forget the dynamic relationship between assets, liabilities, and equity. For reasons that will become clear later, it's also useful to think about the balance sheet as representing a flow of money through the business.

Let's look at a balance sheet and then take a tour of the various asset, liability, and owners' equity accounts.

A Sample Balance Sheet

To make the balance sheet clearer, take a look at the following sample balance sheet for a fictional company.

Balance Sheet for Sample Company, Inc.

December 31	12/31/02	12/31/01
Assets		
Current Assets:		
Cash	$900,000	$600,000
Marketable Securities	1,700,000	920,000
Accounts Receivable (Less: Allowance for Bad Debt of $40,000 in 2002 and $38,000 in 2001)	4,000,000	3,800,000
Inventories	5,400,000	6,000,000
Total Current Assets	$12,000,000	$11,320,000
Property, Plant & Equipment:		
Buildings & Machinery	$9,700,000	$9,090,000
Less: Accumulated Depreciation	(3,600,000)	(3,000,000)
Land	900,000	900,000
Total Property, Plant & Equipment	$7,000,000	$6,990,000
Other Assets:		
Prepayments & Deferred Charges	200,000	180,000
Intangibles (good will, patents)	200,000	200,000
Total Assets	$19,400,000	$18,690,000

December 31	12/31/02	12/31/01
Liabilities & Owners' Equity		
Current Liabilities:		
Accounts Payable	$2,000,000	$1,880,000
Notes Payable	1,700,000	1,800,000
Accrued Expenses Payable	660,000	600,000
Federal Income & Taxes Payable	640,000	380,000
Current Portion of Long-Term Debt	400,000	400,000
Total Current Liabilities	$5,400,000	$5,060,000
Long-Term Liabilities:		
Long-Term Debt	$5,000,000	$5,400,000
Total Liabilities	$10,400,000	$10,460,000
Owners' Equity		
Preferred Stock (6%, $100 par value, 1,200 shares authorized, issued, and outstanding)	$1,200,000	$1,200,000
Common Stock ($10 par value, 300,000 shares authorized, issued, and outstanding)	3,000,000	3,000,000
Additional Paid-in Capital	1,400,000	1,400,000
Retained Earnings	3,400,000	2,630,000
Total Owners' Equity	$9,000,000	$8,230,000
Total Liabilities & Owners' Equity	**$19,400,000**	**$18,690,000**

As you look at this balance sheet, keep a few points in mind:

♦ Remember that each dollar value on the balance sheet is a "snapshot" of the account, meaning its value as of the date of the financial statement (in this case, December 31 of 2002 and 2001).

♦ Total assets must equal total liabilities and owners' equity. It's called a balance sheet because it has to balance.

♦ Parentheses indicate a negative number, one to be subtracted from the column it appears in.

♦ Assets are listed in order of their liquidity; that is, how easily they can be converted to cash. Obviously, cash comes first; next come marketable securities (for example, Treasury bills, because the U.S. government is obligated to pay them).

Then come accounts receivable, because your customers are obligated to pay them. Assets which are more difficult to convert or sell (buildings and land, for instance) come later.

♦ Liabilities and owners' equity are listed in the order in which they are scheduled to be paid (notice that the owners come last!).

MBA Mastery

Only by comparing balance sheets for two or more financial periods can you judge the financial health of the company. Watch the year-to-year changes in the accounts to see what's going on.

♦ Current assets are expected to be liquidated— that is, turned into cash—within one year of the date of the balance sheet. Current liabilities are payable within one year.

♦ You need balance sheets for two (or more) periods so you can compare the values in the accounts for the two periods. A balance sheet for one period offers no basis of comparison and is therefore of little value.

A Tour of the Assets

I realize there are a lot of terms and numbers in this balance sheet that may be new to you. You've probably heard the old joke: "How do you eat an elephant?" Answer: "One bite at a time." So we are going to take these accounts line by line, a bite at a time.

Note that although our sample balance sheet and the following list are not exhaustive, they do present the assets commonly found on the balance sheet of a commercial or industrial company, such as a retailer or manufacturer. Financial services companies, such as banks, and companies in specialized industries, such as power generating or oil refining, have their own specific kinds of assets in addition to these. The assets we cover here are the standard ones you'll find in most companies.

Cash

Cash means the cash in the company's checking and savings accounts, and in petty cash. Often you will see cash and marketable securities together on one line of a balance sheet.

Marketable Securities

Marketable securities are short-term investments, usually in U.S. government securities or the *commercial paper* of other firms. The securities have short maturities and stable prices. Because of their liquidity, these securities are referred to as *near-cash assets*. Companies put money in marketable securities because they often earn higher interest than checking or savings accounts earn.

> **MBA Lingo** _____
>
> **Marketable securities** are short-term investments, usually in U.S. government securities or the commercial paper of other firms. **Commercial paper** is the name for short-term promissory notes issued by large banks and corporations. The maturities run from 2 to 270 days. Marketable securities are often called **near-cash assets** because

Marketable securities are shown on the balance sheet at "the lower of cost or market," meaning at their original cost—the price the company paid for them—or the current market price, if it is lower. This keeps the value shown for these assets conservative. Often when the securities are shown at cost and the current market value is higher, that current value will be shown in parentheses or in a footnote to the financial statement.

Accounts Receivable and Bad Debt

Accounts receivable are amounts owed by customers who have purchased goods or services from the company on trade credit.

In Chapter 10, you learned that some customers do not pay their bills. That is the reason for the allowance for bad debt that is noted on the balance sheet. This allowance is a contra account set up to accumulate an amount for those accounts receivable (or receivables) that will ultimately be uncollectible.

A contra account is an account created to offset potential future changes (usually losses) in another account. For example, retailers use a "Reserve for Returns" to offset their sales, because they know some customers will return the merchandise they bought. By deducting that merchandise from its sales figure, the store is stating sales realistically, because that money is returned to the customer. Contra accounts typically deduct a percentage of sales or accounts receivable (or whatever is being offset) based on experience or an industry average.

The company knows that some percentage (2 percent or so in most lines of business) of accounts receivable will be uncollectible. At the time of the sale, the company sets this amount aside for bad-debt expense.

Inventories

Inventories are goods for sale to customers or goods in the manufacturing process at the time the balance sheet is prepared.

A manufacturer will usually have three kinds of inventory: raw materials, work in process, and finished goods. Raw materials are goods that the company purchased to make its products, while work in process is currently somewhere in the manufacturing process, as the name implies. Work in process is often called unfinished goods. Finished goods are goods awaiting sale.

A retailer has inventory and no raw materials or work in process because it only buys and sells finished goods.

Service companies typically do not sell goods (except as a sideline; for example, when hair salons sell hair-care products) so they usually have minimal or no inventory on their balance sheets.

Property, Plant, and Equipment

Property, plant, and equipment refers to the buildings (offices, factories, warehouses, and so on) and equipment (machinery, furniture, and fixtures, such as lighting and display cases) owned by the company. Often you will see various elements of property, plant, and equipment broken out separately—for example, buildings and equipment, or buildings and fixtures and furniture.

Note that the property, plant, and equipment amounts represent the company's productive capacity and premises, rather than products the company is in business to sell. Thus, property, plant, and equipment are called *fixed assets*.

Accumulated depreciation is a contra account for tracking the depreciation of the value of fixed assets. Because the value of equipment and buildings generally decreases with age, the balance sheet must reflect the true worth of the fixed assets (as opposed

> **MBA Alert**
>
> Be sure to keep your current assets moving. You want your inventories and receivables to keep flowing through the company (or "turning over") because you are then selling product and collecting money more quickly. Ways to speed up the flow of current assets through a company include stocking only fast-moving merchandise, discounting slow-moving items, taking deliveries of merchandise more often to keep inventories low, and collecting accounts receivable aggressively.

> **MBA Lingo**
>
> **Fixed assets** are tangible property used in the operations of a business. They are not expected to be consumed or converted to cash in the ordinary course of business.

to the amounts they were bought for).
Depreciation, which I'll explain fully in
Chapter 14, is a way of *allocating* the cost of a
fixed asset to each year of the asset's life. In
other words, the cost of the asset is charged
against income over the life of the asset, rather
than all in one year.

By the way, in the sample balance sheet, I've
shown depreciation as a separate line on the
statement, while the allowance for bad-debt
contra account was deducted as part of the
accounts receivable line. Either presentation is
correct.

MBA Lingo

Depreciation is a way
of allocating the cost of a fixed
asset with a life of more than one
year. The cost of the asset is
charged against income over the
life of the asset, rather than all in
one year. **Allocating** a cost (any
cost) means assigning portions of
that cost to subsequent operating
periods or to specific areas
within the company.

You do not depreciate assets that are used right away or within one year (for example,
paper or office supplies). But, as I'll explain in Chapter 14, you must under tax law
depreciate assets with a longer life, such as productive equipment or company cars.

Land

Land owned by the company is usually carried at cost (the price paid for it) and listed
separately from other fixed assets.

Prepayments and Deferred Charges

Prepayments and deferred charges are in a sense
not really assets, but rather prepaid liabilities.

The best example of a prepayment is insurance
premiums paid in advance. The company has
paid the bill, say, for five years of insurance coverage in advance. That prepayment creates an
asset that will be used up over the five-year
period. So it is carried as a long-term asset.

Deferred charges are similar. They represent
money already spent that will yield a benefit in

MBA Lingo

**Prepayments and de-
ferred charges** represent monies
that have already been spent that
will yield benefits in upcoming
years. Prepaid insurance premiums and money allocated to
research and development are
examples of prepayments and
deferred charges, respectively.

the coming years. For example, research and development expenses for a new product
may be allocated over the life of that product. The company sets up an asset account
for that amount so it can make that allocation.

Intangibles

Intangibles are assets that provide a business advantage although they do not physically exist. Intangible assets include items such as trademarks, patents, and good will.

MBA Lingo

Intangibles are assets that provide a business advantage although they do not physically exist. Intangible assets include patents, trademarks, and good will.

A trademark is a legally protected brand name, slogan, or design of a product or firm. A registered trademark cannot be used by another company, because the firm that owns it used its resources to develop and establish that trademark.

Patents give an exclusive right to a product or process to the holder of the patent. Like a trademark, this protects the company or person who developed the product or process from having their work exploited by others.

Good will is the amount of money paid for an asset; for example, a product line or another company, above the value it was assigned by the previous owner. Companies vary in their accounting for good will. In most cases, when one company buys another, it must write off any good will within 40 years.

The Major Liabilities

Like assets, the kinds of liabilities listed on the balance sheet will be a bit different for companies in financial services and specialized industries. However, the following sections present the most common liabilities for most types of firms.

Accounts Payable

Accounts payable, or *payables*, are the amounts the company owes to its suppliers. (In other words, one company's receivables are another's accounts payable.)

Notes Payable

Notes payable can include commercial paper or other promissory notes (meaning a written promise to pay) that represent short-term borrowings of the company, meaning those payable within one year.

Accrued Expenses Payable

The *accrued expenses* account sums up all of the other money that the company owes to companies and individuals it does business with, including employees and independent contractors, attorneys and other outside professionals, and utilities such as the electric and telephone companies who have not been paid for services rendered on the date of the balance sheet.

MBA Lingo

Accounts payable, or **payables,** are the amounts the company owes to its suppliers. **Notes payable** can include commercial paper or other promissory notes that represent short-term borrowings of the company.

Federal Income and Other Taxes Payable

Every business that makes a profit must pay federal income taxes and, where applicable, state and city income taxes. There are also real estate taxes, excise taxes, payroll taxes, other business taxes—you get the idea. Taxes are accrued on the books until they're due, and the accrued amount is shown in this account.

MBA Lingo

Accrued means recorded but not paid, collected, or allocated. In the case of the balance sheet, **accrued expenses** sums up the money that the company owes to others (for example, employees, attorneys, and utility companies) who have not been paid for services rendered on the date of the balance sheet.

Current Portion of Long-Term Debt

Remember the distinction between current (or short-term) liabilities and long-term liabilities? *Current liabilities* are those payable within a year, meaning within a year of the date of the balance sheet.

Thus, the current portion of long-term debt is the portion of long-term debt that is due in the coming year. For instance, if the Sample Company took out a three-year term loan on December 31, 2001, the portion of the loan that must be repaid in the first year (that is, 2002) would be shown in this account. The amount to be repaid in the other two years would be shown in the long-term debt account.

MBA Lingo

On the balance sheet, **current liabilities** are those payable within a year, meaning within a year of the date of the balance sheet. **Long-term debt** is all debt due after one year from the date of the balance sheet.

Long-Term Debt

Long-term debt is all debt due after one year from the date of the balance sheet. This debt mostly represents financing from banks and bondholders.

Owner's Equity

Owner's equity refers to the financial stake the owners have in the company. The business has assets, and after you subtract what the business owes to anyone it owes money to, then what is left is the owner's stake. Note that this number can be zero or even negative if the company owes more than it has in assets. (That is, of course, a terrible situation that leads to bankruptcy if not quickly corrected with substantial and profitable growth in sales.)

Any corporation can issue stock. This includes any incorporated business, from a one-person company to a giant outfit that employs thousands of people and issues stock to the public. A corporation will always have an account for stock on the balance sheet as shown in our example.

An unincorporated business, such as a proprietorship or partnership, which you learned about in Chapter 3, will not have accounts for stock but will show the owners' equity in the form of capital contributions (money invested in the business by the owner or owners) and retained earnings (which is the same as retained earnings in our example—money earned by the business and then reinvested in the business).

Stock

Stock, or capital stock, represents ownership in a corporation. A share of stock is one unit of ownership. An owner's percentage of all the outstanding shares indicates his or her percentage of ownership. Investors buy stock in order to share in the company's profits. The company issues stock in order to raise money from investors.

Investors affect the finances and direction of a company in several ways:

◆ An investor purchases a stake in the company's future earnings.

◆ An investor shares in future earnings in the form of dividends (payments made to stockholders out of the company's income).

◆ An investor also gets voting rights, meaning he or she can vote on issues that affect the company, such as who'll be on the board of directors and whether the company will be sold to another company.

Note the difference between an investor and a creditor: While the investor influences and benefits from the growth and direction of the company, a creditor merely lends money to the company.

A company may issue several classes of stock, each with different features such as dividend policies and voting rights. The two broad classes of stock are preferred stock and common stock.

Preferred Stock

Preferred stock pays a dividend at a specific rate, regardless of how the company performs. Owners of preferred stock do not have voting rights. It is called preferred stock because the dividend on this stock must be paid before dividends are paid on the common stock.

Owners of preferred stock do not have a contractual right to a dividend. They only get dividends if the company has earnings to pay them.

MBA Lingo

Stock comes in different classes or types. The most popular classes of stock are preferred stock and common stock. Holders of **preferred stock** have no voting rights, are paid dividends at a fixed rate, and receive dividends before the holders of **common stock**. Common-stock holders have voting rights and do not receive dividends at a fixed rate.

Common Stock

Owners of *common stock* have voting rights, but do not receive dividends at a fixed rate. Because holders of common stock share in the future earnings of the company, the value and price of this stock can rise (appreciate) or fall as the company's business prospects change. Most holders of common stock purchase it as much for the potential for appreciation as for future dividends.

Common stock can pay dividends well in excess of those paid on preferred stock. (I'll cover stocks in more detail in Chapter 16.)

Additional Paid-in Capital

When a company issues stock, the stock has a *par value*, a value assigned to a share of stock by the company (for example, $1 or $5 or $10 a share). This value does not determine the selling price (that is, the market value) of the stock. The selling price, the price the investor actually pays per share, is determined in the market.

MBA Lingo

Par value is the value assigned to a share of stock by the company. The actual selling price of the stock is determined in the market. The amount paid to the company in excess of the par value of the stock is counted as **additional paid-in capital**.

The amount paid to the company in excess of the par value of the stock is counted as *additional paid-in capital*. It is capital paid into the company in addition to the stock's par value. (Additional paid-in capital is also known as paid-in surplus.)

Retained Earnings

When the company earns a profit for a period, it can only do one of two things with the money: distribute it to shareholders in the form of dividends, or retain it in the company to finance more assets. Any income not distributed as dividends goes into retained earnings. It is thus reinvested in the company and becomes part of the capital that finances the company.

Case in Point

Young, growing companies often go for years without paying a dividend. The stock of these companies is often called a growth stock because the company is growing so fast. Instead of paying a dividend, the company retains all of its earnings to finance the growing level of assets it needs in order to support its rapidly growing sales.

Investors who buy growth stocks understand this and target appreciation of the stock price rather than dividends as their investment goal.

The Least You Need to Know

- A balance sheet shows the values in the company's accounts on a certain date.

- The simple formula for the balance sheet is: Assets = Liabilities + Owners' Equity.

- Current assets include cash; marketable securities; accounts receivable; property, plant, and equipment; and intangibles.

- Liabilities include accounts payable, notes payable, accrued expenses payable, taxes, and long-term liabilities.

- Owners' equity includes stock, additional paid-in capital, and retained earnings.

12

Making a Statement: Income and Cash Flow

In This Chapter

- ◆ Using the income statement to understand a company
- ◆ A tour through the income statement accounts
- ◆ How cash flow shows where the money comes from—and goes

In Chapter 11, you took a detailed tour of one of the key financial statements, the balance sheet. Now let's turn to the other two major financial statements—the income statement and the cash flow statement.

The income statement is as important to your understanding of a company as the balance sheet. The cash flow statement is secondary. What it shows—the sources and uses of the cash that flowed through a company during a period—is important, but it is constructed from the balance sheet and income statement accounts. I include it here, though, because with any company, large or small, the way cash flows through a business is key.

Introducing the Income Statement

The *income statement* presents the results of a company's operations for a given period, usually a quarter or fiscal year. The income statement shows the company's sales and expenses for that period. It also shows whether the company had a profit or a loss for the period, so the income statement is also called the profit and loss statement, or the P&L.

The simple formula for the income statement is:

Sales – Expenses = Income

Clearly, the higher the sales and the lower the expenses, the greater the income. But the income statement is not quite that simple, because there are various types of expenses (just as there are various types of assets, liabilities, and owners' equity on the balance sheet). Seeing these various expenses on the income statement tells you how the company is spending its money, and where management is most and least efficient.

While the balance sheet is a snapshot of the company on a certain date, the income statement covers operations over an entire period. Unlike the balance sheet accounts, those on the income statement began at zero at the beginning of the period. So when you see "Sales" or "Salaries" on an income statement, you are seeing the total dollar amount of sales made or salaries paid during the period.

Let's look at a sample income statement to see what all this means.

Income Statement for Sample Company, Inc., December 31, 2002

	2002	2001
Sales	$22,000,000	$20,400,000
Cost of Goods Sold	16,400,000	15,400,000
Gross Income	5,600,000	5,000,000
Selling, General & Administrative Expense	2,800,000	2,650,000
Depreciation Expense	600,000	550,000
Operating Income	2,200,000	1,800,000
Other Expenses:		
Interest Expense	270,000	300,000
Other Income:		
Interest on Marketable Securities	100,000	80,000
Income Before Taxes	$2,030,000	$1,580,000
Provision for Income Taxes	960,000	730,000
Net Income (Loss)	**$1,070,000**	**$850,000**

Here are points to keep in mind when examining an income statement:

♦ As with the balance sheet, you should have at least two years of income state- ments to examine. Trends in sales and income are particularly important to watch. Sales and income growth are management's main responsibilities, so you want to see growth in those areas. Flat or falling sales are usually a sign of trouble.

MBA Lingo

The **income statement** shows the financial results of a company's operations for a given period, usually a year or quarter. It begins with sales during the period and subtracts all expenses incurred during the period to show how much money the busi- ness earned after expenses.

♦ Companies are driven to sell because ulti- mately all their money comes from sales. As you see on the statement, all expenses are deducted from sales. Other income or interest income are not part of the com- pany's regular business.

♦ *Cost of goods sold* captures production expenses, the expenses of producing the products. These are sometimes called direct expenses.

MBA Lingo

Cost of goods sold is the expense of buying goods and producing the product. They are called direct costs or direct ex- penses because they are directly associated with making what the company sells, as opposed to the costs of selling the product or administrative costs. The major components of costs of goods sold are materials and labor.

♦ Selling, general, and administrative expenses capture the costs of selling the products and of operating the administra- tive functions.

♦ The accounts "other expenses" and "other income" record expenses and income not related to operating the business. An example of an "other expense" would be the costs of defending the company against a lawsuit. In contrast, winning a settlement in a lawsuit would generate "other income."

A Tour Through the Income Statement

Let's examine the income statement accounts. Remember: Each account started at zero at the beginning of the period (in this case, the beginning of the year) and accu- mulated the amount shown during that period.

Sales

Sales (also called revenue, revenues, total sales, or total revenue) is the amount of money the company took in, before any expenses, on its operations. This means that sales does not include money the company took in, for example, by selling off old property, plant, and equipment. That would be shown under other income. Nor does sales include interest earned on marketable securities, which would be included under interest income.

Sometimes you'll see a contra account (see Chapter 11) called allowance for returns that is presented with sales. For instance, you might see "Sales $1 Million Less: Allowance for Returns $20,000." That contra account is set up because manufacturers and retailers know that some percentage of their products will be returned by dissatisfied customers or those finding breakage or defects. In this case, the contra account represents 2 percent of total sales ($1 million × .02 = $20,000), which is in the normal range for a manufacturer.

> **CAUTION**
>
> **MBA Alert**
>
> If you manage a company or department that produces a product, be sure to monitor the individual direct expenses that go into making that product. This includes the cost of materials, parts, and hardware, as well as your labor costs (watch overtime, which adds up quickly) and your costs of operating machinery. Those different expenses are the numbers to watch in order to control your production costs and achieve high gross income. It's just another case of "watch out for the dimes and the dollars will take care of themselves."

Cost of Goods Sold

For a retailer, cost of goods sold equals the price the retailer paid to suppliers for the merchandise it sells in the stores. This would also include the transportation costs of getting the goods into the stores.

For a manufacturer, cost of goods sold equals the total cost of producing its products. The major production expenses include the cost of materials; the wages and benefits of production workers; freight and transportation; and the rent, power, lights, maintenance, and other costs of operating the factory.

Cost of goods sold should capture all of the costs directly associated with making (or, for a retailer, acquiring) the product the company sells.

Gross Income

Gross income is the amount of money the company earns on its sales before the selling, general, and administrative expenses, which is the next expense item. Gross income is also called gross profit.

Some income statements don't report income at this level. They don't break out cost of goods sold and instead deduct selling, general, and administrative expenses and go straight to operating income. To me, that's too bad, because it omits important information. You'll see why in the next chapter.

Selling, General, and Administrative Expense (SG&A)

After a manufacturer makes a product (or after a retailer buys it from a supplier), that product must be sold. That means you have to pay salespeople salaries and commissions. They have to use the phone, send out letters, and travel to clients and probably buy them lunch (even drinks and dinner) now and then. All of these expenses, as well as marketing expenses, are included in this account.

On top of that, there are all those support functions—human resources, IS, accounting, and finance—as well as office space, power, light, supplies, and everything else needed to run a company. The salaries and benefits of managers are also included in SG&A, as it's usually called, since they do not work directly on producing the product.

Depreciation Expense

Depreciation expense is the amount of depreciation charged against sales during the period. This is *not* the same as accumulated depreciation on the balance sheet. Accumulated depreciation on the balance sheet is the total of all the past depreciation expense on the company's existing property, plant, and equipment.

This means that depreciation expense on the income statement for a period is added to the amount of accumulated depreciation on the balance sheet at the beginning of the period.

If you examine Sample Company's balance sheet in Chapter 11 and compare it to the income statement in this chapter, you'll see that the difference in accumulated depreciation between the balance sheet dated 2002 and the one dated 2001 is $600,000. That $600,000 is the depreciation expense charged to operations on the company's 2002 income statement.

Operating Income

Subtracting SG&A from gross income gives you *operating income*, also called operating profit, income from operations, or income from continuing operations.

MBA Lingo

Operating income equals sales minus the cost of goods sold and minus selling, general, and administrative expenses. This is the amount earned by the company on sales after deducting the direct expenses of making the product and the expenses of selling it and of all other aspects of running the business itself. Operating income is also called operating profit.

Note that operating income only represents income directly related to operations. Income from other sources—such as from the sale of a division or the settlement of a lawsuit—is listed separately under other income.

Other Expenses

Other expenses include interest expense, plus any extraordinary or nonrecurring expenses, as they are called. Although they are not shown in the earlier statement, other expenses can include costs of litigation, settlements paid in lawsuits, or the expense of closing down a division.

Case in Point

Among its problems, which include a Justice Department investigation of its accounting practices, the telecommunications company Global Crossing took on $12 *billion* of high-yield debt to finance its growth. But it couldn't keep growing after corporate America cut back on telecom purchases when the economy slowed in 2000 and 2001.

In a May 2002 cover story, "Why Companies Fail," *Fortune* contrasted this case with that of BellSouth. This conservatively managed telecom company emerged from the 1990s "with a pristine balance sheet and a strong competitive position" because it kept debt to reasonable levels. Overloading on debt is always a factor in corporate bankruptcies.

Interest Expense

Interest expense is counted separately from both operating and other expenses. Interest expense relates fairly directly to doing business, but it varies with both the amount the company borrows and, often, with the level of interest rates. Managers and investors like to watch interest expense closely because, while there are good reasons to borrow money, too much debt generates high interest expenses that drag on a company's operations.

Other Income

Other income, also called extraordinary or nonrecurring income, is incoming money not generated by regular operations.

Interest income is the most common category of other income. It is counted separately for the same reason that we count interest expense separately. Unless the company is a bank (in which case interest income actually represents sales), interest income is "gravy"— not a source of income from operations.

Although they are not shown in the sample statement, other sources of income can include money paid to the company in settlement of a lawsuit, money from the sale of fixed assets, or money from the sale of an intangible asset, such as a trademark or patent.

MBA Mastery

Because businesspeople (like the rest of us) dislike paying taxes, companies have methods—legal ones, of course—of minimizing their pretax income so that they minimize their taxes. In Chapter 14, I will show you various accounting methods that affect reported income.

Income Before Taxes

Income before taxes is income from all sources—operations as well as extraordinary items—before the government gets a crack at it. Income before taxes is also called pretax income.

Provision for Income Taxes

Corporate income tax rates can vary from year to year at the federal, state, and local levels. In the sample income statement, I've simply assumed a total tax rate of about 30 percent.

This is called a provision for income taxes because the taxes will be charged against the income earned in this period even if they have not actually been paid in this period. In other words, this account shows the total income tax expense charged to income during the period.

Net Income (Loss)

This is the bottom line you've heard so much about. Net income is what's left of sales and other income after you deduct cost of goods sold; selling, general, and administrative expense; other expenses; and taxes.

If all the expenses exceed sales and other income during the period, the company has a

MBA Lingo

People say a company with a loss for a period is **in the red** because losses used to be written in the books in red ink. You'll also hear the expression *red ink*, as in, "If this new product fails, we'll be swimming in red ink."

loss for the period. It is *in the red.* (Note that in the sample statement, parentheses are placed around the word "Loss" in the "Net Income" line to indicate a negative number.)

Get Insights into Income

The income statement represents management's report card for a quarter or a year. Just reading a couple of years of a company's income statements will tell you a lot. Here are some of the questions you'll be able to answer after looking at income statements:

- ◆ Are sales rising, falling, or just plain flat?

- ◆ Are costs rising or falling faster or slower than sales? Or are they keeping pace with the movement in sales?

- ◆ How about interest expense? Did interest expense rise or fall from one year to the next?

- ◆ Is income keeping pace or is it changing in relation to sales? How's the bottom line holding up?

- ◆ Did the company incur any extraordinary windfalls or charges?

How Are Your Employees Doing?

Sales per employee and net income per employee are two quick measures you can easily calculate from an income statement. They can be quite revealing.

- ◆ To calculate sales per employee, simply divide the sales figure on the income statement by the number of employees in the company.

- ◆ To calculate net income per employee, divide the net income figure by the number of employees.

If either of these figures is on a downward trend, it may mean that the company is not efficiently managing its human resources. You can also compare the results of these calculations with the corresponding numbers for other companies in the same industry to see how your use of employee resources rates.

You'll examine a number of calculations for analyzing both the balance sheet and the income statement in Chapter 13.

The Cash Flow Statement

I wrap up this introduction to financial statements with the *cash flow statement*. This is also called the statement of sources and uses of cash, but, for brevity, let's stick with cash flow statement.

Like the balance sheet and income statement, the cash flow statement is presented in a company's annual report. The cash flow statement is important for two reasons:

1. It improves your understanding of what's going on in the balance sheet and income statement, because the cash flow statement is calculated from account values on those statements.

2. It highlights an essential point: Cash is king. A company must generate actual cash (dough, jack, moola) and it must generate it from operations, rather than through borrowing or by selling off pieces of itself.

A company can have high levels of assets, but not much cash. It can have inventory that can't be sold, receivables that can't be collected, and machinery that can't produce what customers want. In those cases the outfit isn't generating cash, and cash is what you need to pay your bills and distribute dividends.

MBA Lingo

The **cash flow statement** shows the sources and uses of the cash that flowed through the company during a period, typically a year, and always the same period that the accompanying balance sheet and income statement covers. This statement shows where the company's money came from and where it was spent during the period.

Easy Come, Easy Go: Cash Flow

The cash flow statement shows where the company's cash came from and where it was spent during the period covered by the statement. (This period is the same one covered by the income statement, the period between the beginning and ending balance sheets.)

A cash flow statement shows the increases or decreases in the various accounts and the effects on the cash account. An increase in an asset is a use of cash, while a decrease in an asset is a source of cash. Conversely, an increase in a liability or owners' equity account is a source of cash, while a decrease in a liability or equity account is a use of cash.

For example, if the ending balance in accounts receivable is higher than the beginning balance, that counts as a use of cash, because the company added more in receivables than it collected. Collecting receivables increases cash. Not collecting them decreases cash. (As you saw in Chapter 11, on Sample Company's 2002 balance sheet, receivables are higher than on the 2001 balance sheet. So that counts as a use of cash.)

Conversely, if the ending balance in accounts receivable is lower than the starting balance, that counts as a source of cash. That's because the company collected more receivables than it added during the period. The net effect on cash is an increase, so that's a source of cash.

The cash flow statement also accounts for "noncash" charges—expenses that were recognized on the income statement but did not require a cash payment. Depreciation is the best example of a noncash charge. The actual cash was spent on the fixed asset before the accounting period, but the expense is allocated (as depreciation) to the operating period. Because no cash was spent on depreciation expense, that counts as a source of cash.

A Sample Cash Flow Statement

Here is a cash flow statement for Sample Company, based on the balance sheet in Chapter 11 and the income statement you saw earlier in this chapter:

Sample Company, Inc. Statement of Sources and Uses of Cash for the Year 2002

Cash Flows from Operating Activities:	
Net Income	$1,070,000
Depreciation	600,000
Decrease (Increase) in Accounts Receivable	(200,000)
Decrease (Increase) in Inventories	600,000
Increase (Decrease) in Accounts Payable	120,000
Increase (Decrease) in Notes Payable	(100,000)
Increase (Decrease) in Accrued Expenses Payable	60,000
Increase (Decrease) in Taxes Payable	260,000
Net Cash Flow from Operations	**$2,410,000**
Cash Flows from Investing Activities:	
Decrease (Increase) in Marketable Securities	(780,000)
Decrease (Increase) in Buildings and Machinery	**(610,000)**
Decrease (Increase) in Prepayed and Deferred Charges	(20,000)
Net Cash Flow from Investing Activities	**($1,410,000)**

Cash Flows from Financing Activities:

Increase (Decrease) in Total Long-Term Debt	(400,000)
Increase (Decrease) in Preferred Stock	——
Increase (Decrease) in Common Stock	——
Increase (Decrease) in Additional Paid-in Capital	——
Dividends Paid	(300,000)
Net Cash Flows from Financing Activities	**(700,000)**
Net Change in Cash	**$ 300,000**

Keep the following in mind as you examine this cash flow statement:

♦ The cash flow statement is largely "constructed" from the balance sheet and income statement, so the underlying numbers have to be sound for the cash flow statement to be accurate.

♦ Like the income statement, the cash flow statement covers only one period (in this case, the year 2002), the period from the beginning balance sheet to the ending balance sheet. It is certainly useful to have two or more years of cash flow statements, but it is not as essential as it is for the other two statements.

♦ There are three parts to the cash flow statement: cash flow from operating activities, cash flow from investing activities, and cash flow from financing activities. The most important one is cash flow from operations. A company cannot sustain itself on borrowings or investments (unless it is a financial institution).

♦ The cash flow statement reconciles all other accounts to the change in the cash account that occurred from the beginning balance sheet to the ending balance sheet for the accounting period.

♦ When more cash comes in from various sources than goes out during a period, cash flow is positive. When the opposite occurs, cash flow is negative.

♦ The term *gross cash flow* or *gross cash flow from operations* usually refers to net income plus depreciation.

Getting Reconciled

Using the cash flow statement, we can easily begin to *reconcile* the accounts listed on the balance sheet and income statements—that is, analyze how changes in one account affect other accounts.

For example, consider Sample Company's retained earnings shown on the balance sheet in Chapter 11. As you may remember from that chapter, net income goes to one of two places: It is either reinvested in the operation as retained earnings, or it is distributed to the shareholders as dividends. Therefore, what is not retained is paid as a dividend. Since dividends are a use of cash, you have to calculate them for the cash flow statement.

You can easily calculate the amount of dividends paid by doing a reconciliation of retained earnings accounts on Sample Company's balance sheet in Chapter 11.

Beginning Retained Earnings (12/31/01)	$2,630,000
Plus: Net Income for 2002	1,070,000
Minus: Ending Retained Earnings (12/3102)	3,400,000
Dividends Paid During 2002	$300,000

This amount is shown on the cash flow statement under "Net Cash Flows from Financing Activities" because paying dividends on stock are part of using stock as a source of financing.

MBA Lingo

A **reconciliation** of an account analyzes the changes in the other accounts that affect the account.

Actually, the cash flow statement is really just one large reconciliation of all accounts to the cash account. If you look back at Sample Company's balance sheets for 2002 and 2001 in Chapter 11, you'll see that cash increased by $300,000. The cash flow statement identifies the changes in the other accounts that led to that $300,000 increase.

The Least You Need to Know

- The income statement, also known as the profit and loss statement or P&L, is management's report card for the quarter or year it covers.

- Examine at least two years of income statements to see trends in sales and key expense categories.

- Cash flow can be more important to a company and its owners than size, growth, or even profits.

- Use the cash flow statement to examine where money comes from and what it is spent on in a given period.

Chapter 13

Digging Deeper: Financial Analysis

In This Chapter

- The basics of financial analysis
- Measuring liquidity ratios
- Understanding solvency ratios
- Analyzing profitability ratios

In Chapter 11 and Chapter 12, I showed you the basics of balance sheets, income statements, and cash flow statements. Simply reading a financial statement will tell you something—but not much. You'll see the dollar amounts of the accounts and, if you have at least two years of statements, you'll see if an account increased or decreased.

But to really understand a company, you must analyze its financial statements. Aside from a basic understanding of the accounts, this requires some simple calculations.

In this chapter, you'll learn basic financial statement analysis—how to look beyond the account values and relate them to one another so you can see into the company's financial structure and performance.

Let's Get Analytical: Financial Ratios

A ratio is a calculation that shows the relationship between two values. A ratio is nothing more than a division problem with a number on top (numerator) divided by a number on the bottom (denominator).

Financial ratios show the relationship between two financial statement accounts. Ratio analysis enables you to measure a company's performance and creditworthiness (capability to pay its liabilities and take on additional debt). While financial ratios are not the only tool of financial analysis, they are among the most powerful.

Liquidity Ratios

The following formulas (aside from working capital, which isn't a ratio) are called liquidity ratios. They measure a company's capability to meet its short-term obligations and to convert receivables and inventory into cash. The liquidity ratios we will cover are current ratio, quick ratio, A/R turnover, collection period, inventory turnover, and days' sales on hand. But first, let's examine working capital.

Working Capital

Working capital measures a company's capability to pay its current obligations. The formula for working capital is:

Working Capital = Current Assets – Current Liabilities

> **MBA Lingo**
>
> **Working capital** measures a company's capability to pay its current obligations. Working capital equals current assets minus current liabilities.

Current assets and current liabilities are listed on the balance sheet.

Based on the financial statements presented in Chapters 11 and 12, let's look at the working capital for Sample Company in 2002:

Working Capital = $12,000,000 – 5,400,000

Working Capital = $6,600,000

For Sample Company in 2001:

Working Capital = $11,320,000 – 5,060,000

Working Capital = $6,260,000

Working capital improved for Sample Company in 2002, rising by $340,000, or 5 percent (340,000 ÷ 6,260,000). This 5 percent increase occurred while sales increased by about 8 percent (22,000,000 − 20,400,000 = 1,600,000, which divided by 20,400,000 = 7.8 percent). Since working capital should grow at about the same rate as sales, this represents good financial management.

Obviously, working capital should, at a minimum, be positive. In general, the higher the working capital, the better. However, positive working capital only tells us that the company's current assets exceed its current liabilities. A ratio can tells us how much greater it is, and a lot more.

MBA Alert

Be careful when you look at working capital. It can at times be inflated by useless current assets. A badly managed company often allows poor-quality receivables or obsolete inventories to build up so that its working capital appears strong. Ratio analysis enables you to look beyond raw numbers like working capital to get a better sense of what's really going on.

Current Ratio

The *current ratio*, also called the working capital ratio, shows the relationship between current assets and current liabilities. Here's the formula:

Current Ratio = Current Assets ÷ Current Liabilities

Again, current assets and current liabilities are on the balance sheet.

For Sample Company in 2002:

Current Ratio = $12,000,000 ÷ $5,400,000

Current Ratio = 2.2

For Sample Company in 2001:

Current Ratio = $11,320,000 ÷ $5,060,000

Current Ratio = 2.2

In most businesses, a current ratio of 2.0 or better is considered good. It means that the company has twice the amount of current assets as current liabilities. Remember, though that some assets are more liquid than others. (See Chapter 11 for a discussion of liquidity.) Therefore, we have another measure of a company's capability to pay its current liabilities: the *quick ratio*.

> ### MBA Lingo
>
> The **current ratio**, also called the working capital ratio, shows the relationship between current assets and current liabilities. The current ratio equals current assets divided by current liabilities.
>
> The **quick ratio**, also called the quick asset ratio or acid test ratio, is a more stringent measure of liquidity. To calculate the quick ratio, find the sum of cash, marketable securities, and accounts receivable and divide by current liabilities.

Quick Ratio

The quick ratio, also called the quick asset ratio or acid test ratio, is a more stringent measure of liquidity. The formula is:

Quick Ratio = (Cash + Marketable Securities + Accounts Receivable) ÷ Current Liabilities

These numbers are all on the balance sheet. This ratio focuses on the capability of the company to meet its current obligations with its most liquid assets, which are cash, marketable securities, and accounts receivable. While industry norms vary, a company with a quick ratio of 1.0 or better is usually positioned to pay its current liabilities out of current assets.

For Sample Company in 2002:

Quick Ratio = ($900,000 + $1,700,000 + $4,000,000) ÷ $5,400,000

Quick Ratio = $6,600,000 ÷ $5,400,000

Quick Ratio = 1.2

This quick ratio of 1.2 indicates that Sample Company has a good portion of its current assets in liquid assets rather than inventories.

Let's turn now to a few ratios that measure the quality of the accounts receivable and the inventories.

Accounts Receivable Turnover

The level of accounts receivable tells us little about the quality of the receivables. Here, the term *quality* refers to the collectability of the receivables. If accounts receivable cannot be collected, they are close to worthless.

It's also a bad sign when receivables are "slow," meaning that the company takes longer than it should to collect. In other words, the customers are not paying the invoices when they're due.

This is bad for two reasons: First, if business conditions worsen, slow receivables can become even slower and perhaps uncollectable. Second, the company has money tied up in those receivables, money that could be used to pay off liabilities or invest in marketable securities.

Here's the formula for receivables *turnover:*

> A/R Turnover = Sales ÷ Average Accounts Receivable

The sales figure is on the income statement. To calculate average accounts receivable, add the accounts receivable at the beginning of the period (from the first balance sheet) to the accounts receivables at the end of the period (from the second period) and divide the sum by two.

> **MBA Mastery**
>
> If you sell to customers on credit, you are financing them for the time you are waiting to be paid. The slower they pay, the longer you are financing them. If you don't want to finance them for free, have a late charge on your invoices.

> **MBA Lingo**
>
> **Turnover** is the number of times the receivables went through a cycle of being created and collected (or turned over) in a period.

Now in strictest terms, the numerator should be credit sales instead of sales, but we're assuming that all of the company's sales are on credit. Usually you won't find credit sales broken out from total sales on financial statements anyway. (If you need to, you can calculate this number for your own company with information available from the accounting department.)

For Sample Company in 2002:

> $22,000,000
>
> (4,000,000 + 3,800,000) ÷ 2
>
> A/R Turnover = $22,000,000 ÷ 3,900,000
>
> A/R Turnover = 5.6 times

In general, the higher the turnover, the better. Why? Because the faster the receivables are turning, the less money you have tied up in them.

It's particularly useful to compare this ratio with the ratio of other companies within the same industry (known as industry norms). A company in an industry that allows customers to pay within 45 days instead of the more common 30 days, for example, will automatically have a lower turnover.

Collection Period

For an even more complete picture of a firm's accounts receivable, convert the receivables turnover to collection period. This measure is also known as days' sales outstanding. Collection period is the average number of days it takes the company to collect its receivables.

Collection Period = 365 ÷ (A/R Turnover)

For Sample Company in 2002:

Collection Period = 365 ÷ 5.6

Collection Period = 65 days

MBA Mastery

To encourage prompt payment, some companies offer terms of "2/10, net 30." This means the customer gets a 2 percent discount if he pays within 10 days of the invoice date, but must pay the full amount if he pays later than 10 days. Whether he takes the discount or not, he must pay within 30 days. Unfortunately, some customers take the discount even when paying beyond 10 days, which creates difficulties.

This means that Sample Company takes an average of 65 days to collect its invoices. This number is "good" or "bad" only in relation to the industry norms and the terms on which the company sells. If Sample Company gives customers 60 days, or even 45 days, to pay, 65 days sales outstanding and 5.6 turns a year is fine. If the terms are 30 days, (which is much more common), then Sample Company is not collecting its receivables quickly enough. In practice, virtually no company that sells on credit is paid on time by all of its customers, so the collection period will always be longer than the actual terms on which the sale is made (for instance, 30 days). In most industries, however, a 65-day collection period is not considered good.

Finally, remember that the collection period is one number that sums up all the accounts—those paying quickly and those paying slowly. In other words, it's an average.

Inventory Turnover

Inventory turnover resembles receivables turnover. You want to sell inventory quickly, just like you want to collect receivables fast. The faster your inventory turns over, the less money you have tied up in inventory to support a given level of sales. Here's the formula for inventory turnover:

Inventory Turnover = Sales ÷ Average Inventories

The sales figure is on the income statement. Inventories are on the balance sheet.

$22,000,000

($5,400,000 + $6,000,000) ÷ 2

To calculate average inventory, add the inventory at the beginning of the period (from the first balance sheet) to the inventory at the end of the period (from the second period) and divide the sum by two.

Inventory Turnover = $22,000,000 ÷ 5,700,000

Inventory Turnover = 3.9 times

As with all ratios, you have to judge inventory turns against industry norms. For example, a jewelry store's inventory may turn only once a year because it carries high-priced items with a large profit margin (a measure we'll discuss later in this chapter) and customers expect a wide selection. However, a grocer may turn his inventory over every three to five days because the prices and profit margins are much lower, many items are perishable, and shelf space is at a premium. A grocer can't afford to carry an item that doesn't sell briskly.

Days' Sales on Hand

As with receivables, it can be useful to convert inventory turns to a measure expressed in days—days' sales on hand. This number reveals the average number of days it takes the company to sell its inventory.

Days' Sales on Hand = 365 ÷ Inventory Turnover

For Sample Company in 2002:

Days' Sales on Hand = 365 ÷ 3.9

Days' Sales on Hand = 94 days

This means that Sample Company has an average of 94 days' worth of sales in inventory. Again, this number is "good" or "bad" only compared with industry norms. (Remember, because it is an average, this number includes the fastest- as well as the slowest-moving merchandise.)

Solvency Ratios

Long-term *solvency* ratios examine two elements. The first is the proportion of debt the company uses in its financial structure. The second is its capability to pay the interest on the debt (that is, to service the debt).

MBA Lingo

Solvency is the capability of a company (or individual) to pay its bills on time.

MBA Lingo

The **debt-to-equity ratio** compares the amount of the company's total financing from creditors compared with the amount of money invested by the shareholders. The debt-to-equity ratio is calculated by dividing total liabilities by total owners' equity, both of which are on the balance sheet.

Debt-to-Equity Ratio

The *debt-to-equity ratio*, also called the debt-equity ratio, is the first of the three long-term solvency ratios we will examine. The debt-to-equity ratio measures the extent to which the owners are using debt—that is, trade credit, liabilities, and borrowings—rather than their own funds to finance the company.

Debt-to-Equity Ratio = Total Liabilities ÷ Total Owners' Equity

Note that total liabilities includes all current and long-term liabilities.

Owners' equity represents the total amount that the owners have invested in the company, both in stock they've purchased and in earnings they've reinvested in the company rather than taken as dividends.

For Sample Company in 2002:

Debt-to-Equity Ratio = $10,400,000 ÷ $9,000,000

Debt-to-Equity Ratio = 1.2

Many analysts look for debt-to-equity of 1.0 or less. That means that half of the company's total financing—or less—comes from debt. However, many analysts also do not mind higher proportions of debt in a company's financial structure (the company financing, as seen on the right-hand side of the balance sheet) as long as they see that the company can handle the interest and principle payments.

Debt Ratio

The *debt ratio* resembles the debt-to-equity ratio. But instead of relating total debt to owner's equity, it measures only long-term debt in relation to all financial resources.

This ratio shows the role of long-term debt in the firm's financial structure. The debt-equity ratio is particularly useful to long-term lenders such as banks.

The formula for the debt ratio is:

Debt Ratio = Long-Term Debt ÷ (Total Liabilities and Equity)

The figures for long-term debt, total liabilities, and equity are on the balance sheet.

For Sample Company in 2002:

Debt Ratio = $5,000,000 ÷ $19,400,000

Debt Ratio = 0.26

> **MBA Lingo** ___
>
> The **debt ratio** compares the company's long-term debt to the company's total financial resources. The debt ratio measures the amount of financing that comes from long-term creditors relative to the amount provided by short-term creditors and invested by shareholders. The debt ratio is calculated by dividing long-term liabilities by total liabilities and owners' equity, both of which are on the balance sheet.

This tells us that 26 percent of Sample Company's total financial resources are in the form of long-term debt. Generally, the lower this number, the better. While you must consider industry practices and norms, if this number approaches 50 percent, you want to be sure the company has a reliable earnings stream.

In this calculation, some analysts would include the current portion of long-term debt in the long-term debt figure (rather than in total liabilities and owners equity). These analysts believe that although it is part of current liabilities, the current portion of long-term debt should be considered long-term debt because it was provided by long-term creditors. I did not include the current portion of long-term debt in the debt figure, in order to keep the calculation simple. Either method is correct.

Times Interest Earned

The *times interest earned ratio* measures the capability of the company to pay the interest on its long-term debt. Here is the formula:

Times Interest Earned = Operating Income ÷ Interest Expense

MBA Mastery

Financial statements are standardized, but different companies use different accounting practices (see Chapter 14). I believe analysts should use the more conservative method of calculating a ratio when there's more than one option. (More conservative means the method that yields the lower value.)

MBA Lingo

The **times interest earned ratio** measures the capability of the company to pay the interest on its long-term debt out of earnings from operations. Times interest earned is calculated by dividing earnings before interest and taxes (or EBIT) by interest expense during a given period, usually a year.

The figures for operating income and interest expense are on the income statement. In this formula, operating income is usually called "earnings before interest and taxes" or EBIT (pronounced *e-bit*). You use EBIT because you want to measure the capability to pay the interest expense out of operating income before you deduct interest out of that income. You use income before taxes because interest is tax-deductible.

Don't include "other income" in this calculation. You want to measure the company's capability to service its debt with cash from the operations only.

For Sample Company in 2002:

Times Interest Earned = $2,200,000 ÷ $270,000

Times Interest Earned = 8 times

In 2002, Sample Company earned operating income of eight times its interest expense. As always, industry norms will dictate the appropriate value for this ratio. Generally, however, EBIT of at least three or four times interest earned is considered safe.

By the way, times interest earned is often called a coverage ratio, meaning coverage of interest expense.

MBA Alert

Look twice at any ratio based on earnings. Earnings may be measured by net income, EBIT, or EBITDA (pronounced *e-bit-da*), which is earnings before interest, taxes, debt payments, and amortization and depreciation. Try to judge the quality of earnings by identifying sources of earnings: continuing operations (which is good), new acquisitions (which may be bad if the company paid too much or took on too much debt for them), sales of assets (which may be bad if the company is selling off pieces of itself to pump up earnings), or improper accounting (which is always bad and is discussed in Chapter 14). Be very suspicious if earnings are rising, but cash flow is falling.

Profitability Ratios

Finally, let's look at the profitability ratios. These ratios measure the company's earning power and management's effectiveness in running operations.

Gross Margin

Gross margin, also called the gross profit margin, is the first profitability ratio we'll examine. The gross margin measures the effectiveness of the company's production management.

Gross Margin = Gross Income ÷ Sales

Gross income and sales are found on the income statement.

For Sample Company in 2002:

Gross Margin = $5,600,000 ÷ $22,000,000

Gross Margin = 25.5%

Obviously, the higher the gross margin, the better. The values for this number will vary widely across industries. Sample Company spends about 75 percent of its total sales on production costs; that is, on cost of goods sold. This means that Sample Company is probably a manufacturer because most retail firms try to keep their cost of goods sold to about 50 percent.

Some businesses have inherently higher margins than others. These "high margin" businesses are often those selling something that customers value highly, particularly if the item can be made cheaply. Designer clothing and other items purchased for their image or status are a good example. For instance, U.S. luxury car models such as General Motors' Cadillac and Ford's Lincoln achieve higher margins than their lower-status products because the luxury models command higher prices for essentially the same components and a lot more sheet metal—and sheet metal is relatively cheap.

> **MBA Lingo**
>
> **Gross margin** is gross income as a percentage of sales. This ratio measures the effectiveness of production and is calculated by dividing gross income by sales.

Another way to achieve high margins is to add a lot of value to a product. For example, a food-processing company will generally have higher margins than a farmer because the food processor adds more value (through the processing and packaging) than the farmer did by growing it.

Case in Point

Innovative high-technology companies often have very high gross margins—some as high as 70 or 80 percent. That's because a high-tech company with a new solution to an expensive problem can charge almost whatever it wants to those who need that solution. Eventually, however, competitors enter the market with competing solutions, and that drives down the prices of the technology because customers then have a choice. This erodes the gross margin of the innovator, who must usually reduce his price in order to compete. Nevertheless, the first company to introduce a new technology, such as the personal digital assistant (PDA) or the VCR, can make a lot of money before those competitors arise.

Operating Margin

The *operating margin* measures operating income as a percentage of sales. In contrast to the gross margin, the operating margin measures management's effectiveness in the nonproduction areas of the company. It measures the contribution (or lack of contribution) of the sales, administrative, and other nonproduction functions.

MBA Lingo

Operating margin is operating income as a percentage of sales. This ratio measures the effectiveness in the nonproduction areas of the company and is calculated by dividing operating income by sales.

If a company has a good gross margin and a poor operating margin, management is somehow mismanaging the areas that account for selling, general, and administrative (SG&A) expense. Perhaps sales costs are too high. Perhaps there are lavish offices, luxury cars, and high entertainment expense being charged to operations. Perhaps the administrative staff is too large. Or maybe management's salaries are too high—a serious problem at some companies, especially at senior levels.

Here's the formula:

Operating Margin = Operating Income ÷ Sales

Operating income and sales are on the income statement.

For Sample Company in 2002:

Operating Margin = $2,200,000 ÷ $22,000,000

Operating Margin = 10%

As is the case with all profitability measures, the higher the operating margin, the better.

Net Margin

The *net margin* measures the bottom line—net income—as a percentage of sales. This shows the percentage of each sales dollar that the company manages to hang on to after production and operating expenses, after interest and other expenses, and after taxes.

Net Margin = Net Income ÷ Sales

Net income and sales are found on the income statement.

For Sample Company in 2002:

Net Margin = $1,070,000 ÷ $22,000,000

Net Margin = 4.9%

A net margin in the 5 percent range is common. Interestingly, several years ago nonbusinesspeople were surveyed and asked, "What percentage of a company's sales do you believe wind up as profits?" The researchers got answers ranging up to 25 and even 50 percent! This highlights the general public's lack of understanding concerning business and profits. The public's understanding of business and the legitimate pursuit of profit was eroded further by the financial accounting scandals of the early 2000s.

A net margin of around 10 percent would be excellent, particularly if the company could consistently achieve it.

MBA Lingo

Net margin is net income as a percentage of sales. This ratio measures the company's capability to deliver on the bottom line. That is, it shows what percentage of sales the company actually delivers to shareholders as after-tax earnings. The net margin is calculated by dividing net income by sales.

Asset Turnover

As you know, management's job is to use the company's assets to generate cash. Assets must therefore generate sales and profits. The *asset turnover* ratio measures management's effectiveness at using assets to generate sales.

The formula for asset turnover is:

Asset Turnover = Sales ÷ Total Assets

The sales figure is on the income statement. Total assets are on the balance sheet.

For Sample Company in 2002:

> Asset Turnover = $22,000,000 ÷ $19,400,000
>
> Asset Turnover = 1.1 times

MBA Lingo

Asset turnover measures sales as a percentage of assets to show how well management is employing the company's assets to generate sales. Asset turnover is calculated by dividing sales by total assets.

Asset turnover, or asset turns, shows how efficiently management uses assets. A ratio of about 1.0, like that of Sample Company, may indicate either inefficient use of assets or an inherently asset-intensive business—that is, one requiring lots of plant and equipment, such as oil refining or heavy manufacturing.

Return on Assets

Return on assets (ROA) measures management's capability to use assets to generate a profit (also known as a return).

Here is the formula for return on assets:

> Return on Assets = Net Income ÷ Total Assets

For Sample Company in 2002:

> Return on Assets = 1,070,000 ÷ 19,400,000
>
> Return on Assets = 5.5%

MBA Lingo

Return on assets shows how well management is using assets to generate income. Return on assets is calculated by dividing net income by total assets.

Over time, a decrease in asset turns or return on assets may mean that management is misusing assets somehow. They may be focused on spending money on assets rather than on selling product to customers. They may be growing the asset base faster than they can grow sales. This can also lead to too much debt, because those assets must be financed.

The company could also be acquiring the wrong mix of assets. If it has equipment that could be rapidly superseded by a better technology, for example, management may soon wish they didn't have all those assets.

Return on Investment

This is *the* key measure of return, especially for shareholders, and therefore for management. *Return on investment* (ROI), also called return on equity, measures the return on the money the shareholders have invested in the company.

This number is critical because management must earn a good return for the owners. If management can't do this, either (1) the shareholders will sell their shares and put their money where it will get a better return, or (2) the board of directors will replace management.

Here is the formula for this important ratio:

Return on Investment = Net Income ÷ Owners' Equity

Net income is found on the income statement; owners' equity is on the balance sheet.

For Sample Company in 2002:

Return on Investment = $1,070,000 ÷ $9,000,000

Return on Investment = 11.9%

Generally, an ROI of 10 percent or better is considered good. Investors compare this number to the returns they can earn elsewhere on their money. They look at the returns earned by other companies and at interest rates on bonds and other securities. So management must always be aware of how they are doing, not just as managers of the business, but as stewards of the owners' money.

MBA Lingo

Return on investment (or ROI, also called return on equity or ROE) measures net income against the investment that it took to generate that income. Return on investment is calculated by dividing net income by owners' equity.

Keep Your Pencils—and Eyes—Sharp

Now that we've covered the main financial ratios, here are a few tips for when you do ratio analysis, particularly if you are analyzing another company's financial statements. Be sure to …

- ◆ *Consider the source.* Sound financial analysis depends on sound financial statements. Beware of accounting games and take any red flags (such as increasing earnings and declining cash flow) seriously. Use the 10-Ks and 10-Qs, which are, respectively, the more detailed annual and quarterly reports that public companies must file with the SEC. Read about the senior managers and their backgrounds and the companies they have managed before, and weigh the statements accordingly.

♦ *Look beyond the ratios.* Read the footnotes to the statements and management's discussion of operations in the annual report. Keep up-to-date with company news on management changes, product announcements, and joint ventures.

♦ *Calculate accurately.* Financial statements can be confusing at first because some accounts, such as depreciation expense and accumulated depreciation, have similar names. Also, the eye can easily misalign numbers and accounts across columns.

♦ *Calculate conservatively.* Remember that most companies, including completely honest ones, put their best foot forward in financial statements. You can make up for that by being conservative in your calculations.

♦ *Compare the trend in the ratio over two or more periods.* A ratio from one period can't tell you nearly as much as a trend over two or more years.

♦ *Cross-check your ratios and look for patterns.* Try to see management's strengths and weaknesses. Do they generate cash? Is their liquidity strong? Do they have too much debt or too many assets? Are they growing the asset base faster than sales? Where are their margins weak or strong?

♦ *Understand industry norms.* Industry norms place financial ratios in context. Industry norms are published by Standard & Poor's, Dun & Bradstreet Inc., and by Robert Morris Associates, a national association of bankers.

The Least You Need to Know

♦ The relationships between various financial statement accounts will tell you about the company's performance and creditworthiness. Financial ratios are the key tools for assessing these relationships.

♦ The liquidity ratios measure the company's capability to meet its short-term obligations as they come due.

♦ The long-term solvency ratios measure an outfit's capability to meet its long-term obligations.

♦ The profitability ratios measure the efficiency of the company's operations. A strong gross margin indicates efficient production management, while a strong operating margin indicates efficient management of sales and administration.

♦ When you calculate ratios and find one that's below par, look for patterns. Whenever possible, compare a company's ratios to industry norms.

Look at the Books: Accounting Systems

In This Chapter

- ◆ How to set up an accounting system
- ◆ Accounting for inventory
- ◆ Calculating depreciation on plant and equipment

Where do financial statements come from? What goes on behind the scenes? What does a bookkeeper do? What decisions go into accounting for various assets, liabilities, and expenses? How do these decisions affect the outfit's finances?

This chapter answers these questions. It will also improve your understanding of financial statements and of business. And it will prepare you to set up an accounting system for your company or department, or help you understand the one that's already in place.

The Major Ledgers

When you hear someone refer to "the books," they are talking about the company's journals or ledgers or "the books of account." They are set up in books with specially ruled ledger paper or, more commonly today, in specialized accounting computer software that replicates ledgers in electronic form.

When setting up an accounting system, you first must decide how often you'll enter transactions into the various ledgers. You can make ledger entries on a daily, weekly, monthly, or quarterly basis. For infrequent transactions, such as purchases of buildings and equipment, you would make an entry when the transaction occurs.

You would enter other transactions on a regular basis. Retail stores or restaurants enter the day's receipts in a daily sales ledger. Assuming that the store or restaurant pays its employees each week, it would make weekly entries in the payroll ledger.

Most companies keep separate ledgers for separate kinds of transactions. They record sales transactions in the sales ledger, payroll checks in the payroll ledger, invoices sent to customers in the accounts receivable ledger, and bills received from suppliers in the accounts payable ledger.

> **MBA Lingo**
>
> A bookkeeper or accountant **posts** an account when he or she enters it into the company's books of account. If an amount is transferred from one account to another, that is also called posting.

These ledgers do not have to be separate books. They can be separate sections of a large book. As a manager, accountant, or bookkeeper, you can choose how to set up your company's books. However, you must follow standard accounting procedures and be understandable by another accountant or bookkeeper (or, heaven forbid, the IRS).

Most businesses need at least three ledgers: one for cash receipts (that is, cash inflows), one for cash disbursements (that is, cash outflows), and a general ledger. In any system, the various journals or subledgers are *posted* to the general ledger at the end of the accounting period.

Posting means "entering an amount." In this case it means "transferred" to the general ledger, which summarizes all the company's accounts. The financial statements are drawn up from the general ledger.

The Double-Entry System

Bookkeeping in the United States employs the double-entry system. This means that two journal entries are made for each transaction. One entry records the transaction itself and the other records the description of the transaction. These two entries offset one another so that the net effect on the books is zero. In other words, the books must balance.

The double-entry system requires two entries: one debit and one credit. A debit is simply an entry on the left-hand side of an account. A credit is an entry on the right-hand side of an account.

The following example shows a $1,200 sale recorded by a double entry into two T-accounts:

Accounts Receivable	Sales
$1,200	$1,200

A sale on credit creates a receivable, which the company will collect later. So we debit accounts receivable and we credit sales. That is, we make a left-hand entry in the accounts receivable account and a right-hand entry in the sales account.

Why?

Because a debit always represents one of the following:

- An increase in an asset account

- A decrease in a liability or equity account

- A decrease in a revenue account

- An increase in an expense account

And because a credit always represents one of the following:

- A decrease in an asset account

- An increase in a liability or owners' equity account

- An increase in a revenue account

- A decrease in an expense account

See Chapter 11 for a description of assets and liabilities.

MBA Lingo

T-accounts represent two sides of an account in a ledger. A ledger may be ruled like a T-account or the bookkeeper can create T-accounts by using a ruler and a pen to add heavier lines to the ledger paper. Another way to indicate a debit or credit is to write next to the entry the abbreviation "Dr." for a debit entry and "Cr." for a credit entry. (I don't know why it's Dr. instead of Db.)

MBA Alert

Some people find the terms *debit* and *credit* confusing at first. Most of us think of credit as something good, as in giving someone credit for something. So it may seem odd that a credit to an asset (like cash) is a decrease, while a debit is an increase. It's best just to think of a debit as a left-side entry and a credit as a right-side entry to a T-account. It might also be useful to remember that when you pay the phone company, they "credit *your* account" (which decreases *their* account receivable).

When the company collects the receivable, that is, when the customer pays his invoice, the following entries will be made:

Cash	Accounts Receivable
$1,200	$1,200

Why these two entries?

We debit cash because when a customer pays an invoice, the asset called cash increases—and a debit represents an increase in an asset. Meanwhile another asset, called accounts receivable, decreases. We record that decrease with a credit to accounts receivable because a credit represents a decrease in an asset.

Remember: In the double-entry system, the accounts must balance. At any time, the sum of the debits must equal the sum of the credits. The debits and credits in a single account do not have to balance, and usually they won't. But the total of all the debits to the various accounts must equal the total of all the credits to the various accounts.

MBA Lingo

You calculate a **trial balance** by first totaling the debits and credits in each account. Usually there will be a debit or credit balance in each account. Then you total the debit balances and the credit balances to ensure that they are equal. If they are, the books balance.

Why?

Because every transaction generates both a debit and a credit of equal amounts. If every transaction generates two entries of equal amounts, then all the transactions must generate total debits equal to total credits. The double entries thus verify the accuracy of the bookkeeping system. In fact, the accountant can calculate a *trial balance* at any time to assure that the debits equal the credits.

What About the Financial Statements?

At the end of the accounting period, after all transactions have been recorded, the totals of the various accounts are posted to the general ledger and then to the balance sheet and the income statement. Thus what you see in the accounts on the financial statements are the account totals, or net balances, after all the entries have been posted and summed.

The Accountant's Opinion

Financial statements for publicly held companies require an opinion written by an independent auditor. The auditor is a *certified public accountant* who has *audited* the company's books and financial statements. For publicly held companies, the accountant's opinion verifies that the company's financial position is accurately represented by the financial statements. If this is not the case, the accountant issues a qualified opinion citing the information that might be inaccurate or incomplete.

MBA Lingo

A **certified public accountant,** or CPA, is licensed by the state in which he or she practices. While requirements vary from state to state, a CPA has acquired a certain level of education, passed certain exams, and accumulated a certain amount of experience. An **audit** is an objective, formal review of the accounting practices and financial records of a company.

If the accountant's opinion is unqualified (that is, the financial statements are approved "without qualification"), then the auditors "found the company's practices and records to be in accord with generally accepted accounting principles (GAAP) and to represent accurately the financial condition of the company," to quote the usual passage.

If the accountant's opinion is "qualified," then the auditors have either discovered a practice or transaction that is not in accord with GAAP or have some other reason to believe the statements do not truly reflect the company's financial condition.

Case in Point

The accounting firm Arthur Andersen was ruined by its failure to audit the books of the energy-trading company Enron properly and to report its financial condition objectively. Investors rely on accounting firms and their auditing procedures to ensure that financial statements are valid. Yet in this case, the auditing process was apparently compromised by Arthur Andersen's relationship with Enron management. This relationship included Andersen's selling consulting services as well as accounting services to Enron (a practice of most major accounting firms). To many observers, Andersen's desire to sell Enron consulting services may have compromised its objectivity as the company's auditor.

Accounting Treatment of Assets

In the chapters on accounting and finance, I've referred to the "accounting treatment" of various items. I've mentioned that accounting treatments can vary and that managers must often decide how to account for certain transactions. And I've pointed out that the accounting treatment can affect the firm's financial statements.

Let's look at two situations in which the accounting treatment of an asset can vary: accounting for inventory and accounting for depreciation.

Accounting for Inventory

In most economies, prices are not completely stable. Inflation occurs in many economies, and deflation—a general decrease in prices—is not unheard of, although it's less common. In addition, even in times of general price stability, prices of specific items can rise and fall.

Because prices change, the way a retailer accounts for the goods it buys and then sells (or the way a manufacturer accounts for the materials it buys) can affect its cost of goods sold and, therefore, its reported income.

Here's what I mean: Suppose a small fuel-oil supplier bought 1,000 gallons of fuel oil in June for $1.00 a gallon, 1,000 gallons in July for $2.00 a gallon, and 1,000 in August for $3.00 a gallon. Suppose in September he sold 1,000 gallons for $4.00 a gallon. (These prices are artificially high and fast moving, just for the example.)

Which 1,000 gallons did he sell in September?

Actually, we don't know. Fuel oil is fuel oil. But here's what happens to his gross income under three different scenarios:

If He Sold:	"June Oil"	"July Oil"	"August Oil"
Revenue	$4,000	$4,000	$4,000
Cost of Goods Sold	$1,000	$2,000	$3,000
Gross Income	$3,000	$2,000	$1,000

See how income can change depending on how the inventory is valued?

The way most businesses track inventory is to count the items (in units, not dollars) at the beginning of the period, count the items purchased for inventory during the period, and then count the inventory at the end of the period. The total at the beginning of the period, plus the purchases during the period, minus the inventory at the end of the period, equals the amount of units sold.

The formula for cost of goods sold is:

Cost of Goods Sold = Beginning Inventory + Purchases – Ending Inventory

Here's how it would work in the fuel-oil example:

Inventory (in gallons)

Beginning Inventory	0
Purchases	1,000
	1,000
	1,000
Total	3,000
Ending Inventory	2,000
Amount Sold	1,000

This is fine, but cost of goods sold must be a dollar figure. When we go to put a dollar value on these 1,000 gallons, the question becomes: Which 1,000 gallons were sold? The answer depends on how we account for inventories.

FIFO and LIFO

The two main methods of inventory valuation are *first in, first out* (FIFO, say *fife-oh*) and *last in, first out* (LIFO, say *life-oh*). Under FIFO, the company assumes that the first inventory it purchased is the first it sells. Under LIFO, the company assumes that the last inventory it purchased is the first it sells.

Regardless of the accounting method used, here are the actual purchases, in dollars, during the period:

Beginning Inventory	0
Purchases 1,000 @ $1.00/gal.	= $1,000
1,000 @ $2.00/gal.	= $2,000
1,000 @ $3.00/gal.	= $3,000
Total 3,000 gallons	= $6,000
Ending Inventory 2,000 gallons	= $????
Amount Sold 1,000 gallons	= $????

Let's look at how we would calculate the amount sold using both FIFO and LIFO.

FIFO Effects

Again, FIFO assumes that inventory is sold in the order in which the company bought it. Sticking with our fuel-oil example, under FIFO the 1,000 gallons sold during September are assumed to be the first 1,000 gallons purchased back in June. This means:

Cost of Goods Sold = Beginning Inventory + Purchases – Ending Inventory

Cost of Goods Sold = 0 + $6,000 – $5,000 (the inventory purchased in July and August)

Cost of Goods Sold = $1,000

Recall that:

Revenue – Cost of Goods Sold = Gross Income

So:

$4,000 – $1,000 = $3,000

FIFO yields a gross income of $3,000.

LIFO Effects

LIFO assumes that the company sells the most recently purchased inventory first. So under LIFO, the fuel-oil company would assume that the last 1,000 gallons of fuel oil, purchased in August, were sold in September. That means:

Cost of Goods Sold = Beginning Inventory + Purchases – Ending Inventory

Cost of Goods Sold = 0 + $6,000 – $3,000 (the inventory purchased in June and July)

Cost of Goods Sold = $3,000

Because:

Revenue – Cost of Goods Sold = Gross Income

$4,000 – $3,000 = $1,000

LIFO yields gross income of $1,000.

Which Method Should You Use?

Think about it: Under FIFO, income equals $3,000. Under LIFO, income equals $1,000. That's a significant swing in income, yet either method is acceptable.

Which one should you use?

Unfortunately, the answer is: "It depends." Here are some points to consider when you are trying to decide:

- If your firm buys and sells inventory, you *must* choose a method of accounting for inventory. Either FIFO or LIFO are permitted for income tax purposes, but once you choose a method you must stick with it or ask the IRS for permission to change.

- Each method has a different effect on income. When prices are rising, FIFO produces a higher ending inventory, and therefore a lower cost of goods sold and higher income. When prices are rising, LIFO yields a lower ending inventory, and therefore a higher cost of goods sold and lower income.

- Each method has pros and cons. Users of FIFO believe that it better represents the way a business actually moves inventory. They see FIFO as valuing inventories at closer to their replacement cost in times of inflation. (The stuff in inventory was purchased most recently, so it's closer to current market prices.)

- Fans of LIFO believe their method better matches current costs (as in cost of goods sold) to current prices. If costs are rising, they believe that the higher value (more recently purchased) inventory should be shown as the inventory that was sold.

MBA Lingo

First in, first out (FIFO) and last in, first out (LIFO) are two different methods of accounting for inventories. Under the FIFO method, the inventory that the company purchased first is assumed to be sold first. Under LIFO, the most recently purchased inventory is assumed to be sold first.

However, the choice of which method to use mainly depends on the effects on income. In times of rising prices, which is most of the time, FIFO will yield a higher income figure—and therefore a larger tax bite—than LIFO. Meanwhile, LIFO will yield a lower income figure—and therefore a smaller tax bite. Since businesspeople in general and accountants in particular hate taxes, LIFO is often the choice.

However, most managers want to show high income to current owners and to prospective investors and lenders. Therefore, FIFO is also often the choice. If raising money is a priority, FIFO may make more sense than LIFO, because you want to show investors and lenders that you can generate high income.

Accounting for Depreciation

The cost of a fixed asset—a piece of equipment or machinery or a computer or a vehicle—is allocated over the productive life of the asset. Actually, businesses would prefer to *expense* the cost of these items in the period they were purchased because that would reduce reported income and thus income taxes by that much more.

From the accounting standpoint there is an excellent reason to depreciate an asset over the years of its life rather than to expense it in the year it is purchased. If the asset is depreciated, its cost is recognized and written off over the period during which it is producing revenue. The accounting principle here is that of matching costs and revenues. If an asset is going to have a productive life of five years and produce product and sales over that period, it only makes logical and financial sense to recognize some of the value of that asset during its productive life.

> **MBA Lingo**
>
> To **expense** an item means to recognize the full cost in the accounting period in which the money was spent.

> **MBA Lingo**
>
> **Salvage value,** or residual value, is the value of the asset after its productive life. Most fixed assets have some salvage value, although it may be minimal.

The matchup between the amount of cost and revenue in any particular year, however, does not have to be perfect. That's just as well because it would literally be impossible to account for depreciation this way. There are just too many assets purchased at different times to allow for that. But there are several methods of accounting for depreciation that do work well, and do what they are supposed to do, which is allocate the cost of the asset over the life of the asset.

Let's examine the three most common depreciation methods:

♦ Straight-line

♦ Double declining balance

♦ Sum of the years' digits

Don't let these names throw you. The calculations involved are at the grade-school level.

In examining these three methods, we will assume that the company is buying a piece of equipment for $10,000 with a productive life of four years and no *salvage value*. We assume no salvage value purely for convenience.

When salvage value exists, just subtract that amount from the asset's full cost to get the depreciable cost (the amount to be depreciated).

Straight-Line Depreciation

In the straight-line method of depreciation, you simply divide the cost of the asset (or the depreciable cost, which is the same thing in our example) by the asset's years of life.

Thus you calculate straight-line depreciation on the machine in our example as shown in the following table.

Year	Depreciation Expense	Accumulated Depreciation
1	$2,500	$2,500
2	2,500	5,000
3	2,500	7,500
4	2,500	10,000

Straight-line depreciation is *not* a method of *accelerated depreciation*. It does not generate higher depreciation in the early years of ownership and does not lower income in those years. Therefore, many companies choose one of the two following methods of accelerated depreciation. Both are permitted by the IRS for tax calculations.

Double Declining Balance

The double declining balance method allows you to calculate depreciation by multiplying the *book value* (undepreciated value) of the asset by twice the straight-line rate. In our example, the straight-line rate is 25 percent per year, so the double declining balance rate would be 50 percent a year. This 50 percent is applied to the asset's book value in each year of its life.

The following table shows how to calculate depreciation on the machine in our example using the double declining balance method.

MBA Lingo

For a fixed asset, **book value** means the undepreciated value of the asset. Recall that an asset is carried on the books at its original cost, less accumulated depreciation. The original cost minus accumulated depreciation equals book value.

Year	Remaining Value	Depreciation Expense	Accumulated Depreciation
1	$10,000	$5,000	$5,000
2	5,000	2,500	7,500
3	2,500	1,250	8,750
4	1,250	625	9,375

They don't call it accelerated depreciation for nothing. With this method, 75 percent of the value of the asset in our example is charged to depreciation in the first two years of its life.

MBA Lingo

Accelerated depreciation allows a company to allocate more of the cost of the asset to the early years of ownership. The more costs a company can charge against current revenue, the lower the income, and therefore the lower the taxes.

Two points about the double declining method: First, you don't consider salvage value, even if it exists. At twice the straight-line rate, the asset is depreciated to a negligible value by the end of its life. Second, the IRS allows you to switch over to straight-line depreciation one time in the life of the asset. In our example, the logical point to do so would be year three.

If you do switch to the straight-line method, you must then consider salvage value. So if the salvage value were $250 and the company switched over in year three, the calculation would look like this:

To figure book value at start of year three:

$10,000	original cost
– 7,500	accumulated depreciation
– 250	salvage value
$ 2,250	book value

Then, dividing book value by two (for the two years left in the asset's life) yields straight-line depreciation of $1,125 in year three and year four. The company gets a bit less depreciation in year three than it would if it continued using double declining balance, but a lot more in year four.

Sum of the Years' Digits

The sum of the years' digits method, also called the sum of the digits, calculates depreciation on what may at first seem an odd basis. (At least it seemed odd to me at first.)

In this method, you first add up the numbers of years in the life of the asset. Then you use that number as the denominator (the bottom one) in fractions you apply to the depreciable cost of the asset.

Confused?

I don't blame you. But here's how it works.

For example, for an asset with a six-year life, you add up the numbers 1 + 2 + 3 + 4 + 5 + 6 = 21. That 21 is your denominator. The numerator goes in the reverse order of the years, meaning that the first year's depreciation is 6/21 of the asset's value, the second year's depreciation is 5/21, the third year's is 4/21, and so on. These fractions are applied to the asset's original cost (*not* to book value).

See?

Let's use this method in our example, which you'll recall is a $10,000 asset with a four-year life and no salvage value. The sum of the years' digits is 1 + 2 + 3 + 4 = 10.

Year	Value × Fraction = Depreciation Expense			Accumulated Depreciation
1	$10,000	4/10	$4,000	$4,000
2	10,000	3/10	3,000	7,000
3	10,000	2/10	2,000	9,000
4	10,000	1/10	1,000	10,000

The sum of the years' digits method will depreciate the full value of the asset by the end of the process (unlike double declining balance). Also unlike double declining balance, it first deducts salvage value if there is any.

Comparing the Three Methods of Depreciation

The method you choose will depend on your goals. As with inventory valuation, you have to consider the effects on income and taxes.

Let's compare depreciation expense from our example under the three methods. (In the double declining balance method, we are *not* switching to straight-line depreciation.)

Annual Depreciation Expense Under the Three Methods

Year	Straight-Line	Double Declining	Sum of the Balance Years' Digits
1	$2,500	$5,000	$4,000
2	2,500	2,500	3,000
3	2,500	1,250	2,000
4	2,500	625	1,000

Here the double declining balance method depreciates half of the cost of the asset in the first year, and 75 percent in the first two years. For assets with longer life, the percentage charged to depreciation in these years would be lower—but would still be twice the straight-line rate.

The sum of the years' digits is not quite as accelerated a method, but in our example it still charges off 70 percent of the value in the first two years. This is comparable to the double declining balance rate.

Thus, under the double declining balance method, first-year income would be $2,500 lower than under the straight-line method. Under the sum of the years' digits method, income would be $1,500 lower than under the straight-line method.

You might be asking, "What about the later years? What about the years when things 'flip over' and the straight-line method yields the lower reported income?"

Those are valid questions, but for now, just take the "least and latest rule" of taxes on faith: You want to pay the least amount of taxes you can and pay them as late as you can.

Matching Depreciation to Productive Life

Aside from the income and tax effects, there's the issue of matching depreciation to the life of the asset. Fans of accelerated depreciation point out that an asset is more productive in its early years. In those years, machinery incurs less downtime and requires less maintenance, so there's an economic argument for accelerated depreciation.

Fans of straight-line depreciation believe the asset is productive throughout its life, so you may as well allocate its cost equally over that time. Also, perhaps they prefer to show higher income in the early years, just like users of FIFO inventory accounting. Again, investors and lenders like to see high income.

As with inventory valuation, the choice of depreciation method is up to you, considering your tax and income situation.

Clearly, a lot goes into financial statements, and the better you understand accounting systems and practices, the better you'll understand financial statements.

If you're in a position to make these decisions, you will certainly need to understand the effects of these choices. In fact, no matter what your position, your efforts to look behind financial statements will always be repaid. Understanding the financials is the only way to know what's really going on in a company.

Number Games

As this edition is being prepared, accountants, managers, and regulatory bodies are dealing with the aftermath of improper accounting procedures at Enron, WorldCom, Global Crossing, and other companies. This aftermath includes an erosion of investors' trust in financial statements and a stock market that's stalled at least partly as a result.

The goal of financial statements is accurate reporting of the company's financial condition and performance. This is often referred to as "transparency"—nothing should be hidden from investors or lenders who are, after all, committing their funds and the funds of others to these companies. Transparency goes hand in hand with the rule of disclosure, which states that a public company must divulge all information—positive and negative—that could affect an investor's decision to buy, sell, or hold the company's stock.

Chapter 27 examines the ethical issues involved in business. However, even aside from the ethical issues, attempting to improve a company's performance by falsifying its financial statements is like trying to cure cancer by touching up the

MBA Lingo

Off-balance-sheet financing includes certain loans, leases, partnerships, and other means by which a company can raise funds without creating a liability that must be reported on the balance sheet. These methods are usually legal and often must be reported in the footnotes to the financial statements. However, while off-balance-sheet financing has its uses, it can easily be subject to abuse, as was the case with Enron's myriad off-balance-sheet partnerships.

patient's X-rays. Even certain legal practices, such as some forms of *off-balance-sheet financing*, can harm a company because managers often act as if the lack of reporting means the situation (that is, the debt) doesn't exist when, in fact, it does.

As noted in Chapter 4, every relationship rests on trust. Trust cannot exist in an atmosphere of accounting games. Therefore any manager who employs them essentially dooms his company and himself to failure in the long run, no matter how well the games seem to work in the short run.

The Least You Need to Know

♦ Because you can use various accounting treatments for certain transactions, you must often decide which one will provide greater benefit to your company. The flip side of this is that if you are looking at a company from the outside, you must be aware of which accounting treatments were used—and of their effects.

♦ A transaction generates a debit and a credit. A debit is an entry to the left side of an account and a credit is an entry to the right side.

♦ A debit represents an increase in an asset account, a decrease in a liability or equity account, a decrease in a revenue account, or an increase in an expense account. A credit represents a decrease in an asset account, an increase in a liability or equity account, an increase in a revenue account, or a decrease in an expense account.

♦ Of the two main methods of accounting for inventories—first in, first out (FIFO) and last in, first out (LIFO)—LIFO will, in times of rising prices, yield lower net income and thus a smaller tax bite than FIFO.

♦ Methods of accelerated depreciation, such as double declining balance and sum of the years' digits, allocate more of the asset's cost to the early years of its life than straight-line depreciation. Therefore, accelerated depreciation yields lower income in those early years of life.

15

Making Investment Decisions

In This Chapter

- ◆ The time value of money
- ◆ Understanding major investment decisions
- ◆ Three ways to analyze a business investment
- ◆ Deciding whether to lease or buy an asset

Major investment decisions are among the most important—and difficult—decisions you will face as a manager. They involve large sums of money and affect the company's long-term future. These decisions also affect people's jobs.

They can even affect *your* job. Company shareholders and boards of directors take an extremely dim view of poor investment decisions.

Decisions with so much at stake require careful analysis. This chapter shows you how to analyze major business investment decisions. But first you need to know some basic concepts.

Time Is Money

The key concept in investment analysis is the time value of money. The time value of money refers to the fact that a dollar you receive today is worth more than a dollar you receive a year from now. It's also worth more than a dollar you receive two years from now. It's worth more than a dollar you receive at any time in the future.

Why is that? After all, it's still one dollar, right?

> **MBA Lingo**
>
> **Present value** is the current value of an amount to be paid in the future. The **discount rate** is the interest rate an analyst uses to calculate the present value of future cash payments. This rate is chosen by the analyst making the evaluation.

The dollar you receive today is worth more because you can invest it at some interest rate for one year or two years (or for however long you want to invest it). You can't invest the dollar you'll receive next year today.

Let's look at this another way. Suppose you do not have a dollar right now; instead, you have an absolute guarantee that you will receive a dollar in one year, or two years, or five years. What exactly is that dollar worth today? In other words, what is the *present value* of that dollar?

Financial professionals have the answer: The present value of that dollar is an amount that, when multiplied by the proper interest rate, becomes a dollar in the time allowed.

Here's what I mean: At a 10 percent interest rate, that dollar you have coming to you in one year is worth 90.9¢ today. Why? Because 90.9¢ multiplied by 1.10 (for the 10 percent interest) equals $1.00.

At 15 percent interest, that dollar you have coming to you in one year is worth 87¢ today. That's because 87¢ times 1.20 is $1.00. At 5 percent interest, that dollar is worth 95.2¢ today, and at 1 percent it's worth 99.9¢.

These interest rates that I'm using are called *discount rates*. We call them discount rates because we are using them to discount the value of the future payment to its present value.

Believe it or not, this is the essence of investment analysis: You discount future payments (that is, future cash flows) produced by the investment to their present value. Then you compare these cash flows to the amount you have to invest to produce those cash flows. Then you ask yourself, "Is this worth it?"

A Present Value Table

The following table shows the present value of $1.00 for the years and discount rates indicated. For example, the present value of $1.00 discounted at 10 percent for five years is 62.1 cents.

The following table is hardly exhaustive. Complete tables give more interest rates (for example, from 1 percent to 40 percent), and cover every period from 1 to 50 years or more. The interest rates and periods in this table will be enough for our purposes. You can find extensive present value tables in finance textbooks. In fact, you can find books with nothing but present value tables. (Talk about bedtime reading!)

Present Value of $1.00

Years	5%	6%	7%	8%	9%	10%	11%	12%	15%
					Interest Rate				
1	.952	.943	.936	.926	.917	.909	.901	.893	.870
2	.907	.890	.873	.857	.842	.826	.812	.797	.756
3	.864	.840	.816	.794	.772	.751	.731	.712	.658
4	.823	.792	.763	.735	.708	.683	.659	.636	.572
5	.784	.747	.713	.681	.650	.621	.593	.567	.497
6	.746	.705	.666	.630	.596	.564	.535	.507	.432
7	.711	.665	.623	.583	.547	.513	.482	.452	.376
8	.677	.627	.582	.540	.502	.467	.434	.404	.327
9	.645	.592	.544	.500	.460	.424	.390	.361	.284
10	.614	.558	.508	.463	.422	.386	.352	.323	.247
12	.557	.497	.444	.397	.355	.319	.286	.257	.187
15	.481	.417	.362	.315	.271	.239	.209	.183	.123
20	.377	.312	.258	.214	.178	.148	.124	.104	.061

You will see how to use this table a bit later in this chapter. For now, just know that it's best to evaluate major investments with a method that considers the time value of money. Before we look at these methods, let's look at the kinds of investments we're talking about.

Major Business Investment Decisions

The investment decisions we need to evaluate concern *capital expenditures*. These are investments in new plant and equipment, improvements to existing capacity, or perhaps the acquisition of another company.

MBA Lingo _____

A **capital expenditure** cannot be charged as an expense in the current accounting period. It must be recognized over time because the asset associated with the expense will last longer than one year. (This resembles depreciation.) Instead, a capital expenditure must be capitalized, which means placed on the balance sheet as an asset with its cost to be allocated to subsequent accounting periods.

Investment in Plant and Equipment

An investment in new plant and equipment is the classic investment decision for a manufacturer. Adding capacity is a serious move because it's expensive and affects future costs. The company must spend its cash, borrow money, or issue stock to raise cash. So management better be sure that the added sales and profits will make the investment worthwhile.

Every investment takes money, but building new capacity (like a new factory) is a long-term decision. You can't unload it like a bad stock. It's hard to say after a year or two, "Gee, this wasn't a good idea. Let's sell this factory we just built." You probably won't get the true value of the assets, and there will be costs associated with disposing of them.

Major improvements to existing plant and equipment require similar care and analysis. Many companies expand their current operations or lease additional space in response to rising sales. And many of these find that when sales decrease or level off (typically with the arrival of the next recession), they are saddled with expensive, upgraded equipment or office space that they cannot easily unload.

Expand carefully and get all you can out of assets already on the books. Study your asset turnover and return on assets (see Chapter 13 for more on ratios) before adding new capacity. Seriously consider your growth prospects when analyzing any investment in plant and equipment.

Acquisition of a Company

The acquisition of another company is even more complex. The acquiring company must have a plan for either integrating the acquired company into its operations or leaving it as a separate outfit. Both of these choices have their own complexities (which we won't go into here).

Case in Point

Many acquisitions paid for with stock occurred in the late 1990s. Critics argue that companies with overvalued stock (stock that had risen to an unrealistic price based mainly on investor enthusiasm) were able to make acquisitions that would have been unjustified and impossible if they had had to pay for them in cash rather than in overvalued stock.

For example, AOL (America Online) used its stock to acquire media giant Time Warner in January 2000. Just prior to the acquisition, the total value of AOL's stock was $164 billion while that of Time Warner's was $97 billion, even though Time Warner had five times the revenue of AOL. In fact, from March 1992 (when AOL first issued stock) to January 2000, AOL's stock rose 59,000 percent (that's right, 59,000) while Time Warner's rose a mere 400 percent. To the astonishment of many observers, this enabled the young, web-based, "new media" AOL to use its stock to acquire the "old media" Time Warner, publisher of magazines and books, operator of cable TV systems, and producer of movies and television programs.

Just after the acquisition, AOL Time Warner's stock price stood at $75. By August 2002, the stock had nose-dived to about $10 a share—a staggering 85 percent loss of the merged entity's value. This reflected the overall downturn in the market, but also the gross overvaluation of AOL relative to Time Warner. The lesson? Just because a deal can be done doesn't mean it should be done.

A company can pay for an acquisition with cash, stock, or a mix of cash and stock. Accounting for acquisitions is a field unto itself. Nonetheless, the decision to acquire a company—and, for that matter, the price that should be paid for that company— should be based on the present value of the future cash flows.

A merger, in which two companies combine their operations, requires analysis on the part of each party to the deal similar to that for an acquisition.

GIGO, Once Again

You've probably heard the expression GIGO (pronounced *gee-goo*). (No, it's not another method of accounting for inventory.) GIGO is a saying from computer professionals. It means Garbage In, Garbage Out. (Hmmm ... maybe it could refer to inventory!)

Here's the point: If you put bad data into a computer, you'll get bad information out. Similarly, when you analyze an investment, the accuracy of your result depends on the reliability of the numbers you use. You need solid estimates of future cash flows, and the best possible fix on the discount rate to use in the analysis. We'll examine ways of choosing the discount rate after we look at the investment analysis methods.

Three Ways to Analyze Investments

We will examine three methods of analyzing business investments:

1. Net present value

2. Internal rate of return

3. Payback period

The first two, net present value and internal rate of return, consider the time value of money. The payback period does not.

Net Present Value

In the net present value (NPV) method, you calculate the net present value of all future cash outflows (the money you'll invest) and cash inflows (the money the investment will produce). *Net* here means you subtract the outflows from the inflows. If this net amount is positive—if the discounted cash inflows exceed the outflows—then the net present value is positive and the investment may be worth undertaking.

The discount rate you use is your *required rate of return*, that is, the return you need to achieve on the investment.

MBA Lingo

The **required rate of return** on an investment is the rate that the company or person doing the analysis and making the investment has defined as the rate that they must achieve for the investment to be worth making.

MBA Lingo

The investment **horizon** refers to the length of time of the investment. The horizon is either the natural life of the investment (for example, a bond that matures on a certain date) or the time you want to take your money out of the investment.

Calculating NPV

Suppose you are a regional manufacturer based in Phoenix. You see an opportunity to expand into the Southeast by building a production and distribution facility near Atlanta. Building the facility requires a $22 million investment..

You have a seven-year *horizon* for the investment because after seven years you may, for personal reasons, sell the entire business. But you're not sure. So one way or another, you want this deal to work as seven-year investment.

Over the next seven years you estimate the income from the new facility to be:

Year 1	$2 million
Year 2	5 million
Year 3	7 million
Year 4	8 million
Year 5	10 million
Total	$32 million

You thus have a total of $32 million in future cash inflows associated with this investment.

Let's say you need at least a 10 percent return on investment for this deal to work. That 10 percent is the discount rate you'll use to calculate the net present value of the investment.

You do not discount the initial $22 million investment because it's an outflow now, not in the future. It's the amount of the investment. However, if you had to invest more money over the investment horizon, for example, another $5 million in Year 3, you would discount that amount at the 10 percent rate using the value in the earlier table for 10 percent at three years (that is, .751).

To discount the future cash inflows, you do the following calculations (the amounts in column three—"Present Value of $1"—are from the present value table presented earlier in the chapter):

Year	Cash Inflows	Present Value of $1	Present Value of Cash Inflow
1	$2,000,000	× 0.909	$1,818,000
2	5,000,000	× 0.826	4,130,000
3	7,000,000	× 0.751	5,257,000
4	8,000,000	× 0.683	5,464,000
5	10,000,000	× 0.621	6,210,000
			$22,879,000

Again, that $22,879,000 is just the present value of the future cash inflows. To calculate the *net* present value of the investment, you subtract the initial investment (the outflows) from the discounted inflows:

Present value of inflows	$22,879,000
Minus initial investment	$22,000,000
Net present value of investment	$879,000

This $879,000 is the net present value of the investment. It is the current value of the money the investment will make.

Seeing the Time Value of Money

To see the impact of discounting—and the importance of the time value of money—consider how this investment would look if you did not discount the cash inflows and outflows:

Undiscounted cash inflows	$32,000,000
Initial investment	$22,000,000
Net undiscounted return	$10,000,000

Because the time value of money is real, not theoretical, it would be quite wrong to think this investment is worth $10 million today. There's a big difference between $10 million and $879,000. That's why it's best to think in terms of rates and not just dollars when considering investments.

You'll make over a 10 percent return on the investment. Since 10 percent is your discount rate and the net present value of the investment is positive at that discount rate, you would say yes to this investment.

If you were analyzing more than one investment opportunity with the NPV method, you would choose the one (or the ones) with the highest net present value. (For the purposes of this analysis, we are ignoring other, nonfinancial factors that would affect the decision, such as the strategic fit with the business and the ease or complexity of managing the opportunity.)

Internal Rate of Return

The internal rate of return, or IRR, also considers the time value of money. However, the approach and calculations differ slightly from those in the NPV method.

The internal rate of return on an investment is the discount rate that brings the present value of the future net cash flows to zero. In other words, you must find the discount rate that will make the future cash inflows equal to the up-front cash outflow.

In this method, you don't know the discount rate. You must find it by trial and error.

The discount rate that makes the future net cash flows equal zero is the internal rate of return on the investment. When you find that rate, you compare it to your *hurdle* (target) *rate*. If the internal rate of return exceeds your hurdle rate, you say yes to the investment.

By the way, it's called the *internal* rate of return because it's the rate of return that the investment itself produces. The investment has only three components—the cash outflow, the cash inflows, and the number of years. Those three items are all you need to calculate the investment's internal rate of return.

MBA Lingo

The **hurdle rate** is the return—expressed as a percentage or interest rate—that you require on an investment. To be acceptable, the investment must clear this target rate, or hurdle.

Figuring the Internal Rate of Return

Let's stick with the example of the manufacturer expanding into the Southeast and assume that our hurdle rate is still 10 percent.

To calculate the internal rate of return, let's start by discounting the cash flows at 12 percent (again, the values in the present value column come from the present value table earlier in the chapter):

Year	Cash Inflows	Present Value of $1 of Cash Inflow	Present Value
1	$2,000,000	× 0.893	$1,786,000
2	5,000,000	× 0.797	3,985,000
3	7,000,000	× 0.712	4,984,000
4	8,000,000	× 0.636	5,088,000
5	10,000,000	× 0.567	5,670,000
			$21,513,000

Discounted cash inflows	$21,513,000
Minus initial investment	22,000,000
Net amount	($487,000)

(Remember: In finance and accounting, a number in parentheses is usually negative.)

This tells us that the internal rate of return is *below* 12 percent, because 12 percent discounts the net cash flows to less than zero. So the internal rate of return is a bit lower than 12 percent. Let's try 11 percent.

Year	Cash Inflows	Present Value of $1	Present Value of Cash Inflow
1	$2,000,000	× 0.901	$1,802,000
2	5,000,000	× 0.812	4,060,000
3	7,000,000	× 0.731	5,117,000
4	8,000,000	× 0.659	5,272,000
5	10,000,000	× 0.593	5,930,000
			$22,181,000

Discounted cash inflows	$22,181,000
Minus initial investment	22,000,000
Net amount	$181,000

Because 11 percent yields a positive net amount and 12 percent yields a negative net amount, the internal rate of return on the investment is between 11 and 12 percent. In this case, it looks like it's a bit above 11 percent, meaning closer to 11 percent than to 12 percent.

We don't need to calculate the internal rate of return out to one or two decimal places—especially because our hurdle rate is 10 percent. In that case, an investment with an IRR a little over 11 percent would be acceptable.

As with NPV, if you are evaluating several competing investments, you would choose the one (or ones) with the highest internal rate of return. (Again, we are ignoring other, nonfinancial factors that might affect the investment decision.)

Payback Period

The payback period does not consider the time value of money. This makes it a lot easier to "do the numbers" but produces numbers with a lot less value.

The payback period is simply the amount of time that it will take to earn back the original amount invested. The amounts involved are not discounted.

In the example we've been using, the amount invested is $22 million. The annual returns are shown in the following table.

Year	Cash Flow	Cumulative Return
1	$2 million	$2 million
2	5 million	7 million
3	7 million	14 million
4	8 million	*22 million*
5	10 million	32 million
	$32 million	

The payback period is exactly four years. After four years, the original $22 million investment will be recouped. If the payback period fell between any two years, you could divide the return in the final year of the payback period by 12 months and *prorate* the return to come up with a period expressed in years and months.

Aside from ignoring the time value of money, the payback period has another serious drawback: It does not consider returns after the payback period. For instance, let's say you're comparing two five-year investments: one with the returns in our example, and one with the same returns in the first four years, but with $15 million instead of $10 million in the fifth year. The payback period doesn't take that fifth year into account.

So what good is the payback period?

The payback period is most useful for short-term investments, meaning those of a year or less, where you can measure the payback period in months. Also, you might calculate the payback period for longer-term investments as extra information to use along with net present value or internal rate of return, or both.

MBA Lingo

You **prorate** an amount any time you apportion it in some mathematical manner. Depending on the situation, you may prorate an amount by the months in the year, by contractual share, or by some other means. For example, in a liability suit, a judge may prorate the damage award according to the plaintiffs' share of the suffering.

Pick a Rate, but Not Just Any Rate

There are two good ways to choose the discount rate you apply to future cash flows in the NPV method or the hurdle rate you use for comparison with the internal rate of return:

1. You can use the opportunity cost.

2. You can use your cost of capital, or more properly, your incremental cost of capital.

Let's examine each of these methods.

Using the Opportunity Cost

In general, the opportunity cost is the return you could earn on the next-best investment. Here, "next-best investment" refers to one you could actually make and earn that return on. "Opportunity cost" means the cost of forgoing the opportunity.

One good way to think of opportunity cost is to use the rate you would get by investing in an interest-paying security, such as a bond. If you can invest in a low-risk bond with 8 percent interest instead of pursuing a business investment with a similar return, why not just buy the bond?

Case in Point

I've seen a number of business investments that didn't work out well. Often, after they didn't work, someone would say, "You know, we could have done better just putting the money into Treasury notes." Those people were referring to the opportunity cost, and it was something they should have considered more carefully beforehand.

Of course, that's easy to say *after* the investment sours. The trick is to consider it before investing. Far too many companies make investments with marginal or risky returns. Sometimes they kid themselves into thinking the returns are higher or more certain. But other times they fail to ask themselves, "What could we get by just investing the money in securities until we find a *great* opportunity?"

If you have a next-best investment and you know its return, you can use that rate in your NPV and IRR calculations.

Using the Cost of Capital

The cost of capital is a good rate to use in investment analysis because it is "the price you pay for money" and you can calculate that from your balance sheet. A company's cost of capital is a weighted average of its cost of debt and its cost of equity. These, as you know, finance long-term (as opposed to current) assets.

Of course, the company must have cash to invest over on the asset side of the balance sheet, or be willing to sell some assets and invest the proceeds in other assets. In other words, the actual cash to be invested is not in the debt and equity accounts but rather in the cash and marketable securities accounts. Or the company must raise the cash from lenders or investors.

CAUTION   ## MBA Alert _____

As with other costs a company faces, the lower the cost of capital the better. If the company's cost of capital is low, then it will not only have a larger range of investments to choose from (because of its lower hurdle rate), it will also make more money on an investment with a given return. In other words, a company with a cost of capital of 12 percent will make more on an investment with a 20 percent return than will a company with a cost of capital of 14 percent. Savvy financial managers, particularly in large companies, are always on the lookout for less expensive capital from sources such as foreign investors and competitive banks.

To calculate the weighted average cost of capital, first multiply the company's cost of debt by the percentage of debt in its long-term financing, then multiply the company's cost of equity by the percentage of equity in its long-term financing. Then add up the results.

The following table shows you what I mean.

ABC Company Liabilities and Owners' Equity

Source of Funds	Cost	Amount on Balance Sheet	Percent of Total Capitalization
Bank Loan	prime +1%	$1,000,000	10
Bond	8%	2,000,000	20
Total Long-Term Debt		**$3,000,000**	**30**
Preferred Stock	5%	$1,000,000	10
Common Stock	???	3,000,000	30
Retained Earnings	???	3,000,000	30
Total Owners' Equity		**$7,000,000**	**70**
Total Capitalization		**$10,000,000**	**100**

ABC Company has 30 percent of its capitalization in long-term debt and 70 percent in equity. More specifically, the company gets 10 percent of its capital from a bank loan at prime plus 1 percent, 20 percent from a bond on which it pays 8 percent interest, 10 percent from preferred stock, and 70 percent from common stock and retained earnings.

What's the Cost of Equity?

You may be wondering why I've shown question marks rather than the cost of common stock and retained earnings in the earlier table. That's because the cost of common equity and retained earnings is often not precisely known.

There is no guaranteed return on common stock. And retained earnings simply represent profits that were reinvested in the company rather than distributed as dividends.

The calculation of the "cost" of common equity is complex and subject to theory. The complexity concerns the rate of return required by equity investors in the market as a whole and in the company in particular. Because the return on common stock has two components—dividends and price appreciation—and both are uncertain, the calculation of the cost of equity is controversial.

So let's just say that for ABC Company, the cost of equity is 12 percent. This doesn't mean the company has to pay 12 percent to stockholders the way it pays interest on the bank loan and the bond. Instead, it means that its investors expect a return of 12 percent on their investment over the long term.

Calculate the Cost of Capital

In any event, assuming the costs presented in the earlier table and a prime rate of 6 percent, the weighted average cost of capital for ABC Company would be calculated as follows:

ABC Company Weighted Average Cost of Capital

Source of Funds	Cost	Percent of Total Capitalization	Weighted Cost
Bank Loan	.07	× .10	= .007
Bond	.08	× .20	= .016
Preferred Stock	.05	× .10	= .005
Common Stock and Returned Earnings	.12	× .60	= .072
Total Weighted Average Cost of Capital		.100	= 10%

The total weighted average cost of capital for ABC Company is 10 percent. This would be a good rate for the company to use as its discount rate or hurdle rate.

Why? Because if the outfit's cost of capital is 10 percent and it can get more than that on an investment, then it will be making money on that investment.

Beyond the Numbers

When analyzing investments, look beyond the numbers. Here are some practical guidelines for doing that:

- Many investments look great on paper but fall apart in reality. Be sure you understand the operating and technical aspects of an investment, not just the financial aspects.

- Think for yourself. Don't let competitive threats or senior management's enthusiasm lead you astray. You should find creative ways to "make the deal work," but apply that creativity only to deals you believe in.

- In my experience, most companies don't develop enough really good investment alternatives. The more good choices you have, the better.

- Seek projects that can be self-funding to at least some degree. The investment itself should throw off money that can be used to fund the project as it proceeds.

- Remember that *not* investing is always an option. If there are no good opportunities, invest in securities or buy back your stock, which can be an excellent move.

The problem with investment analysis is that the amount you must invest is certain, but the returns are not. Take all reasonable precautions. But remember, you must invest in order to get a return.

The Lease-Versus-Buy Decision

You can often finance property, plant, and equipment through a lease rather than a purchase. There are two major types of leases: financial and operating.

A financial lease goes on the balance sheet as an asset, to record the fixed asset being financed, and as a liability, to record the payments due under the lease.

In a financial lease, the lessee (the party getting the equipment) assumes the maintenance, insurance, and taxes. The lessor just provides financing. According to generally accepted accounting principles, these leases must be capitalized (that is, shown on the balance sheet), because they are contractual obligations and usually cannot be canceled.

An operating lease does not go on the balance sheet, but is usually shown in the footnotes to the financial statements. The lessor usually remains responsible for maintenance, so this is often called a service lease. These leases are mostly used for equipment, such as vehicles, computers, and copiers, and usually can be canceled.

I won't go into the calculations for a lease-versus-buy decision. Basically they involve examining the total cash inflows and outflows if you were to buy the asset and if you were to lease it. Then you consider service arrangements, tax implications (due to depreciation), and the likelihood of the equipment becoming obsolete (if it might, an operating lease may be better).

The Least You Need to Know

- The time value of money refers to the fact that a dollar you have now is worth more than a dollar you would receive in the future. That's because you can invest the dollar you have in hand and earn a return on it.

- Two major investment analysis tools—net present value and internal rate of return—consider the time value of money. Thus, they are better than the other major analytical tool, the payback period.

- Use the best discount rate you can for net present value or internal rate of return analyses.

- Always look beyond the numbers, even if your job is to "just do the numbers." A project must fit the company's strategy and be suited to its people if it is to succeed.

Chapter 16

Ups and Downs:
The Financial Markets

In This Chapter

- ◆ Key financial markets
- ◆ Major types of financial securities
- ◆ How the markets work
- ◆ Interpreting market activity

The financial markets have always played a key role in business, and in recent years that role has become even more important. More companies are issuing an ever-increasing range of financial instruments to an ever-broader base of investors. As a result, the financial markets now affect every business on some level. In addition, over the course of your career, you will probably be investing your company's money or your own, if you are not already doing so. Moreover, the financial markets are barometers of business psychology and a daily demonstration of economics in action.

You don't need deep knowledge of the financial markets to understand their impact, or even to invest wisely. But you do need to understand the overall workings of the markets and the characteristics of the major types of securities, and you will gain that understanding in this chapter.

What Are the Financial Markets?

Broadly, the financial markets are organized forums for buying and selling securities and other financial instruments, such as foreign currencies. Securities are documents that evidence ownership in a company (stocks) or debts owed by a company or government entity (bonds). While the financial markets include physical markets in actual buildings, such as the New York Stock Exchange and the Chicago Board of Options Exchange, the financial markets actually comprise millions of buyers and sellers linked by national and global telecommunications networks.

A financial market provides mechanisms for ensuring that transactions occur in an orderly manner and are accurately reported and tracked. An exchange is such a mechanism. For example, the New York Stock Exchange (NYSE) reports the prices of stocks that are listed on that exchange. The NYSE, the oldest stock exchange in the United States, maintains certain listing requirements—including minimum levels of income, shares outstanding, and total value of shares—for companies traded on the "Big Board," as the NYSE is commonly called. To maintain order, the NYSE can halt trading of a particular stock or of all stocks, as it did after terrorist attacks on the World Trade Center and the Pentagon on September 11, 2001.

The Players in the Market

Aside from the exchanges, several other parties play key roles in the financial markets:

- **Institutional investors** include insurance companies, commercial banks, mutual funds, pension funds, and other financial institutions that invest as part of their business. For instance, insurance companies invest a large portion of policyholders' premiums in stocks and bonds (and in real estate). Institutional investors are often collectively referred to as the "buy side."

- **Individual investors** are people who invest their own money in securities to meet their financial goals.

- **Investment banks** enable corporations to issue and sell stocks and bonds to institutional and individual investors (in contrast to commercial banks, which take deposits from and make loans to businesses and individuals). Investment banks often employ traders of stocks and bonds, who facilitate the sale of securities in the *secondary market*.

MBA Lingo

Secondary markets are markets where securities are bought and sold after they are issued. (They are issued in the primary market, where the issuing entity sells them to the public and receives the proceeds.) The proceeds of sales in the secondary market go to the seller, not the issuer, of the security.

◆ **Brokers** act as intermediaries between buyers and sellers of securities. Brokers are also called registered representatives because they must register with the exchange where the securities they handle are traded.

◆ **Dealers** buy and sell securities for their own or their employer's account (rather than facilitate transactions for buyers and sellers). Most brokerage firms employ brokers and dealers, and when the firm sells securities out of its own inventory the buyer must be notified of that fact. Collectively, investment banks and brokerage firms are known as the "sell side" because selling securities is their main line of business.

Other key players include the Securities and Exchange Commission, which I'll cover later in this chapter, and, of course, corporations and other issuers of securities.

Why Companies Sell—and Investors Buy—Stock

AS we discussed in Chapter 11, there are two broad classes of stock: common and preferred. Common stock represents ownership shares in a corporation, and holders of this stock vote on proposed members for the board of directors and receive *dividends* (when the company pays them). Preferred stock pays dividends at a specified rate, and holders of this stock receive their dividends before dividends can be paid to holders of common stock. However, preferred stock usually carries no voting rights. Convertible preferred stock, a hybrid of the two, can be converted to a specified number of common shares.

A company sells shares to the public in order to raise capital. Buyers of stock actually buy a share in the future earnings of the company, to be paid as dividends. (In the language of Chapter 15, they are buying a share of those future cash inflows.) Investors buy and sell a particular stock for various reasons, often based on their financial situation. But mainly, investors buy and sell a stock based on differing estimates of the company's future earnings. Those differing estimates are based upon each investor's view of the company's industry, management, operations, finances, products, and strategy, all of which will determine the magnitude of those future earnings. The higher an investor believes those earnings will be, the more he will be willing to pay for the stock.

Thus, when a company announces a new product that's expected to be wildly popular, investors bid up the price of the stock. They expect the new product to generate higher sales and earnings than they expected before the announcement. (Essentially, the stock price rises thanks to the law of supply and demand. The greater the number of investors who want the stock, the higher the price.)

In practice, the stockholder expects something in addition to a share of future earnings. He expects the price of the stock to appreciate as the company grows and increases its earnings. Higher earnings command a higher stock price. In fact, many investors buy stocks more for expected appreciation than expected dividends, and that generates some of the more fascinating dynamics of the stock market.

The Price/Earnings Ratio

Before we look at those dynamics, let's examine the relationship between a company's earnings and its stock price. The *price/earnings ratio* neatly captures that relationship, and therefore is widely used in equity investing and reported in newspapers' listings of stocks.

The price/earnings ratio, or P/E ratio, is just what it sounds like: the ratio of the company's stock price to its earnings—actually, *earnings per share*. A company's earnings per share is calculated by dividing its total net profit for the most recent 12 months by the number of shares of common stock outstanding. Thus, if the company earned $50 million last year and it has 50 million shares outstanding, it earned $1 per share.

MBA Lingo

The **price/earnings ratio** (P/E ratio) equals the price of one share of stock divided by earnings per share. **Earnings per share,** a widely reported measure of a company's performance, equals total net income divided by the number of shares of common stock outstanding. The P/E ratio is commonly referred to as the stock's **multiple,** meaning the multiple of earnings per share at which the stock is selling.

Now, if a stock with earnings per share of $1 is selling at $10, its P/E ratio (or *multiple*) is 10. If the stock were selling at $20, it would be selling at a multiple of 20.

Why would the stock of Company A with earnings per share of $1 sell for $10 and the stock of Company B with the same earnings per share sell for $20? Because investors believe that the *future* earnings of Company B will be higher than those of Company A. Remember, investors in common stock are buying a share of the future earnings.

From 1965 to 1995, before high-technology and dot-com stocks drove average stock prices to unsustainably high levels, the average multiple for the U.S. stock market as a whole was about 14.

Stocks with extremely high multiples—for instance, 40, 60, 80 times earnings, and higher—are considered growth stocks. Investors purchasing these stocks expect the future earnings—or, more realistically, future earnings and appreciation—to justify those multiples. Investors who won't purchase those stocks don't believe that those multiples (that is, those prices) are justified.

Stocks selling at low multiples—for instance, in the single digits—are viewed by most investors as either slow-growth stocks or "dogs" (stocks in troubled companies). However, some investors search for stocks with low multiples in an effort to find and buy undervalued stocks or those with "slow and steady" performance.

Case in Point

Some investment professionals believe that the P/E ratio has become less relevant than it once was. The P/E ratio's reputation took a beating during the bull market of the 1990s as the stocks of dot-coms with little-to-no earnings reached stratospheric levels. On top of that, the accounting scandals of 2002 cast suspicion on reported earnings, and the P/E is based on earnings. However, the P/E ratio remains relevant for most investment professionals because earnings are still relevant. After all, ignoring the link between earnings and stock prices helped fuel the dot-com bubble. Moreover, if a company's income figures can't be trusted, what would be the point of buying its stock?

Bulls, Bears, Bubbles, and Crashes

An investor is bullish on a stock if he believes the price is going to rise and is buying it. He's bearish if he believes the price will fall and is selling the stock. Investors are said to be bullish on the stock market if they are buying stocks—bidding up prices—and are said to be bearish if they are selling stocks—sending prices lower. Hence, the popularity of the terms *bull market* and *bear market.*

Again, as in all markets, the dynamics of supply and demand determine prices. In the short run, the supply of stock in a company and of stocks in the overall market is fairly fixed. Publicly held companies don't frequently issue new stock (which would increase the supply) or buy back existing stock (which would decrease it—yes, as noted in Chapter 15, companies do buy their own stock).

MBA Lingo

A **bear market** is usually defined as a 20-percent decrease from the previous high in the market averages.

You might also think that demand for stock should be fairly stable. After all, events in a company or the economy that could change the earnings outlook for a stock, let alone for the market as a whole, don't happen every day. Therefore demand should be fairly stable. In reality, however, demand for a stock and for stocks in general can vary wildly, even in the short term, based on market psychology.

Market psychology moves the overall market—which is measured by various market averages that I'll explain later in this chapter—up or down as often as expectations about the earnings of a specific company change.

When market psychology becomes too optimistic, a bull market can turn into a bubble. When "the bulls run loose on Wall Street" they can bid up the prices of stocks too far, too fast. If this goes on long enough or the prices go up high enough, a bubble results. In a bubble, the overall market or a segment of it (for instance, technology stocks) becomes highly overvalued. Prices become too high relative to potential future earnings and the stocks' collective multiple rises to historically high levels.

When prices become too high, demand falls (as it will in any market) and when demand for stocks falls, market psychology—which feeds on itself—becomes pessimistic. If market sentiment becomes pessimistic enough for long enough, "the bears run loose" and a sell-off occurs. Investors sell in order to lock in, or realize, the gains they made on paper when the price of their stocks rose in the bull market. Or they sell to limit their losses. A massive sell-off signals falling demand and prices spiral downward. If prices fall far and fast, it's called a crash.

A bear market ends and recovery from a crash begins when investors see that the prices of stocks are low relative to expected earnings and start buying again.

> ### MBA Mastery
>
> The main U.S. market averages are the Dow Jones Industrial Average, the S&P Composite Index of 500 Stocks, and the NASDAQ-OTC Price Index, each of which have shorter nicknames. "The Dow," a weighted average of 30 large-company stocks, is the most widely reported market average. The S&P 500, based on 500 stocks selected by the financial information company Standard & Poor's, obviously represents a broader measure of the market's performance. The NASDAQ (National Association of Securities Dealers Automatic Quotations system) is a broad average of stocks of smaller companies traded "over the counter." These OTC stocks are not listed on a major exchange, but are nonetheless bought and sold through brokers.

Information and the Market

Information is, and has always been, the lifeblood of the financial markets: information on the companies issuing securities, on current and historical prices and returns, on buying and selling activity, and on economic and market trends. As noted in Chapter 14, the principles of disclosure and transparency underlie financial statements. Those principles also underlie the financial markets because a truly free market can exist only when buyers and sellers have equal access to information. Of course, the conclusions they draw from the information will vary as will the information they actually employ.

Yet efficient financial markets depend on open access to information. In fact, the efficient market theory holds that the market price of a stock reflects all known information about the stock and the collective expectations of all investors. According to the theory, any new development that affects the stock will be immediately assessed by millions of market participants who will, through the market mechanisms of selling and buying, correctly assign a new price to the stock.

The efficient market theory has been debated for decades. Supporters believe that information spreads so quickly and investors respond so rapidly that it's impossible to "beat the market." Detractors believe that inefficiencies in the distribution of information and investors' varying analytical skills and judgment render the theory only theoretical. Although the theory may not perfectly describe reality, the stock price is set by the market, which is the sum total of millions of buy and sell decisions.

Case in Point

Supporters of the efficient market theory hold that investors may as well throw darts at the pages of stock listings from the newspaper as carefully analyze their stock picks. *The Wall Street Journal* put this to a test. *The Journal's* editors asked professional fund managers to pick stocks and then, several months later, compared the returns on their stocks to those on stocks chosen at random. Seldom did the choices of the money managers do significantly better than the randomly chosen ones. So maybe there is something to the efficient market theory.

The most widely used sources of information for equity investors include the business news, investment newsletters, brokerage-house analyst reports, and research services such as Standard & Poor's and Value Line. The company's financial statements are essential sources, and form the basis for much of the other information that firms such as Value Line and Standard & Poor's issue on a company's stock. These statements are required of all public companies by the *Securities and Exchange Commission (SEC)*.

MBA Lingo

The **Securities and Exchange Commission (SEC)** regulates the securities markets and specifies the type and frequency of the information that companies issuing securities must make available to the public.

The SEC is the federal agency charged with protecting investors from fraud, supervising the exchanges, and regulating the process by which companies issue securities. The SEC requires that detailed quarterly and annual financial statements (the 10-Q and 10-K, respectively) be filed with the SEC and made available for public distribution. The SEC's rule of disclosure calls for the release of all information, positive or negative, that would affect an investor's decision.

Types of Investors and Traders

Investing entails a longer-term commitment than trading, which aims for gains on short-term price appreciation. In addition, there are various styles of investing and trading.

Value investors seek companies with strong management teams, earnings histories, and balance sheets. (A strong balance sheet has little to no debt, high levels of equity capital, and valuable, productive assets.) They often use a *buy-and-hold* strategy, which aims for returns from dividends and long-term appreciation. Although some value investors will sell when they believe the stock has reached a peak, others will hold it as it goes down (and even buy more, at the lower price) because they expect a higher peak further in the future.

MBA Lingo

A **buy-and-hold** investment strategy seeks to identify companies with above-average long-term growth prospects and to make money from dividends and long-term price appreciation.

So-called bottom-feeders look for undervalued stocks. These stocks often have some characteristics of value stocks, such as strong balance sheets, but their prices may be depressed by current conditions or lack of investor interest. Bottom-feeders expect to reap gains when conditions change, the companies turn around, or investors rediscover the stock.

Growth-oriented investors seek growth stocks, typically those of companies with new technologies or products, vigorous expansion plans, or both. Growth investors are willing to forgo dividends, which growth companies usually do not pay, for the prospect of high short- to long-term appreciation. They often hold stocks for shorter periods than buy-and-hold investors. Although some growth investors purchase stocks for long-term appreciation, most prefer to sell when the stock reaches a cyclical peak or a target level they had set, and then to invest that money in the stock of another, newer company with prospects for more dramatic growth and price appreciation.

Unlike investors, traders hope for very short-term gains—within hours, in the case of day traders. In general, traders try to profit from very short-term inefficiencies in the market by closely following news and events that could affect the company's business.

They sometimes play their hunches, in effect betting that the stock price will rise when the event occurs.

In short selling, a short-term investor or trader believes that a stock is going to go down. He borrows (rather than purchases), say, 100 shares of the stock from a broker, sells them immediately, and sets that money aside in a bank account or other risk-free vehicle. Then, when the price of the stock has fallen, he buys 100 shares and repays the broker with those shares. The successful short-seller pockets the difference between the price of the stock when he borrowed and sold it, and the price when he purchased it and repaid the broker. However, if the stock goes up, rather than down, the short-seller loses because to repay his broker he must buy the 100 shares on the open market at a higher price.

Short selling is a good introduction to stock options, which also involve judgments about the price of a stock in the near-term future.

Options: Puts and Calls

In general, an option gives a person the right to purchase or sell something in the future. For instance, when a Hollywood producer options a best-selling novel, he or she pays the author an amount of money—for instance, $25,000—for the right to buy the book as the basis of a movie, at a certain price—let's say $500,000—within a certain period of time, usually one to two years.

An option has value because it locks in the price of an item for a certain period of time as well as the right to buy it. The price of the option is usually a small fraction of the price of the item. Also, an option is not an obligation to buy or sell something. The decision to buy or sell remains with the holder of the option (which is why it's called an option rather than a purchase or sale agreement).

Puts and calls are both stock options. A put gives its holder the right to *sell* a specific number of shares of a specific stock at a specific price—known as the exercise price ("or strike price")—by a certain date. A call gives its holder the right to *buy* 100 shares of a stock, at a specific strike price by a certain date. Puts and calls are sold by the person or institution that owns the underlying stock. Companies do not sell options on their own stocks, which in effect would be "betting" on the price movements of its own stock when their focus should be improving the value of the stock.

Calls

Let's start with call options. The buyer of a call option hopes that the price of the stock will rise above the strike price before the option expires. The buyer of the option wants to buy the stock at a (strike) price *below* its market value before the option expires, and then sell the stock at the market price and pocket the difference. For this to be profitable, the difference between the strike price and market price must be greater than the amount paid for the option.

Example: Say you have an option to buy stock in XYZ Inc. at a strike price of $50 and you paid $5 per share for that option. If the price rises to $55 before the option expires you make no money if you exercise the option. That's because if you exercised the option you would buy 100 shares at the strike price of $5,000 and sell them for $5,500—but you paid $500 for the calls, and therefore you would make nothing. (In fact, you would lose money because of transaction costs, which are omitted here to simplify the calculations.) Thus, you would not exercise the option if the price rose to $55 a share or less, nor, of course, would you exercise it if the stock fell (or remained) below the strike price of $50.

However, if the price of the stock were to rise to, say, $60, you would definitely exercise the option. You would buy the 100 shares at the strike price of $50, promptly sell them for $6,000, deduct your costs of $500 for the option and $5,000 for the 100 shares, and pocket a $500 profit.

What's so great about call options? You just made $500 on an investment of $500—a return of 100 percent on your investment!—in 90 days, a matter of a several weeks, or a few months.

Yes, this is a simplified example and, true, options are a sophisticated investment vehicle where money can be lost as easily as it is gained (perhaps more easily). Moreover, most options are not exercised before the expiration date because the stock price is such that the holder allows them to expire (because the price of the stock vis-a-vis the strike price of the options would not allow the holder to make any money by exercising them). However, the fact that calls enable an investor to profit from a rising stock price without actually buying the stock is the underlying logic and motivation for buying them.

Case in Point

The incentive stock options given to managers and employees at start-ups or to senior executives at large, established companies as part of their compensation are essentially calls. The holders have the right to buy shares in the company at a certain price. The intent is to give the holders of the options added motivation to work hard and make the stock price as high as possible.

In practice, however, when a company pays employees in stock options, it is also potentially issuing new stock that will dilute the company's earnings per share and the value of the stock already in the hands of investors. Therefore the options should be accounted for as an expense, but they usually have not been, which up to now has been legal. Because of this and the incentives that stock options gave managers to falsify reported earnings, reforms are underway in the United States to change the way companies use and account for employee stock options.

Puts

Again, a put option confers on its holder the right to sell a stock at the strike price to the seller of the put (known as the "writer"). (In other words, the writer of the put agrees to buy the stock at the strike price from the holder of the put by the strike date.) The buyer of a put is betting that the price of the stock will *fall* before the option expires. He makes his profit by buying the stock on the open market at a price below the strike price, then exercising the option, which forces the writer of the put to buy the stock at the strike price from the holder of the put.

Example: Suppose you hold an option to sell 100 shares of ABC Company to Joe Smith (the writer of the put) at a strike price of $50. Suppose, again, that you paid $5 per share for the option. If the price of the stock falls to, say, $40, you would buy 100 shares on the open market and then exercise the put. That put option compels Joe to buy 100 shares from you at the strike price of $50 a share, for a total price of $5,000. You make $500, which is the $5,000 Joe paid you, minus the $4,000 you paid for the stock on the open market and minus the $500 you paid for the option.

As with call options, the difference between the strike price and the stock price must exceed the price of the put (plus transactions costs) or there is no point in exercising it. If the holder does not exercise the put option then, as with calls, he loses the amount he paid for the option. Finally, like calls, puts offer the *possibility* of high returns.

Meanwhile, the writer of the put is hoping that the stock prices rises, remains the same, or falls by less than the price of the put. If any of those things occur, then the put is not exercised and the writer of the put, Joe Smith in our example, does not have to buy the 100 shares. Smith's profit on the transaction is the $500 paid to him for the put.

Again, both puts and calls enable investors to profit on the movement of a stock's price—upward in the case of calls, downward in the case of puts—without having to buy the stock itself. This limits the potential loss to the amount paid for the options.

Fundamental Analysis vs. Technical Analysis

No discussion of stocks would be complete without touching on the two schools of equity analysis. All analysis aims to develop enough information about a security so that a wise investment decision can be made. Fundamental analysis deals with information about the company that has issued the stock. Technical analysis deals with information about the stock's price, particularly its historical levels and trends.

Fundamental analysis focuses on the company's "fundamentals"—including its record of sales and earnings, the strength of its balance sheet and cash flow, the quality of management, and the health of its industry—and uses these to determine the company's prospects for profitable growth. Fundamental analysts judge the company's quality of earnings—for instance, how much of profit comes from operations and how much from selling off assets—and its levels of debt, R&D spending, and exposure to lawsuits. They also use techniques, such as forecasting earnings per share over the next year and applying the stock's multiple to that EPS figure, to forecast the stock's price.

The goals of fundamental analysis are to assess the company's prospects and to decide whether the stock is overvalued, undervalued, or fairly valued. If the stock is overvalued, fundamental analysis says to sell it, because sooner or later the fundamentals will always affect the stock's price. If the stock is undervalued, it should be purchased. Fairly valued stocks may be bought, sold, or held depending on the investor's goals and preferences.

MBA Alert

Completely ignoring a company's fundamentals can be dangerous. The few reporters and observers who warned of the Enron debacle in 2001 were focused on the company's business methods and financial condition, not on the skyrocketing price of its stock.

Technical analysis ignores financial statements and instead focuses on the price, past prices, sales trends, and trading volume of the stock itself. Using mathematical formulas, graphic analysis, and computing firepower, technical analysts (or technicians) chart the supply and demand for a stock based on past patterns and trends. Important concepts in technical analysis include the stock's resistance level (its previous high price), support level (its previous low), horizontal price movement (fluctuations within a narrow range over time), and correction (usually downward and temporary reversal of direction in a trend). Most technical analysis is geared to the short to intermediate term.

Although fundamental and technical analysis each have their fans, the wise investor considers the company's financial performance *and* the stock's price movements.

Corporate Bonds: Big IOUs

Corporate bonds represent long-term borrowings on which the company pays interest and principal at regular intervals. At maturity, the bondholder redeems the bond and receives any interest due and the remaining unpaid principal. Bondholders are lenders rather than owners of the corporation (who are shareholders) and they have no voting rights. They do, however, have a written agreement to be repaid in the form of the bond.

Key features of corporate bonds include the following:

♦ Bonds may be secured or unsecured. An unsecured bond, also known as a debenture, is backed only by the creditworthiness of the issuer. A secured bond is backed by collateral, financial or physical assets that may be sold by the bondholders in the event of *default*.

♦ Bearer bonds pay the interest and principal to whomever holds the bonds. Registered bonds pay interest to the owner who is registered in the company's records.

♦ A convertible bond can be exchanged for other securities, usually preferred or common stock.

> **MBA Lingo**
>
> Long-term **maturities** are those of one year or longer, and short-term are those of up to one year.
>
> A company is in **default** when it cannot pay the interest and principal on a bond or loan when they are due.

♦ Bonds may be purchased at the time they are issued or in the market after they are issued. Over its life, the price of a bond will fluctuate with supply and demand, interest rates, and investors' judgments about the creditworthiness of the issuer.

The interest rate on a bond is a function of the length of the maturity, the creditworthiness of the issuer, and the bond rating. Generally, the longer the *maturity* and the lower the creditworthiness, the higher the interest rate, because both factors increase the risk for investors, who must be compensated with a greater reward.

There are three major bond-rating services: Standard & Poor's, Moody's Investors Service, and Fitch's Investors Service. These companies assess the creditworthiness of companies that sell bonds to the public by analyzing their operations and finances. Then they assign letter grades that range from AAA (highly unlikely to default) to D (in default). (The letter grade systems vary slightly among the three services.)

Only bonds rated B or higher are considered investment grade. Bonds rated lower are considered noninvestment grade, also known as high-yield bonds (because they carry high interest rates) or, less charitably, junk bonds. Regulations usually stipulate that insurance companies and other financial institutions cannot invest their customers' funds in junk bonds.

In general, bonds are considered more conservative investments than stocks because of the agreement to pay a fixed amount of interest. (Incidentally, bonds are also referred to as "fixed-income" securities.) Before we look more closely into bonds, let's quickly examine a common and important type of corporate investment.

Commercial Paper

Commercial paper is issued by large, extremely creditworthy corporations and financial institutions with short-term borrowing needs. These IOUs, with maturities ranging from 2 to 270 days, are traded among large corporations and financial institutions in the commercial paper market.

Commercial paper has several advantages for both issuers and buyers. The market is active and the issuers are creditworthy, so commercial paper can be issued, bought, and sold relatively easily. Issuers like the flexibility of the maturities and the rates they pay on the paper, which are lower than the prime rate. Buyers like the range of available maturities, the ease of purchase, and the ability to "park" excess cash in a security offering a higher return than a bank account or short-term government securities, but comparable levels of safety and liquidity.

Government Securities

The U.S. federal government issues securities of varying maturities to finance the public debt. These securities are negotiable and are backed by the full faith and credit of the U.S. government, which, if it has to, can raise taxes or print money to pay its debts. The interest earned on government securities—also known as government obligations and "treasuries" (because they are issued by the U.S. Treasury)—is exempt from state and local, but not federal, taxes.

CAUTION MBA Alert _____

The U.S. government can always issue securities to finance budgetary shortfalls created when it spends more than it collects in taxes, fees, and other revenue. It can also print money to pay these debts. However, when the government issues securities, it is borrowing money that could be used by private industry. This can create a phenomenon know as crowding out—because the government's demand for funds "crowds out" private-sector borrowers. Also, when the government prints money to pay its debts, it puts more money into circulation, which can contribute to inflation, the situation covered in Chapter 6 of "too many dollars chasing too few goods."

The most common U.S. treasury issues are the following:

♦ **Treasury bills,** known as T-bills, have maturities of one year or less and are sold at auction at specific intervals and traded in the secondary market. T-bills come in denominations of $10,000 and up.

♦ **Treasury notes** carry maturities of 1 to 10 years and are sold at auction or in exchange for outstanding or maturing treasuries. Treasury notes come in denominations ranging from $1,000 to $1 million and up.

♦ **Treasury bonds** carry maturities of at least 10 years and come in denominations of $1,000 and up.

Because they are backed by the U.S. government, treasuries are viewed as a "risk-free" investment. As such, they carry interest rates lower than those of corporate bonds or commercial paper, or other types of government securities.

Other Government Securities

A variety of U.S. government agencies, such as the Federal Home Loan Bank, issue bonds. Although these are relatively safe investments, they are not backed by the U.S. Treasury, but rather by the creditworthiness of the issuing agency.

State and municipal governments and government agencies also issue bonds to finance their operations and manage their budgets. These securities, known as "munies," are relatively low-risk investments because they are backed by the taxing power of the state or local government or (often, but not always) a reliable source of income, such as highway tolls. However, they are not risk-free and therefore, unlike treasuries, they are rated by the rating agencies. Munies are usually free of federal, state, and local taxes if they have been issued solely for a public purpose rather than for one that also benefits private parties.

How Bond Prices Fluctuate

Bonds are issued with a face value and a stated interest rate. Corporate bonds are generally issued with a face value of $1,000, federal government bonds for $10,000, and municipal bonds for $5,000. Face value is also known as par value.

Bonds also carry a stated interest rate and interest is paid at that rate, applied to the face value of the bond. However, each time a bond is sold, its price may be more or less than the face value. The price of the bond fluctuates in this manner because of changing interest rates and changes in investors' judgment of the creditworthiness of the issuer.

Therefore, if a bond issued by XYZ Inc. has a face value of $1,000 and pays 10 percent, that means that each year the company pays the bondholder $100. Now if the price of the bond falls and XYZ continues to pay whoever owns the bond $100, then the effective interest rate on the bond has risen. For example, if you purchased this bond in the market for $950, the effective interest is $10\frac{1}{2}$ percent (= $100 ÷ $950). Conversely, if the price of the bond rose and you paid $1,050 for it, then the effective interest rate falls to $9\frac{1}{2}$ percent (= $100 ÷ $1,050).

In this way, the bond market and the mechanism of supply and demand adjusts the price of the bond to reflect investors' judgments about the company's creditworthiness and the prevailing level of interest rates. A bond can gain or lose value, and the investor can see price appreciation or erosion, although usually not of the magnitude customarily seen in equities.

The following key factors affect bond prices:

- If investors sell off stocks and move into bonds, which are inherently safer, demand for bonds increases and bond prices will rise as the buying continues.

- Conversely, if investors move into stocks because they seem more attractive, demand for bonds decreases and bond prices will fall.

- Bond prices are also affected by the general level of interest rates. If interest rates are generally high relative to the effective yield on stocks (dividends plus appreciation), investors will buy bonds, driving up demand for them and their prices. In a low-interest-rate environment, investors normally seek the higher returns offered by the stock market.

This is not to say that the stock and bond markets move in opposite directions. However, investors seeking healthy returns have a limited number of securities in which to invest. Therefore, the markets for stocks and for bonds *tend* to behave in complementary ways.

The Risk/Return Tradeoff

Purchasers of financial securities assume a degree of risk that the value of their investment will decrease. (Even treasuries can lose value if inflation runs high.) Investors take this risk expecting a return on their investment in the form of dividends or interest plus appreciation. The actual degree of risk and the actual return are unknown because they lie in the future. Yet historical performance and the features of various securities provide a general guideline regarding the risks and returns associated with them.

For instance, stocks are riskier than bonds because a stockholder owns a share in the company's future profits and those profits might not materialize. But a bondholder is a lender whose money must be repaid as an expense of doing business, whether or not the company actually earns a profit. For accepting more risk, the stockholder expects a higher return. Stockholders expect the company to earn a profit and expect to share in those profits in the form of dividends. They assume greater risk in expectation of a greater return. Yet a stockholder is *not owed* a portion of the profits. In fact, the company may choose not to pay any dividends and instead reinvest the money in the company.

Bondholders also expect the company to earn a profit. An unprofitable company will eventually go bankrupt and be unable to pay its debts in full, including those owed to bondholders. But bondholders typically have a lower tolerance for risk than an equity investor. Therefore, they want a bond that states that the company *owes* them their interest and principal.

Other Financial Markets and Investment Vehicles

While the markets for stocks, bonds, and treasuries are the key financial markets, others include:

♦ **Commodities markets,** where buyers and sellers trade contracts to deliver agricultural staples such as wheat, corn, soybeans, and pork bellies. The spot market deals in goods for immediate delivery while the futures market deals in goods for delivery on a future date. Oil is also traded in spot and futures markets.

- **Foreign exchange markets,** where buyers and sellers trade currencies. Foreign exchange (or FX) futures are also traded, with the goal of reducing the risks inherent in future currency fluctuations.

- **Precious metals,** such as gold and platinum, are actively traded. A "goldbug" is an investor who invests relatively heavily in gold as a hedge against inflation or because he or she believes that a depression or other disaster lay ahead.

MBA Mastery

Gold has traditionally been viewed as an extremely safe and conservative investment, but not one noted for high returns. For this reason, a rising price for gold indicates investor pessimism about the economic or political future, and a falling price signals optimism.

Other investments include those in tangible assets, rather than financial securities or precious metals. The most popular of these by far is real estate, followed by a huge range of collectibles, including art, antiques, vintage automobiles, coins, and memorabilia. While real estate has proven itself as a reliable long-term investment, collectibles are generally purchased as much for their aesthetic value and emotional appeal as for their investment value. In other words, if you love Elvis buy Elvis memorabilia, but don't count on it to fund your retirement.

The Least You Need to Know

- The financial markets are organized forums for buying and selling securities and other financial instruments, such as foreign currencies.

- Common stock provides an ownership share in a company and the potential for dividends and price appreciation. Bonds are IOUs from a company, government, or government agency and offer returns mainly in the form of interest payments.

- U.S. government obligations, or treasuries, are essentially a risk-free investment because they are backed by the full faith and credit of the U.S. government, which has both taxing authority and the ability to print money.

Part 4

Managing Marketing for Maximum Sales

Everything you do as a manager comes down to the customer. All your work will be for nothing if customers don't buy what you sell. People in marketing and sales spend their working lives focusing on the customer. Who is the customer? What does the customer want? What will the customer pay for it? When is the customer satisfied? Where can we find new customers? How can we beat our competitors in the fight for customers?

Because customers make or break a business, the human factor dominates marketing and sales more than any other area of business. This makes these areas the most exciting part of business to many people. But marketing and sales are also where business competition can be toughest.

So hang on as we charge into the battle for markets and the quest for customers.

WE NEED A NEW MARKETING STRATEGY HERE AT PETER'S POULTRY. WE PUT ALL OUR EGGS IN ONE BASKET AND COUNTED THE CHICKENS BEFORE THEY'VE HATCHED.

Chapter 17

Ready, Aim, Sell

In This Chapter

- ◆ The difference between marketing and sales
- ◆ How marketing and sales work together
- ◆ Basic concepts in marketing and sales

You'll recall from the income statement in Chapter 12 that a company's financial health starts with sales. Every company must sell its products or services to make money to pay its bills and earn a profit.

This makes marketing and sales two of the most important functions in a company. Their job is finding people to buy what the company sells. In most businesses, this isn't easy. When it is easy, it doesn't stay that way because competitors quickly come along. So marketing and sales offer some of the most challenging work in business. But it's some of the most satisfying and financially rewarding work as well.

In this chapter, we examine marketing and sales and how they serve the company and its customers. We also cover some basic marketing and sales concepts.

Marketing, Sales—What's the Difference?

Think of marketing as selling to groups of people, while selling is done one on one. Marketing raises people's awareness of a product and generates interest in buying it. However, it takes selling to get an individual to hand over money or a check.

Advertising and direct mail are great examples of "selling to groups." But marketing goes beyond advertising and direct mail to include many other activities.

Selling means getting a person or a company—a customer—to pay for your product or service. But selling goes beyond "pitch the product" and "ask for an order."

MBA Lingo

Strategic initiatives operate on a larger scale than **tactical** initiatives. Managers craft a strategy in order to achieve a goal. For instance, in order to achieve the goal of increased sales, management may adopt a strategy of pursuing a new market. To implement that strategy, the company will have to develop the right tactics, which might include developing new products. In general, tactics implement strategy.

In most organizations, marketing exists to support the salespeople. That's good, because selling is the toughest job in business. Most people will not part with their money, or their organization's money, without a good reason. The marketing and sales departments are there to supply those reasons.

Marketing is a staff activity, usually located at the company's headquarters. Selling is a line activity, and salespeople are said to work "in the field."

Marketing also tends to be *strategic*, while sales tends to be *tactical*. This flows from the idea that marketing supports sales. That support often takes the form of planning and guidance. For example, marketing identifies groups that appear to need the company's products. Then salespeople go to individuals within those groups to try to meet those needs with the company's product.

People in marketing and sales approach business a bit differently. Marketing people tend to view their work in more intellectual and abstract terms than salespeople. The issue of "selling to groups" insulates marketing people from the hurly-burly of face-to-face selling. A marketing person researching product features faces less difficulty than the salesperson phoning busy people for appointments or trying to persuade a reluctant buyer.

There is often some tension between marketing and sales. Marketing can view salespeople as mere tools in its grand strategy, people who exist simply to execute the wonderful plans that marketing geniuses hatch. Meanwhile, sales can view marketers as hopelessly out-of-touch "staff-types" who would starve to death if they had to actually make sales.

People in marketing and sales must either eliminate this tension by fostering mutual respect, or at least manage it creatively.

MBA Mastery _____

To get marketing and salespeople to understand one another, force them to work together. Be sure marketing includes salespeople in its planning process and decisions. Be sure salespeople tell marketing about competitors and problems they face in the field. Get salespeople to take marketing people along on sales calls now and then, just so they can observe the process. Get marketing people to solicit ideas from the salespeople about how marketing can best support them.

Commercial vs. Consumer Sales

In business, there's a distinction between consumer and commercial—or business-to-business—marketing and sales.

If the person is buying the product or service for himself or herself as an individual, we're talking about *consumer sales*. If he or she is buying it for his or her organization, we are talking about *commercial, corporate, industrial,* or *business-to-business sales*, which all mean the same thing.

The product or service usually dictates the type of sales. For example, breakfast cereal and toothpaste are sold to consumers. (In fact, they're in a category known as consumer packaged goods.) Meanwhile, office supplies and photocopiers are business-to-business items.

But it gets tricky. For example, the 1990s boom in home-based businesses created a whole new market for personal computers, fax machines, and office supplies. This market has characteristics of both the commercial market and the consumer market.

Each type of sale—consumer and commercial—presents its own challenges, which we'll examine as they arise in this part.

MBA Lingo _____

In **consumer sales** the customers buy the product or service with their own money for their own personal use. In **commercial sales** (also called **corporate, industrial,** or **business-to-business**) the customers buy the product or service with their organization's money for professional use by themselves or others on the job.

Marketing Strategy Basics

Companies compete largely on price and quality. Basically, a company can deliver either high quality at a high price (like Mercedes Benz) or lower quality at a low price (like Hyundai). The economics of our planet will not allow a company to manufacture a car with the quality of a Mercedes for the price of a Hyundai.

So the first strategic decision for a company is to choose the basis on which it will compete: price or quality. Then marketing delivers that message to the marketplace. John's Bargain Store says, "Come here if you want to pay a low price and get commonplace goods." Neiman Marcus says, "Come here if you can pay top dollar for the very best."

There's another dimension: service. Here service means everything not included in price and quality—selection, post-purchase support, warranties, and so on. In some businesses and markets, service can be as important as price and quality. And there are other elements such as novelty, design, prestige, ease of use, and technical sophistication.

Of course, I've simplified things considerably, but essentially the goal of marketing strategy is to have a competitive advantage and to get word of that advantage out to the marketplace.

Sales Tactics, Summarized

After marketing strategy identifies markets, prospects, and a competitive position, sales must win customers. So after marketing gets the word out and customers come to the store, salespeople help them find what they want, explain how the products work, and so on. In retail, the sales challenges are typically lower than in industrial sales because the customer comes to the store. And they don't go to John's Bargain Store looking for gold cuff links or to Neiman Marcus to buy clothespins.

MBA Lingo

Prospecting means looking for prospects, specifically prospects who will agree to see or speak with a salesperson. Prospecting includes everything from randomly telephoning people for appointments to carefully targeting specific individuals from annual reports.

In many businesses, the salespeople must go *prospecting* for customers. They must telephone them for appointments and make sales calls. Then the salesperson guides the prospect through the sales process, which I show you in Chapter 21.

A sales call is a visit or phone call a salesperson makes to a customer or prospect in order to sell them something.

Translating Sales Goals into Marketing Plans

Every company wants to grow, which means that the dollar volume of sales must always be higher next year. There are several ways to achieve a sales increase:

- Increase your prices

- Sell more existing products to current customers

- Sell new products to current customers

- Sell existing products to new customers

- Sell new products to new customers

Let's briefly look at each of these strategies.

Increase Your Prices

A price increase would seem to be the simplest way to increase your sales. All you have to do is raise your prices 5 percent, then sell the same amount of product next year as you did this year, and your sales increase by 5 percent. Great, huh?

There's only one problem: *price resistance*. That's MBA-ese for customers not wanting to pay a higher price. When they see higher prices for the same products, they look for other places to buy or they try to get along with less of it, or without it. They'll also bargain harder with your salespeople.

If you have the market power—that is, if you face few competitors and your customers have no options—your price increase may "stick." But it's not a strategy you can count on for long. A product that commands constantly increasing prices will quickly attract competition. Also, customers often learn to live without companies they see gouging them.

The other four goals all involve selling more units of product, rather than selling the same amount of product at a higher price.

MBA Lingo

Price resistance refers to the fact that customers who face high or increasing prices for a product or service will generally seek cheaper alternative products or services, try to get a lower price from the seller, or go to a different seller with lower prices.

Sell More Existing Products to Current Customers

This comes down to "pushing product," and it can work. It is based on the reasonable idea that your best prospects are your current customers.

> **MBA Lingo**
>
> **Cross-selling** means going to a customer who is buying one kind of product from you and selling him another kind, too. The question "Would you like fries with that?" is surely the most common example of cross-selling.

This strategy can work if your current customers are underserved or your product line is broad, or both. If you have only scratched the surface of your current customers and you have a broad product line to sell, you have ample opportunity to *cross-sell* them—that is, sell them other products that you offer.

You can also offer volume discounts and find ways of binding the customers closer to you, perhaps by setting them up on an electronic system for automatic purchasing and billing. Anything you can do to make doing business with your company easier can help.

Sell New Products to Current Customers

New products are so vital that Chapter 22 is devoted to new-product development. Even if you have what you think are satisfied customers, someone is out there working on ways to satisfy them even better or more cheaply. So you must always be improving your current products and developing new ones to meet your customers' needs.

Current customers can be your best prospects for new products, particularly products that solve problems you learned about when selling them old products.

Sell Existing Products to New Customers

Some companies get into a rut by just serving the same old set of customers. When you have a successful product or service, constantly ask yourself: "Who else might buy this? Who else can use this?"

The search for new customers should never stop. Even the most successful companies lose at least some customers each year. Even your best accounts may leave you, for any number of reasons—a better product or price from a competitor, a snafu with a salesperson, or a simple desire for change.

Also, any potential customer that you don't approach is one that a competitor will probably win. Why give away business without a fight?

Case in Point

New markets for existing products can even give rise to entirely new businesses. For example, the office-supply retailers Staples and Office Depot did not exist before the home-office boom. But then the need arose.

Companies selling office supplies commercially were not about to start calling on consumers. However, consumers, who are used to going to a store when they need something, have no problem going to one for paper, toner, or folders.

Sell New Products to New Customers

When sales of your product begin to slope off—often in the phase of *market maturity* or *saturation*—you have three choices: (1) close up shop or sell the business, (2) try to survive on repeat and replacement business, or (3) sell new products to new customers. The third choice is the best—provided you want a growing business. But don't make the mistake of waiting until your markets are saturated with your old products before developing new ones.

Selling new products to new customers can be the most powerful of the five growth strategies.

However, new products for new markets can be the hardest to develop. Even if you stay close to your main business (and generally you should), it's tough to come up with something new for a new market. That's why companies usually develop new products for their current markets, even when they enter a new business. For example, Disney entered theme parks in the 1950s. That was different from films, but Disney was already established in family entertainment. Nike, Adidas, and Reebok now offer active wear, but their target customers were already buying their athletic shoes.

Most senior managers and all marketing and salespeople think constantly about ways to increase sales. These five strategies can move those thoughts in practical directions.

MBA Lingo

Market maturity means that the product has achieved wide acceptance and that growth in sales has leveled off. **Saturation** means that every potential customer who wants, needs, and can pay for your product already has one. It can be hard to know when your product has saturated its markets, because it depends on the true market potential for the product.

Product Differentiation

Product differentiation means making your product different from the others like it. Successful products offer customers a difference, something better. Even products that compete mainly on price should offer some difference.

Marketing plays a big role in making and highlighting product differences. In the following sections, I'll discuss certain proven ways of achieving product differentiation.

Improved Performance

Performance improvements actually make the product better. The Japanese challenge to U.S. automakers in the 1970s was one of improved performance. Gas mileage, durability, and value for the price improved dramatically in Japanese cars during this decade.

Improved performance may strike you as a manufacturing issue rather than a marketing issue. But product improvements must be announced and "made real" in the marketplace, and that's a marketing challenge. It's not enough to build a better mousetrap. You have to show and tell people that it's better.

A company can decide to improve the performance of its product in various ways, including ease of use, durability, freedom from maintenance, economy of operation, and characteristics such as speed, weight, or water resistance.

One caution: Worthwhile performance improvements are those that people want and will pay for. If you make improvements that customers don't care about, you're not differentiating your product in a meaningful way. The result is often "a gold-plated crowbar." You get nothing but added production costs, which are the last thing you need.

Case in Point

Some products have succeeded largely on their design. Examples include Braun's kitchen appliances and the Miata sports car from Mazda.

The sleek lines of Braun's coffeemaker and the symbols instead of words on the controls give it a futuristic look. Let's face it: A coffeemaker is a coffeemaker. You have to differentiate it somehow, and Braun does it with design.

The Mazda Miata became the darling of automotive writers and car buyers with a design that evoked the venerable British roadsters by MG and Austin Healy. Designed more as a toy than a machine, everything about the car says "I'm here for fun."

Improved Appearance

Modern society is visually oriented. Today, the appearance of a product can be as important as its performance. Therefore, design—the blend of form and function that dictates the appearance of a product—is now a powerful product differentiator.

Improved Image

In our society, many people define themselves at least partly by what they buy and use. Thanks to advertising, television, and movies, products convey certain images, both to ourselves and others. These images involve wealth, youth, status, sophistication, sexuality, health, caring, environmental consciousness, power, and danger (and in some cases, a social critic would surely add, stupidity).

Product images pervade our culture. Consider the various images cultivated by products as diverse as Marlboro cigarettes (rugged and manly), Chivas Regal scotch (smooth and sophisticated), Sears Kenmore appliances (sensible and reliable), Campbell's soups (wholesome and comforting), Kellogg's corn flakes (pure and simple), *New Yorker* magazine (urbane and literary), Harley-Davidson motorcycles (big and American), and the MGM Grand Hotel in Las Vegas (entertaining and swingin').

These images often go beyond mere product qualities. They attempt to create an experience for the customer that says, "When I buy this product, I am saying that I value these qualities, and that I have them myself."

Marketing Basics

Like every area of business, marketing and sales have their own ways of describing things. In the rest of this chapter, we'll cover several major concepts in marketing and sales that are worth knowing.

Who Drives Your Company?

A market-driven company looks to the market—to groups of customers—to learn what it should be doing. A market-driven company listens to customers to learn why and how customers use what they sell. A market-driven firm watches trends in the marketplace in technology, pricing, packaging, and distribution (where and how it sells its products). It also watches competitors.

CAUTION

MBA Alert _____

It's hard to find customer-focused employees in the United States because many people see being of service as somehow beneath them. (This is recognized as a major problem in the retail business.) This makes building a company culture that values customer service challenging. But when companies do manage to make service a priority, the results can be spectacular.

A customer-focused company also listens to customers for cues on what it should do. However, the term "customer-focused" emphasizes an effort to make each customer's experience satisfying. A customer-focused company believes that every customer is important and tries to ensure that each customer is treated as an individual. These companies tend to be very accommodating when they face customer requests, taking a "can-do" approach. Many companies say they're customer-focused, but few truly are.

Sales-driven companies are focused on the top line. They want sales. I'm not saying they ignore their markets and customers. No company can do that. I'm saying that those are not the main priorities. Increasing sales is the main priority.

Case in Point

Nike, the athletic shoe and clothing manufacturer, is very market-driven. By studying the running-shoe market, Nike saw many markets it didn't know it had: markets for basketball shoes, walking shoes, racquetball shoes, cross-trainers, beach shoes, and so on. So Nike made special shoes for these activities.

If you want to see what customer-focused means, try this: Call several major car-rental chains at two or three airports and ask to rent a car. Then watch how you're treated. Is the service person courteous? How long are you kept on hold? Does he or she ask if you have any discounts? Will he or she honor your request for a special model? You'll quickly see which companies have their act together.

Many insurance and securities firms are sales-driven. They often hire salespeople focused on "making the numbers." This works because many prospects can't distinguish among financial services firms and the product is intangible, so the outfit that pushes hardest can often close the sale.

Of course, all companies want increasing sales. But sales-driven companies take a very direct route to this goal. They hire salespeople who "push product" rather than discover and satisfy needs. They take a "get-the-money" approach to customers, which can close sales but fail to win long-term customers.

The Product Adoption Curve

The Product Adoption Curve states that a successful new product will be adopted by various categories of buyers in a predictable order. That's because not all buyers are willing to try something new. Many people need to see other, more innovative buyers adopt the product first.

The Product Adoption Curve and the categories of buyers are shown in the following figure.

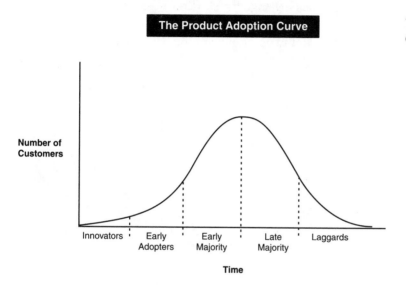

The Product Adoption Curve

The Product Adoption Curve.

By definition, the following percentages apply to each category of buyer:

Innovators	=	the first $2^{1}/_{2}$ percent of buyers
Early Adopters	=	the next $13^{1}/_{2}$ percent
Early Majority	=	the next 34 percent
Late Majority	=	the next 34 percent
Laggards	=	the final 16 percent

These categories present different marketing and sales challenges. Innovators have to be located, which can take some doing, and then persuaded to try something new and unproven. Early Adopters present similar challenges, but at least you have some earlier customers to point to as success stories.

You have to get to the Early Majority quickly, because you're soon going to face competitors if the product is successful. You may have to broaden your marketing effort and increase the size of the sales force. The Late Majority will probably require discounts and other inducements, such as service plans. At this stage you're in a battle for market share. You'll also be trying to find completely new markets for the product, perhaps overseas.

By the time you're selling a product to the Laggards, the challenge has shifted to controlling your sales and manufacturing costs to squeezing all the profitability you can from the product while it's still alive.

The Product Adoption Curve is also called the Technology Adoption Curve because it applies to a technology (such as the VCR or personal computer) as well as to new products.

> **MBA Mastery**
>
> Different types of customers respond differently to different marketing messages and sales approaches. For example, Innovators and Early Adopters get excited when they hear that something is new and different. In contrast, you have to sell the Late Majority on the reliability and wide acceptance of the product.

The Product Life Cycle

Like people and organizations, products have lives. They are conceived, they are born, they grow, they have a period of maturity, and they go into decline. The product life cycle was developed in the 1960s to describe the predictable phases in the life of a product. Those phases are as follows:

- Introduction
- Growth
- Maturity
- Decline

Usually these phases are shown on a curve that plots sales over time, as shown in the following figure.

Each phase presents a different marketing and sales challenge. In the introductory phase, the challenge is "missionary work"—spreading word of the new product and finding the first customers. During growth, the challenge is to beat competitors, who introduce similar products when they see one that makes money, and win as many customers as possible. In maturity, the challenge becomes controlling sales costs, fighting for market share, and developing variations of the product. In decline, the challenge is deciding what to do with the product: Can it be revitalized? Is it still profitable enough for you to sell?

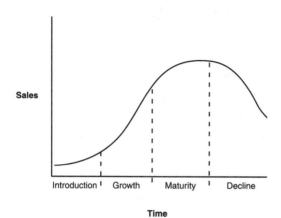

The Product Life Cycle Curve.

MBA Mastery

Few things in business are predictable, but the product life cycle is one of them. Unfortunately, the *timing* of the phases is not very predictable. The key thing to watch is the sales trend. When sales are slow early in the product's life, it is in the introductory phase. When sales rise sharply, it is in the growth phase. When sales growth levels off for an extended time, it is in maturity. And when sales decrease, it is in decline.

The length of any particular phase can vary for different products. A fad item such as Tamaguchis ("virtual pets") can have a life of a couple of years, with phases measured in months. A car brand like the Ford Mustang can take off rapidly, moving quickly from introduction to rapid growth, then enjoy a long maturity and gentle decline with periods of revitalization. The product life cycle can be applied to entire product categories such as healthy frozen dinners (now in maturity) or steam locomotives (now defunct).

Occasionally, a product or category can go into decline, then stage a comeback. Large-engine, gas-guzzling cars and vans bounced back from their 1970s decline with the economic boom of the 1990s. Sales of fur coats also rose in 1997 after several years in decline due to antifur activism.

By the way, the product life cycle applies only to successful products. Those that don't make it past the introductory phase are product failures (products that are introduced but do not win market acceptance). Such failures are more common than most non-businesspeople realize.

The Least You Need to Know

- Think of marketing as selling to groups, while sales is done one on one. Marketing, which tends to be strategic, exists to support sales, which tends to be more tactical.

- Since companies basically compete on price and quality, a company must first decide where it wants to be in terms of price and quality. Then it must establish and reinforce that position through its products and marketing message.

- There are several ways to increase sales: increase prices, sell more existing products to current customers, sell new products to current customers, sell existing products to new customers, or sell new products to new customers.

- To differentiate your products, you can improve their performance, appearance, or image relative to competitive products.

- Successful products go through a life cycle from introduction, to growth, to maturity, to decline. Each phase of the life cycle presents a different marketing and sales challenge.

- A product will usually be adopted—either rapidly or gradually—first by Innovators, then by Early Adopters, then by the Early Majority, followed by the Late Majority, and finally the Laggards.

Chapter 18

Who Are Your Customers, Anyway?

In This Chapter

- ◆ The purpose of market research
- ◆ The characteristics of market segments
- ◆ How to conduct a market research study

In Chapter 17, you learned that marketing deals with two flows of information, one coming into the company and one going out. Market research, the study of a company's customers and prospects, can generate very useful incoming information. This research helps the company create and modify the information it sends out to the marketplace.

This chapter examines the goals and tasks of market research. It also tells you how to plan and launch a good market research study.

What Is a Market?

A *market* is a group of customers or potential customers. A company focuses its market research on its particular market. Coca-Cola studies the soft-drink market. Merrill Lynch researches the market for financial services. Sony wants to know about the entertainment and home-electronics markets. You research a market to get practical information your company can use in its sales, marketing, and product-development efforts.

Most companies think of their markets in two ways: First, there is the broad market the company serves, such as the soft-drink or financial-services or home-electronics market. Second, there are *market segments*, which are specific markets within markets.

MBA Lingo

A **market** is a group of customers or prospects—usually a group made up of individual people or organizations with certain shared characteristics, if only a need for a certain product or service. **Market segments** are parts of a market that have some characteristic in common. For example, the market for personal computers has two broad segments—homes and businesses. **Targeting** refers to the practice of developing specific advertising, products, or services for specific markets. These markets are referred to as target markets.

Divide and Conquer: Market-Segmentation Strategies

A market segment is a section or a slice of a broader market. Market segmentation recognizes that different customers have different needs and motivations. There are a number of standard market segments, such as the baby-boomer and Hispanic markets. However, most companies also define their own market segments using one or more of the following segmentation strategies:

- **Geographic segmentation** divides the broad market into regional or local markets. Managers in a company using geographic segments will talk about the "Northeast market" or the "Dallas–Fort Worth market."

- **Demographic segmentation** classifies the broad market by customer characteristics such as age, gender, income, and race. Television shows, radio stations, magazines, and other media aim for specific segments (such as males 18–34 years old, working mothers, senior citizens, or African Americans). This helps companies *target* these demographic segments with their advertising messages.

- **Product segmentation** divides the broad market by the products the company sells. For example, the automotive industry deals with the markets for luxury, midsize, compact, subcompact, and sport-utility vehicles.

◆ **Sales-channel segmentation** divides the market according to the way in which a product is sold. For instance, Coca-Cola is sold in grocery stores, restaurants, stadiums, movie theaters, and vending machine markets.

Large companies can use several segmentation strategies at once to better target their markets. For example, combining geographic and product segmentation enables General Motors to approach the California luxury-car market. Combining demographics and sales channels lets Coca-Cola divide the working-mother segment into working mothers who buy beverages in grocery stores, at restaurants, and from vending machines.

By segmenting markets, a company can better understand customer needs, motivations, and behavior. That understanding is also the goal of market research.

Why Do Market Research?

The better a company understands its customers and potential customers, the better it can serve them. Market research helps companies understand and analyze their customers.

Most market research focuses on one or more of the following types of information:

◆ **Demographic characteristics** include descriptive information about the customer. In consumer markets, *demographic* data includes age, sex, income, education, race, marital status, housing, and number of children. In business markets, it includes industry classification, annual sales, number of employees, number of locations, and years in business.

◆ **Buying behaviors** are the ways in which customers buy (such as retail stores and websites), frequency of purchase, and influences in the buying decision (such as advertising or recommendations from friends).

◆ **Customer satisfaction** is the buyer's happiness (or disappointment) with the product or service. Components of satisfaction include perceived value for the price, ease of use and maintenance, product defects, most and least important features, desired features, and likelihood of repeat purchase.

MBA Lingo

Demographics are characteristics of a market or market segment. These characteristics are usually statistical information such as age, gender, income, and so on. **Psychographics** are characteristics of a market or market segment that usually focus more on attitudes (such as political affiliation) and lifestyles (such as attendance at sporting events or museums).

♦ **Attitudes and lifestyle**—often called *psychographics*, these are relatively new concerns for marketers. These include hobbies, participation in sports, frequency of dining out, vacation plans, favorite magazines and television shows, concerns for the future, political leanings, religion, even personality traits and sexual orientation.

Case in Point

Among the newest identified lifestyle segments is the gay market. Since many gay people are urban dwellers without children, some marketers target them as prospects for leisure-time services such as vacations and fine dining. Companies in fields such as financial services and consumer packaged goods are considering specific ways to approach this market segment.

Who Needs Market Research?

Companies vary in their need for market research. For example, large companies tend to do more market research than small ones. Small companies often see research as costly and feel they already know their customers.

MBA Lingo

A **commodity** is a product whose characteristics and performance are indistinguishable across the companies that sell it. Petroleum products, coal, and grain are examples of commodities. Product **differentiation** presents real or perceived product differences as beneficial to customers. A **homogenous market** is one where all the customers and prospects share most characteristics. If you sell only to government agencies, you have a homogenous market.

Often companies that shun market research sell *commodity* products (products such as coal or grain that are indistinguishable across companies that sell them) and believe their customers care only about low prices and fast service.

Others have a *homogenous* market, meaning that they sell to only one type of customer. For example, manufacturers of professional dental equipment sell only to dentists, and defense contractors sell only to governments.

These firms have a point, but often research can discover something new that would help them *differentiate* their product or further understand their customer. For example, a company might emphasize that its petroleum products are purer, its coal burns longer, or its grain is more nutritious than that of competitors.

Some companies avoid market research because they feel that their sales force does a good job of reading their customers. Some managers don't believe that market research yields accurate or useful results.

These attitudes are understandable. However, most companies benefit from at least occasional research on their customers and prospects.

The Two Types of Market Research

The two broad types of market research are primary market research, which usually means asking people prepared questions, and secondary market research, which examines published material, such as newspapers, magazines, and books.

This chapter focuses on primary market research, but secondary research has its place. It will give you a good overview of a product or service. This can help you focus your primary research, particularly in an area completely new to your firm. Secondary research is also faster and cheaper than primary research.

In primary research, you go directly to sources of information. This usually means surveying customers or prospects (or both). Sometimes, primary research is essential. Only someone who has used a product can discuss customer satisfaction. Only a prospect can tell you whether he'd buy a new service you're offering.

Specific information directly from the source is the main advantage of primary research. But this comes at a price: Primary research costs more than secondary research of comparable scope.

Primary research delivers very structured information. Since you design the questions, you can use primary research to develop *quantitative* (numerical) or *qualitative* (verbal) responses.

The rest of this chapter will focus on how to conduct a primary research study.

MBA Lingo

Quantitative information involves numbers and data that can be analyzed mathematically. For example, "29 percent of the survey respondents said the Mighty Vac was an excellent value" is quantitative information. Qualitative information tends to be verbal and less subject to mathematical analysis. For example, "The Mighty Vac lets me clean in hard-to-reach places" is **qualitative**.

Creating a Market-Research Study

Let's say you've decided to prepare a market-research study in order to uncover primary information about your customers. A market research study has five steps:

1. Define the goal of the research.

2. Design the study.

3. Develop the questionnaire.

4. Field the survey.

5. Analyze and present the results.

How well you carry out each step will determine the quality of the results of your study. Let's consider each step in turn.

Define Your Goal

Good market research—either primary or secondary—starts with a goal. Your goal may be "to assess customer satisfaction with our Mighty Vac vacuum cleaner" or "to develop a profile of our customer base."

In defining your goal, consider how you will use the results. Think about the behaviors and attitudes you want to understand about your customers and prospects. Think ahead to the analysis phase and the final presentation and gear the research accordingly.

> **MBA Alert**
>
> People tend to load market research with too many goals. They'll often say, "As long as we're doing a survey, let's be sure to cover X, Y, and Z." This makes the questionnaire too long and can muddy the results. If people try to overload your survey, explain the goal and point out that you can explore other issues in the next round of research. Try to stick with one goal.

Design the Study

Study design results from a series of decisions about who you will survey, how you will conduct the survey, and what questions you will ask.

Who you survey depends on what you want to learn. If you want to know how to win back former customers, you must survey former customers. If you want to know how young single people perceive your company, you must survey young single people.

Who you survey also depends on the size of the sample you intend to survey. A cable-television company trying to learn why people do not subscribe doesn't have to ask every nonsubscriber in the area. It merely has to ask a sample of them.

The medium you use—mail survey, telephone interviews, in-person interviews (either through informal methods, such as "sidewalk surveys," or through more structured focus groups), or the Internet—depends on the budget, sample size, and goals of your research.

Let's briefly consider the pros and cons of each medium:

Survey Structure

Survey Medium	Benefits	Disadvantages
Mail	Least expensive survey method per respondent. Ideal for conducting a large survey (with easily answered questions) on a tight budget.	Yields low response (many surveys get thrown out). Those who do respond may have extreme feelings on the subject, leading to a skewed sample. You cannot control how readers respond (they may skip questions, answer incoherently, etc.). You cannot ask for more information.
Telephone	Generally yields better response rates than mail surveys. You control the order of the questions and can ask for more information. An excellent choice for in-depth data on customers' experiences with your products.	More expensive than mail surveys.
In-person	Best if your sample can be reached at a certain place (i.e., a health club or supermarket). Yields in-depth information. Necessary if you have a product prototype that must be demonstrated in person.	Getting interviewees can be difficult. Extremely expensive for large samples.
Internet	Inexpensive survey method (assuming established website and straightforward programming). You control the order of the questions, and can make respondent answer before proceeding. Best for conducting surveys with respondents you do business with on the web.	Requires a website with a good volume of activity. Not good for in-depth questions or long questionnaires.

Finally, during the study-design phase you must decide how you will handle the mechanics of getting the questions answered. The main decision is whether to do it in-house (with company employees or independent contractors) or to use a market research firm (or "vendor").

Obviously, you may want to use a vendor if you do not have the in-house time or resources to complete the survey. Certain research subjects are best left to market research firms. If the subject is sensitive or will elicit negative comments, a vendor may get more honest answers. Many people will withhold negative comments about your product if they're speaking with someone from your company.

MBA Lingo

A **focus group** is a panel of 5 to 10 individuals brought together to respond to questions requiring in-depth discussion. Issues range from a company's service or image, reactions to new-product ideas, or feelings about political matters. Respondents are paid for their time (from $50 to $150) and the session is run by an experienced facilitator. Managers from the company often observe the session from behind a mirrored wall (with the participants' knowledge) and most sessions are taped for later viewing.

You might also hire a vendor if you want outside, independent research on issues that affect key company decisions, such as whether to enter a new market or where to place a large retail chain store. If you need totally objective information about a thorny subject, use a vendor.

However you choose to handle your survey, you have to make sure it is something your company can afford.

Whether research is done in-house or jobbed out, someone at your company must closely supervise the project from start to finish and ultimately be responsible for the costs and the results.

Develop the Questionnaire

Questionnaire design is a field unto itself. The guidelines here will enable you to either write a questionnaire or work well with the person who is writing it.

First, list the issues you want covered and the questions you want asked. Brainstorm. Write down anything that may be pertinent. Include identifying questions such as name, address, and general characteristics (such as "education" for consumers or "industry" or "annual sales" for companies).

Here are the major kinds of questions and their uses, along with some examples.

Open-end questions cannot be answered yes or no, nor do they prompt for a specific response. Open-end questions are particularly good for eliciting opinions, attitudes, and feelings. They tend to get honest answers, because without prompting the respondent has no choice but to say what he or she thinks (or refuse to answer). Examples of open-end questions include:

MBA Mastery

Many market research firms will offer to do an analysis, written report, and even a presentation of the results. In my experience, it is best for in-house managers to conduct the analysis. They know the company, product, customers, and internal politics best.

- ◆ Which features of the Mighty Vac are most important to you?

- ◆ What is your opinion of the service you receive from Acme Industries?

Closed-end questions can be answered yes or no or they prompt for a response. They can be standardized so the answers are easy to compile and compare when you do your analysis. Closed-end questions are also easy for respondents to answer. Here are some sample closed-end questions:

- ◆ Which of the following features of the Mighty Vac are important to you? (Check all that apply.)

  ❏ Extra-long hose

  ❏ Extra-long cord

  ❏ Extra-high horsepower

  ❏ Square head

  ❏ Other *(Please specify)* _____

- ◆ How would you rate the service you receive from Acme Industries? (Check one.)

  ❏ Excellent

  ❏ Good

  ❏ Fair

  ❏ Poor

With closed-end questions, you must often give directions to the respondent (such as "Check one" or "Please rate from one to five, with five being the best ").

Identifying questions ask the respondent to verify his or her name, title, address, and similar information. These questions make good icebreakers for telephone or personal interviews.

Qualifying questions are asked early in a survey when you must determine whether the person is qualified to take part in the survey. For example, a customer-satisfaction survey requires a respondent who has actually used the product ("Have you ever used the Mighty Vac?" is a qualifying question).

Follow-up questions, also called probing questions, ask the respondent to add more to the answer he or she gave to the previous question. These questions let you dig deeper into a subject. For example, you might first ask a respondent for her opinion of the service she has received from Acme Industries. Whatever her response, you then ask why she feels that way.

> **MBA Mastery**
>
> Often on a rating scale with five elements (such as 1–5 or Excellent, Very Good, Good, Fair, or Poor), many respondents just check the middle value. You may force a more positive or negative answer if you give the respondent a choice of only four ratings. This forces the respondent to make a positive or negative judgment.

Don't overuse follow-up questions or you'll fatigue the respondent and eventually produce cursory answers. Don't waste a follow-up question asking the obvious (such as, "Why do you prefer a low price?").

Once you've brainstormed a list of questions, pare the list down to the necessary questions. Keep questionnaires short; long surveys annoy or fatigue respondents. Ask only what you need to ask and you'll get a better response rate and more accurate information. A written questionnaire should be kept to one page, two at most, if possible. Telephone questionnaires should ideally be kept to five minutes. You can go over these limits, of course, but your response rate will fall.

Do's and Don'ts of Questionnaire Design

Here are some general guidelines for questionnaire design:

- **DO** think ahead to the analysis phase and ask questions that will produce answers you can compile and analyze.

- **DO** keep the survey as short as possible, while asking all questions pertinent to your goal.

- **DO** try to ask important questions early in the survey in case the respondent chooses not to finish it.

- **DO** be careful when you give instructions for answering the survey.

- **DO** leave enough space for respondents or interviewers to write answers to open-end questions.

- **DO** write a one-page cover letter that politely tells a respondent to a mail survey why the survey is important.

- **DON'T** be afraid to ask sensitive questions if they're important to your goal. The respondent always has the right to refuse to answer.

- **DON'T** let others load up the survey with questions that don't relate to the goal.

> **MBA Mastery**
>
> Be absolutely certain to test your questionnaire before you field it. See which questions work and which don't. Modify or omit any confusing questions. (And don't blame the respondents. If they say it isn't clear, it isn't clear.)

- **DON'T** crowd the questions to fit them onto a certain number of pages.

- **DON'T** expect a huge response. And don't rule out making a second request of those who have not replied to a mail survey after three weeks.

- **DON'T** go to the same sample too often. They will lose interest and may become hostile.

Fielding the Questionnaire

If you have handled the first three steps properly, actually fielding (conducting) the survey should be straightforward. However, depending on your particular study, there will be details to oversee. For example, mail questionnaires must be sent on time, and at a time free of predictable distractions, such as after the winter holidays. Telephone interviewers need up-to-date lists of phone numbers. They should also be instructed to schedule a specific time later with any respondent who is busy but will agree to be interviewed at another time.

Be reasonable in your expectations and don't become overly excited or disappointed by the early responses. It's often a good idea to not look at early results very closely (except to ascertain that the surveys are being properly completed).

In this step, your goal is to get the target number of completed surveys (or "completes"). This can take more time and effort than you originally thought.

If glitches occur (okay, *when* they occur), work with the interviewers or others, such as your mailroom or mail house, to resolve them. You may even have to enlarge the sample. As you work to resolve problems, just be sure to project an air of calm confidence. Ultimately, you'll get to your target number of completed surveys.

Analysis and Presentation of Results

I have always found analysis of results to be the most interesting part of any market research project. It's investigative work and it brings out the detective in most of us.

If your study and questionnaire were properly designed—and if the questionnaires were properly completed—you'll have the information that you set out to capture. Now you merely have to make sense of it.

Here are some guidelines:

- **Be as objective as you can.** We all like to believe that we approach research results with an open mind, but most of us would prefer a certain outcome. Be sure you're aware of your biases and those of others on your team, and trust the survey respondents to tell the truth as they see it.

- **Look for patterns in the answers.** The more you see an answer, the more likely it is to be true.

- **Don't be swayed by wildly positive or negative answers to open-end questions.** Especially if they are, uh, colorfully worded, it's easy to latch onto them. Unless they're part of a pattern, they only represent one person's opinion.

- **Consider who is saying what.** Often you must evaluate responses in light of the characteristics of the respondents. If the opinions of newer customers diverge from those of longer-term customers, if those of city dwellers differ from those of suburbanites, if those of your customers in financial services do not match those of industrial clients, that may tell you something.

- **Think back to the goal of the research and evaluate the results in light of that goal.** If the research was done to support a decision—for example, to pursue a new market or change a product—what did the respondents tell the company to do? If the research was done for purely informational purposes—for example, to compile a profile of your clients—what are you hearing? These conclusions will make up your major findings.

- **Given the research results, decide what recommendations you would make.** Most market research (actually, most research of any kind) should produce "actionable results." That is, the results should point to some kind of action the company should take, now that this information has been unearthed.

Various statistical tools beyond the scope of this book are available for analyzing research results. However, provided the base of respondents is large enough for your purposes, simple percentage readings of various responses (that is, the percent that answered this way or that) will tell you what you need to know. Most political poll data reported in newspapers, such as approval ratings and voters' positions on issues, are based on simple percentages.

Use common sense when analyzing market research results. If most respondents say something, and your common sense supports their view, you can safely believe that most of the population represented by that sample feels similarly.

Powerful Presentations Pack a Punch

In presenting the results of market research, you have powerful information to announce: the opinions of customers and prospects. With that kind of ammunition, it's best to let the results—good, bad, or otherwise—speak for themselves to the extent possible.

Here is a general outline for a written report of typical market research results:

- ◆ **Executive summary**—a one- to two-page summary of the study and its goals, findings, and recommendations.

- ◆ **Purpose**—the first section of the body of the report. This should mention the goal and scope of the study and when it was conducted.

- ◆ **Major findings**—how the key questions were answered by the survey respondents.

- ◆ **Secondary findings**—how the less important questions were answered.

- ◆ **Recommendations**—what actions the company should take in light of the findings.

- ◆ **Appendix 1**—methodology of the study, telling how the study was conducted and how the sample was developed, and showing a sample questionnaire.

- ◆ **Appendix 2**—respondents to the survey.

This outline is only an example. An actual report of research results might easily contain more, fewer, or different sections.

Market research represents one of the best foundations for making decisions available to a company. It can also be tailored to very precise needs and conducted on virtually any scale.

Whatever your needs and resources, market research often spells the difference between flying blind and following a clearly lighted course.

The Least You Need to Know

♦ Be clear about the goal of a market research study and gear the survey accordingly.

♦ The five major steps in a market research project are to define the goal, design the study, develop the questionnaire, field the survey, and analyze and present the results.

♦ The quality of the sample often dictates the quality of the research. Unless you are doing "quick and dirty" research as a simple double-check, be sure that your sample is representative of the population.

♦ Avoid the tendency to load up a study with more than one goal or to make the questionnaire too long.

♦ If you see the budget for a market-research project going too high for the value of the information you seek, reduce the number of questions. Or try doing half of the survey first and then do the second half only if it would add useful information.

♦ If you are in a company that doesn't believe in market research, patiently try to sell the idea. Meanwhile, conduct secondary research, which costs relatively little, to learn as much as you can about your markets and customers.

Chapter 19

The Five Ps of Marketing

In This Chapter

- ◆ Understanding the marketing mix
- ◆ Using product, pricing, packaging, place, and promotion properly
- ◆ How to think about product positioning

How do they do it? How do companies like Nike, Absolut, Disney, Honda, Bird's Eye, EverReady, McDonald's, Coca-Cola, and Merrill Lynch sell so much to so many people year in, year out? You might at first say, "They advertise like crazy." But advertising can't do it all. In early 1998 mighty Nike suffered at the hands of competitors, and even McDonald's periodically rethinks its products. No, advertising is just one piece of the marketing mix, and a company has to get most of the pieces right.

The term *marketing mix* refers to the combination of elements that a company uses to market its product. It takes work to combine them to create the best marketing mix for a product. You have to gauge both the market (your prospects and customers) and your competitors properly.

This chapter explains each element in the marketing mix. All five of them can help you gain a competitive advantage, if you know how to use them. Let's learn how.

The Marketing Mix Made Easy

The five Ps of marketing are:

- **Product.** The product or service you are selling. For a new product to succeed, it must be well conceived, well executed, and fill a customer need.

MBA Lingo

In the marketing mix, which is designated by the Five Ps, **product** refers to what the company actually sells. **Price** refers to the money customers must pay for it. **Packaging** refers to what a product comes in and how it is displayed. **Place** refers to where the product or service is sold, and **promotion** includes advertising and promotion.

MBA Lingo

Distribution refers to the ways you get your product into the customer's hands. It can even include the methods of transportation by which you ship your products. In the marketing sense of the term, however, distribution focuses mainly on sales channels. **Sales channels** (also called distribution channels) are the specific means of getting the product to customers. These include retailers, wholesalers, telemarketers, direct-mail campaigns, websites, and so on.

In most companies, marketing and sales play a big role in any decision affecting the company's products. That's because they understand market trends and customer needs, and they know what makes new products or services sell.

- **Price.** After the product itself, price is the key element in the marketing mix. Price affects the rest of the mix and can generate strong responses in customers and competitors. So your pricing strategy is quite important.

While a purely mathematical approach might work in setting your price (for example, you might choose to set your price 10 percent below your nearest competitor or 30 percent above your costs), there really is as much art as science in pricing decisions.

- **Packaging.** A product (particularly a product as opposed to a service) needs a package. A package must protect your product and present it in the best way. Attractive, efficient packaging is so important (and difficult to design) that entire design firms focus exclusively on this area of marketing.

- **Place.** In the marketing mix, place really means *sales channels*, which relate to *distribution*—the specific means through which you get your product to your customers. (But "distribution" begins with the letter D, not P, and these are the Five Ps, not the Five Ds, of marketing.) A product needs the right distribution in order to reach the right customers in the right way.

◆ *Promotion.* Promotion is what most people think of when they hear the word "marketing." Promotion, which includes publicity and advertising, is how you choose to get the word out about your product.

The rest of this chapter examines each of the five Ps in more depth. Put them all together and you have the marketing mix.

Product Is Paramount

There are people who believe that great marketing can overcome a product's flaws. While that does happen, I believe that it's a rare occurrence and almost never works in the long run. Most truly successful products do fulfill their purpose for those who buy them.

You will see how to develop great products in more detail in Chapter 22. For now, here are the characteristics your product must have to succeed in the marketing mix:

◆ Fulfillment of a customer need

◆ Ease of use

◆ Quality in keeping with the price

◆ Product safety

◆ A good "fit" with the rest of your company's business

Now, any of these characteristics—such as ease of use or quality—can be pitched to customers in your marketing messages and sales presentations. However, the way you pitch them can make a real difference. That's because most customers are more interested in *benefits* than *features*.

A product should have features—such as a convenient size, a special technology, or an appealing color—that distinguish it from other products in its category. These features should not be included in your product for the heck of it. (What's the point of producing a pocket-sized waffle iron, for example, if portability isn't a feature anyone wants in waffle irons?)

MBA Lingo

A **feature** is a characteristic of a product—for example, its color, size, power, or something it can do. A **benefit** is what the customer receives because of the product and its features.

MBA Mastery

Try to work with engineering, research and development, product development, and senior management to always improve products in ways that are important to your customers. Ask yourself: Is it really an improvement if nobody will pay extra for it?

Rather, every feature you include in your product must deliver a benefit to the customer. That benefit is what you must focus on when you market and sell your product.

Here's the difference between a feature and a benefit: A feature is a characteristic or quality of your product. A benefit is the way that feature helps your customer.

For example, consider these features and benefits for a sports car:

Feature	Benefit
320-horsepower engine	Enjoy fast cruising and easy passing
No tune-ups for 50,000 miles	Money in your pocket; more time to enjoy your car
Huge 18-inch wheels	You stay upright in your seat on sharp turns
Candy-apple-red exterior	Draw attention and project fun-loving image

Customers care about benefits, not features. A feature that doesn't deliver a benefit is useless from a marketing standpoint.

If you're a marketing pro, you must always think in terms of the customer. If you can make your product smaller, you as a marketer must tell customers what that means to them. Does it make the product easier to hold? Easier to store? More portable? More compatible with something else? If your product is more durable, what should you tell the customer? That he or she will never have to buy another one? That he or she will save money in maintenance cost? Find the benefit, and market it.

Case in Point

Some companies are tempted to develop ways of drawing more money from customers for products that are essentially the same as the previous model or that add only marginal value. For instance, *planned obsolescence* is the tactic of making your product "outdated" (which Microsoft does with each successive operating system it issues) or building it to last for an artificially short time (which U.S. automakers were accused of doing before the Japanese quality challenge of the 1970s).

Deceptive or confusing pricing schemes are another popular way of parting customers from their money without adding value. Many phone companies and banks lead customers on with a low base price (for long-distance minutes or a mortgage), but then add arcane fees and charges that more than make up the difference.

Consistently successful companies put their energy into creating products and services that customers want, and then marketing them aggressively, but honestly. (And yes, Microsoft is consistently successful but was also found to have engaged in anticompetitive business practices.)

Pricing Problems

Pricing mistakes can kill a good product—and even a good company. The first requirement for a "proper" price is that you must be able to make money at the product's *price point*. If the product costs more to make than you are selling it for, there is almost no sense in making it. (I say "almost" because you may be able to use the product as a *loss leader*—that is, a product that does not make a profit, but lures customers to try other products.)

You must be able to sell the product at a competitive price. If your competitors can underprice you on a product of similar quality, how will you get business? Don't rely on your relationships with customers or the skill of your sales force to overcome prices that are above the competition's. There are, however, other ways to justify high prices that deliver the high profits we all crave.

MBA Lingo

Price point means price level or price in relation to the prices of similar products. A **loss leader** is a product on which a manufacturer or, more commonly, a retailer does not make a profit, but carries in order to attract customers.

MBA Lingo

A company engages in **competitive pricing** when it attempts to price its products below the prices for similar products from competitors.

In **cost-plus pricing** a company assesses the total cost of producing the item or of delivering the service that it sells, and then adds on what it believes to be a reasonable profit.

In **value pricing,** a company charges a price that reflects the value of what it is delivering to the customer. This is the alternative to competitive and cost-plus pricing.

If you sell aspirins, competitive pricing says to charge a lower price than competitors, cost-plus says to charge what it cost to make them plus a profit, and value pricing says to charge what the customer will pay to have his headache gone.

Pricing Strategies

There are three basic pricing strategies: competitive pricing, cost-plus pricing, and value pricing. Let's examine each one.

If your product sells at the lowest price of all your competitors, you are practicing *competitive pricing.* Your prices certainly *don't* have to be the lowest in order to succeed in the marketplace. (Just look at the price of a Mercedes.) But low prices are one way to compete effectively.

Sometimes competitive pricing is essential. For instance, in a commodity business—where the products are basically the same no matter who sells them—the outfit with the lowest price will usually succeed. That's because when the products themselves are not differentiated, price becomes the differentiator. Iron ore, coal, lumber, rice, and many other products drawn from the earth are commodities.

Competitive pricing is not just for commodities, however. In retail, portable CD players are not a commodity, but once a customer decides to buy a portable CD player, price will play a big role in which type he or she buys. So competitive pricing is common in retailing. In fact, some retailers offer to beat any other advertised price.

In general, the success of a competitive pricing strategy depends on achieving high volume and low costs.

In *cost-plus pricing*, you look at the cost of what you sell (that is, your costs), then add on the profit you need to make. That's your price. Cost-plus means "cost plus profit."

MBA Alert

Cost-plus pricing can be particularly useful in labor-intensive service businesses such as consulting. However, the costs in these businesses can be more difficult to estimate than those in manufacturing businesses. You can lose money unless you closely figure the labor needed on each project beforehand, add your profit, and keep your costs within the budgeted amount.

So if a stereo equipment retailer buys a Sony Discman for $60 and he needs to make a gross margin of 40 percent, then he has to sell the Discman for $100 (because 100 − 60 = 40 and 40 ÷ 100 = 40%). (There are various other ways to figure out your price using cost-plus pricing, but all are based on clearing a certain level of profit above your costs.)

This method is straightforward and ensures that you will make money on what you sell. Unfortunately, it does not ensure that you will sell it.

The success of this pricing strategy depends on your not being underpriced by a competitor. It also depends on controlling your costs and targeting a "reasonable" profit.

Value pricing is the alternative to basing your prices on your competitors' prices or on your costs. Instead, you base your prices on the value you deliver to customers. In this strategy, you deliver as much value as possible to your customers—and charge them for it. With this strategy, you can charge a high price and justify it by delivering high value.

Value pricing is common in high-technology and luxury items, such as clothing, restaurants, and travel.

Value pricing works well for new, high-tech products. When a new technology either has very high appeal or solves an expensive problem, it has extremely high value. In other words, if customers really want it or need it, they will pay a high price for it.

You will notice that after a technology is established, the price falls. In fact, when a technology (like VCRs or high-definition television or the next wave of personal computers) is released, you hear some people say, "I'm going to wait until the price comes down." In other words, the technology doesn't have enough value to them to warrant the high price. But other customers, who are much less price-sensitive and who need the new technology, will buy it first.

Value pricing in other markets depends on the ability to deliver value and the perception of value. Service is one way to create value. Many outfits justify high prices by servicing their customers like crazy. Another way is to be "the best" in terms of quality, materials, construction, and features. This then delivers benefits such as long life, high performance, and freedom from maintenance.

Often the perception of value can be as important—or more important—than actual product qualities. Value is in the eye of the buyer. Does a Hermes silk scarf really deliver 10 times the value of a $25 silk scarf? Does Johnnie Walker Black deliver three times the value of Passport Scotch? The buyers seem to think so.

This leads to an odd situation in some product categories: The higher the price of your product, the more you sell. This phenomenon is called the Veblen Effect, for the American economist who identified it. The Veblen Effect runs contrary to normal *price theory*, which states that the lower the price of your product, the more you will sell. Veblen saw that some products sold in greater amounts if their price was increased. In other words, high prices can create the perception of value.

Mix Pricing Strategies

In practice, you must consider all three pricing strategies. You have to consider your competitor's prices, even if you're not competing on price. You also have to consider your costs, or your profits will suffer. You must consider the value you deliver because no matter what you sell, customers want value for their money.

There's a dynamic aspect and an element of trial and error inherent in successful pricing. Pricing is dynamic because your products, customers, and competitors often change, and your prices often must change in response. Pricing involves trial and error because your prices affect your sales, income, and growth. So you must monitor the effects of your prices on these measures, and then decide what do to next.

Packaging Presents Your Products

Packaging includes all aspects of the package that holds your product. Your product's package must be practical and promotional. Issues of engineering, design, graphics, distribution, and marketing enter into packaging decisions.

Different products present different packaging challenges. For fragile products, protection during shipment is the key consideration. For retail products, the ability to attract customers in the store is paramount. Many retail products also must vie for overcrowded display space, and packaging can impact the retailer's decision on where to place the product. The cost of packaging is always a consideration, too.

In the past two decades, three new packaging issues have emerged: environmental concerns, safety concerns, and what I call "packaging as product."

Environmental or "green" concerns still drive a relatively small proportion of the U.S. population's purchase decisions. Nonetheless, this proportion appears to be growing, and it tends to place high value on environmentally friendly products. These products are made from or packaged in recyclable or biodegradable materials, or can otherwise claim to be "earth-friendly."

For example, customer reaction to the waste involved in the packaging originally used for musical compact discs—long cardboard boxes—prompted a move to the shrink-wrapped jewel cases.

Safety concerns arose after several product-tampering cases and scares in the 1970s and 1980s. Tamperproof packaging is now standard for many foods and consumer packaged goods. We also now have childproof caps for prescription and over-the-counter medicines. However, this new packaging strategy had an unintended consequence: Elderly people or others whose hands are weak or arthritic often find childproof caps on medicines difficult or impossible to open.

MBA Alert

Surveys in the mid-1990s revealed that far more consumers say they buy only "earth-friendly" products than could be possible given the sales of regular, "nongreen" products. However, consumers who are highly motivated by environmental concerns are known to heavily favor "green" products.

In "packaging as product," the package becomes integral to the product and acts as a differentiator. This can work well in commodity-like product categories. For example, unrefrigerated milk packaged in boxes has found broad acceptance in Europe, although it's been a tougher sell in the U.S. However, juices in boxes have proven quite successful in the states.

At its best, packaging provides physical protection, attractive display, and ease of use, as well as product differentiation and a form of competitive advantage. Like every part of the marketing mix, packaging demands thought and effort.

A Proper Place Produces Profits

Today, there are more places to sell your product than ever before, including:

- **Direct sales force**—salespeople who are employees of the company and sell only the company's products.

- **Wholesalers**—companies that sell the products of other companies to outfits that will resell them. Wholesalers are sometimes called "middlemen" because they are between the maker of the product and the outfit that sells it to the customer. A food wholesaler buys food from the food-processing companies and sells it to the grocery stores.

- **Retailers**—stores that sell to individual and (sometimes, but much less often) business customers. A retail chain is a company that owns more than one location of the same store, such as Macy's or Barnes and Noble.

- **Original equipment manufacturers (OEMs)**—Companies that assemble and sell equipment made from components and products made by other companies. OEMs operate mainly in computers and other high-technology businesses.

- **Independent sales reps**—Salespeople who sell products for a company without being employees of the company and generally work purely on commission.

- **Direct response**—Selling only through the mail or by means of advertisements in magazines or on television or radio that asks customers to mail or phone in their order.

- **Telemarketing**—Involves calling lists of people and selling to them over the telephone.

- **Internet**—Selling over the Internet, or more accurately over the World Wide Web (the graphical interface between the Internet and the user) is relatively new. It involves asking for orders on an "electronic order blank" at the website. To date relatively few products have been sold successfully on the web, with software, books, and travel services among the best sellers.

- **International**—For a business in any country, foreign markets are becoming increasingly important. While exporting can be a complex and costly means of selling, the U.S. Department of Commerce in Washington, D.C., offers businesses lots of free information on how to go about it.

♦ **Joint marketing agreements**—When one company supplies a product for another (usually larger) company to sell.

These are all distribution channels. How many of them you can use depends on your product, pricing, and target markets. But you should try to use all that you profitably can.

Case in Point

As marketers seek to reach customers through a variety of sales channels, the issue of channel management arises. Channel management entails matching the sales channel to your goals and products and minimizing "channel conflict."

For example, a window manufacturer with a line of windows ranging from economy to quality to specialty, employs a variety of sales channels—and brands. The economy model is sold through major chains, such as Home Depot, under one name. The quality model is sold under another name to large contractors by the company's sales force. The specialty (or super-premium) windows—for instance, skylights that change their degree of tint for sunrooms in expensive homes—are sold to architects through distributors and the sales force.

Channel conflict arose in the specialty category when distributors found themselves competing with the company's sales force for sales to certain architects. When distributors complained, the company agreed to pay a commission to any distributor who had called on the architect in the previous 12 months, even if the distributor did not make the sale. The company felt it was worthwhile and fair to pay a distributor a commission even though a company salesperson had made the sale, to keep the distributor happy and reduce channel conflict.

When formulating a distribution strategy, ask yourself:

♦ What am I selling?

♦ Who are my prospects?

♦ Where are they?

♦ How can I reach them?

♦ How does the distribution channel work?

♦ What does it cost to sell through this channel?

♦ How many channels should I use?

Answering these questions will help you choose the right sales channel—however, there may be no single "right" channel. The choice may be which two or three to use (or at least try) and whether to start using them together or one at a time in a certain sequence.

Promotion Boosts Purchases

Defined narrowly, *promotion* means ways of creating awareness or inducing people to buy. Tactics include cents-off coupons, limited-time offers, and special events, such as sponsoring concerts or athletic competitions. *Premiums,* which include standard promotional items such as pens, T-shirts, calendars, and coffee mugs, are another example of a promotion. (I'll discuss premiums more in Chapter 20.)

More broadly, promotion includes these tactics, along with everything you do to tell the market about your product—most importantly, advertising and public relations.

Because most markets are crowded, good promotion can make or break a product. Its importance is underscored by the existence of advertising agencies and public relations firms, which help companies promote their products and themselves.

We will look at advertising, promotion, and public relations more closely in the next chapter.

Proper Positioning Prevents Poor Performance

All the five Ps add up to one final piece of the program—positioning, which refers to the position of the product in relation to others in its category and in the minds of prospects and customers. Positioning is linked to quality and price. In most categories, there are two extremes—high-quality, high-price offerings and low-quality, low-price offerings—and various spots in between.

Please understand: Every company would like to be able to deliver high quality at a low price. Unfortunately, that is just not economically possible. So individual companies have to decide where they want to be. Mercedes decided to produce high-quality cars at a high price. Hyundai decided to produce lower-quality cars at a lower price.

Essentially, positioning hinges on two elements of your business:

- Your target market
- Your operating costs

A target market of lower- or middle-income people with a lower demographic profile dictates different positioning than a higher-income target market.

And, again, you have to be able to make money on the product, which goes back to your costs. If your costs dictate a high price, you cannot position your products as low-price, lower-quality offerings. You will lose money and ultimately fail.

Case in Point

One of the best positioning strategies in business history is that of General Motors. GM maintained five different divisions, with each division geared to a different level of price and quality, from lowest to highest: Chevrolet, Pontiac, Oldsmobile (now defunct), Buick, and Cadillac.

The GM strategy offers a product positioned for each income and status level, and to give customers something to aspire to on their next purchase. Ideally, as a GM customer earns more money, he or she would trade up to the next level of automobile. More recently GM established the Saturn division, to make popularly priced cars sold in a "no haggling" environment, which women find particularly appealing.

Thus, positioning grows out of the strategic choices underlying the entire enterprise: Who are your customers? What business are you in? What are you selling? What are your financial objectives? We examine these decisions more deeply in Chapter 23.

From the marketing standpoint, every element in the mix must establish or reinforce the product's positioning. The product itself, its price and packaging, the places that sell it, and the way it is promoted all play their role in positioning the product.

The Least You Need to Know

- The marketing mix has five elements: product, price, packaging, place, and promotion.

- The best marketing is generally in service of the best products. Marketing can do the best job on products that meet a genuine customer need reliably, effectively, and economically.

- When pricing your products, consider competitors' prices, your costs, and the product's value to customers.

- Packaging must ensure that the product gets to the store or customer in one piece. But it can also help the product competitively.

- Promotion is the essence of marketing.

Chapter 20

You Can Understand Advertising (and That's a Promise!)

In This Chapter

- Developing advertising messages that work
- How to create an advertising budget
- Where should you advertise?

Advertising is everywhere. None of us can escape it, even if we want to—and many of us do. Yet despite criticism, which has been around as long as advertising itself, the volume of ads in any medium continually increases over the long term.

Why?

Because it works. That is, advertising works enough to encourage companies to keep doing it.

This chapter will give you a general overview of what makes advertising work and why so many companies use it in so many different forms. You also learn a bit about public relations, another method of business communication.

What Is Advertising and What Does It Do?

Advertising is a positive message about a product, service, or organization in a communication medium that is paid to carry the message. In any advertisement, the sender of the message is identified. (Note that the sender does not have to be a business. Many nonbusiness outfits, including the military and nonprofit organizations such as the American Heart Association, use advertising, as do individuals, such as political candidates and people selling their cars in the classified ads of a newspaper.)

> **MBA Mastery**
>
> *Advertising Age* and *Adweek* are weekly publications that cover trends and issues in the advertising industry. If you are interested in influencing your company's advertising strategy, they may be worth a look. They're available at large newsstands, by subscription, and at many libraries.

Since the rise of television advertising in the 1950s, critics have said that advertising manipulates people.

The manipulation allegedly takes the form of using constant repetition, overpromising benefits, hiding products' disadvantages, and, in the minds of some critics, even hiding subconscious messages that in effect "hypnotize" people into buying. Other criticism states that advertising uses constant intrusion, bad grammar, and, worst of all, bad taste to appeal to the lowest common denominator. Finally, some people oppose advertising on the grounds that it needlessly raises the price of the products being advertised.

Defenders of advertising point out that consumers realize that advertising is self-serving, so they view it skeptically. Defenders also believe that people's purchase decisions are influenced by many factors besides advertising: recommendations from friends, their own experiences and observations, and elements such as salespeople, service, warranties, financing, and, of course, price. While a lot of advertising deserves criticism, no one has proven that it forces people to buy products.

Advertising's place in the marketing mix is simple: It is part of promotion, the fifth P (as I discussed in Chapter 19). It plays a role in establishing and reinforcing the product's positioning. As a marketing tool, advertising supports the sales force.

Advertising, and any advertising campaign, works with the other elements in the mix to present the product to prospects, along with reasons to buy. Advertising cannot make up for failings in the product or in other parts of the marketing mix.

> ### Case in Point
>
> Over the past several years, direct-to-customer (DTC) advertising of prescription medications has generated controversy. Print and television DTC advertising creates awareness of medications among consumers, who ask their doctors to prescribe them. Until recently, these drugs were advertised only to physicians.
>
> Opponents of DTC advertising contend that it raises the marketing costs and thus the price of medications. They also believe that this advertising prompts consumers to request the newest, most expensive medications. The pharmaceutical companies counter that consumers have a right to know about all available medications and that the more users there are for a given medication, the lower its price becomes (as increased volume spreads development and manufacturing costs over a wider customer base). As usual in such controversies, both parties make valid points.

Components of Advertising

Many questions arise in any advertising decision. The major ones center on

- Message: What should you say in advertisements?
- Money: How much should you spend on advertising?
- Media: Where should you run the advertisements?

Let's examine these one at a time.

Ad Messages: Say What?

Basically, there are three types of advertising messages: creative messages, selling messages, and those that that try to sell creatively.

A creative message tries to capture the audience's attention by standing out from the clutter (advertising overload). Advertisements that rely on humor are good examples of creative messages. So are most MTV-influenced television ads, such as those for Levi's jeans, soft drinks, and some luxury cars.

These approaches are often called image advertising, because they aim to create a mood, a feeling, and an image around the product rather than to sell it on its features, benefits, or competitive merits. Jeans could be sold on their merits. In fact, Levi's once were, showing their durability with a picture of two mules trying to pull the pants apart. Soft drinks and luxury cars could also be sold on features and benefits, and sometimes are. But creative messages tend to ignore standard descriptions of features and benefits, and instead focus on getting attention and generating an attractive product image.

Selling messages are more matter-of-fact in their approach and oriented toward features, benefits, and requests for action ("Buy now and save up to 30 percent on any Black and Decker power tool").

Slice-of-life commercials for detergents, cleaners, head-ache and indigestion remedies, and diet products are good examples of selling messages. You know the kind I mean: A woman suffering from a cold can't get to sleep. She gets out of bed, goes to the medicine cabinet, opens it, and takes some NyQuil. Next, she is sleeping soundly. This is straightforward and, for these kinds of products, effective advertising.

The best advertising aims to combine the factual in-formation of a selling message with the humor or visual appeal of a creative message. This is extremely hard to do. The Energizer Bunny ad campaign was a great example of a creative (and funny) ad that constantly sold the main feature of the battery: long life. People even started referring to their most energetic co-workers or tireless friends as "Energizer bunnies." This kind of advertising is the exception rather than the rule.

> **MBA Lingo**
>
> A **brand** is a company name (Levi's, Chevrolet) or product name (501 jeans, Corvette), together with its logo (that is, a distinctive graphic associated with the name) and any other identifiers, which can even include the shape of a bottle (as for Perrier water).

Most advertisers want either image-oriented ads that create an ambiance of luxury or "hipness," or reality-based pitches that tout a benefit ("Get better checkups with Crest") or incite customers to action ("Only three days left in the Toyota sell-a-thon"). At the same time, a major goal of almost all advertising is to establish or reinforce a *brand*.

Hot Copy

The kind of message you use depends on your product, its positioning, the audience, and the medium you are using. So does the content of your message. Various guidelines developed over the years offer hints on developing *ad copy*. Two of the most famous, which I find useful, are the AIDA formula and the Unique Selling Proposition.

The AIDA formula helps you remember the four key things that good copy must do: get **A**ttention, capture **I**nterest, create **D**esire, and request **A**ction. Let's briefly examine each of these goals:

◆ Getting *attention* is essential because people are busy, clutter is everywhere, and you can't sell to people until you have their focus. Humor, color, movement, design, offbeat situations, and astonishingly attractive models are major tools for getting attention.

◆ After the audience notices the ad, you have to get them *interested* in it. Copy that starts with a provocative question ("Can you afford to die?") or statement ("Don't throw money away") are trusty tactics. Others include dramatizing a problem, offering an escape, or using a celebrity endorsement—which can also get attention.

◆ A good ad must create *desire* for the product. Appeal to the heart, the head, the stomach, the wallet, the whatever. Tell customers about the money they'll save, the fun they'll have, or the affection they'll win with your product. Show the luscious turkey, the happy family, the headache-free worker, the beautiful lawn—whatever your product or service offers. Make them want it.

> **MBA Lingo**
>
> **Copy** narrowly refers to the text in a print ad or the words read by an announcer. More broadly, it means the total ad as presented to the audience. This includes not only the text, but the color, graphics, photos, video, and so on. Copy strategy refers to all the choices that you have to make in developing an ad.

◆ Then you ask for *action*. Tell your customers what they have to do to quench this flaming desire you have created. Sample actions you can suggest: "Call now." "For a limited time only." "Send no money." (No money??) "Operators are standing by." "Be the first on your block." "Saturday only." "Don't let this once-in-a-lifetime opportunity slip through your fingers."

Another excellent concept for developing a message—or a theme for an entire campaign—is the Unique Selling Proposition (or USP). The USP is, as the name indicates, the unique thing about your product or service that provides a motivation for people to buy it.

This can be something real, such as Federal Express's "Guaranteed overnight delivery," or something made up, such as "Wonder Bread builds strong bodies 12 ways." (I say this is made up because no one in the target audience can name even 3 of the 12 ways—and that doesn't matter.)

A really great USP is not just a memorable tag line, like Sprite's "Obey your thirst." Instead, it's something unique about the product that provides motivation to buy. The

USP can begin in the product-development process. "Guaranteed overnight delivery" is a feature, benefit, product, and selling proposition—all in one. And when FedEx started, it was unique.

If you can't create a USP around a wonderful and intrinsic feature of your product, you have to come up with something almost as good. "You deserve a break today" is great because it reminds people who are too tired and overworked to cook that there's a fast way to get a tasty meal. It's not in itself unique—any fast-food outfit can make that claim—but through advertising it became unique because it was McDonald's message.

Money: Your Advertising Budget

The advertising budget is part of the marketing budget. It's the amount the company will spend on paid messages in the media. This will include any ad agency fees as well as money spent on the media itself. If your account is large enough, the advertising agency works for 15 percent of the bill for *media buys*. If not, the agency bills you directly for its services.

The advertising budget can include the direct-mail budget, since technically direct mail is an advertising medium.

There are several ways of setting your advertising budget. One easy way is just to set the amount of the ad budget as some percentage of sales. If you do well spending 5 percent of total sales on advertising, do that. Or move it higher. Or lower. This method has the advantage of tying this cost to revenues, but it does little else.

Other approaches are to just pick a number (yes, this is done), or to spend the industry average, or to spend a bit above or below the industry average. Many advertisers fall into habits, believing that since they've always advertised in certain media, they should continue to do so. Habit is a bad way to budget.

> **MBA Lingo**
>
> A **media buy** is the purchase of space (in print media) or time (in broadcast media) for running your advertisement.

> **MBA Mastery**
>
> If you are shopping for advertising or are curious about a particular media's demographics and audience, call and ask for a rate card, which details the prices for various ads. Most media sales departments can also send you a media kit that provides even more information, including demographics.

There is a more thoughtful approach: Decide what you want to achieve, then see how much you must spend on advertising to get there. This could result in your spending either more or less than you did as a percent of sales last year or compared with the industry average. However, it ties the expenditures to what you're trying to accomplish. You may not have the money to do all you would like to do. But at least you can then back off the "ideal" number and spend where you believe it will do the most good.

Please understand, however, that there's an element of risk in advertising expenditures. Advertising is an inexact medium in that there is no message that is guaranteed to work and the correlation between expenditures can vary. There is also the issue of luck. A massive distraction, such as a natural disaster, snowstorm, or major trial on television can distract people or even keep them from buying. For instance, warm winters hurt ski resorts even though they can make snow and usually have temperatures cold enough to ski. It is just that people don't think about skiing as much during a warm winter.

If you've hired an advertising agency to handle your advertising budget, a media planner in the agency will determine the best use of your money. He or she will calculate the cost per thousand—that is, the cost of reaching 1,000 people—for the media being considered. Cost per thousand (or CPM) places the costs of various media on an equal basis.

Cost per thousand enables you to compare the costs of media that deliver different-size audiences at different prices. Be careful, however. A low CPM is of no value unless the audience being delivered is *your* audience.

Media: Who's Watching?

As you develop your advertising message, you have to consider which media you will use to deliver that message to your target audience. The major media you have to choose from are print and broadcast. More specifically, they include

- Magazines
- Newspapers
- Broadcast television
- Cable television
- Radio

MBA Lingo

Awareness is a major goal in advertising. On one level, it means that people know your product exists. On another, it means they think of your product when making a purchase. (This is called top-of-mind awareness.) On another, very specific level, awareness means that people recall seeing your ad. Market research can measure these kinds of awareness.

Other media include

- Direct mail
- Outdoor advertising (billboards, posters)
- Internet

Different media have varying potential for displaying your product, explaining its uses, and dramatizing the satisfaction customers will get from it. Some products, such as exercise machines, benefit from live demonstration, which television provides. Others, such as mutual funds, benefit from printed charts and graphs, and newspapers and magazines work well for that. Still others benefit from a quick reminder to customers that you're always available. A billboard can generate that kind of *awareness*.

Before you choose the media in which to run your ad, you have to decide what you're trying to do with your ad. Are you demonstrating? Dramatizing? Explaining? Displaying? Motivating an immediate purchase? Then you must consider the media's ability to help you do that.

Consider the Demographics

The demographics of a medium are the demographics of the audience that the medium delivers to the advertiser. (I covered demographics in Chapter 18.) The desirability of a medium's demographics depends on your target market or markets. In other words, it depends on what you are selling and to whom you are selling it.

It's no coincidence that you'll find rock 'n' roll CDs advertised in *Rolling Stone* and investment CDs in *Money*. Movies are advertised during television shows for 18- to 34-year-olds because they are the most frequent moviegoers. Products for babies and the elderly are advertised during soap operas because mothers with young children and housebound elderly people tend to watch those shows. (In fact, soap operas got their name because detergents were originally the most heavily advertised products on daytime dramas.)

These examples may lead you to believe that choosing the right media for your target market is a no-brainer. It often isn't. First, there's the issue of cost: Getting your ad in a major national magazine or during prime-time TV can be expensive. Second, the psychographics (see Chapter 18) can be impossible to determine. Third, there's the chance that your target audience will not even see the ad due to clutter (too many ads competing for attention) or "channel surfing."

Case in Point

As a new medium, the World Wide Web is carving out a role among the "old media" of print (magazines and newspapers), television, radio, and outdoor platforms (billboards and posters). But as of this writing, marketers are questioning the effectiveness of web-based advertising. This is to be expected, given the number of dot-com failures in recent years and the recession-related downturn in ad spending.

Measures of web-based advertising's reach, frequency, and impact are being developed because metrics such as hits and click-throughs have proven inadequate. Moreover, most users ignore banner ads and see pop-up ads as intrusive (or infuriating). Yet readers ignore magazine ads and hate television commercials, too.

As a new medium, the web is still evolving, and so is its role in marketing. The novelty has worn off for most users, who now turn to the web for information more than entertainment. Given this, marketers must carefully tailor their messages and offers to fit their product and audience. For instance, compare several sites for prescription medications and universities with those for resorts and music CDs to see how information-rich sites (for the medications and schools) differ from those geared more toward "straight selling."

Other Media Characteristics

When deciding where to place your ad, you must also consider some other—somewhat technical—media characteristics, specifically

◆ **Reach** is an inexact number that attempts to quantify how many people or households have been exposed once to a single ad. Reach calculates the number of people using the media (that is, the number who read a publication, watch a particular television show, or listen to a particular radio station at a certain time of day) when the ad ran in that media. Reach tells you the number of people who were *potentially* exposed to the ad, not the number who actually saw it or can recall it.

◆ **Frequency** is the number of times these people will see or hear the advertisement. There's a way to measure frequency. Let's say a monthly magazine has 500,000 readers. Let's say that in a month, 200,000 will see the ad once, 200,000 will see the ad twice, and 100,000 will see it three times. The ad's frequency would equal 1.8, as calculated below:

$$(200{,}000 \times 1) + (200{,}000 \times 2) + (100{,}000 \times 3) = 900{,}000 \div 500{,}000 = 1.8$$

This number, which is more precise than the value for reach or measures of impact, can be compared with the frequencies of other media to evaluate them as potential advertising venues. In general, the higher the frequency, the better.

◆ **Impact** determines whether the advertisement is remembered and communicates what it's supposed to. Ultimately, impact should be evident in increased sales. However, the connection between advertising and sales can be fuzzy since factors other than advertising, including the competition and even social trends, can affect sales. Impact can be assessed by market research designed to measure ad recall and even purchase behavior after recall.

Before choosing the correct media for your ad campaign, you must compare media on reach, frequency, and impact as well as on cost and demographics. Then choose. After that, await the market's response.

Promotional Tools

Promotional items have their place: You've probably got several corporate coffee mugs in your cabinet, or T-shirts and tote bags emblazoned with company logos in your closet. These and similar *premiums* carrying the name of your company or product should be part of an advertising or marketing campaign—but just a part.

Other tools of promotion include

◆ Discounts

◆ Coupons

◆ Incentives and rebates

◆ Free samples and demonstration models

◆ Contests

◆ Special events

MBA Lingo

A **premium** is a token item such as a coffee mug or tote bag that features the company name and logo. Premiums are given away either free or with a purchase. The goal of a free premium is to get your company name out there.

Briefly, discounts, coupons, incentives, and rebates all have one goal: to get people to buy your product. A discount, coupon, or rebate reduces the price, usually for a limited time. Technically, incentives are any inducement to buy, but more narrowly include items such as optional features, related products, or special services offered for a limited time.

Free samples can be very effective with consumer packaged goods such as cereals, snack foods, mouthwash, and candy. Demonstration models (demos), such as a test drive for a car or a "demo disc" for a video game, let people try a product when free samples are impossible.

Contests work in three ways: First, they attract attention and associate your product with an exciting experience. (A chance to win concert tickets if you buy a CD is one example.) Second, those who enter the contest become more bonded with your product by having taken the trouble to enter. Third, by collecting entry forms, you are getting the names of potential prospects.

Sponsoring special events can take many forms. These include sporting events or teams, racing cars, marathons, or parts of an event (such as the Miller Half-Time Report for NBA games) or even the stadiums themselves (such as the Fleet Center in Boston, sponsored by Fleet Financial Services). These are not incentives to buy, but rather a means of advertising and associating the product or company and the event in the minds of the target market.

Of course, these promotional tools should reinforce one another and your advertising. For instance, a promotional tie-in with a movie combines premium items (figures of the characters), a special event (the release of the movie), and advertising (for the movie and the promotional item).

Public Relations Programs

Public relations (PR), broadly defined, includes nonadvertising communications aimed at the company's existing and potential customers and shareholders, and at the general public. In many businesses, especially consulting, financial services, and health care, PR aims to establish the company's people as experts whom the media can call for interviews. These spokespeople boost the name recognition of the organization and represent the interests of the company and its industry to the public.

More narrowly, public relations focuses on developing article ideas for editors of print media and ideas for segments for producers of broadcast and cable media. These should, of course, place the company, its products, and its people in a positive light.

Public relations services also include writing speeches and press releases. Another key service is assisting executives in dealing with reporters and interviewers, especially in times of a company crisis.

Depending on your industry, good PR can be more powerful than advertising. People realize that an advertisement is a paid announcement intended to sell. But a positive story about your company or its people or products is generally viewed as fact, and therefore builds credibility in a way that is close to impossible with advertising.

Case in Point

In the early 1980s, a public panic ensued when poison was found in some Tylenol capsules. This could have led to a full-fledged public relations nightmare, but Johnson & Johnson, the manufacturer of Tylenol, acted instantly. First, the company immediately pulled all existing product off the shelves. Then the CEO quickly addressed the media to discuss the manufacturing process, the investigation of how the poison got there, and the development of tamperproof packaging. The company also explained the situation in newspaper ads.

Johnson & Johnson's open, intelligent approach to this crisis is widely credited with earning back the public's trust in the product and regaining Tylenol's sales.

On the other hand, in August 2000, the U.S. government began investigating deaths related to Ford Explorers and Firestone tires. Firestone recalled over 6.5 million tires, about two thirds of which were on Ford SUVs and trucks. Initially, the companies supported one another in their public communications. Yet before the month was over, Ford released documents showing that Firestone had received complaints about tires in 1997. Firestone, of course, became defensive and cited problems with Ford's SUVs. Congressional hearings worsened the strain, and both companies wound up publicly brawling and blaming one another, to the detriment of both their images.

The Least You Need to Know

◆ Advertising is a paid-for, positive message in a communication medium. The sender of the message is identified. Advertising doesn't force anyone to buy a product, although getting people to buy is its ultimate goal.

◆ The best way to set the advertising budget is to decide what you want to achieve, then see how much you must spend on advertising to achieve it, and then look to your costs and your competition to reach a final figure.

◆ Ad copy must get attention, capture interest, create desire, and request action.

◆ Advertising media can be viewed in terms of reach, frequency, and impact. These three measures, plus cost per thousand and demographics, enable you to use similar measures to compare different media.

◆ Various promotional tools can reinforce advertising and help prompt people to buy. Public relations can build credibility in a way that advertising cannot, and good PR is essential during a company crisis.

Chapter 21

Selling to Customers and Keeping Them Happy

In This Chapter

- ◆ The critical mission of the sales force
- ◆ How the sales process really works
- ◆ Creating customer service that shines

Salespeople play several crucial roles in a company. First, they are the primary source of revenue. Star salespeople are often called "rainmakers." In traditional cultures, a rainmaker could conjure the clouds to produce rain to grow the crops and put food on the table. Salespeople put food on the table for a company. They bring in the money.

Second, salespeople are the link between the company and its customers. On the one hand, prospects and customers know the company mainly through its salespeople. On the other hand, the company knows its customers mainly through its salespeople.

Finally, the sales force represents the company's frontline offense and defense. They are the foot soldiers in any business. They are directly exposed to the pressures of finding prospects, solving problems, making deals, handling complaints, and beating competitors.

Given these critical roles, a company must do all it can to develop and support the best possible sales force. This chapter will show you how to do that.

Types of Sales

Sales can be characterized in several ways, which I'll discuss over the following pages. Here are a few:

♦ Order taking occurs at a movie theater or sporting event. The customer asks for a ticket and the vendor sells one. It occurs when a delivery person (for example, fora brewery or bakery) takes the order for the next delivery from a restaurant or store. In order taking, the customer either approaches the company or is purchasing a steady stream of product on a schedule.

♦ Active selling, on the other hand, involves prospecting, presentation, problem solving, and persuasion. In active selling—the focus of this chapter—the salesperson approaches the customer, and to some degree the customer resists purchasing. Thus, active selling involves overcoming *sales resistance.*

You'll sometimes hear a salesperson mocked as an "order taker." This means that the salesperson is supposed to be actively selling, but isn't. Instead he or she is getting by on current accounts, going for easy sales, and avoiding the hard work of prospecting and persuasion.

MBA Mastery

Sales resistance takes various forms, including delay, evasiveness, indecisiveness, budgetary excuses, and simple reluctance, plus, in commercial sales, bureaucracy.

♦ Inside sales refers to selling done mainly by telephone. This may include telemarketing, but also allows for situations in which the customer comes to the salesperson's place of business. Inside sales usually does not mean retail sales, which is yet another type of selling.

♦ Outside sales involves going to the customer, and starts with getting appointments to meet with businesspeople or to see consumers in their homes.

The Sales Process

The sales force has two goals: selling to current customers and finding new ones. Every company and salesperson must strike a balance between the two, but let's focus on winning new customers because it includes all three parts of the sales process:

◆ Prospecting

◆ Problem solving and presenting the product

◆ Persuading

I'll explain these steps in the following pages.

Prospecting: On the Hunt

Prospecting involves finding people to sell to, and there are various ways of doing this. *Cold calling* means picking up the phone and calling people that you don't know for appointments (or trying to sell products to them on the phone).

> **MBA Lingo**
>
> **Prospecting** is the act of finding prospects for the product or service you sell. A **cold call** is a telephone call or (much less often) a visit to someone who does not know you. A **lead** is the name of a person who has been identified as a prospect. A **referral** occurs when a current customer refers the salesperson to a friend or acquaintance who may be interested in the product.

Most salespeople have a strong preference for cold calling *leads* or *referrals*—people who have already been identified as prospective customers. Leads are identified in various ways by salespeople, their assistants, or the marketing department. Public records at courthouses (for example, for recent home purchases) are one source. The newspapers are another (for example, for people recently promoted). Many companies generate leads through advertising, and of course through inquiries coming in by telephone or mail. (For example, frequently targeted leads involve new businesses or people who recently bought a home, got married, or had a child.) In those cases it is still a cold call, since the salesperson doesn't know the person he's calling. But, as with the weather, there are degrees of coldness.

After making contact, the salesperson must qualify the prospect early in the sales process. This means somehow getting the answer to two questions:

1. Does the prospect have a need for or an interest in the product or service?

2. Does the prospect have the money and, in commercial sales, the authority to buy the product?

If the prospect doesn't meet these two criteria, most salespeople move on to the next prospect. But there's a judgment call here: Will the prospect qualify at some later point?

For example, you may not need a new car now. Maybe you can't afford one. Maybe you just bought one. But next month, if you get a raise or total your car, you may be in the market for one. So most salespeople keep a file of active prospects—people who may buy in the future—and contact them regularly.

Problem Solving and Presenting: Show and Ask

Assuming a prospect qualifies, the salesperson will then move to problem solving and presenting the product. The salesperson must explore the customer's problems—the ones that relate to the product, that is—and show how the product or service will solve these problems.

Customers buy solutions rather than a product or service. For this reason, the best professionals in both consumer and industrial sales frame much of their sales presentation in terms of questions.

Let's take an example of a salesperson selling a desktop-publishing system to a business account. Useful questions to pose in the sales presentation might include

- What volume of desktop publishing do you do in your shop?
- What system are you currently using?
- How are the original documents created (for example, in WordPerfect or Microsoft Word)?
- What problems do you encounter most often?
- How much training do new people need on the system?
- What complaints do you hear most often about your current system?
- Do you have a maintenance contract for the system? What are the key terms of the contract?
- Which features of your current system do you like best?
- How does this system perform during crunch times?
- Would you be interested in a system that can reduce your costs and manpower requirements while delivering better quality in less time?

And so on. Questions like these work as well for a lawn-care service or personal trainer as they do for a computer networking or advertising firm. With the answers to these questions, the salesperson can finish the job that marketing began—proper positioning of the product.

Persuasion: Overcoming Objections

Most people think of persuasion when they think of selling. But today the *hard sell* (use of high-pressure sales tactics) turns off many prospects. This is not to say that it is not used or that it doesn't work. It is, and sometimes it does. But it produces a lot of wear and tear on salespeople and customers.

However, persuasion is often necessary to close a sale. The professional approach is to use questions to lead the prospect to a logical conclusion: I should buy, now. These questions center on the problem, the product, and the solution. As the salesperson forges these links—a process called "tying down" issues such as cost, operating requirements, and installation—he or she uses questions to keep the prospect involved and moving toward the close.

But logic is not the only tool. Good salespeople appeal to the emotions as well as to reason. Motivators such as being up-to-date, doing the smart thing, joining a select group of companies, and so on can be just as important as the cost-benefit analysis.

MBA Lingo

The **hard sell** employs high-pressure sales to close sales. This pressure can include large discounts (often on inflated prices) for acting now, aggressive questioning of resistant prospects ("Can't you make a simple decision?"), and even wearing down the prospect by not leaving his or her premises.

Case in Point

You'll see a startling array of personality types and selling tactics in sales. I've known salespeople who've told customers that they need this sale—or they'll lose their jobs. One guy I knew would pull out a photo of his three kids and tell the prospect they needed shoes.

I've known salespeople who literally wouldn't leave a prospect's office without a signed contract. Others would directly question the sanity of resistant prospects.

But I've also known great sales pros. Several even told me their product was not really for me, given my needs. Others fought their companies to get me a better deal, faster delivery, or higher quality. These people win business—and referrals.

A sales force, like any other department or resource, must be actively managed. This means the salespeople must be properly organized, motivated, compensated, and supported. Let's examine these issues in more detail.

Organizing a Sales Force

The two major issues in organizing a sales force are

◆ Size of the sales force

◆ Alignment of the sales force

Let's look at both.

Sales-Force Size: When Is Bigger Better?

Remember the law of diminishing returns? It says that more of a good thing is good, but only up to a point—the point of diminishing returns. So one way to get the right-size sales force is to add salespeople until the last one does not produce more in sales than he or she earns. In other words, add salespeople as long as they profitably add sales. This is actually one sensible method of sizing the sales force.

There is, however, another consideration: the proper workload.

The average salesperson's workload should also guide decisions about the size of the sales force. You have to think about this carefully, because sometimes small accounts require more sales effort than large ones. Large accounts are often large because they routinely place an order every month.

The sales force has to be large enough so that each prospect and customer receives adequate *coverage* (communication and attention). Management, even the sales manager, can quickly lose track of how well accounts are being serviced, especially if the poor coverage is masked by growing sales. Poor coverage is an open invitation to competitors.

> **MBA Lingo**
>
> **Coverage** means regular sales calls and other forms of communication, and enough service to keep the account from ever feeling neglected.

To judge the workload properly, the sales manager must carefully analyze how many tasks the salesperson must complete to cover his or her accounts, prospect properly, and solve the inevitable problems that arise every week or month. Then the manager must examine the number of working hours in the week or month, and adjust the number of salespeople accordingly.

Sales-Force Alignment: Three Choices

The alignment of the sales force refers to the way in which the sales force is organized in relation to who and what it is selling. There are three ways of aligning the sales force:

◆ **Alignment by territory** divides the company's market into geographical areas. For a regional company, this might mean by cities. For a national company, it might mean by states. An international company may divide its markets by countries.

However it's done, alignment by territory has the advantage of simplicity. A salesperson or sales team sells all the company's products to consumers or companies in their territory. The disadvantage is that a company with lots of product lines may find that *product knowledge* suffers. The next type of organization addresses that issue.

◆ **Alignment by product** means that each salesperson or sales team specializes in a product or product line. For example, an office-supply company might have one sales group for computers and related equipment, another for general office equipment, and another for furniture and fixtures.

> **MBA Lingo**
>
> **Product knowledge** includes everything the salesperson has to know about the product. First-rate salespeople can answer virtually every question about the product they sell: its construction, use, installation, and maintenance. They will also know how their product differs from competitive products. In some businesses, especially high tech, this is too much to ask of a salesperson, so the salesperson teams with a technician who has complete product knowledge.

The advantage of this arrangement is that each salesperson offers deep product knowledge and total coverage of each customer. The disadvantages are a potentially too-large sales force and numerous salespeople calling on the same customer.

The best way to handle this may be to have an overall account manager who then calls in a product manager or a brand manager for a particular product line.

◆ **Alignment by customers** calls for coverage of certain types of customers by certain salespeople. Alignment by the customer's industry is quite common. Many commercial banks have account teams for specific industries, such as consumer-packaged goods, telecommunications, high technology, and so on. This reflects the customers desire for account managers who "understand my business."

Customer characteristics other than industry can also be used: a common one is size. Many banks have special account reps for "high-net-worth individuals" in their retail (that is, consumer) divisions. In commercial sales, various levels of sales volume will move an account to a different sales team. And many companies have national account reps who sell to corporate customers with nationwide operations.

Companies often use more than one of these methods of aligning their sales forces. A company can even combine all three methods, having sales teams for different product lines covering different-size customers by geographical territory. The idea is to get the best alignment for both the company and the customer.

Compensating and Motivating Your Sales Force

We look at the issues of compensating and motivating salespeople together because most salespeople are heavily motivated by money. Their compensation has to reflect this.

Salespeople can be compensated by straight commission, straight salary, or salary plus commission.

- ◆ Salespeople on straight commission are paid a percentage of the amount of each sale they make. They are paid only their commission. They get no salary, although they may receive a draw (advance against future sales), or benefits, or both.

- ◆ Salespeople on straight salary receive a salary, but no additional commission based on sales.

- ◆ Salespeople on salary plus commission get paid a base salary (also called the "base") plus some percentage of the sale.

Benefits as well as bonuses can be added to any of these compensation systems as well.

Commission plans are often structured so that the salesperson makes a certain percentage on the first, say, $100,000 of business he or she sells, then a higher percentage on the next $100,000, and then an even higher percentage on sales above that.

The big advantage of a commission plan—particularly straight commission—is that it ties pay directly to performance. It also ties sales costs to sales. What's more, commissions can be tweaked in various ways to focus the sales force on particular goals. For instance, many firms pay a higher commission on new business than on repeat business. Some outfits pay higher rates on sales of new products.

There are also disadvantages to commission compensation. First, these systems can be complex and costly to administer. Second, some salespeople get so focused on selling that they resent anything that cuts into selling time and any initiative they see as "fiddling with their income." Third, if sales decrease (which may or may not be their fault), they may become depressed or desperate when their incomes dwindle. Finally, while most people are honest, there is greater temptation to abuse a commission system.

Case in Point

When their incomes depend on how much they sell, some people resort to an aggressive hard sell that can alienate customers. Salespeople may also be more prone to dishonestly report sales in ways that generate higher commissions. One way this is done is to report sales they'll make in January as December sales to pump up the current year's revenue.

It gets worse. Sales teams have moved business around among salespeople to manipulate commissions, and then shared the artificially high payments. There are also illegal "kickbacks"—bribes paid by dishonest salespeople to dishonest customers out of their commissions.

Straight salary is easy to administer and not prone to abuse, but most salespeople do not find it very motivating. Most companies shoot for the best of both worlds: a base salary plus a commission on sales.

Surveys have shown that money is the biggest motivator for most salespeople. There are, however, other ways of motivating salespeople, some of which relate to money, some of which do not.

Sales quotas (the amount of revenue an individual salesperson or team is budgeted to bring in) tend to work, provided they are neither too high nor too low. They work because financial rewards such as higher commissions and most bonuses are tied to quotas. If they're too high, they frustrate and anger the salesperson. If they're too low, the company will overpay for the amount of sales it gets. That's because commissions are usually based on the salesperson making his quota and then exceeding it by various amounts. Quotas have another built-in advantage: You can terminate salespeople who consistently fail to meet their quotas.

MBA Mastery

A good portion (say, 30 to 50 percent) of a salesperson's salary should be in commissions or bonuses. This is critical for small firms, which really can't afford to pay nonproducers.

Sales meetings, particularly off-site meetings that include golf, tennis, and banquets (and, yes, cocktails) are popular with salespeople and build camaraderie (to put it mildly).

Sales contests work for many companies, even companies that think they might be "too sophisticated" for them. The winners usually must beat their quotas significantly and are ranked by performance for the grand prize—usually a vacation at a nice resort on company time or a cash payment—and subsidiary prizes. Structuring these contests takes skill. For example, there can be monthly winners and various ways of qualifying for the grand prize in order to keep the sales force pumped up for the entire year.

Some relatively inexpensive (and less impressive) motivators include plaques, awards, membership in the "CEO's Roundtable," and so on. Access to senior management in meetings or special luncheons and inclusion on special task forces are useful, inexpensive rewards that are generally underused.

Finally, the opportunity for advancement can be a powerful motivator. But watch out. Many a first-rate salesperson has found managing others, not to mention meetings and paperwork, boring and worse than what he or she was doing before. I've heard a few salespeople promoted to sales manager or product manager yell, "Give me a bag and put me back on the road!" after two months.

Supporting a Sales Force

Salespeople are "out there," exposed, competing, and facing daily rejection. To do their job, they need the best support a company can give them.

This support starts with the best products, service, and marketing that the company can deliver. The products have to be the best in their class and price range. The service has to have one goal: total customer satisfaction. The marketing has to be connected with the real world of customers and their problems and buying motives.

Support also means a sensible and (key point) consistent credit policy and good credit management. Having a salesperson break his or her neck to make a sale only to have it killed by the credit department makes no sense. It helps if the credit policy is predictable and if salespeople can get an early reading on a prospect's creditworthiness, with a call to the credit department, for example.

Support includes good management. Unfortunately, some sales managers believe fear and threats are motivational. Maybe firing the three lowest producers is a good idea, but doing it publicly is not. Salespeople, like everyone, need trust and the authority to make decisions. And more than most people, they need minimal paperwork and bureaucracy and the freedom to manage their own time.

Finally, rapid resolution of customer complaints about quality, defects, and delivery is essential. That's where a good customer service department comes in handy.

Customer Service

Many companies of all types have customer service departments separate from the sales function. They usually report to sales or to marketing (the best ones work closely with sales). They deal mainly with customers—people who have purchased the company's products—but some also answer inquiries from prospects.

Customer service has two goals: to keep customers happy (or make them happy if they aren't) and to do it without burdening the salespeople.

That second function is essential. Everyone in a company wants the customer to be happy, especially the salespeople. But the time that salespeople must spend resolving disputes, answering routine questions, and fielding requests for price lists and product literature erodes selling time.

So customer service should be staffed with individuals who have people skills (including patience), product knowledge, and an understanding of what can be done operationally, procedurally, and legally to resolve customer complaints.

Customer service can be a great training ground for future salespeople. In fact, if they develop leads that later become customers, they should get some kind of compensation or recognition. It's a small price to pay to someone with the sales orientation that keeps a company growing.

MBA Mastery

Be sure to give your customer service people the authority they need to resolve problems. Customers find it extremely irritating to deal with people who can't help them. Some companies get customer service right, while others seem to use it as an obstacle to service. Hire good people for this function and let them do their jobs. Dissatisfied customers can hurt your company far worse than competitors.

A Few Words on Sales Training

Too often new salespeople are given a bunch of product literature to read, taken on a couple of sales calls, and then given a desk, phone, and phone book. Some outfits view salespeople as cannon fodder and hire ten for every one they figure will make the grade.

Smart companies take a different approach. They do their best to hire smart. When they seek experienced people, they take the time to locate good performers who will fit in well. When they seek entry-level people, they hire just as carefully and train them in sales. They also train everyone, new or seasoned, in the company's products and procedures.

General sales training can be valuable, and any good-size city has firms that provide it. But I believe that the training will help only those people who have that special motivation that real salespeople have: They are competitors. When they sell, they win—and they hate to lose. More than being outgoing or gregarious or "a people person," that motivation, plus an interest in solving customers' problems, make a true salesperson.

The Least You Need to Know

- Salespeople are a company's source of revenue, link to customers, and frontline offense and defense. They find prospects, solve problems, make deals, handle complaints, and fight competitors, so they need lots of support.

- The major parts of the sales process are prospecting, problem solving and presenting the product, and persuading prospects to purchase.

- When figuring the best size for a sales force, consider the added sales of each additional salesperson as well as workload per salesperson. A sales force can be aligned by territories, products, or customers—or all three.

- In most businesses, salary plus commission is the best way to compensate salespeople.

- A customer service department can make life easier for salespeople while perhaps delivering better service than a busy salesperson might. It can also generate leads and be a training ground for future salespeople.

Chapter 22

Product Development: Pioneers at Work

In This Chapter

- ◆ How to develop successful products—and quickly kill the duds
- ◆ Where to get ideas for great new products
- ◆ Why new products are the key to growth

As I'm sure you've noticed, in our economy new products are introduced with amazing frequency. At times it seems that if a product isn't new or improved—or new *and* improved—then it isn't worth selling. This focus on new products is driven by market demand, competitive concerns, and our ability to improve products with better technology.

New products are the lifeblood of many companies. Remember that aside from raising prices, you have only four ways to increase sales, and two of them involve new products: You can sell new products to current customers or new products to new customers. The other two ways involve existing products.

In most companies, the marketing department plays a key role in new-product development. This chapter examines that role and shows you how to develop successful new products.

The Value of Cross-Functional Teams

Until fairly recently, product development was done by various departments within an organization that did not work closely together.

Marketing might dream up a product concept, then throw the idea to the design people, who would design the product, and then throw it to the engineers. The engineers would make a *prototype* (sample model). Production could then manufacture it. Then the salespeople could start selling. This process was not only time-consuming, but often created products that nobody would buy.

> **MBA Lingo**
>
> A **prototype** is a model of how a product looks. A working prototype also shows how the product would work, although it might not include every function.

Today, managers recognize that development is best accomplished with a *cross-functional* approach. A cross-functional team (which you learned about in Chapter 5) includes someone from every department that will deal with the product. That way each department has input at each stage of development. This helps the company minimize problems and secure support for the new product at each step.

The Product-Development Process

Managers have a process for product development. There are six steps in the process:

1. Idea generation
2. Concept testing
3. Prototype and product design
4. Product testing
5. Market testing
6. Product launch

Each step plays an important role in the process: You can kill a product that isn't succeeding at any time. Therefore you don't start this process with the fixed goal of seeing it through. Rather, you view each step as a hurdle that the product must get over in order to get to the next step. There's no point launching a product that can't make it through the previous steps.

Let's examine each of these steps in turn.

Step One: Get a Good Idea

Product ideas come from a variety of sources. The best source is the marketplace. The market never stops generating product ideas because that is where the problems are, and the best products are the ones that solve problems.

Listen to Your Customers

To get product ideas, listen to your customers. Welcome their complaints; they can point the way to new products.

Also, market research should periodically seek the answers to questions like these:

- What do customers want to see the product do?

- How do customers use the product?

- How does the product fit into their operation?

- What problems do they have with the product?

- What would make them use the product more?

Many customers will only tell you, "Just lower the price," but others will tell you things that you'd never know unless you asked—things that can lead you to new products.

MBA Mastery

You can get customer input by sponsoring a customer council or user group. A customer council consists of 6 to 10 customers who will devote time to discuss your products and service, and how to improve them. A user group can be larger and more informal. They're often used in high-tech companies, where they're sometimes formed by users themselves.

Ask Your Salespeople

Your salespeople are out there in the market, dealing with problems. Their biggest goal is selling more product. If you're in marketing, you should regularly ask your salespeople these questions:

- What are the biggest barriers to a sale?

- How could you sell more?

- What product modifications do customers ask for?

MBA Alert

In too many companies there's an invisible "wall" between marketing and sales. The two departments don't communicate. If you're in marketing, talk to everyone you can in sales. If you're in sales, talk to marketing. It's the best way to develop good products and marketing programs.

- Do you see any "holes" in our product line?

- What competitive products beat us to the sale?

Watch Your Competitors

Let's face it: Sometimes the other guy has a better idea. When he does, grab it if you can. Better yet, improve on it.

Patent laws protect true inventions, yet many products are not inventions but just new ideas, and you can't patent an idea. In the beverage industry, a new flavor can be readily copied. In consumer goods, many packaging ideas can be copied. So can most styles in the clothing, home furnishings, and entertainment industries.

Recently, readily copied developments have included home-equity credit lines and platinum credit cards in banking, microbeers and caffeinated water in the beverage industry, and run-flat tires in the automotive business.

Sometimes regulations drive new products. Home-equity lines were developed after interest on credit card debt was no longer tax deductible. Trends and fads generate products (for instance, the national obsession with health and fitness has spawned products ranging from organic TV dinners to nicotine patches); so do safety concerns and technology, particularly in automobiles and equipment.

> **MBA Lingo**
>
> A **parity product** copies a competitor's product or service more or less directly, in order to give you parity (that is, equality) in the market. In **reverse engineering,** your engineers take apart a competitor's product to see its materials, assembly, and workings, and then replicate the design.

Copycat or *parity products* are often developed by *reverse engineering*. It is fairly easy to copy successful products, and to "twist" their design or operation slightly, in order to bring out a competitive one.

I prefer creativity rather than copycat tactics. I'll talk about that later in this chapter. But you may someday need a parity product in order to stay competitive, so it's silly to rule them out.

Step Two: Test the Concept

Once you have a product concept, it's essential to test it among potential prospects for the product. These prospects may or may not be among your company's current customers.

Concept testing is market research for getting reactions to a product idea. This can be done by just describing the product idea in detail and then asking the respondents a set of structured questions about the concept. Or you can build a prototype and get reactions to that, also with structured questions.

With or without a prototype, typical questions to ask in a concept test include the following:

♦ Do you understand the product and what it would do?

♦ How do you now accomplish what this product would do?

♦ What would you change about the product?

♦ Would this product solve a large, costly problem?

♦ How frequently would you use this product?

♦ What products do you see as competitive with this?

You may be tempted to ask the prospects how much they would pay for the product, but it's very hard to get a good reading on price at this stage. You may as well ask, but take the answers with a grain of salt.

In most cases, your company will benefit by concept testing product ideas. Yet there are situations when you should probably limit or even omit concept testing. For instance, if the idea represents a small change (such as introducing a hot 'n' spicy flavor for an existing line of snack foods), you can omit testing the idea and go directly to the product test, particularly if you know you need that product offering in order to stay competitive.

MBA Mastery

The prototype needed for a concept test varies with the industry and budget. In the magazine business, you can do a mock-up to show how the cover and pages would look. In the software business, you can show how the computer screens would look, without doing any programming. For tools, appliances, or cars, you can use clay models, computer simulations, or actual working models.

Step Three: Design the Prototype and Product

There is, of course, the matter of developing the actual product or service. This stage calls for marketing's input, but not much hands-on involvement. Rather, this is the point where designers, engineers, materials specialists, programmers, and others with the technical skills to bring the product to life go to work.

Marketing must, however, make sure that any barrier to making, selling, or using the product is eliminated at the design stage. So ease of use and installation, freedom from maintenance, and control of manufacturing costs are all considerations that marketing should talk about with those making the prototype and the product.

Step Four: Test the Product

Once the product or service exists—ideally, before it's ready to go into production—a product test should be conducted jointly by marketing and the design and production team.

The product test is often lumped in with the next step, the market test, but if possible keep these two steps separate because they address two distinct issues. The product test addresses product issues: Does it work? Can customers use it? How do they use it? What would they change? Do they like it? Does it fit into their operation? The market test addresses marketing issues.

MBA Lingo

A **beta site** is an organization or individual (usually a customer) who uses a product and reports his or her experiences to the company developing it. Beta sites are used mainly for industrial products and most often for high-tech products such as computers and software. Many businesspeople call a product test a *beta test*.

In many businesses, product tests involve recruiting *beta-site* customers for the product who agree to act as guinea pigs and provide feedback by field-testing the product. Some companies do their own field testing, for example, in their own company's offices, which is fine. But only objective parties using the product under real conditions can pass final judgment.

By the way, beta-site participants are not motivated simply by the joy of helping a company develop a product. They are typically Innovators or Early Adopters (as described in Chapter 17) who want exposure to something new that may give them a competitive advantage. You may also have to give them discounts or free usage for some period of time, even beyond the beta test.

Step Five: Do a Market Test

A market test gathers information about the customer as a buyer, rather than user, of the product. As much as possible, a market test should gauge buying behavior.

By this time, you should have a good fix on the product's positioning. You do a market test to learn whether that fix is correct, so you can adjust whatever isn't. You want to get reactions to your advertisements, sales pitches, and product literature. These can all be in close-to-final form, but not written in stone. They may need fine-tuning, or more.

The major issue to nail down is pricing, which may be a fuzzy issue even at this stage, particularly if the product is completely new. There are several ways to test various price levels. One of the best ways is to start high and then slide the price downward during the market test to see if lower prices boost sales. An even better way is to try two or three different prices in various customer samples. These samples can be sub-sets of customers divided by geography, industry, or size.

Avoid introducing a new product at a price that's too low. While you may be stunned at the high volume of business, if the price is too low you're leaving money on the table. Also, it's far tougher to raise prices than to lower them.

Aside from pricing, the main things to study are purchase motivations, buying patterns, frequency of purchase, favorite features and benefits, and customer satisfaction.

> **CAUTION**
>
> **MBA Alert**
>
> Be sure to include difficult prospects as well as easy sales in the market test. Going only to Innovators who like your other products will skew the results. If you intend to reach the masses with the product, include some Early and Late Majority types.

Step Six: Launch the Product

A product launch, or rollout, can be done in various ways. It can be gradual, starting with several cities or states. Or it can be a broad regional, or even a national, rollout.

Provided you've done the first five steps properly and have geared up production and shipping, all that's left is to execute the promotional program and support the sales force. This is easier said than done, but at least it represents a concrete set of tasks that you should be prepared for.

Know When to Stop

As I mentioned earlier, a product can be killed at any one of these stages. Clearly, if a product is going to be a loser, the earlier you figure that out, the better. Of course, that's because the sooner you stop, the less time, effort, and money you've spent on it. But the issue goes a bit deeper.

The more time, effort, and money a company spends on something, the more likely it is to continue on that path. People find it hard at the product-test or market-test phase to say, "Well, this isn't working. Let's bag it." After all, they've gone through the idea generation, concept testing, prototype development, and some development of the actual product. The further you proceed the more you have invested, in ego as well as money, in a product.

So, rigorous idea generation and concept testing are essential. If the concept does not address a real customer need, what good will the product be? If customers are lukewarm in the concept test, how can they be thrilled when they're asked to pay for it? Kill bad product ideas early.

Extending Your Line

MBA Lingo

A **product-line extension** is a new product for an existing product line. The new product basically offers a variation on the other products in the line. Examples include a sugar-free version of a breakfast beverage, a cordless model of an electric appliance, or a deluxe model of just about any existing product. An extension is not the same as a **breakthrough,** which is an entirely new product or product category.

The process I've presented will help you manage product development in an orderly way. You may, however, find that this much structure is not always necessary. For example, a simple *product-line extension* might not call for several steps. In fact, going through them might cost more than just slinging the product into the market and seeing if it works.

Product-line extensions are less risky and do not call for much creativity. Product-line extensions may be necessary from the competitive standpoint—for example, to address a competitor's product or to offer a complete selection. However, product-line extensions will rarely, if ever, lead to a *breakthrough*—an entirely new product line or category—that will transform your business. The microwave oven, microcomputer, VCR, and DVD are examples of breakthrough products.

Case in Point

Companies that invent new products, or product categories, can grow so large so rapidly that they virtually invent—and dominate—an entirely new industry. Federal Express invented overnight delivery. Microsoft invented the disk operating system (DOS) for microcomputers.

These and other firms became leaders because they had the creativity and discipline to address problems that others didn't see or couldn't solve. And these companies continue to reap the rewards to this day.

Only genuine creativity will develop a breakthrough. There is nothing wrong with leaving the development of breakthroughs to other companies. But a real break-through can raise a company and its shareholders to an entirely new level of wealth.

What About R&D?

R&D—research and development—refers to a more technical function than product development. A true R&D function, which may be called product development in some companies, is usually staffed by scientists and technicians rather than marketers.

The *R* in R&D—research—creates the need for scientists. Many companies in high-technology industries such as aerospace, chemicals, pharmaceuticals, telecommunications, medical instruments, and materials conduct basic research in the hope of a breakthrough. Basic research is a long-term, intellectual activity with frequent failure as part of the process.

Yet product development (the *D* in R&D) is a shorter-term, profit-oriented activity that seeks to minimize failures. So managing R&D calls for understanding the inter-action of research and development. It requires faith in both processes. Researchers must understand that they are not pursuing knowledge for its own sake but for com-mercial reasons. Product developers must understand that research is a trial-and-error process with a long-term payoff.

Case in Point

In November 1995, the credit card giant MBNA decided to launch a super-premium credit card called Platinum Plus. (Although American Express had introduced its platinum card by then, this was the first platinum card ever issued by a bank.) Management believed that competitors would copy the product almost instantly, so they decided to move very quickly and in total secrecy, with no product or market testing.

A cross-functional team from marketing, credit, and operations worked intensely to design the card itself and its financial features (unprecedented high credit lines and a bundle of services) and to set up the credit approval and transactions processing opera-tions. They managed to do this in three months and launched their first mailing in February 1996.

As MBNA expected, competitors introduced parity products as soon as they saw the Platinum Plus offerings in their own mailboxes. However, by moving quickly and quietly, MBNA had the market largely to themselves for about five months, which was enough time to gain a permanent edge over competitors in this highly profitable market seg-ment.

Often the best way to manage R&D is to get it away from the rest of the outfit. That way the scientists can be free to pursue research, and when they come up with something the company can develop into a product, they can hand it off to the right people.

Today, because markets and technology move so quickly, a company can gain a major competitive advantage by being able to develop new products quickly.

The Least You Need to Know

- ◆ A cross-functional product-development team includes someone from every department that will deal with the product. This gives each department input into the process, which minimizes problems and gets everyone's buy-in at each step.

- ◆ There are six steps in the product-development process: idea generation, concept testing, prototype and product design, product testing, market testing, and product launch.

- ◆ You can save time, energy, and money by quickly eliminating bad ideas. Be tough when judging product ideas and be sure the concept test reveals enthusiasm for (not just interest in) the product.

- ◆ A product test ensures that the product operates the way it should. The market test ensures that customers respond to it the way you thought they would. The market test also helps you fine-tune the product's positioning.

- ◆ The best products meet a need or solve a problem. There is nothing wrong with product-line extensions or parity products. But the really huge returns go to companies that come up with breakthrough ideas.

Part 5

Steering the Business into the Future

When you steer a car, you're not supposed to focus on your dashboard or even on the car in front of you. Instead, you are supposed to look at what driving instructors call the Big Picture.

So, it's time to look up from your desk and gaze out on the Big Picture. Think about strategy and plotting a course for your company. Ponder the nature of business information and how to use it to your advantage. Think about improving productivity and quality. And consider your company's legal obligations and your role as an ethical manager.

If you have set your sights on a senior management position in a large company—or if you are an entrepreneur starting or managing a small company—you need to understand the Big Picture in order to do your day-to-day job. This part will show you how.

Chapter 23

Charting a Course with Strategic Planning

In This Chapter

♦ The role of strategic planning in the future of your company

♦ How to assess threats and opportunities

♦ Classic business strategies and action steps

All of the activities and tools we've covered so far have to serve the larger needs of the company. All of the things that finance, accounting, marketing, and sales do must be coordinated so they work together smoothly.

This calls for a long-term strategic plan. You need a plan to give managers the framework for making good decisions. That plan must relate to the major goals of the whole company, and management's decisions must serve those goals.

This chapter explains long-range strategic planning, which is usually just called strategic planning. It tells you why you need a strategic plan and covers steps and techniques that will help you create one. (The business plan—a document that explains the operations, finances, and marketing goals of a small business or a business unit—is covered in Chapter 26.)

What Is Strategic Planning?

Strategic planning typically involves five steps:

1. Define the company's goals.

2. Analyze the company's environment.

3. Consider the company's resources.

4. Identify actions that will move the company toward its goals.

5. Implement the actions and monitor progress.

Through the rest of this chapter, I'll explain each of these elements.

Define the Company's Goals

The company must have a large, unifying goal that will organize the thinking and activities of everyone in the outfit. The most widely accepted goal of a company is to maximize long-term *shareholder value*—that is, to improve the worth of the company.

Unfortunately, having the goal of maximizing shareholder value does not tell you *how* to maximize shareholder value. So most companies need one or more other strategic goals that will help them do that.

Your goals should help you direct the assessments of the environment and your resources. They can be broad ("to increase sales and operating profits by 10 percent") or more specific ("to increase European sales of the Mixmaster to $3 million next year").

Later, you may find that these goals are too low or too high. Or you may find that you can develop several specific goals that would support one overall goal. For instance, you might identify product lines that can increase sales and profits by more than 10 percent.

MBA Lingo

Shareholder value is the investment of the owners of the company. The most common measure of this is the stock price multiplied by the number of shares of stock outstanding. The higher the stock's price, the higher the shareholder value.

In setting a corporate goal you must

♦ Define your business in the broadest terms possible.

♦ Make your goal measurable.

♦ Consider the basic sales-growth strategies.

Let's look at each of these guidelines.

Define Your Business Broadly

Many companies have gotten themselves in trouble by defining their business too narrowly. Management consultant Peter Drucker uses the example of the railroads to illustrate this. Before the development of air travel, the senior managers of railroads believed they were in the railroad business. If they had seen themselves in the transportation business instead, they would have been prepared to compete when airplanes came along.

While it hardly guarantees success, looking at your business broadly will open your mind to possibilities you might otherwise miss. For example, if you are in training or consulting, think of yourself as being in the information business. This may open up possibilities in publishing and software. If you are in the restaurant business, think of it as food services or entertainment. You may find that corporate catering, cooking classes, or dinner theater are avenues of growth for you.

MBA Mastery

Many companies fail because they are one-product firms. For long-term success, most companies need a "second act."

How Will You Know You've Arrived?

To be "real," a goal must be measurable, as noted in Chapter 2. Vague goals don't motivate people. Be precise. Define a goal in numerical terms, if possible. Useful measures include revenue and profit gains, number and size of accounts, market share in certain product and customer groups, and percentage of sales and profits in certain areas of the business. These goals are measurable. And if you fail to achieve them, at least you'll know how close you came.

Consider the Sales-Growth Strategies

The key strategic question that recurs every year is, "Where will growth come from?" As a starting point, consider the sales-growth strategies covered in Chapter 17.

Thinking about these strategies as goals—for example, to sell new products to existing customers—will help you identify markets, customers, products, and price sensitivities as you assess the environment and your resources.

Analyze the Company's Environment

The company's environment includes the economy, market, competitive landscape, and regulatory and social climate. You have to analyze each of these aspects because threats and opportunities can emerge in any one of them. Most companies make a strategic plan every year or two because the environment changes, and as it does so do the threats and opportunities.

Nonetheless, many companies have been blindsided by change—succumbing to competitors they failed to take seriously and missing opportunities that once stared them in the face.

Case in Point

Here are some examples of major threats and opportunities that have challenged various industries in the last 25 years:

The U.S. auto industry faces an ongoing competitive threat from foreign automakers. The rise of microcomputers radically altered the market for minicomputers and mainframes. The tobacco industry faces serious regulatory and social challenges, as does health care, which also faces rising costs due to the aging of the population.

However, opportunities also abound, often imbedded in threats. The microcomputer brought tremendous opportunities to many companies of all kinds. While foreign competitors pose threats, foreign nations have also become more robust export markets for U.S. goods. The entire "green revolution" has generated profits for companies that address environmental concerns.

Let's talk about the different parts of your environment that you need to continually monitor.

Customers and Prospects

Any sales-growth strategies you suggest must take into account your customers' needs, satisfaction, price sensitivity, and alternative product choices. Be sure to get the views of the sales force on these issues. Market research and the business press can also be good sources of information on consumer preferences and habits.

Competitors

You must closely monitor your competitors and—key point—your *potential* competitors by analyzing annual reports, reading announcements of personnel changes, examining new products, keeping up with acquisitions and alliances, and even speaking with former employees or current customers to gain insight into competitors' plans and operations. Again, your sales force can offer excellent insights into your competitors.

Suppliers

Keep an eye on your suppliers because they can affect your future. If they plan to increase their prices or phase out a product, it could impact your outfit. Plan accordingly. Pay special attention to the financial condition of your major suppliers.

To monitor suppliers, talk—and listen—to their salespeople and read the business press. Read the annual report of any supplier upon whom you depend heavily. Suppliers don't always warn customers of adverse changes. The sooner you know of any, the sooner you can respond.

> **MBA Mastery**
>
> Keep abreast of any public company you compete with or do business with by asking for information as a potential investor. You can receive company announcements, quarterly and annual reports, and press releases.

Regulatory and Social Change

The strategic-planning process must include an analysis of changes in regulations that affect your business. These changes are often driven by social change. Cigarettes are a good example of a product affected by both regulatory and social change. Since the 1960s, when television commercials for cigarettes were banned, the tobacco industry has seen increasing restrictions on its business.

Deregulation—the full or partial lifting of restrictions on business activity—can change the landscape, too. Deregulation of power generation, for example, has created an environment of change and competition in a business that had been stable and predictable.

> **MBA Lingo**
>
> **Deregulation** occurs when an industry that had been operating under close government restrictions sees those restrictions loosened or removed.

Your local, state, and federal representatives and your trade association can help you keep abreast of regulatory change. In large, publicly held companies, this is the job of the government affairs or legal staff.

Economic Trends

Depending on your business, the major economic factors you should consider might include interest rates; housing starts; consumer confidence; consumer spending; monetary and fiscal policies; and local, state, regional, and national (and perhaps international) growth trends.

As noted in Chapter 7, economic information, including news of the latest statistics and forecasts, is continually reported in the business press. Many large banks and investment firms make forecasts available to their customers. There are also consulting firms that sell economic forecasts and data, with DRI/WEFA and Economy.com among the most prominent.

Add It Up

After you assess the environment, you must examine each development you have identified and decide whether it is a threat or an opportunity. The following table shows how this kind of assessment might look for a U.S. auto manufacturer.

Development	Threat	Opportunity	Comment
Customers			
Larger vehicles falling out of favor	✓		We get 60% of profits from mid- to large-size cars and sport-utilities.
Desire more comfort and performance in smaller cars	✓	✓	See above, but we can respond by repositioning our compacts.
Spending lower percentage of income on transportation	✓		May hurt sales and profits. Stress economic benefits of our cars?
Competitors			
Several new competitive compact models	✓		We must distinguish our lower-end models, perhaps by adding luxury features.
Lower-priced smaller cars added to Mercedes and BMW lines	✓		We can deliver luxury in a small car at a much lower price.
Suppliers			
Rising steel prices	✓		Can we nail down low prices in contracts now?
Small firm has a new accident-prevention technology		✓	Should we test it? Can we get an exclusive? At what cost?

Development	Threat	Opportunity	Comment
Economic			
Growth will slow next year	✓		This will make it hard to match this year's sales level.
Rising interest rates ahead	✓	✓	Threat to sales volume but can benefit our financing subsidiary.
Regulatory/Social			
Environmental groups more visibly opposing large vehicles	✓		Marketing must stress environmental friendliness.
Possibly higher gas prices		✓	Could work in favor of our economy models.

As you see, some developments pose both a threat and an opportunity. This is often the case because changes in various areas actually open up opportunities while posing a threat. (Remember: The Chinese character for "crisis" combines the symbols for "threat" and "opportunity.")

Consider the Company's Resources

Most companies do a decent, if incomplete, job of considering their resources.

In assessing your company's resources, you must consider the resources you need, as well as those you have. These needs are dictated by the company's goals and by the threats and opportunities in the environment. Your most important resources include

◆ Product profitability and growth

◆ People

◆ Productive capacity

◆ Other resources

Let's examine each of these.

Profitability and Growth

Regarding the profitability of current products, you must answer the questions: Which product lines and activities are making money? Which are not? How do we create more money-making ones? How do we phase out unprofitable ones?

Regarding growth, you must answer the questions: Which product lines and activities are growing the fastest? Which are stagnant or declining? How can we boost the growing products and eliminate the others?

> **MBA Alert** _____
>
> To protect themselves, some managers do not want their financial results to be very clear. They usually construct complicated systems, keep poor records, and argue about whose costs are whose. Senior management must insist that accounting work with department managers to develop clear, accurate, comparable numbers that fairly reflect their performance.

A straight accounting analysis will tell you a lot about the profitability and growth of your company or products. This means that you need accurate numbers from your accountants that clearly identify revenues and costs.

There is an excellent tool to help you evaluate the relative strength and profitability of your products or product lines: the growth-share matrix. The Boston Consulting Group (BCG) developed the growth-share matrix (or growth/market-share matrix) to help managers of multidivisional companies classify their subsidiaries. However, it also helps managers of a single company or division to classify products and product lines.

The classification system works along two dimensions: market growth and market share. Basically, growth is a measure of how much investment—that is, cash—the company or product requires. High growth requires lots of cash; low growth needs less cash. Market share is a measure of the company's or product's position in its market, which can range from dominant to weak. In general, the larger the market share, the more cash the company or product should be generating for the owners.

Here's how the growth-share matrix looks:

Market Growth	High	Star	?
	Low	Cash Cow	Dog
		High	Low
		Market Share	

Here's how to read the growth-share matrix:

- A star has high market share in a rapidly growing market. It needs a high level of investment, but it can generate lots of cash. That's why it's a star. To manage a star, invest whatever you can in it, because if you have a high share of a growing market you're going to make money.

- A cash cow has high market share in a slowly growing market. This kind of company or product should yield lots of cash, particularly if the market is large, yet requires relatively little investment. That's why it's called a cash cow. Invest only what you need to invest to keep a cash cow healthy. It should be a net source of cash.

- A question mark is a product in a high-growth market, but it has not achieved high share of that market. Like the star, it requires investment in order to expand capacity to win high share. The question is, if you make the investment in more capacity, will the product or division win high share? If you believe you can move it into the star area, you should invest in it. Otherwise, you shouldn't.

- A dog offers the worst of both worlds: low market share in a low-growth market. On the one hand, it does not require much investment. On the other hand, it's not going to generate much cash. It's a dog. A dog should be sold or phased out.

People Are the Company

At most companies, the resource assessment tends to be incomplete in the area of human resources. That's because the assets on the balance sheet are easier to inventory than the knowledge in people's heads. However, certain human resources can give a company a competitive edge that physical resources cannot.

In considering your resources, consider the skills, education, expertise, and experience of your employees. Consider knowledge they could apply to your business as well as what they are now applying.

Many companies with sophisticated human resources departments use a knowledge and skills inventory of their employees. A formal knowledge and skills inventory asks employees to list their skills, education, experience, and other characteristics, often for entry into a computerized database. This kind of inventory can help managers make sure they are making the most of their employees.

Productive Capacity

To determine your true productive capacity, you need to look beyond the fixed assets on your balance sheet. You need to understand everything about your equipment: downtime, maintenance requirements, ease or difficulty of operation, amount of training required, and the productivity of the machinery and of the people using it.

You must go to the machinery operators and their managers to get this information. These people have the information you need to assess productive capacity realistically.

Other Resources

Other resources to consider are less tangible—and perhaps lie outside the company—but they can be important nonetheless. These include …

- Patents, trademarks, and brands.
- Sales channels and distribution systems.
- Alliances or joint ventures with other companies.

Importantly, the potential to develop these kinds of resources can often point the way toward useful ways of acquiring resources that the outfit currently lacks. In fact, developing these resources is often among the action steps that fall out of a strategic plan.

Add It Up Again

As you consider the company's resources, you must decide whether they are adequate to meeting the threats and capitalizing on the opportunities posed by the environment. The following table shows how this assessment might look for a U.S. auto manufacturer.

Resource	Strength	Weakness	Comment
Profitability & Growth			
Minivan and SUV lines are aging (cash cow)		✓	Lines continue to be profitable but we haven't invested in them recently and we don't want to.
Midsize sedan line is losing ground (dog)		✓	Competitors have overtaken us in midsize market because we placed our bets on vans and SUVs.

Resource	Strength	Weakness	Comment
Our new high performance sports coupe has sold well (question mark)	✓		We may be able to capitalize on this key product strength to build a line of high performance small cars.
People			
Our dealer network has not been happy but remains committed to us.		✓	We must improve dealer relations by helping them improve their profits.
Our U.S. workforce is aging as we have emphasized production in Mexico.		✓	We cannot function without a solid, well-trained U.S. workforce.
Productive Capacity			
We have large amounts of capacity, but we have not updated it in some time.	✓	✓	This reflects our investment in minivan and SUV capacity, which we may need to retool for sedans.
Outsourcing has left us dependent on two major suppliers of key components.		✓	This exposes us to price increases that can be difficult to resist. We must bring some of this work back inside.
Other Resources			
We have filed a number of patents that we haven't used or exploited in any way.	✓		We must look into commercializing these inventions by applying them ourselves or licensing them to other companies.
Our financial structure remains strong.	✓		Although we have new products, our reliance on cash cows has left us financially underinvested.

As with environmental developments, a resource can now and then represent both a strength and a weakness. Also, the preceding list represents a sample of resources to be considered. In reality, an automobile manufacturer would have many more resources to consider in every category, and perhaps several other categories as well.

What's SWOT?

From time to time you will hear the acronym SWOT, another example of MBA-ese. SWOT stands for an analysis of Strengths, Weaknesses, Opportunities, and Threats. Thus, SWOT also sums up the second step (analyze the company's environment) and the third step (consider the company's resources) of the strategic-planning process presented here.

That is, the product of step 2, analyzing the environment, should be an assessment of the threats and opportunities that the company faces in the marketplace. And the product of step 3, considering the company's resources, should be an assessment of its strengths and weaknesses.

Although SWOT is widely discussed and used, it's only part of the strategic-planning story, which many managers forget. I believe that a SWOT analysis works best when performed *after* the company sets at least a preliminary goal. I also believe that it's best to analyze the environment (opportunities and threats) *before* you consider the company's resources (strengths and weaknesses). That way, you can evaluate the resources in light of the opportunities and threats you must address.

In sum, SWOT is an excellent mnemonic, but the process it represents must occur in context. Company goals provide that context. Also, if you literally follow the SWOT sequence and analyze strengths and weaknesses before identifying opportunities and threats, you are in a sense putting the cart before the horse.

That said, any strategic plan worthy of the name must include actions that will move the company toward its goals, our fourth step.

MBA Mastery

A staggering amount of information on goals, environmental developments, and resources can go into a strategic plan. Several software packages have been developed to assist the strategic planner. These range from cheap to pricey, and new packages and updates of existing packages are always being introduced. The key features to look for are the ability to handle various types of information—that is, text as well as columns of numbers—and to create alternative planning scenarios easily.

Alternative scenarios might include those based on assumptions of slow, medium, and fast economic growth. Or a resource assessment based on an optimistic, pessimistic, and best-guess levels of sales or market share. Software enables the planner to change the assumption and automatically generate new figures for any value tied to that assumption (such as equipment or number of people needed). In this way, the effects of different assumptions about the future can be considered more realistically.

Identify Actions

On the basis of the information resulting from the first three steps, you should now be positioned to decide what action the company should take to move toward its goals. These actions must

♦ Neutralize or eliminate threats.

♦ Capitalize on opportunities.

♦ Exploit existing resources and develop or acquire needed resources.

Actions are the heart of the strategic plan. The result of this step should be the actual "To Do" items that operations, marketing, sales, finance, and other departments must undertake. Examples of useful action steps for key departments that would typically come out of a strategic plan include:

Marketing

Develop new products.

Develop a new marketing campaign.

Replace advertising agency.

Reposition existing products.

Identify new markets.

Develop new sales channels.

Sales

Explain price increase to customers.

Employ new sales tactics.

Restructure sales-force alignment.

Restructure sales territories.

Restructure sales compensation.

Improve customer service.

Finance

Secure debt financing.

Issue stock.

Refinance debt.

Adjust capital structure.

Improve financial controls.

Start a cost-cutting effort.

Secure international financing.

Production

Expand capacity.

Improve product quality.

Increase productivity.

Outsource production tasks.

Find new suppliers.

Improve inventory methods.

General Management/Human Resources

Expand certain areas of the organization.

Develop hiring or downsizing campaigns.

Increase use of independent contractors.

Form business alliances or joint ventures.

Merge with or acquire another company.

Of course, this list is not exhaustive, nor would all of these steps be taken at once.

Implement the Steps

If you are new to business, you may be surprised to learn that strategic plans are often created, presented to management, and even approved—but never implemented.

This occurs most often in companies with strategic-planning functions that are isolated from the company's real business and operating managers. These "ivory tower" planners are typically either too removed from the business to create a relevant plan or seen by operating managers as useless, or both.

To lessen the chances of this, you must get input from all managers before the plan is formulated. Then, after it is completed, you must tie their individual goals to the plan and tie their raises, bonuses, and promotions to those goals. Both of these tactics will make the plan much more relevant to them.

Also, the management and leadership skills covered in Part 1 are essential to implementing strategic plans. For instance, managers must communicate the plan and its goals throughout the entire organization. Effective leaders link the strategic plan to the organizational vision. They focus people on the tasks that will get the plan implemented and hold them accountable for taking action and achieving the goals of the plan. They also ensure that the organization is aligned with the plan, and they take the time to coach and mentor people in the context of the plan.

Many strategic plans fail not because they're poor plans, but because they're poorly implemented. Implementation is the toughest step in the process, yet in a sense it lies outside strategic planning. That's because strategic planning is largely an analytical function, while implementing is a management function—getting things done through others.

Throughout the planning process, and especially when you are crafting the action steps, be sure that you can implement the plan. The plan is not an end in itself, but rather a tool to move the company toward its goals. It can do that only if the goals, analysis, and action steps are rooted in reality.

Strategic-Planning Guidelines

While no part of strategic planning is easy, there are guidelines as well as tools and techniques that can help you in the process. Let's turn to them now.

Set a Time Frame

The most common time frame for a strategic plan is one year and five years; that is, you have a plan for the coming year and for the coming five years. Most companies prepare the plan for the coming year in detail. Outfits vary in the detail they go into for the subsequent four years.

Get Everyone Involved

A plan that originates with senior management and is then dictated to the troops is called a top-down plan. A bottom-up plan begins with input from the department managers, who may in turn get input from their employees.

Top-down and bottom-up represent two extremes. In reality, if senior managers try to impose a plan they develop unilaterally, they'll have trouble implementing it because they won't have buy-in from those who must implement the plan. On the other hand, if senior managers rely only on the input of departmental managers as the basis for the plan, they may miss a major development outside the day-to-day operations that are the main focus of the departmental managers. So a mix of the two approaches works best.

Who Needs a Plan?

Virtually every business of any size needs a strategic plan if it plans on being around for more than a year. Poor planning and lack of planning are repeatedly cited among the top reasons for business failure.

There is no valid excuse for not planning. Attempting to perform the basic managerial functions of organizing and controlling the company is difficult to impossible without a good plan. Planning brings the future into the present, so you can think about it more clearly and more productively than you can when it comes hurtling toward you. Remember: Proper planning prevents poor performance.

The Least You Need to Know

- A long-term strategic plan gives managers a framework for making good decisions that serve the long-term goals of the company. A strategic plan can ensure that day-to-day decisions and tactics move the company toward its major goals.

- A strategic plan should start with a goal, even if that goal will be modified as more information is gathered during the planning process.

- Since companies are affected by the business environment, you must assess the environment for threats and opportunities.

- Use Boston Consulting Group's growth-share matrix to examine your company's divisions (or products) for their growth rate and market share, and to assess current and future profitability.

- Be certain that the identified actions can be carried out by those who will be accountable for doing so. Align your incentives and communicate management's support of those who carry out the plan. Use management and leadership skills to implement the plan.

Chapter 24

Information, Please

In This Chapter

- ◆ Why information is a crucial resource
- ◆ Securing and exploiting your information
- ◆ Managing the IS function
- ◆ Getting the most from e-commerce

Information has become a business resource on par with the traditional business resources, which are money, labor, and productive capacity. These days, information itself has become very valuable from the competitive standpoint.

This is most obvious in financial services. Walter Wriston, retired chairman of Citicorp, said—in the early 1980s!—"Information about money has become as important as money." In finance, information about deposits, investments, interest rates, currencies, and every other aspect of money affect growth and profitability every day.

But it's not only information about money that is so important. Information about customers, competitors, suppliers, technology, trends, and regulations have all become extremely valuable in today's economy.

In this chapter, you learn why information is so important and what you as a manager need to do about it. We also examine ways of safeguarding your information and of getting your information systems, including your Internet-based efforts, to support your company's strategy.

Let's get informed about information.

Why Information Has Become a Strategic Resource

Information has become so important in business because

♦ Computing power (as measured by calculations performed on a microchip per second) is getting cheaper. Throughout the 1990s and continuing to the present, the computing power that we can get onto a single microchip has doubled about every 18 months. Meanwhile, the price of computers has been dropping. In other words, the price-performance ratio of *information technology*, or IT, has been improving at a phenomenal rate.

♦ With IT equipment, such as microcomputers, software, networks, Internet, EDI (electronic data interchange, which is computer-to-computer communication), and e-mail, information can be created and distributed in new and faster ways. Companies that use this technology gain an edge, so their competitors must also use it.

> **MBA Lingo**
>
> **Information technology** includes computers, software, networks, memory (data storage), and e-mail. It also includes telecommunications, computerized voice response, satellite and wireless communications, and even fax machines.

♦ IT enables companies to decentralize decision making by pushing information down to lower levels. Information moves more quickly now. This changes the ways in which people work, managers manage, and companies operate.

♦ Broad social and economic trends, such as individualism, globalization, the fall of Soviet communism, and increasing economic aspirations worldwide, have been produced by information and drive the demand for more information.

These and similar trends suggest that in some ways we have moved out of the Industrial Age and into the Information Age.

I'm not saying that the requirements of success in the Industrial Age no longer apply in the Information Age. They still do, especially in businesses such as heavy manufacturing. However, they are generally less important. As many high-tech firms including Microsoft, Amazon.com, and eBay have proven, you can go awfully far awfully fast in the Information Age with relatively little in initial capital.

The Intelligence Pyramid

I've found it useful to think about information in terms of the Intelligence Pyramid, shown in the following figure.

The Intelligence Pyramid.

This pyramid shows a hierarchy with various kinds of information. Each kind has a different level of value.

Data is the lowest level of information. A piece of data is a fact. Data is raw and un-analyzed and must be enriched through analysis to become information. Examples of data include sales figures, delivery times, or manufacturing defects per thousand units. Data is usually the first result, or finding, of research or an investigation.

You produce **information** by analyzing data. Analysis and analytical tools help you understand the relationships among data. Information describes the conditions and behaviors behind the data—for instance, the factors that affect sales figures, delivery times, or manufacturing defects.

With information, you're on your way to developing **knowledge** (and maybe even wisdom). Knowledge is informed by experience, education, and reasoning. Large amounts of it

MBA Mastery

Know when enough information is enough. Cost-benefit analysis can help here. When you face a decision that calls for information, try to weigh the cost of buying or developing the information versus the potential benefits of having the information. In other words, there's no sense in spending $100 to develop a credit profile of a new account to which you're going to sell it only one $99 item, with a $33 profit.

equal expertise. You can now understand the conditions and behaviors and make informed decisions.

Wisdom goes beyond knowledge to include decision making on the basis of sound moral and intellectual judgment. Wisdom is the result of knowledge plus character applied to difficult situations that demand a decision. As you know, wisdom is in short supply. (Demand for it even appears to dry up occasionally.)

Using Information to Gain Competitive Advantage

The saying "Knowledge is power" is an old one, but it has never been truer. Knowledge and information give a company a competitive edge.

Let's consider some ways in which information works in business.

Financial Information: Where's the Money?

Walter Wriston's comment at the beginning of the chapter could be updated to "Information *is* money." Or rather, money is information. In our $10-trillion-plus economy, most transactions are conducted with no exchange of cash. In many transactions no paper, checks, or receipts even change hands. Funds are transferred electronically, by electronic bookkeeping entries.

These entries, and the information they generate, make sophisticated corporate cash management possible. If you are the financial manager of a company, and you always know how much is owed to whom, how much is due from whom, and where all of the firm's money is, you can make sure that the funds are put to use in the most effective way.

This means that money can be moved from low-yield accounts to higher-yield investments, collection efforts can be speeded up, disbursements can be slowed down, and loans taken or repaid electronically—all as soon and as profitably as possible.

Internal financial reporting systems can provide timely, accurate feedback on sales, earnings, investment performance, price changes, and similar matters. This enables you to adjust your strategy and tactics to correct mistakes, adjust to changing conditions, and exploit new opportunities more quickly than ever.

Marketing Information: What Do Customers Want?

As you learned in Part 4, information on customers can help you create successful marketing and pricing strategies, promotional and sales tactics, and products and services. Strategically, information on trends in prospects' attitudes can help you see how to increase sales. Tactically, this information can help you identify the best ways of approaching them.

IT has led to an explosion of marketing information in the past 20 years. This is particularly true in consumer sales, where new information on buying patterns has been compiled from sources such as credit card companies, mail-order houses, and retail stores. This has created *database marketing*, a relatively new area of direct-response marketing, which mainly includes direct mail and telemarketing.

Bar codes have proven useful for tracking inventory and sales down to very specific levels. A major retailer can run a special promotion in one or two stores, then judge its effectiveness precisely—and instantly—before rolling it out to other stores. If you run a special on Cheer detergent on Thursday, for example, you know the result Thursday night and, given your margins, whether it was worthwhile. In fact, if the customer uses a credit card, you can know exactly what he bought—and can then send him cents-off coupons through the mail.

MBA Lingo

Database marketing involves compiling large amounts of data on customers and prospects to help you tailor an approach in a direct mail or telephone offer. The data includes buying behavior coupled with demographic and often psychographic data.

Information Flows

As you saw in Chapter 23, much of strategy development, and therefore strategy itself, hinges on information. You need information about your business and the environment. To implement strategy, you must both disseminate information and get information back to ensure that the strategy is (a) being implemented, and (b) succeeding as planned.

Because the business and the environment are dynamic, this process must be continual. You must create a "feedback loop" in which you continually gather information, understand that information, and provide new information. This flow of information into, through, and out

MBA Alert

A potential backlash against companies that compile consumer information is underway. Federal legislation proposed in recent years would limit the ability of companies to compile, sell, or share information they gather while doing business with individuals. No serious action has yet been taken, but in the future it may, as real and perceived invasions of privacy continue.

of the company is as important as the flow of cash that goes into, through, and out of it.

The following are among the key information flows, some of which are informal yet, nonetheless, important.

MBA Mastery

Companies that solidly align their communications stand the best chance of success. If the marketing department says one thing to customers and the salespeople say something else, there is a lack of alignment. Management must ensure that everyone at all levels communicates a consistent message. This requires open sharing of information, honest interpretation of it, and a consensus on the company's message.

Information that flows into and out of the company includes

♦ Information from customers to the company, through the sales force, customer service, market research, and sales records.

♦ Information on competitors, gathered from the media, salespeople, and customers.

♦ Information from suppliers, particularly those supplying a critical material or service.

♦ Information from the financial markets.

♦ Information from regulatory agencies, particularly those overseeing the industry.

♦ Information from trade associations and the media.

Information that flows through the company includes

♦ Information from senior management to managers and employees, and from employees and managers to senior management.

♦ Interdepartmental information, particularly regarding sales, budgets, and employee and customer satisfaction.

♦ Informal communication between people at all levels, including casual conversations and even gossip, all of which affect the company.

Information that flows from the company includes

♦ Information sent to customers, including everything from product literature to statements by salespeople.

♦ Information for the financial markets, particularly reports and commentary on sales and profits.

♦ Information to suppliers, particularly regarding quality, cost, and delivery of materials and services.

♦ Information to the public through the various media, which affects customers, prospects, employees, suppliers, and investors.

The more accurate, understood, and aligned all these information flows are, the better. In addition, the company must ensure that its information is secure and that it exploits its information aggressively.

Securing Corporate Knowledge

Securing your company's knowledge generally involves administrative tasks. That means having good records of what you've done in the past. Then you need security measures to protect these materials.

Here are six ways to secure corporate knowledge:

♦ **Document what you do.** Every project worthy of the name should have some kind of final report (or at least a memo) that sums it up. In addition, legal agreements, customer records, accounting records, and so on all must be properly filed and maintained. Proper record keeping is essential to compiling corporate knowledge.

♦ **Apply for trademarks and patents.** A trademark protects your brands and logos from exploitation by others, while a patent protects your products and processes. In a large company, the legal department will work with senior management and operating managers to ensure that trademark and patent protection is in place. This involves applying to the U.S. Patent and Trademark Office in Washington, D.C., and following the application procedure.

♦ **Have a document-retention schedule and use it.** According to tax law as of this writing, records that document your revenues, expenses, and income must be retained for seven years. Contracts and other legal agreements must be retained for the life of the agreement, and in most cases should be kept longer. In large companies, the corporate secretary can define the document retention schedule.

> **CAUTION**
>
> **MBA Alert**
>
> Without patent or trademark protection, a company has a much more difficult time establishing and maintaining ownership of its brands and technological developments. Whenever the company has a brand it values or develops a technology it believes is unique and useful, it is worth investigating trademarking (in the case of a brand) or patenting (in the case of a technological development).

◆ **Install proper security systems.** Whether your files are computerized or on paper, access to sensitive information should be controlled. This information may include client lists, employee data, books of account, banking records, tax records, loan agreements, agreements with other companies, information on proprietary products, processes and technologies, and strategic plans. Grant access to sensitive information on a need-to-know basis; that is, grant access only to those who need the information in order to do their jobs.

MBA Lingo

A **document-retention schedule** specifies how long a certain type of document must be retained. For example, a bank's policy may call for five years of financial statements on each business borrower. That means that when a new set of statements arrives from a borrower, the earliest set (the one from six years back) can be discarded.

MBA Alert

The big issue with security is not corporate espionage, but employee turnover. If someone leaves your company and goes to work for a competitor, they may give your competitor intimate knowledge of your technology, strategic plans, or compensation policies. They may also attempt to solicit business by using your client list. This is why nondisclosure agreements are important.

◆ **Use nondisclosure agreements.** A nondisclosure agreement is a document, signed by one or more individuals, that prohibits them from revealing certain information to other people. The information is usually considered proprietary, confidential, or at least sensitive by the party requesting nondisclosure. Companies routinely request that vendors, freelancers, consultants (and even potential vendors, freelancers, and consultants) sign a nondisclosure agreement because they may be privy to sensitive company information. Companies require these agreements less often from employees, but it does happen.

Often an agreement (for example, to provide consulting services) will have a nondisclosure clause. A typical nondisclosure clause might read:

I, _____ (name of consultant), agree to keep all information regarding the products, processes, technologies, employees, suppliers, customers, prospects, contracts, and plans of ABC Company strictly confidential during and after the period of my engagement to perform the consulting services described in this agreement. I will in no way reveal any proprietary information regarding any aspect of the company's business to anyone, except during the project and as necessary to complete the project.

Should you sign a nondisclosure agreement? Generally the answer is yes, provided you want to do business with whomever is requesting it. There are three reasons. First, refusal to sign can be a "deal breaker." Few outfits will work with someone they suspect might reveal their trade secrets. Second, if the agreement is properly worded, it will not stop you from communicating on the project or job. Third, a nondisclosure agreement cannot restrict you from making a living. (In the interests of full disclosure, I must point out that I am not an attorney. Your corporate counsel or attorney should be your guide on legal agreements.)

Exploiting Corporate Knowledge

Having and securing a body of knowledge is one thing. Making money with it is another. To get a competitive advantage from information, you have to put the information to use. You have to act on the information.

In the following sections, we'll explore several ways to exploit corporate knowledge.

Apply Corporate Knowledge to New Products

I've covered product development in Chapter 22, so I'll make this point quickly. Corporate knowledge will find the most profitable application in products. The reason is simple: Products are what you sell. That's where the money is.

We've explored ways of developing product-related information. The point of doing market research is to develop knowledge of customer needs so that you can address those needs with products they will buy. The point of having an accounting and finance function is to tell you which products you are making money on. The whole point of having a research and development function is to develop knowledge that can be used to build better products.

You have to act on all this information by using it to make profitable products.

Apply Corporate Knowledge to Your Processes

The other most profitable use of corporate information is to apply it to your processes, particularly production processes, to improve them. If you can make these processes better, faster, or cheaper, that is certainly using information for competitive advantage.

Keep up-to-date on your industry and on the technologies and techniques that drive it. Join and become active in your trade association. Read everything that has anything to do with your business. Keep asking yourself, "How can I use this?"

Use Templates to Stop Reinventing the Wheel

So many companies approach a task as if it were the first time they were doing it—even when they have done it many times before. These tasks may include almost any business activity—analyzing an opportunity, creating a marketing campaign, developing a product, building a team, conducting a consulting assignment—just about anything.

MBA Mastery

When you face a task, ask yourself and others: "What did we do last time?" This is particularly important if you are young or new to an outfit, or both. Few of the tasks an established organization faces are completely new, and the people who faced them last time probably did something you should know about. Don't be chained to the past, but don't ignore it, either.

It's great to have a fresh approach. But it will be freshest if you avoid repeating past patterns or if you repeat them with a new twist. Either way, it helps to know what those past patterns are. The costs of reinventing the wheel are too high, in wasted time and effort, for you to be lazy about keeping or consulting records. In these days of frequent layoffs and high employee turnover, these records are more important than ever.

Leverage Your Information

Say you have knowledge—about a market or method—but you don't have the resources needed to profit from that knowledge. Ask yourself: "Who does have these resources?" Your company's knowledge, coupled with another company's resources, can be a powerful combination. An alliance or joint venture with another company can enable you to get something from that information without having all the resources necessary to fully exploit it.

Business alliances and joint ventures have become increasingly popular over the past several decades, particularly between large and small companies.

Whether you work in a large or small firm, be aware of these benefits and think in terms of potential combinations as you monitor the business scene.

Case in Point

When a small firm with a new technology links with a larger firm with access to markets—the way Microsoft licensed its disk operating system (DOS) to IBM in the early 1980s—it can get its technology into the marketplace much faster. Microsoft was able to leverage its technology off of IBM's huge base of corporate customers, achieving in a few years what would have taken a decade or more to achieve, if indeed it would have been possible. IBM's base of existing customers, built up over 50 years, comprised a ready-made market for Microsoft. Through the licensing arrangement, Microsoft was able to capture that market through the efforts of IBM's superb sales force. Thus, the arrangement gave Microsoft both the market and the means of selling to the market. To this day, it is probably the best deal Bill Gates ever made.

Another way that information is shared and leveraged is through *technology transfer*, a process by which technology becomes *commercialized*. Smart companies watch what's going on in university and government laboratories and even monitor patent filings for technological developments that can affect their business.

MBA Lingo

Technology transfer refers to the movement of technology either out of the laboratory and into commercial application or from one area (such as a country) to another. A technology is **commercialized** when it finds expression in a product. For example, fiber-optic technology has been commercialized in high-speed cable for television and Internet transmission.

Be Your Own Best Competitor

Being your own best competitor means never resting on past achievements. It means always looking for ways to improve what you sell and do—before a competitor does. It means looking at your products and processes the way your customers and competitors do: objectively and with an eye toward what could be better.

The Role of IS

Let's turn to some of the nuts and bolts of producing and distributing information. The management information systems—or IS—department plays a key role in this process. IS is charged with establishing and maintaining computer and communication systems to ensure that the right information is delivered in the right amounts to the right person at the right time.

IS cannot do this alone. The department must work with managers at all levels to learn who needs what information in what amounts and when. This endeavor is complicated by the psychological distance between managers and technical personnel in some companies. Fortunately, most companies have taken steps to close this gap by recognizing the chief information officer (CIO) as a full-fledged member of the senior management team and according IS the status that's given to marketing, accounting, finance, and operations.

They also encourage IS to investigate the practices of competitors and to review (but not necessarily buy) promising new products. And they give IS the clearest possible picture of the business and of the information needs of its managers and employees.

Most companies are long past the days when IS (or data processing, as it used to be called) was viewed as a corporate backwater inhabited by geeks. Instead, they focus IS on getting the information systems to serve the company's strategic goals.

For instance, suppose your goal is improved customer service. In almost any business, IS can help you achieve that goal. Think about it: Customer service representatives can have access to a database of troubleshooting information to assist customers on the other end of the phone. Records of resolved problems can be computerized and reviewed a few days later to ensure that the problem stayed solved. Records can also be analyzed to pinpoint recurrent product defects by product, sales outlet, or type of user.

Case in Point

Wal-Mart is not only the most successful retail chain in the United States, but also now tops the list of the Fortune 500 (a list of the nation's 500 largest companies, compiled by *Fortune* magazine). Much of Wal-Mart's recent growth has come from making its operations more efficient, particularly in the area of inventory management.

Wal-Mart works with suppliers, such as Rubbermaid, to minimize Wal-Mart's inventory through just-in-time inventory management. Ideally, when a Wal-Mart store sells a green Rubbermaid garbage can, it wants Rubbermaid to send that store a new green garbage can to replace the one it just sold. Moreover, this should occur automatically through placement of a computer-to-computer order between the two companies' inventory control systems. (Several years ago, Rubbermaid invested significant amounts in new, sophisticated injection-molding technology in order to keep pace with Wal-Mart's needs.)

Wal-Mart has the market power to demand just-in-time efficiency from its suppliers. However, it is the creative application of information technology that makes that kind of efficiency possible.

If your goal is to improve the quality of a manufactured product, computerized quality assurance (QA) devices can help the cause. For example, parts traveling on a conveyor belt can be scanned for defects by a monitor. An operator can be alerted and the information on the defect fed into a database and into a report of defects, so that problems can be pinpointed.

The application of information technology (IT) to efforts to reach strategic goals are too numerous too mention. *Just-in-time* (JIT) inventory practices are almost impossible without computerized information on sales, inventory, and production levels. The efficiency of routing, dispatching, and tracking trucks, planes, and trains is enhanced tremendously. The entire world of finance is being revolutionized by computer technology. For example, the trading of securities now takes place at a much faster pace than was possible even 10 years ago. Moreover, there is every reason to believe that IT will continue to be the enabling force behind productivity gains and competitive improvements for the foreseeable future.

The strategic goals of increased quality, efficiency, speed, and accuracy can all be served by IT. The challenge is to use the fundamental practices of management to ensure that these goals are served. As a starting point, the more that business managers educate IS managers and professionals about the business, the better the alignment between IS and the business.

The Promise of E-Commerce

E-commerce broadly refers to all commercial transactions that occur on the World Wide Web. This includes web-based advertising, selling, shopping, and purchasing and, more broadly, all Internet- or *intranet*-based functions that support these activities, such as online order tracking and inventory systems. For instance, e-commerce includes the mechanism by which a customer can place an order with Federal Express online *and* the online mechanism by which the customer can track his or her package as it travels to its destination.

MBA Lingo

Just-in-time, or JIT, inventory refers to the practice of keeping very low levels of inventory, either at the factory or at the customer site, or both. Companies using just-in-time practices use sophisticated ordering and manufacturing methods to get the product into inventory just in time to be shipped. The goal of just-in-time is to maximize inventory turnover and minimize the money tied up in inventory.

MBA Lingo

E-commerce includes web-based advertising, selling, shopping, and purchasing, as well as all Internet- or intranet-based functions and functions that support these activities. An **intranet** is a company-owned communication network that uses the technology of the Internet and the World Wide Web, but is dedicated to the needs of the company and is not available to the public.

There's wide agreement in the business community that the full potential of e-commerce has not been tapped. At the moment, many companies that made a mad dash to "get something up on the web" or who made large investments in ill-conceived efforts are trying to digest the lessons of the experience and of the bursting of the dot-com bubble.

At this point, the basic e-commerce lessons learned so far appear to be:

♦ Web-based efforts must be based on, justified by, and applied to the actual business needs of a company's customers, suppliers, employees, investors, and other stakeholders. They should not be "technology driven." Web-based efforts must also be aligned with the company's strategy and operations.

♦ There is no "New Economy" in which the workings of traditional economics have been suspended.

♦ Every web-based effort requires a business plan and a team that includes both businesspeople and technologists. Without technologists, businesspeople may underutilize (or fail to utilize) the web. Without businesspeople, technologists can lose sight of business realities.

♦ The web is a new medium with its own characteristics and uses. Like other media, it does some things better than others. It is best suited to maintaining interactive contact, conveying information, and communicating with and among large groups.

♦ The web works better for information that users "pull" rather than information that companies "push." (In other words, users will look for information they want, but will ignore junk e-mail.) Also, not everyone has constant access to the web or an interest in using it.

♦ Despite the hundreds of billions of dollars misallocated by investors during the dot-com bubble of the late 1990s, the web has been and will be profitably, productively applied to numerous information-management and commercial tasks.

The following are just a few of the many web-based applications that have proven themselves:

♦ The web provides a worldwide, round-the-clock, low-cost order-taking mechanism for many types of businesses, including personal computer and other equipment manufacturers, airlines, resorts, and makers of food, clothing, sporting goods, and office supplies.

♦ Virtually every publicly held company communicates with investors through its website.

◆ Distance learning—training and education conducted over the web—is now a reality, and web-based learning is among the fastest-growing areas of higher education. Many companies also participate in, or develop their own, distance-learning programs.

◆ A huge range of companies make customer service information, online diagnostic tools, and searchable, full-text, continually updated technical manuals and product documentation available to customers and to their own technicians anytime, anywhere.

◆ Telecommunications, publishing, credit card, investment, and other financial-services companies and government agencies provide continually updated online account information to customers. Intranets give employees and retirees online access to their benefits accounts.

◆ E-mail, which the web has enabled, has provided a whole new means of communication on both a person-to-person and companywide basis.

These applications are in addition to the advertising and selling done on the web by millions of businesses. In the process, the web has driven down the cost and raised the productivity of the people engaged in these tasks. This increase in productivity has been a major payoff of the huge investment in information technology that companies, nonprofits, government agencies, and households have made in the past decade. (Recall the economic effects of increased productivity that I explained in Chapter 6.)

As of this writing, U.S. businesses are still absorbing the investment they made in technology and telecommunications during the 1990s expansion. However, they will gradually renew their efforts to gain competitive advantage and increase productivity through e-commerce as the economy recovers and new applications for the web are developed.

The Least You Need to Know

◆ Because information has become so valuable, it is a strategic resource equal to the traditional resources of money, labor, and productive capacity.

◆ The Information Age demands speed, flexibility, knowledge, rapid communications, decentralized decision making, and the ability to customize. Size, money, physical location, market share, and the ability to standardize are becoming less important.

◆ Information that flows to, from, and within the company must be accurate, aligned, and well understood if you are to achieve your business goals.

◆ A company can secure its information by documenting it using a document-retention schedule, installing proper security systems, and issuing nondisclosure agreements.

◆ A company can best exploit its corporate knowledge by applying it to new products and productive processes, using templates, forming alliances and joint ventures, and competing hardest against itself.

◆ The full potential of e-commerce is far from realized, even though many companies have used the World Wide Web in various functions. Any company not working to apply the power of the Internet to information distribution and transaction processing will soon find itself outflanked by more creative competitors.

Chapter 25

Mind Your Ps and Qs: Productivity and Quality

In This Chapter

- ◆ How to measure productivity
- ◆ Ways to increase productivity
- ◆ Creating a "culture of quality" in your organization

Have you ever given someone a job and heard them ask, "Do you want it done fast or do you want it done right?" Although you may not have liked hearing it, it's a good question. There is often a trade-off between productivity and quality.

For a company, department, or other operation, productivity is usually measured by how fast something happens—how many units of product come off the assembly line per hour, how many hours it takes to build a car, how many tons of steel are produced by a mill in a year, how many customers a restaurant can serve per day. Productivity is about time and quantity: How long it takes to do how much.

Quality is measured by how well something is done. It's about how many defects occur, how many products break down, how many customers are satisfied rather than dissatisfied.

In this chapter, you'll learn about productivity and quality and ways of promoting them in your business.

What Is Productivity?

Productivity is the amount of output created by a person, machine, or organization (or a nation, as we saw in Chapter 6). Output can be measured in dollars of value, units of product, number of customers served, kilowatts, or any another measure that makes sense for a business. The more output, the greater the productivity.

Productivity is really another way of saying efficiency. An efficient worker or machine produces more output than an inefficient one. An efficient use of funds produces a greater return than an inefficient one. This last point is key: Money itself must be put to the most productive uses available.

These elements—workers, machines, and money—are what economists call factors of production. It is management's job to make sure that each factor of production is used as efficiently as possible.

There is a wonderful saying in management: To manage it, you must measure it. Therefore, let's look at some ways of measuring and managing productivity.

Measuring Productivity

Productivity can be measured in various ways. Productivity as we are analyzing it here is not a total concept (as it is to an economist assessing a nation's productivity growth). Here we are concerned with productivity per worker or per machine. In a business, you increase productivity by increasing output per worker or per machine. If you increase the output of the business by simply adding more workers or equipment, you are not increasing productivity, but instead expanding your workforce or capacity. That may be desirable or necessary, but it is not increasing productivity.

Calculating Worker Productivity

You can use the following formula to measure worker productivity:

$$\text{Worker Productivity} \quad = \quad \frac{\text{Output in units or dollars}}{\text{Worker hours}}$$

So if a staff of 15 production workers produces 9,000 gewgaws a week and the work week is 40 hours:

$$\text{Worker Productivity} \quad = \quad \frac{9{,}000}{600\ (=15\times40)}$$

Worker Productivity = 15 gewgaws per hour

Each worker produces 15 gewgaws per hour. This is, of course, an average. As a manager, in many situations you can also assess individual productivity. If some workers can produce more than 15 per hour, you can perhaps study their methods and try to apply them to other workers.

Calculating Machine Productivity

You can use a similar formula to calculate machine productivity:

$$\text{Machine Productivity} \quad = \quad \frac{\text{Output in units or dollars}}{\text{Machine hours}}$$

Suppose you have five machines and each one operates 40 hours a week:

$$\text{Machine Productivity} \quad = \quad \frac{9{,}000}{200\ (=5\times40)}$$

Machine Productivity = 45 gewgaws per hour

Again, this measure is an average and could be put to various uses—for example, to see how much more productive a newer machine may be compared with an older one.

More, More! Faster, Faster!

Everyone wants to increase productivity. There are several ways of doing this, including

♦ Improving worker skills and motivation.

♦ Improving the equipment.

♦ Improving production methods.

MBA Mastery

However you measure productivity, be sure that you *do* measure it. In some businesses this can present challenges, but even an imperfect measure of productivity will enable you to manage it, provided you apply it consistently.

Each of these methods of increasing productivity involves an investment on the part of management. You must invest time, effort, and usually money to increase productivity. Why bother? Because the greater the productivity of an operation, the greater the financial returns it produces.

Let's look at each of these ways of increasing productivity.

Boosting Employee Skills and Motivation

To improve worker productivity, you generally must invest in workers. This can involve either hiring workers who have better skills, experience, and education, or training workers to become more productive.

To get higher productivity by investing in workers, you must invest in skills, experience, education, and training related to their jobs and day-to-day duties. Most companies with company-sponsored training or tuition reimbursement plans for education use them only for courses that apply to the worker's current job. That's smart, because you don't want to be in the business of training and educating people so they can leave your company for a better position elsewhere.

> **MBA Mastery**
>
> In some situations, employees "take the training and run" or "take the experience and run" to another company. If you tend to pay low and hire young workers, you can be especially vulnerable to this.

A number of companies see high employee turnover as a way to control labor costs by constantly replacing experienced workers with less experienced but cheaper ones. These firms tend not to invest much in training. But if you do invest in training, remember that you lose that investment when the employee leaves. So if you invest in training you should try to limit your employee turnover.

Paying for Production

Another way to improve worker productivity is to provide incentives for them to be more productive. These incentives may be financial; perhaps you pay workers by the number of products they produce rather than the number of hours they work. Incentives can also be in the form of awards or special recognition, which tends to be less effective. You can offer productivity bonuses for individuals or teams, or provide awards or recognition on a team or individual basis.

You saw in Chapter 17 that salespeople tend to be more productive when they have financial incentives. But you also saw that financial incentives, particularly straight commission, can cause trouble. For production workers, they can cause quality to suffer. If you send workers the message that quantity is the overriding goal, you can wind up with more product—and a lot more defects, breakdowns, and returns.

MBA Lingo

The **limiting factor** in a situation is the element that will stop the process, even when other factors are still operating. For example, the limiting factor in the distance a vehicle can travel is the amount of gasoline it can carry.

Another problem with paying for high production is that after awhile it doesn't work. There are usually very real limitations on how much workers can produce. A worker can physically go only so fast. A machine can pop out only so many units. So unless the *limiting factor* in your operation is the speed at which employees work, you simply can't increase productivity significantly with financial incentives.

What's the Motivation?

Worker motivation is a major determinant of worker productivity. As we learned in Part 1, motivating workers and teams calls for management and leadership skills.

To raise worker motivation to the highest possible levels, leaders must create and sustain a sense of mission in employees by building trust and sharing a vision of what the company could be. They must focus people on the right tasks (and have them stop performing unproductive tasks) and foster a sense of personal accountability in each employee. Effective leaders also coach their people to be more productive. Other tools for motivating people include mission statements (which set forth the corporate ideals), high expectations (which call on people to put forth their best efforts or leave the outfit), and participative management (which gives employees a greater role in setting and achieving goals).

There is no perfect way to increase and maintain motivation. But companies that truly excel do manage to create corporate cultures in which people are motivated to work very hard and to be very productive.

For a variety of reasons, once you have a skilled, educated, trained, well-paid, and motivated workforce, productivity comes down to managing well and requesting extraordinary time and effort from workers when the business demands extraordinary production.

Case in Point

Companies with the most productive workforces tend to be rapidly growing companies with strong leaders and clear goals. The rapid growth creates an external demand (from customers) for high productivity. The strong leader creates an internal demand for productivity and sets an example. The vision and the goals—for example, to be the biggest, the first, the best, or to reach a certain size by a certain time—bind everyone into a cohesive team. In this environment, unproductive people leave or are forced out.

Good examples include any number of firms that once experienced rapid growth with strong leaders and big goals. Several that come to mind include Digital Equipment, Apple Computer, Federal Express, and Starbucks. That kind of growth, unfortunately, does not last forever. So the challenge of managing to motivate people to stay highly productive never ends.

Improving Equipment

Perhaps the easiest, if not the cheapest, way to increase productivity is to give workers better equipment. There are several ways that this investment can boost productivity:

♦ New equipment is often more productive simply because it runs better.

♦ New equipment (for example, an improved or higher-end model) often offers more productive capacity.

♦ New equipment can often be run with fewer workers, thus enabling you to replace labor with capital.

♦ New equipment can improve quality (I'll cover this later in the chapter).

MBA Mastery

Substituting capital for labor—that is, workers with machinery—is perhaps the oldest way of boosting productivity. In the long run, equipment is generally cheaper than employees. It requires less management and never gets sick or leaves for another employer. This substitution can, however, be tougher to achieve in service businesses than in manufacturing.

Returning to our earlier example, recall that the average worker can make 15 gewgaws an hour. That's worker productivity. Recall also that the average machine can make 45 gewgaws an hour. That's machine productivity. There were five machines in the shop and each machine required three workers. The 15 workers operating the five machines produce 9,000 gewgaws per week, assuming a 40-hour week.

What would happen if we replaced one of those five machines with a new one that required only one worker and could produce 75 gewgaws per hour?

Productivity would increase. In fact, the five machines (which include the new one) could now produce a total of 9,000 gewgaws in a little over 35 hours rather than 40 hours. This would allow you to reduce the workers' hours (thereby saving labor costs) while maintaining the same level of production.

Why?

Because in 35 hours, four machines producing 45 gewgaws an hour will make 6,300 gewgaws (= $4 \times 35 \times 45$). And in 35 hours, one machine producing 75 gewgaws an hour will make 2,625 gewgaws (= $1 \times 35 \times 75$). The total production of all the machines in 35 hours will be 8,925 (= 6,300 + 2,625).

Case in Point

Many service business have harnessed information technology, and the energy of their own customers, to raise their productivity. For example, when bank customers use ATMs, they enable the bank to reduce the number of tellers. When Federal Express enabled customers to track the status of their packages on the web, they also reduced the number of incoming phone calls that employees had to field. Any company that enables customers to check the status of their accounts or troubleshoot their product problems on the web uses technology in the same way.

Ideally, this is a win-win strategy: It's more productive for the company and easier for the customer. However, reality often falls short of the ideal, for example, when customers can't reach a human receptionist or have no alternative to the technical manual on the website. Smart companies enable customers to serve themselves, but give them the option of being served.

That 8,925 is only 75 gewgaws short of 9,000. You can get to the 9,000 by keeping one additional worker on overtime for one hour to run the new machine for one extra hour and produce the final 75 gewgaws.

Again, thanks to this productivity increase, you can reduce your outfit's work week from 40 hours to 35 hours. This reduction will create significant savings for your company on labor costs. In fact, new and improved equipment can often kick an operation up to a completely new level.

Improve the Processes

A final way to boost productivity is to examine the processes in your operation with an eye toward improving them. Process improvements are a major goal in *reengineering* a company.

Process improvements come from examining all the ways in which the work is performed and seeing how the tasks could be redesigned for greater efficiency, that is, for greater productivity. This can include examining and redesigning the type or the number of tasks performed by a single worker, the way work gets to the worker (for example, conveyor belts versus handoff from another worker), and the layout of the work area.

Improvements can be realized by training workers in new methods and in the use of new equipment. Thus, a process improvement can include both an investment in workers and an investment in equipment.

> **MBA Lingo**
>
> **Reengineering** means analyzing a company or an operation, carefully deciding which activities the company should continue, abandon, or outsource, and then designing the most efficient way of doing this. The term *reengineering* has often been misused to refer to massive layoffs and redistribution of the same work to the remaining staff. This is not really reengineering.

You can identify ways to improve work processes by interviewing the people actually doing the work. These interviews should be conducted by outside consultants who grant "amnesty" to workers who cite inefficiencies. That way, you'll get honest answers. The interviews should focus on identifying waste in all its forms, including wasted time, equipment, effort, materials, heat, and electricity. Focus especially on the time that people spend waiting for something or someone, working on a task that does not really require their skills, or tracking down information that should be readily available. When properly conducted, these interviews usually identify easy ways to save time and other resources and thus raise productivity.

Work studies are another way to understand your work processes. In a work study, some employees are asked to list all of the tasks they perform in an average week. Then, for about a month, they wear a beeper set to go off at random intervals. When the beeper goes off, they place a checkmark next to the task on the list that they were performing at the moment. (Few employees enjoy doing this, but dedicated people who realize that the work, and not their performance, is being studied will cooperate.)

Work studies break down processes and show how people actually spend their time. This enables management to eliminate waste by asking, "Why do we have people doing this?" Eliminating waste in a process is the surest way to increase the productivity of that process.

Case in Point

Studies conducted in supermarkets by Conway Management Company, a consulting firm, show that the average chain can increase its overall productivity by 20 to 30 percent by reducing wasted resources, including time, produce, baked goods, heat, and electricity. For instance, one chain had all stores constantly rearranging their produce displays to convey an image of freshness. This practice wasted employees' time, damaged produce (with added handling), *and* irritated customers, who couldn't find what they wanted because it was never in the same place. Why were the stores rearranging produce displays? Because they had always done it that way.

At another chain a program of preventive maintenance—in which a part for, say, a freezer, is replaced on a schedule rather than waiting for it to break down—saved tens of thousands of dollars annually. The program reduced the time employees spent responding to crises, overtime pay for repair crews, and wasted food.

What Is Quality, Anyway?

We usually think of quality as *goodness* or *excellence* or *superiority*. In business it can mean these things, and often does. However, it is best to think of quality as a decision and a goal.

First, let's consider quality as a decision. As mentioned in Chapter 1, you can have relatively low quality at a low price or relatively high quality at a high price. Customers know this, and so do companies. So a company has to decide what level of quality it wants to pursue.

That level of quality becomes the goal. For products, the goal is often best formulated in terms of the number of defects you can tolerate. These defects can be discovered by inspection or by the less desirable means of merchandise returns, warranty claims, and breakdowns. In service businesses, the goal may be formulated by calculating the average waiting time for customers in a store or restaurant, customer satisfaction, and number of complaints.

The decision about quality flows from your company's business philosophy, image, costs, target markets, and prices, and its human, financial, and other resources. Here we focus on the pursuit of quality, once you have decided on a level of quality.

Quality Assurance

Quality assurance (also known as *quality control*) has several meanings. First, it can encompass all of the activities that go into achieving the level of quality the company desires and customers demand. This could include everything from designing the product's specifications, to creating standards for suppliers of the materials used in the product, to various inspections done during manufacturing.

Second, it refers to the final inspection performed before a product is shipped. Note that this inspection can be performed by a human being or through technology. For example, the manufacturing process can include running the product by a computerized scanner that is programmed to recognize any defects.

Third, quality control refers to mathematical tools involving statistics and probability that are applied in manufacturing for tasks such as sampling products and minimizing defects. For instance, in many situations it would be too costly to inspect every product. So an inspector may pull a mathematically determined sample of each hour's or each day's production and use the results of that inspection to measure the quality of the entire production run. (Recall the example in Chapter 9 of chickens that had to weigh 3 to 5 pounds for shipment.)

> **MBA Lingo**
>
> **Quality assurance** (or **quality control**) refers both to policies, programs, and efforts to minimize product defects and ensure a high degree of quality, and to the formal function that conducts these activities within a company.

Finally, quality control can refer to the quality control department that inspects products and performs other activities associated with maintaining product quality. Most operations have someone responsible for a quality check, while major manufacturers have large departments dedicated to the task.

How to Control Quality

Over the past 20 years, towering stacks of books and more conferences than you could attend in a lifetime have been devoted to the issue of quality. The wake-up call for U.S. manufacturers was Japan's success in the U.S. auto market in the 1970s. Before then, U.S. manufacturers of autos—and of many other products—had grown complacent about quality. Some even designed their products for *planned obsolescence*.

> **MBA Lingo**
>
> **Planned obsolescence** refers to the tactic of withholding a feature from a product so you can introduce a "new and improved" product later, or repeatedly making cosmetic changes to a product so it constantly "goes out of style," or building the product so it breaks down at some future point and requires replacement. The product becomes obsolete, but you planned it that way.

Here are three practical steps in the quality control process:

- Developing quality standards
- Applying the quality standards
- Creating a corporate "culture of quality"

As you read about these steps, keep in mind that quality control has two basic purposes: first, to meet the customers' expectations and create satisfied customers, and second, to find cost-effective ways of fulfilling the first purpose.

Developing Quality Standards

One big issue in quality control centers on the number or percentage of defects that are acceptable. Traditionally, manufacturers believed that because manufacturing processes are imperfect—machines go out of alignment, people get tired, mistakes are made—you cannot eliminate defects.

With this approach, quality control means deciding what number and what types of defects are acceptable. These decisions amount to your standards, which must factor in customer expectations. For example, you might say that defects that affect performance are not acceptable, but that small defects in appearance are. Or you may say that you are willing to discard only 2 percent of the production run for defects, and you ship the rest.

Of course, you have important decisions to make regarding the number and type of defects you will accept. Too many defects will result in poor quality. And the wrong type of defects—for instance, those affecting customer safety—can bankrupt the company in product liability claims.

What About Zero Defects?

Quality consultant Philip Crosby has made the quest for zero defects his cause. This clearly goes against the traditional approach of deciding which defects to accept. Crosby believes that a policy of knowingly accepting *any* defects will lead to accepting too many. The standard should be zero defects, because to have a standard that accepts *any* defects is to tell employees that defects are okay. A common side effect of accepting defects is a loss of focus on customer needs. After all, the customer wants zero defects.

Also underlying the zero-defects goal is the notion that it is easier to do something right the first time than to fix it later.

Nevertheless, perfection is a tough—and more to the point, expensive—goal to pursue. What's more, if you try to use it as a selling point, you may be going out on a limb. Customers may not believe it, and worse, it will amplify the impact of any defects or quality problems that do occur.

In the end, each company must define its own approach to quality standards.

What Are Quality Standards?

Whether you accept some level of defects or shoot for zero, the way you define and measure standards will depend on your operation and industry. For most manufacturing operations, you will need standards in the following areas and of the following types:

Area	Type of Standard
Performance	Product fulfills its functions
	Product meets performance specifications
Appearance	Adherence to design specifications
	Uniformity of color
Workmanship	Smoothness of finish
	Tightness of joints and fittings
Content	Purity (for foods, drugs) and percentages of allowed content (for fat or other ingredients)
Safety	Resistance to fire or to breakage that would endanger the user

Management, marketing, engineering, operations, and the design team must all be involved in developing quality standards. The product must be as safe as the company can possibly make it. But beyond that, the standards must be developed with a sharp eye on costs, target market, and company image.

Applying Quality Standards

Applying the quality standards is traditionally the work of the quality control department. Most of us think of quality control as the department that inspects the final product to see whether or not it passes and is fit for shipment. However, you must apply quality standards more broadly than that.

You must apply quality standards in the purchasing function, where the company decides which materials to buy and where to buy them. You must apply them in the receiving department, so that someone checks to see that materials shipped to the company meet the standards. You must apply quality standards in operations, so that products are properly made at each step of production.

For most manufacturing processes, this constant quality control is more effective and less expensive than waiting until the product is completed before giving it a passing or failing grade.

Aside from applying quality standards to materials and products at various stages of production, quality control faces the task of discovering the reasons for variations in quality. Discovering defects is good, but preventing them is even better. So when quality control people notice a pattern of standards not being met, they must learn why and try to fix it.

Creating a Corporate "Culture of Quality"

Some people think of quality as something that only applies to high-quality, high-priced products. However, quality control applies to every company, because the real issue is maintaining the desired level of quality—the level of quality that the customer wants and is willing to pay for.

For any company, when it comes to quality, the real management challenge is to create a culture of quality. In a culture of quality, every product and every customer is important. Every stage of production is important. In a culture of quality, every employee internalizes these ideas and works on quality.

How do you create a culture of quality?

It begins with the goals, strategies, and plans presented by management. It goes on to hiring, training, compensation, and promotion practices. It has to do with the marketing messages and sales stories you send to customers. It must permeate the customer service function. It affects purchasing, receiving, operations, and shipping. It extends to your suppliers and distribution channels. All of this amounts to *total quality management.*

MBA Alert

Good quality control can actually be more important to the company with a lower-quality, lower-priced strategy. There is less variation and fewer mistakes when you pay top dollar for labor and materials. With a low-cost, low-price strategy you have more chance of trouble as well as a smaller profit margin to absorb the costs of repairs, replacements, recalls, and warranty claims.

MBA Lingo

The term **total quality management,** or TQM, refers to every area of the organization involved in creating quality. TQM means that everyone is responsible for quality. It also assumes that quality must be designed in and built in, rather than be something added at the last step of production. TQM was something of a "fad" in the 1990s, but became a permanent effort in some companies.

One excellent way to create a culture of quality is to have everyone in the company think of themselves as serving customers—even if they don't actually deal with "real" customers on a daily basis. Everyone has internal customers to serve. For example, the accounting function delivers reports to other managers, who are its internal customers. The marketing department has the sales department as its key internal customer. The purchasing department has operations as its internal customer. And so on.

Thus, the notions of customer service and customer satisfaction can be used as motivators and standards in every area and for every person in the outfit.

In a culture of quality, everyone works to high standards within the context of the company's costs and values. They hold themselves and they hold one another to these standards. Those who cannot or will not join the culture, or those who undermine the effort of the larger group, eventually either choose to leave or are forced out—if they even get into the company in the first place.

Tools for Quality Control

In addition to the tasks of developing standards, applying standards, and creating a culture of quality, there are several tools that can assist you in the quest for quality. These tools include the following:

♦ Supplier programs

♦ Quality circles

♦ Control charts

♦ Best practices and benchmarking

Let's talk briefly about each one.

Supplier Programs

Various large manufacturers, including Ford Motor Company, have supplier programs that involve suppliers of materials and components in achieving and maintaining high quality. In a supplier program, the company issues strict specifications and works closely with suppliers to get the levels of quality it desires.

These programs often require the company to formally rate suppliers on their quality. The company will then, on the basis of these ratings, designate certain suppliers as "star suppliers" or a "prime source" and give them longer contracts or larger orders, or both, compared with other suppliers.

> **MBA Mastery**
>
> Supplier programs actually fall within the larger framework of supply-chain management. A company's supply chain includes its suppliers and the processes by which materials move from supplier to purchaser. Supply-chain management coordinates sales forecasts, production plans, inventory targets, costs, and quality between a company and its suppliers. This differs from the way companies used to purchase materials. Today companies and suppliers work together on common goals instead of constantly bargaining hard.

Quality Circles

Quality circles are regular meetings of representatives from every part of the production function. In these meetings workers discuss quality problems, reasons for problems, and potential solutions. This is an effort by management to involve employees in maintaining quality and to educate them about the entire issue of quality.

Quality circles push both the responsibility and authority for quality down to those on the production line. This puts the tasks of identifying problems and creating solutions on the workers themselves. The result is greater worker involvement and cooperation and more pride in workmanship.

Control Charts

A control chart shows the *control limits* for various dimensions of the product in a manufacturing process. These help us control the variations that occur in any manufacturing process and which affect product quality.

Suppose we are milling wooden two-by-fours. Let's say that they are supposed to measure $1^3/_4$ inches (the thickness) by $3^1/_2$ inches (the width) when they come off the saw at the mill. Our control chart might look like this:

> **MBA Lingo**
>
> In a manufacturing process, **control limits** are the maximum acceptable deviations above and below a standard. The term **tolerance** refers to the maximum physical limits that the deviation from the standard could reach in a manufacturing process.

Control Chart

Thickness	Specification & Control Limits	Width	Specification & Control Limits
$1^{13}/_{16}$"	Upper limit	$3^7/_8$"	Upper limit
$1^3/_4$"	Specification	$3^1/_2$"	Specification
$1^{11}/_{16}$"	Lower limit	$3^5/_8$"	Lower limit

This chart says that for the thickness of the piece of wood, the lower control limit is $1^1/_2$ and the upper limit is $1^{13}/_{16}$. For the width, the lower limit is $3^5/_8$ and the upper limit is $3^7/_8$.

These limits are generally defined more tightly than the *tolerances*, which are the maximum potential physical deviation from the standard. For instance, in this case the mill may actually produce some two-by-fours that measure two and a quarter inches by four inches. That would define the upper tolerance. In common parlance, people often use the term tolerance to mean control limit, but technically they are distinct.

Referring to this chart—or better yet, incorporating it into an automated measurement process—will tell the production workers when the product is exceeding its control limits and thus moving toward substandard quality. Any pieces which were outside the limits would be recut, if possible, or discarded or sold as "seconds."

Best Practices and Benchmarking

The term best practices refers to the most efficient and most effective way of structuring and conducting a business process. Best practices in product development, for example, indicate the use of cross-functional teams. Best practices in a certain type of electronics manufacturing may indicate the use of printed circuits rather than wiring.

Broadly, best practices means the best way of doing something. It means doing something in the way that those who do it best do it.

Benchmarking refers to a method of comparing your company's practices and performance with those of companies with the best practices that you wish to employ. Benchmarking measures the results of best practices and describes how to get that performance in your processes.

For example, if another company can reduce the time it takes to develop a new product by using cross-functional teams or reduce the number of defects with the use of printed circuits, then you want to know the time they need in order to develop a new product or their number of defects. Those become the benchmarks, the targets you use in your business.

One way to get benchmarking going in your company is to have a task force drawn from key areas of the outfit to investigate best practices in their respective areas. This "best practices task force" can represent their areas and draw on the experience of their people (some of whom may have worked at companies with best practices) and direct their people to do some investigating as well. Much of the research can be drawn from news stories and articles about other companies.

Finally, you actually adapt the best practice to your needs. You begin using cross-functional product-development teams, or start making printed circuits or getting a supplier to make them for you.

MBA Alert

Employing best practices and benchmarking is not copying, or at least it shouldn't be. Instead, you must examine the logic and reasoning behind the practices and performance and then adapt the methods to your operation. Every company is different. Each has its own traditions, culture, and interactions. These "human factors" usually mean that simply trying to copy another company's practice rarely works.

Case in Point

The Baldridge Award, officially known as the Malcolm Baldridge National Quality Award, goes to companies judged to best meet the Baldridge criteria for quality. The U.S. Congress created the award to recognize companies that achieve extraordinary levels of quality and named it after Secretary of Commerce Malcolm Baldridge, who held the post from 1981 until his accidental death in 1987.

Companies that apply for the award are judged in seven areas: leadership, strategic planning, customer and market focus, information and analysis, human resources focus, process management, and business results. Applying for the award represents a significant project, and most companies that do so learn a lot about themselves from the process. Past recipients of the Baldridge Award include Ritz Carlton Hotels, Motorola, Cadillac, AT&T, and Corning Telecommunications Products.

The Challenge of Global Competition

Until fairly recently, U.S. companies had the U.S. markets pretty much to themselves. In other countries, most companies had the domestic market to themselves. In today's global market, however, this is not the case.

When goods, services, money, people, and information can flow freely across national borders—the way they do across state lines in the United States—then competition occurs on a global scale. A company in Ohio or Oregon can see its markets seriously eroded by an outfit in Poland or Paraguay. And it can work the other way around, too.

Competition on a global scale means that productivity and quality are now the two most effective competitive weapons. A marketing strategy or promotional tactic may or may not translate well overseas. Sales methods and distribution channels vary widely from nation to nation. Accounting and financial tactics may or may not work under another nation's accounting policies or financial system.

However, cost, price, value, and satisfaction are universal. A focus on productivity enables a company to control its costs by making the most of its resources. A focus on quality enables a company to deliver the best possible products to its customers. A company that offers good quality at a reasonable price can compete in any environment.

The Least You Need to Know

- Productivity is usually measured by how efficiently something happens. It is about time and quantity: how long it takes to do how much.

- To compare productivity, dollars or units of output are the most common measures. You can calculate both the productivity of workers and of machinery.

- To increase productivity, you can improve worker productivity, improve productive equipment, or improve production processes. Any of these moves involves an investment of time, effort, and (usually) money.

- Quality is measured by how well something is done. It's about how many defects occur, how many products break down, and how many customers are satisfied.

- To maintain or improve quality you must develop quality standards, apply the quality standards, and, if at all possible, create a corporate "culture of quality."

- Specific tools that can help you achieve high quality include supplier programs, quality circles, control charts, and best practices and benchmarking.

Chapter 26

Growing Oaks from Acorns: Entrepreneurship and Small Business Management

In This Chapter

◆ Creating a great business plan

◆ How to find funds to start a business

◆ Buying an existing business

◆ Predictable problems in growing a business

Being an entrepreneur differs sharply from being an administrator. An administrator assumes responsibility for an established department or function within a larger organization. An *entrepreneur* must create a business from scratch and with very limited resources. Although MBA stands for Master of Business Administration, most business schools have established or expanded their course offerings for those who want to become entrepreneurs. This recognizes that many students would rather start a company or join a small company rather than work for a large corporation. They would rather be entrepreneurs than administrators.

But it also recognizes that many large companies want to hire people capable of managing entrepreneurially. These companies realize that sometimes they can compete in a market only by starting a totally new business, apart from or within the larger organization. They have also learned that developing these new businesses calls for approaches different from those required to manage their traditional, established businesses. Thus, they seek entrepreneurial managers for certain areas of the business.

This chapter examines the process of starting a business and managing the growth of a small business. It also touches on ways in which large companies tap entrepreneurs.

Big Plans

The entrepreneur faces three broad tasks. He or she must finance the business, produce the product or service, and bring it to market. Clearly, there are other tasks, such as finding suppliers and setting up an accounting system, but financing, producing, and marketing the product are the big ones.

These tasks are also linked in chicken-and-egg fashion. How do you market a product if you haven't produced it? How do you produce a product if you don't have much money? How do you raise money if you don't have a proven product?

The business plan answers these questions. A business plan describes the product or service, its market and its production and distribution requirements, the background and qualifications of the entrepreneurs, and the amount of money that the business will require.

MBA Lingo

An **entrepreneur** organizes resources into an enterprise that brings a product or service to people who need it, while making a profit for him- or herself and the investors. A **start-up** is a new business created to bring a product or service to market. Most start-ups begin with one product or service, or an idea for one.

The business plan is a blueprint for the business as well as a sales tool. (The business may be either a *start-up* or an existing operation, but I'll discuss plans in terms of start-ups.) As a blueprint, a business plan guides the entrepreneurs through the steps necessary to get the business up and running. Therefore, the business plan must be complete and realistic. As a sales tool it tells potential investors and lenders about the company's business, prospects, and financial requirements. Therefore, it must also be positive and optimistic.

Outline for a Business Plan

Although the exact section titles and their order may vary, every business plan must include the following information:

- Table of Contents

- Executive Summary

- Business, Products, and Services

- Market Analysis

- Management Team

- Operations

- Financial Projections

A business plan should be written in plain English and answer the major questions that prospective investors, lenders, employees, and suppliers have about the enterprise:

- What is the product?

- How large and needy is the market?

- Who are the managers of the business?

- Can this business make and sell the product?

- What are the potential sales and earnings?

Do not load up the main sections of the plan with too much detail. That material should go into appendixes. The outline presented here would work for a proprietorship, partnership, or corporation, but assumes that the business is a corporation seeking equity investors.

Describe the Business, Products, and Services

Describe the location, nature, industry, and history of the business, and its current products and services and those in development. Mention brand names, trademarks, service marks, and patents, as well as any licensing arrangements, alliances, or joint ventures. Although financial information will be covered later, it's good to note sales and profits, and the proportion of sales and profits derived from key products and services, in this section. Also note any trends and government regulations affecting the business.

Particularly if the only products are still in development, briefly describe the underlying technology and the functions it performs and customer needs that it meets. Note the stage of development. For example, is there a prototype? Has it been tested? How will the product be produced, packaged, distributed, serviced, and maintained?

This section is also where basic data on the company—year founded, locations, facilities, number of employees, and so on—should go.

Analyze the Market

Market analysis is a key section of the plan and one of the hardest to write for a business with no track record. In those cases, the analysis will depend almost solely on market research, which should be conducted in each major target market (and which you learned about in Chapter 18).

It is not enough to determine that a good portion of the respondents say they "like" the product concept or are "likely to purchase" it. Survey respondents often give positive answers just to be agreeable. Therefore, the research must ascertain *how and how often they would use* the product, *how they are currently addressing the need* the product addresses, and *how much money they would make or save* by using the product. These questions prompt respondents to relate their needs and behavior to the product.

Market research can also bolster the case for products already in the marketplace. In those instances, the research should substantiate that there is still a large, untapped market for the product even though it is already available.

Finally, the market analysis should describe existing and potential competitors and substitute products. Take care with this section and never assume that your business will face no competition. Even if it has no competition in the beginning, if the business succeeds it soon will have plenty.

Case in Point

Research is not necessarily the last word on a product's feasibility. When a product or service is totally new, a company may just have to launch it to build a market. For example, Citibank developed and introduced the ATM (automatic teller machine) even though survey respondents said they would never use it. People said they needed a live teller, they wouldn't trust a machine, and they feared being robbed. Today, however, most people could barely get along without ATMs.

Note, however, that although Citibank acted in a highly entrepreneurial manner, it was at the time the largest bank in New York. Its branch network and its base of accounts positioned it to win customers over to the new technology.

Marketing and Sales Strategy

Many start-up companies fail not because they have a poor product, but because they cannot sell it or get it distributed. The business plan must therefore present realistic marketing, sales, and distribution strategies (see Part 4). Also mention any firm orders you have for your products or services, and the expected delivery date.

Introduce the Management Team

Investors and lenders must know the qualifications and track records of the business's senior managers. If the product or service depends on technology, they need the same information on the key technical people.

At a minimum, the business needs an experienced general manager, a sales or marketing professional who can close sales, a production manager, a manager of information systems, and an office manager. Perhaps one person can cover two of these functions, but attempting to attract financing without the right people on board is foolhardy.

The plan should include the resumés of key employees and emphasize each individual's qualifications for his or her role. If any key positions have not yet been filled, mention that and a time frame for filling them.

Describe the Operation

The plan must describe how the company's products will be produced and how its services will be delivered. When and how will the production facilities be built, leased, or purchased? What equipment will be necessary and will it be leased or purchased? If production will be done by a *contract manufacturer*, describe the outfit. What are its capabilities? What is its track record? Mention any details, such as packaging, shelf life, and other product characteristics, that affect production, distribution, and storage. Also identify major suppliers and their record of quality and reliability.

MBA Lingo

A **contract manufacturer** produces products to the specifications of another company, which has designed the product and handles the marketing, sales, and distribution. This allows the entrepreneur to minimize his investment in productive plant and equipment.

Discuss the staffing requirements in the various operating functions and the qualifications and sources of any highly specialized personnel (for instance, software engineers).

Other questions to address at this point include the following:

♦ Which distribution channels will be used for the product? Who are the wholesalers, retail chains, or other middlemen involved in the process?

♦ What are the product's transportation and storage requirements?

♦ Are there seasonal variances in the sales and production cycles of the business?

♦ What are the anticipated needs for facilities, equipment, staff, and distribution?

Analyze the Financial Needs and Potential Returns

For an established business, the plan should include historical financial statements for the past five years through the most recent quarter. It should also include *pro forma* statements for the next five years. Present monthly projections for the next two years and quarterly projections for following three years.

> ### MBA Lingo
>
> **Pro forma** financial statements project the values for the various accounts on the balance sheet, income statement, and cash flow statement. Underlying pro forma statements are assumptions about future sales growth, financial requirements, and other factors. Thus, the believability of the pro forma statements depends on the believability of the assumptions, which should be included as footnotes to the statements.

If the company has not yet opened for business, only pro forma statements can be presented. However, an accounting of the money invested so far by the founders and other investors should be presented. How much has been invested and raised? How has it been used? How much cash is on hand? Mention other investors who have backed the business or made firm commitments to back it. Note the current distribution of the company's stock and the effect that new investors will have on that distribution.

The financial section should also include the owners' compensation plan and benefit plan (if any) and those of other employees. Most important, this section must explicitly state how much money you are trying to raise and the uses to which that money will be put.

Keep It Short and Substantive

Some business plans are long on sales pitches and short on substance. While many insubstantial plans did raise money in the 1990s, today's business plans must be true plans rather than sales pitches. That does not, however, mean that a plan should bury the reader in information. Investors "get it" very quickly and can decide whether they are interested on the basis of the two-page executive summary. If they are interested, they will want to meet with you and will request more detailed information.

Incidentally, the planning process may reveal that the business would not, in fact, become successful. If that happens, that's good. You have just saved yourself (and others) huge amounts of time, energy, and money by avoiding a situation that was destined to fail.

Finding Financing

A new venture offers investors an equity stake in the business. If the business grows, they will receive a share of the proceeds when the company goes public or a share of the sales price if the company is sold to a larger company or to new owners. Where do you find venture investors?

The traditional sources of funds for new businesses include the following:

♦ **Managers of the business and their relatives and friends:** Typically, the founders—the senior managers—of a business first use savings, personal bank loans, and even credit cards to raise money for their business. Then they go to family members, relatives, and friends. This can be uncomfortable and must be handled in a businesslike manner.

♦ **Wealthy individuals, known as "angels":** Angels invest directly in the business and are typically savvy businesspeople with a background in the type of businesses they back. Entrepreneurs locate them through personal contacts and flat-out networking.

♦ **Small Business Administration (SBA):** The SBA is an agency within the U.S. Department of Commerce that supports small businesses through information, advice, training, and loan programs. It has far too many loan programs to list here, so it would be best to check out its website at www.sba.gov.

♦ **Venture capital firms:** A venture capital (or VC) firm manages funds that invest money gathered from individual and institutional investors in early-stage companies. The average venture capital firm receives about 100 business plans for every 10 it seriously considers, and then invests in only 1 of those 10.

> **MBA Mastery**
>
> Venture capitalists almost always want a substantial block of stock, a seat on the board of directors, and a role in major decisions. In other words, you give up some control when a venture fund invests in your business. Yet good venture capitalists bring more than money to the table. They bring experience, contacts, and expertise that can help the company grow faster and larger than it otherwise could. A venture capital firm also knows how to go about taking a company through its initial public offering (IPO), meaning the first offering of a corporations stock to the investing public.

♦ **Large corporations, suppliers, and other sources:** Some large corporations realize that the Next Big Thing could be launched by a very small outfit.

Therefore, some of them are open to investing in or forming an alliance with a new or small business with a high-potential product that fits their business. Suppliers rarely invest in a new company, but it does happen. More often a supplier will extend favorable terms to a start-up with the potential to grow into a large customer, particularly if the start-up agrees to use the supplier as its sole source for a key component of its product.

Managing Growth

No matter how well a business has been planned, things rarely proceed according to that plan. After the business begins operating, entrepreneurs generally face one of two problems: growing too slowly or growing too quickly.

If the business is growing too slowly, you should

- Evaluate your salespeople and sales process to ensure that both are able to close sales, rather than just generate interest. New businesses need "missionaries" and "rainmakers"—enthusiastic people who can close sales.

- Adjust your marketing message by examining each of the Five Ps, which I covered in Chapter 19, and experimenting with different combinations.

- If you have a new product, be sure you've identified and reached the relevant innovators and early adopters.

- Find out, through informal and formal research, why customers are not buying or not buying repeatedly—and address those issues.

- Learn whether or not the company is delivering as promised. Great sales efforts must be backed up by great products and service. Early customers will tolerate a few glitches from a new company with a new product. But sloppy service or unsolved problems will inevitably generate bad word of mouth.

- Get hold of the resources needed to grow the business. If the business could grow more quickly with more money, people, and other resources, work hard to get them.

In some cases, patience and persistence are the keys to surviving a slow start. But you must learn why things are starting slowly and remedy the situation.

If the business starts growing too quickly, you have another set of problems. You may be thinking, "We should all have such problems," but business history is filled with companies that grew too fast and flamed out as a result.

If the business is growing too fast, you should

- Exercise leadership to motivate people through the long hours and high demands that growth imposes on a rapidly growing company. Let them share in the rewards of growth (for example, through bonuses).

- Collect your accounts receivable as quickly as possible. Booking sales without collecting the cash will not enable you to pay your employees and suppliers. Consider using the receivables to secure a loan or line of credit in order to speed up your cash flow.

- Do all you can to expand production without compromising quality. Make and ship product as fast as you can, but when quality problems arise, fix them fast, even if it costs a lot. A disappointed customer—particularly a large disappointed customer—can quickly spread the word that you don't have your act together.

- If you're strapped for resources, outsource some of the production, installation, and even customer service, instead of expanding permanently and increasing your fixed costs.

- Keep your investors informed about your success and your problems. They may well be willing to invest more money in what now looks like a success, if that money will help you grow. This would also be a good time to meet with your banker about a loan or line of credit.

- Get all the advice you can from your board of directors, network of advisers, and your accountant, suppliers, and industry association.

- If production, quality, delivery, or financial problems overwhelm the company, seriously consider hiring a competent operating executive to put the right management systems and controls in place.

Never underestimate the power of systems and controls, which are necessary in every company. Management systems provide vital information on the needs and performance of the business—for instance, on sales, expenses, inventory, time usage, customers, transactions, and other aspects of the business. Controls involve understanding the contribution that each activity makes to the business and creating policies and procedures that cut less productive activities and increase the more productive ones.

Systems and controls also send employees, customers, investors, and other stakeholders the message that this is a true business, rather than a fly-by-night operation. Most of all, systems and controls, especially financial controls, keep management in touch with reality.

MBA Mastery

Data must be developed into information by cross-referencing, examining trends, and identifying patterns. For example, data on customers—who they are, where they are, how much they spend on which of your products, how they heard about your company, their creditworthiness, and so on—can be used to develop customer profiles.

A customer profile can enable marketing to target and tailor your company's message to the most promising prospects. It can also help sales understand how best to close deals with them. And this is just one type of information that can be developed from the data generated by good systems.

Policies and procedures distinguish a well-managed business from a seat-of-the-pants outfit. A business needs policies and procedures to guide people in areas such as accepting deliveries, using overnight delivery, purchasing materials, handling customer complaints, and responding to emergencies—to name a few.

This means that in the midst of all the production and sales activity, someone must see to the administrative side of the business. In the early stages, the business may get by with an office manager, a bookkeeper, and a sales assistant, and perhaps with a few people performing multiple functions. However, as the company grows, it will need specialists and even more sophisticated systems.

For instance, when enough money is flowing through the business (the amount varies by industry and company size), an on-staff accountant or controller becomes necessary. In many jurisdictions, once a business has a certain number of employees, it must begin complying with a new level of regulation and perhaps institute an employee benefits plan. At that point, a knowledgeable head of human resources may become necessary. To get to "the next level," a company may need a seasoned vice president of marketing or sales, or even a new CEO. Many companies flounder when an entrepreneur can't let go of the company he or she founded even though he or she is not equal to the managerial demands.

Financing Growth

As the saying goes, it takes money to make money. Start-up capital is only the beginning. It takes money to grow a business, and that money can come from only two places: inside the company or outside the company.

Internally generated funds—the earnings generated by the business—are the cheapest source of growth capital. They carry no interest rate and no promise of future dividends. Internally generated funds also enable the founders to maintain the most control over the company.

Yet insisting that the business stick to self-funding may hamper its growth. If the company is growing—or is positioned to grow—faster than it can fund itself, then it's quite likely that external financing is necessary to bring the company to its greatest potential.

To finance growth, the business must usually locate additional financing from the original investors, new investors, or one or more banks. At a certain point, most truly successful companies at least consider the ultimate step in gaining access to capital: going public.

The IPO

A successful initial public offering will provide long-term capital at a lower cost than borrowing. An IPO also usually enables the early investors in the company—management, angels, venture capitalists, and so on—to reap huge profits.

An IPO comprises a series of steps, which include working up in-depth information on the business and its history and plans (in the form of a prospectus), notifying the SEC of the owners' intention to sell stock to the public, registering the securities with the SEC, setting a price, and deciding how the stock will be sold and distributed.

An investment bank usually guides the owners through this process. Aside from providing the legal and financial expertise to make the IPO happen, the investment bank has the distribution network needed to sell the stock to investors. The investment bank is compensated with a fee, at least some of which is tied to the amount of money raised by the IPO.

A successful IPO, meaning one that raises the targeted amount of capital or close to it, often identifies the issuer as a growth company in the minds of investors. As noted in Chapter 16, these investors expect any profits to be reinvested in the business to finance its growth. For that reason, and for the ability to raise additional capital in the public markets if necessary, going public is the ultimate in financing strategies.

Buying a Business

While the image of the entrepreneur starting on his or her kitchen table or garage and going public several years later may be the popular one, many entrepreneurs prefer to buy a business. While it may take a bit more creativity to start a business from scratch than it does to buy a going concern, the business challenges are quite similar.

Anyone buying a business, whether it's a small retail store or a division of a large company, must understand its products and services, market and customers, facilities

MBA Lingo

Due diligence refers to the process of discovering and understanding all aspects of the business and all the factors that could affect the prospects of the business. Due diligence must be undertaken by brokers representing securities for sale, managers, and investment bankers involved in a merger or acquisition, and anyone buying a business.

MBA Mastery

Leveraged buyouts can be used to take a public company private. The company's senior managers (or other purchasers of the company) pledge the company's assets as collateral for the loans to finance the purchase of the stock. Then they use the proceeds of the loan to buy the stock from the existing shareholders, usually at a premium over the current market price.

and operations, and financial history and prospects. Understanding the impact of current legal actions, tax matters, and regulatory issues on the company is also part of the *due diligence* required when you purchase a business. Rather than deal only with the owners or brokers of the business, speak to key employees, customers, suppliers, and lenders about their history with the business and their role in its future.

In addition to the sources of financing already mentioned in this chapter, the buyers of the business may be able to use a leveraged buyout to raise some or most of the funding. In a leveraged buyout, or LBO, the new owners use the assets of the company to finance the purchase of the company. The borrowings are then repaid out of the company's future cash flow. If the current managers of a company are buying the business from the owners, the transaction is often referred to as a management buyout.

However they finance the purchase, people buying a company must understand the business, develop a plan to keep the company growing or to boost its growth, and avoid paying too high a price. Any key employees, and for that matter the former owners, should be available in at least a consulting capacity to see that the new owners get off to a good start. This is particularly important for buyers of a service business, where the relationships and skills of the former owners probably played a big role in the success of the business.

As always, *caveat emptor* (buyer beware) are the watchwords. It is easy for a buyer to overpay for a successful business. Savvy founders are motivated to sell when the value of the company has peaked. They may know that competitors are entering the market, that the company's technology is about to be superceded, or that the fad that drove their success is about to end. It's difficult to know these things if you're not in the industry. In other words, there is almost no way to overdo due diligence.

CAUTION

MBA Alert _____

If you buy a business, try to structure the deal so that part of the purchase price depends on the future earnings of the company. This can be tough to do, because the seller (a) wants his or her money, and (b) doesn't want his or her payments to depend on your competence. Yet to the extent that at least some of the price can be linked to certain contingencies (for example, continuance of a contract with a major account), you as a buyer have some protection.

Corporate Ventures

Many major companies understand the value of entrepreneurial behavior and realize that their organizations are too large and rigid to encourage such behavior. While these companies need the creativity, drive, and willingness to take risks of the entrepreneur, most true entrepreneurs do not want to work for them. The standard salary structures and bonus policies of most large companies don't offer the entrepreneur the earnings potential of starting a company, particularly one that might go public. Bureaucracy stifles entrepreneurs, and they lack the patience to sit through unproductive meetings, deal with the chain of command, and have their ideas reviewed, altered, and, perhaps, killed.

Recognizing this, a number of large companies have launched efforts, called corporate venture programs, to find and tap into entrepreneurial businesses in their industry. Others try to give their "home-grown entrepreneurs" the environment and compensation they need in order to act like entrepreneurs.

A corporate venture program looks for new businesses, solicits and reviews business plans, and provides financial, distribution, and other resources needed by a small company. As noted, the deals may range from distribution or licensing agreements to direct investment in the smaller company.

Efforts to grow in-house entrepreneurs are often related to product development, R&D, or business-development efforts. The company will form a small team under the leadership of a creative executive with both technical and business skills and give it a mission. Ideally, the team is cut off geographically from the rest of the company, provided with extra financial incentives, and given funding, a goal, and freedom to find ways of reaching that goal.

However, true entrepreneurs put their own capital at risk and want complete autonomy. Thus, it is difficult for a large company to create and hold on to true entrepreneurs, because that element of risk (and extraordinary reward) cannot really be duplicated in a large, relatively secure organization. Yet large companies can encourage a certain amount of entrepreneurial behavior, and some have had some success in doing so.

Entrepreneur Away

Not everyone is suited to the entrepreneurial way of work. It takes dedication, high energy, tolerance for risk, willingness to fail, and the ability to form relationships and get things done with minimal organizational structure. That last item is key. Most of us spend most of our early years in structured environments—family, school, scout troop, baseball or soccer team, band or debating squad, and military service. In contrast, entrepreneurs must function with very little structure. They make it up as they go along.

That ability to improvise—to make it up as they go along, and to do it productively and profitably—may be the signal characteristic of true entrepreneurs. That is a difficult thing to learn. But many entrepreneurs have learned how to improvise, if only because they had to in response to the demands of the market and their business. Moreover, very few entrepreneurs would change their way of working. Most people who "go out on their own" never regret it, and that even includes the ones who fail.

The Least You Need to Know

- ◆ An entrepreneur identifies a need and organizes the financial, productive, human, and other resources required to fill that need, and then, if he or she succeeds, fills it profitably.

- ◆ Entrepreneurs either buy a business or start their own. The latter is the more challenging undertaking, but both require a true entrepreneurial approach.

- ◆ Successful start-up companies are built around a product or service that meets a genuine need, by founders with management skills, access to financing, and the means to make, market, deliver, and distribute the product or service.

- ◆ A business plan is the sales tool for the entrepreneur seeking investors.

- ◆ Sources of financing include the founders themselves, individual investors (or "angels"), large companies, venture capital firms, and sometimes banks.

- ◆ Large companies that have tried to encourage entrepreneurial behavior have a mixed record, but those that have succeeded have reaped rewards.

Chapter 27

Doing Well by Doing Good: Business Law and Ethics

In This Chapter

- ◆ How business and society interact
- ◆ Key areas of the law that concern managers
- ◆ The importance of business ethics

The financial accounting and stock trading scandals of the early 2000s revealed a high level of greed and self-dealing among senior managers of some companies. Enron, Global Crossing, Qwest, Computer Associates, and AOL were subject to criminal investigation. Executives at Arthur Andersen, WorldCom, Tyco, Aldelphia Communications, and Imclone Systems were charged with crimes ranging from fraud to obstruction of justice. Merrill Lynch paid a $100 million fine to New York State for violations of securities law.

Moreover, scores of publicly held companies have had to restate their earnings over the past two years due to "aggressive" or improper accounting practices. Millions of investors collectively lost billions of dollars because they followed the recommendations of Wall Street analysts touting stocks that their own employers had a stake in (including stocks that they knew were worthless). The staggering levels of senior executive pay at some large companies—even when they perform poorly—and the tight link between politics and corporate contributions among members of both major political parties have further eroded people's trust in business, or at least "Big Business."

Of course, wrongdoing occurs in all institutions and professions, so business has not cornered the market on legal trouble and ethical lapses. Yet, given the scale of business wrongdoing in recent years, it's clearly time for every businessperson to take time to understand his or her legal and ethical responsibilities.

This chapter aims to assist you in developing that understanding by providing an overview of the major legal and ethical issues in business.

Society, Business, and the Law

Any society worthy of the name has laws. Many people believe laws form the very basis of society. Traditional tribal societies are governed by laws, and modern societies have extremely elaborate systems governing both criminal behavior and civil matters.

CAUTION

MBA Alert

Please understand that I am not an attorney, nor am I dispensing legal advice. Rather, I am pointing out the areas of the law that managers should be aware of, and underscoring the value of ethical behavior in business.

Society makes laws to govern people's behavior. The criminal code, the set of laws that define criminal behavior, simply forbids certain behavior. The civil code governs property rights and the rights of organizations and individuals. Each of us has a right to buy and own property, to enjoy using it, and to live without suffering because of someone else's negligent behavior. Similarly, each of us has an obligation to act responsibly, and that includes acting responsibly in our business dealings.

Business Law

Business law governs the conduct of people and organizations engaged in business. Major areas of business law include the following:

- Antitrust
- Consumer protection
- Product liability
- Bankruptcy

- Real estate and insurance
- Employment
- Intellectual property
- Securities regulation

- Business organization
- Contracts
- Uniform commercial code
- Taxation

Let's look at the legal issues surrounding each of these areas.

Antitrust

The antitrust laws ensure that competition remains fair. The *monopolies* of the late 1800s and early 1900s in industries such as railroads, oil, and steel prompted the federal government to pass antitrust laws. Antitrust law prohibits companies from merging with one another or acquiring one another to form monopolies.

Restraint of trade can include monopolistic practices and other attempts to limit competition in an industry or business. For instance, an agreement that "punishes" customers for doing business elsewhere would be an attempt to restrain trade.

> **MBA Lingo**
>
> A **monopoly** exists when there is only one supplier of some product or service. The monopoly can usually charge whatever prices it wants to, because it has no competition.

Case in Point

In the late 1990s, several competitors of Microsoft filed a federal suit alleging unfair trade practices that effectively limited competition in the software market. For instance, among other practices they cited Microsoft's practice of *bundling products*—that is, packaging its Internet Explorer browser with its operating system and making retailers buy the whole bundle. This limited opportunities for other companies, such as Netscape, one of the companies that filed the suit, from selling Internet browsers.

The case was tried, and a federal judge found merit in the charges and ordered that Microsoft separate its operating system and applications software businesses. Microsoft is appealing the decision.

Consumer Protection

Consumer-protection laws are regulations regarding products, services, and credit practices. Some of these laws (such as the ban on cigarette advertising on television) are federal, while others (such as the "lemon laws" covering automobiles) are state law.

Consumer-protection laws arise as the need demands. For example, in the 1970s many health clubs used hard-sell tactics to sign people up. So New York passed a law giving anyone who bought a health-club membership three days to reverse the decision without penalty.

> **MBA Lingo**
>
> **Implied warranties** are not explicitly stated by the seller but can reasonably be assumed by the buyer to exist. For instance, consumers should be able to assume that food is safe and that a car has working windshield wipers.

Opponents of these laws believe that it is the buyer's responsibility to carefully inspect all purchases before buying (summed up in the saying *caveat emptor*, let the buyer beware), but regulatory authorities believe that the seller makes certain *implied warranties* about the products offered for sale. At the minimum, for example, the product should be safe to use.

Product Liability

Product liability comes under consumer protection, yet there have recently been so many lawsuits in this area, with some resulting in awards against companies well into the millions of dollars, that it warrants separate mention.

Essentially, case law in this area says that a company cannot knowingly sell a product that it believes will be unsafe or harmful when it is used for its intended purpose. This logic underlies the investigations of the tobacco companies to discover when, if ever, management knew that smoking caused life-threatening diseases.

Most product-liability suits seek to prove that the company either knowingly sold an unsafe product or that the outfit's negligence in manufacturing created a dangerous defect. Or the plaintiff—the party bringing the lawsuit against the defendant—tries to prove that the company should have issued warnings about the product's dangers.

> ### Case in Point
>
> Product-liability suits are the reason for the warnings we see on everything from coffee-cup lids ("The beverage you are about to enjoy is very hot") to children's sleds ("Wear a helmet and use in an open area under adult supervision").
>
> Many people believe product-liability suits have gotten out of hand. They see a "victim culture" in the United States and believe juries are manipulated by attorneys. Defenders of the suits believe that safer products and useful warnings are the result.

Bankruptcy

The bankruptcy laws let a company that is having financial problems "seek protection" from the demands of creditors in order to either *reorganize* or *liquidate* the business.

You might hear about Chapter 11, as in, "If this doesn't work out, we're headed for Chapter 11." This refers to Chapter 11 of the bankruptcy code, the chapter of the code that regulates liquidation. Chapter 7 of the code regulates reorganizations.

Business Organization

Laws govern the formation of businesses such as partnerships and corporations. As you learned in Chapter 3, a corporation is a "legal person," and this means it has certain rights, such as the right to purchase and own property, and responsibilities, such as paying taxes, just as a person does.

MBA Lingo

The term **reorganization** more commonly refers to major changes in the way a company is structured. In connection with bankruptcy, it means a court-supervised procedure to reorganize the business while its creditors wait for payment. **Liquidation** means closing the company and selling its assets to pay creditors. The expression "10 cents on the dollar" refers to the fact that creditors usually wind up getting about 10 cents for each dollar they are owed.

Contracts

Contract law is complex and constantly evolving. Many people find it hard to understand how two parties who have agreed to a transaction can then spend more time and money on the details of the contract. But the days when business was done "on a handshake" are gone.

A lot of the complexity of contracts comes from the terms and conditions that people (especially attorneys) put into them. These terms and conditions govern every aspect of the contract, such as "right to terminate" and so on.

MBA Alert

In all your business (and personal) dealings, be very careful when you sign a contract. Many naive people have unwittingly signed away valuable rights. Have an attorney, or at least a very knowledgeable person, review any contract that you are about to sign but do not fully understand.

Most lawsuits over contracts occur when one party fails to perform, or is seen as failing to perform, as agreed. This is called "breach of contract" and the usual remedy, if you cannot negotiate, is to sue the nonperforming party.

Real Estate and Insurance

Both real estate and insurance broadly come under contract law. However, these contracts can become extremely complex. For example, real estate transactions involving legal structures such as condominiums and cooperatives can become quite intricate. And insurance attorneys spend a lot of time, effort, and money deciding whether or not a major claim under an insurance policy is valid.

> **MBA Mastery**
>
> If you are a hiring authority or manage others, know your responsibilities under employment law. For example, it is illegal to ask certain questions in a job interview, such as those relating to age or child-bearing intentions. In most companies, the human resources function can advise managers of their responsibilities in this area. But it is your responsibility to ask.

Employment

Employment laws regulate the hours and conditions under which people work and who can work. For example, the child-labor laws prohibit the hiring of children. The minimum wage sets a minimum level of hourly pay.

The most significant recent federal employment law was the Americans with Disabilities Act (ADA) of 1990. This law expanded the rights of disabled people in employment.

Employment laws, including those against racial, religious, age, and gender discrimination, impact most managers' day-to-day activities.

Intellectual Property

Intellectual property includes innovations, ideas, know-how, methods, processes, and other intangible elements of the business. Intellectual property rights are protected by copyrights, trademarks, and patents. These devices are key to protecting your business and to establishing ownership in the event that someone else tries to exploit these rights.

Securities Regulation

In the late 1800s and early 1900s, securities fraud was common. Bogus stocks and bonds, dishonest investment schemes, and various forms of market manipulation (running up the price of a stock) were common. The U.S. government realized that a honest, open, regulated securities market was essential to a capitalist economy, so it created the Securities and Exchange Commission (SEC), which you learned about in Chapter 16.

The SEC has the ongoing job of policing all players in the financial markets. Among the most common and challenging situations the SEC faces are

◆ Insider trading, in which managers, board members, and other people who have information not available to the public buy or sell stocks on the basis of that information.

◆ Stock price manipulation, such as "pump-and-dump" schemes in which a group of investors trade a stock among themselves to raise the price to artificially high levels and then sell it to unsuspecting investors attracted by the stock's rapid rise.

◆ Improper financial reporting by publicly held companies, as you learned in Chapter 14.

◆ Improper and illegal practices at brokerage firms, including overcharging customers, appropriating or "borrowing" funds from customers' accounts, "pushing" stocks that the firm wants to unload from its inventory, and allowing "good customers" to buy an IPO early in the day so they can sell it later that day or soon thereafter when the price has skyrocketed.

Case in Point

Unfortunately, relatively few securities-law violators go to jail. The March 18, 2002, *Fortune* reported that from 1992 to 2002 the SEC referred 609 cases to the Justice Department for possible prosecution. The Justice Department prosecuted about 335 of these cases and won guilty verdicts an impressive 76 percent of the time. But only 87 people spent any time in jail.

Also, when these white-collar criminals do land in jail, it is usually for a stay of one to two years in a minimum-security federal prison (known as "Club Fed").

Uniform Commercial Code

The Uniform Commercial Code, or UCC, is a set of laws governing business transactions. Areas governed include sales of goods, commercial paper, bank deposits, shipping and delivery of goods, and so on. The UCC was prepared by the National Conference of Commissioners on Uniform State Laws and has been adopted by all 50 states except Louisiana, which has adopted most of it.

This body of law does what the name implies: It standardizes the laws that govern business transactions across all the states, which makes it easier to do business.

Taxation

The federal tax code, as you probably know, is one of the most lengthy, complex, and impenetrable documents ever created by political, legal, and accounting minds (and that's saying a lot). Major companies employ batteries of attorneys and accountants to interpret tax law and, if necessary, to defend the company's decisions in tax court, where differences with the IRS are decided (unless they are settled before going to court).

Rules and Regulations

In addition to all of these areas (and some I have not mentioned, such as maritime law, which governs the seas and shipping), businesses must cope with regulations issued by federal and state agencies.

Some of the more important federal agencies include

- ◆ The Food and Drug Administration (FDA), which regulates the quality of products for human consumption.

- ◆ The Environmental Protection Agency (EPA), which regulates air and water quality.

- ◆ The Federal Aviation Administration (FAA), which regulates air transportation.

- ◆ The Federal Reserve Board (the Fed), which regulates banks.

- ◆ The Equal Employment Opportunity Commission (EEOC), which enforces antidiscrimination laws.

While all types of businesses are subject to the EEOC, a company's involvement with any particular agency depends on its business. Pharmaceutical companies such as Eli Lilly must deal with the FDA. American Airlines has to be concerned with the FAA. Merrill Lynch has the SEC to think about.

If you are in a large company in a regulated business, you'll become familiar with the major regulatory requirements and how they affect your job. But what about other managers and other laws? What do managers generally have to be concerned about in the law?

What Does This Mean to Managers?

As a manager, it is not your responsibility to know the tiny details of the law in every area. Each legal area is its own field, employing attorneys focused on only that area.

This specialization is necessary because the law is complex and constantly changing. In addition, most laws have an international aspect, which adds to the complexity.

Despite all this, your responsibilities as a manager are fairly straightforward. Here are some general guidelines, from one business person to another:

◆ Use common sense and think before you act. Most of us have learned the difference between right and wrong. For instance, if someone offers you a kickback if you'll do business with them, you don't need an attorney to tell you to refuse it and to take your business elsewhere.

◆ When in doubt about whether you need legal advice, ask for help. Your boss, legal department, or attorney can advise you, but only if you ask. It's wise to avoid legal difficulties rather than try to fix them later.

◆ Be very careful about what you sign. If a contract was drawn up by an attorney, have your attorney review it before you sign it.

◆ If the other party has an attorney, you should probably have one, too. If the other party brings an attorney to a transaction, you should have yours along.

◆ If you're ever actually accused of a crime, such as fraud, or something serious but not a crime, such as negligence, get an attorney. Say as little as possible (and nothing in a criminal case) until you get legal advice. Many innocent people have blurted something out that "sounded bad" or was misinterpreted and wound up in serious trouble.

Finally, conduct yourself as ethically as you possibly can on the job.

About Business Ethics

Ethics are moral guidelines that tell you right from wrong. Business ethics tell you what is right or wrong in a business situation, while professional ethics tell you the same thing regarding your profession. Ideally, there should be no conflict between your personal ethics and your business or professional ethics. However, ethical conflicts can arise when what might be best for the company is wrong morally or professionally.

Here's a real-life example of what I mean. Your ethics probably tell you that child labor is wrong. Yet in some countries, children are put to work at a young age, and often in poor working conditions. They have no choice in the matter, and from our point of view are basically being exploited.

Suppose your company purchases well-made, inexpensive products from a foreign company that uses child labor in poor working conditions. The good quality and low price helps your company stay competitive. But is it right to purchase these products?

This is an ethical dilemma, particularly because no law is being broken. The foreign nation does not prohibit child labor, and the United States does not prohibit these imports. It may be legal, but is it right?

Case in Point

In the early to mid-1990s, controversy intensified in the United States regarding the payment of bribes by some U.S. companies to people in foreign countries. The U.S. government opposed these payments.

However, some U.S. companies argued that these payments are part of the process of doing business in some countries. They said that payments that we call "bribes" were so customary that they were really just a cost of doing business. They pointed out that other foreign firms paid the bribes, and that U.S. companies would lose out if they stopped the practice.

The ethical situation was resolved by the United States passing a law against U.S. companies paying bribes in foreign countries.

The child-labor situation has other complexities. Suppose you believe the purchase is wrong because children are being exploited, but the families of these children need their income for food and shelter. Is it still wrong? Under the circumstances, perhaps buying those products provides a *greater good*.

Sometimes your professional or personal ethics may conflict with your business ethics. From the business standpoint, you are paid to further your employer's interests. But you also have professional and personal ethics to uphold. To minimize moral and psychological conflict, and to wind up consistently doing the right thing, it's best to work in a business—an industry and a company—that closely matches your own sense of ethics. It is also best to bring your own highest ethical standards to bear in your place of business.

Many people believe in having two sets of ethics, one for their business lives and one for their personal lives. They see business as a game in which honesty and fairness are relative terms and in which money made or lost is the only measure of value. A few of these people actually are honest and fair in their

> **MBA Lingo**
>
> The **greater good** in a situation is the outcome that provides more benefit, at the expense of sacrificing an ethical standard or a smaller benefit to another party. For example, murder is wrong, but the state sanctions killing in war because the defense of our nation is the greater good.

personal, as opposed to business, dealings. But people who behave unethically on the job have corrupted business and eroded the public's faith in business institutions.

Business sometimes does pose genuine ethical dilemmas. In those situations, each of us must do what our conscience tells us is right. This may well involve overcoming the "business reason" that we give ourselves or that someone else gives us for going against our conscience.

Case in Point

Every profession has an explicit or implicit code of ethics. When auditors at accounting firms such as Arthur Andersen overlooked improper accounting practices of clients such as Enron, they did so at least partly to protect the consulting revenues that their firms earned from these clients. Any senior manager aware of these auditors' actions could justify them by saying "Well, we need those consulting revenues."

However, accounting's professional standards state that audits must be conducted objectively and that certified financial statements must fairly reflect a company's condition. These standards exist in order to help auditors overcome the kind of conflicts of interest that the consulting revenues posed. But those standards were ignored, which undermined investors' trust in financial statements and in the accounting profession.

Hot Legal and Ethical Topics

You should be particularly aware of several "hot topics" that often come up in discussions of modern-day business ethics:

♦ **White collar crime** is a fact of business life, so be on the lookout for it. Billions of dollars are lost annually due to fraud, embezzlement, theft of equipment and supplies, false insurance claims, bribery, kickbacks, and various schemes. Customers, suppliers, shareholders, and everyone else pays a price for this. If you learn of such activity, bring it to the attention of your company's chief of security or legal services.

♦ **Whistle-blowing** refers to going to the authorities or the media with proof that your company is engaged in wrongdoing. Some people see whistle-blowers as "squealers," while others see them as heroes. Extreme situations call for extreme measures, and whistle-blowing usually serves an important purpose.

♦ **Conflicts of interest** arise when you must play two conflicting roles in a situation. For example, if you are part-owner of a company that could become a supplier to your current employer, you have a conflict of interest. How can you be objective regarding who should become the supplier when you stand to gain from the decision? When you face a conflict of interest, it's best to inform someone responsible about the situation or to relinquish one of your roles.

MBA Alert _____

Most companies and agencies of the federal government, as well as most other levels of government, do not allow employees to accept gifts of any kind. I've seen a high-ranking U.S. government official return a $79 pen he received in appreciation for a public-speaking engagement for which he was not paid. Accepting gifts is prohibited because it could create a conflict of interest. Most companies also forbid giving gifts—for example, to customers or suppliers—for the same reason.

◆ **Fiduciary responsibilities** are typically those that an attorney, financial adviser, or executor of an estate have toward a client. In a fiduciary relationship you must put your client's interests ahead of your own because the client has placed significant trust in you and your professional abilities. You must never harm the client's interests, must remove yourself from serving him or her if you judge yourself not fully competent, and must protect the client's rights at all costs.

◆ **Privacy** is the right of everyone, and I must say that I personally have strong feelings on this matter. I believe that our rights to privacy are being eroded by the ability of technology to capture and record personal information, and by government, corporate, and media intrusion into private matters. So I make a policy of vigorously supporting everyone's right to privacy.

MBA Mastery _____

You may have heard that the *customer* is always right. That's a good policy, but the fact is that the *client* is not always right. An attorney, accountant, financial adviser, or consultant must tell the client when he or she is wrong. The client relies on the professional's judgment, even if the client doesn't like it or disagrees.

◆ **Sexual harassment** is defined as unwanted repeated or aggressive sexual commentary or advances of a sexual nature toward another person. It is wrong, and it can amount to professional suicide.

◆ **Discrimination** based on race, religion, ethnicity, gender, age, marital status, or sexual preference is to be avoided on both legal and ethical grounds. Most of us, if we are honest with ourselves, understand that we all have prejudices to some degree. The goal is to be aware of them and not let them affect our behavior or relationships, especially on the job. In fact, many companies are seeing the benefits of developing a diverse staff, if only because the market is becoming more diverse and companies with diverse staffs will be best able to serve these markets.

◆ **Business and politics** have become linked in ways that distort the behavior and undermine the standing of both institutions. When legislators accept corporate campaign contributions and then sponsor and vote for bills that clearly benefit the contributors, the legislators and contributors erode trust in government and business. As noted in Chapter 4, trust is the foundation for the relationship between leaders and followers. So any "leadership crisis" we may be experiencing stems at least in part from self-dealing, cynical behavior by those in leadership positions in business and in both parties at all levels of government.

Governing the Corporation

Business scandals have moved the topic of corporate governance into the spotlight. The term *corporate governance* refers both to the policies by which a company operates and the system of controls and oversight that enables the company to operate according to those policies.

Policies are broad guidelines for behavior and decisions. For example, many companies once had a "no-layoffs" policy (few do today). In tough times, they might have asked employees to take a pay cut, but they would not lay anyone off. Some companies' financial policies call for them to minimize their debt, while others believe in using debt as a large element in their financial structure. Some companies have a policy of paying as little tax as possible, and use off-shore tax havens (such as Bermuda) and other means of eliminating their taxes. Other companies have a policy of paying at least some tax as part of their obligation as corporate citizens.

As you learned in Chapter 3, the ultimate authority over the corporation rests in the board of directors, who are elected by the shareholders. Thus, ultimate responsibility for corporate governance rests with the board. That is why, when the scandals of the early 2000s were unfolding, many observers asked, "Where was the board of directors?" (The answer was often, "In management's back pocket.")

MBA Lingo

Corporate governance refers both to a company's policies and to the system of controls that enables the organization to operate according to those policies. Ultimately, corporate governance is the responsibility of the board of directors, which oversees the company at the policy level. **Policies** are broad guides for acceptable behavior and decisions in specific areas, such as financial policies and human resources policies.

The board, which includes members of senior management (who are the "inside directors"), governs the corporation through two major means: quarterly meetings to discuss, review, and advise management on major developments and decisions; and various committees that oversee specific aspects of the organization.

Sound corporate governance demands that board meetings be well-informed, substantive debates about developments and decisions. Boards with outside directors who rubber-stamp every management decision are useless and do not represent the shareholders or other stakeholders effectively.

Good corporate governance also calls for board-level committees that can act forcefully. Typical oversight committees include the finance committee, which oversees major financial decisions; the audit committee, which oversees audits of the company's financial statements; the human resources committee, which reviews matters such as compensation policy and major layoffs; and the legal affairs committee, which deals with matters such as lawsuits.

While it will take time for corporate governance in the United States to improve, it will certainly do so. Large shareholders, which include major pension funds, have the power to demand change, and they are demanding it. The erosion of investor confidence and the public's outrage over management abuses of power virtually guarantee that improvement will occur. But again, it will take time.

Act with Integrity

As a manager, you have an obligation to your superiors, subordinates, peers, shareholders, customers, and suppliers to act with integrity. You have the same obligation to the community and to society.

The word *integrity* has the same linguistic roots as the words *integrate* and *integral*. With various shades of meaning, all of these words indicate states of being whole and undivided. Thus, a manager with integrity does not have one set of ethics for business and another set for the rest of his life. Nor does he hold one set of ethics for all areas of his life, which he then betrays when he can profit by doing so.

Integrity comes from within the individual, from his conscience. Managers with integrity don't wonder whether or not they'll be caught violating the law or sound business ethics. They will catch themselves and when they do, they will think less of themselves. Most importantly, they don't want to place themselves in that position in the first place.

The manager with integrity has one set of sound ethics based on honesty, fairness, and decency, and she applies them to all aspects of her life, including—make that especially—her business dealings.

Big businesses are often reviled by people outside business as being greedy, corrupt, and impersonal. But that can only be true to the extent that most people in business—people like you and me—walk away from doing what we know to be fair and right. Millions and millions of businesspeople, the vast majority of whom never are covered by the media, have proven that you can do well by doing good in business.

The Least You Need to Know

- ◆ Society makes laws to govern people's behavior. Business law governs business transactions, such as contracts, as well as issues such as monopolistic practices, employment, and taxes.

- ◆ In the United States, laws can be created by legislatures, which write codes and statutes, and by courts, which create case law.

- ◆ Key areas of the law for most managers to be concerned about include consumer protection, contracts, employment, and product liability.

- ◆ As a manager you don't have to be a legal expert, but you must use your common sense, distinguish between right and wrong, and act with integrity. Also, get legal advice when you need it, be careful what you sign, and use an attorney if the other party has one.

- ◆ Although some managers see conflicts between business goals and ethical behavior, conducting business ethically is good from a business and financial perspective. A number of companies in the news (and executives under indictment) have proven this to be the case.

Index

A

accountability
  creating, 47
  defined, 20-21
accountants, 186-187
accounting
  audits, 187
  departments, 31-32
  GAAP, 187
accounts
  CPAs, 187
  national, 35
  payable, 31, 150
  receivable, 147
    departments, 31
    turnover, 171-172
  reconciling, 165-166
  T-accounts, 185
accrued expenses, 151
acquiring companies (investment), 202-203
actions (strategic planning), 323-324
active selling, 288
ad copy, 278-280
additional paid-in capital, 153
administration (business), 4
administrators, 53
advertising, 276
  budget, 280-281
  demographics, 282
  DTC, 277
  frequency, 283
  image advertising, 277
  impact, 284
  media, selecting, 281-282
  messages, 277-280
  promotions, 284-285
  reach, 283

AIDA (Attention, capture Interest, create Desire, and request Action), 278
alignment
  maintaining, 48
  sales force, 292-294
allocating resources, 92
analysts
  compensation, 53
  credit, 135
analytical tools, 104
  break-even point, 104-106
  crossover analysis, 107-108
analyzing
  break-even, 104-106
  company environments, 314-317
  cost-benefit, 93-95
  crossover, 107-108
  financial needs, 366
  financial statements
    calculations, 182
    financial ratios, 168
    industry norms, 182
    liquidity ratios, 168-173
    patterns, 182
    profitability ratios, 177-181
    solvency ratios, 174-176
    source, 182
    tips, 181
    trends, 182
  fundamental, 226-227
  information (decision making), 18
  investments, 204, 213
  market research studies, 260-261
  markets, 364
antitrusts, 377
AOL Time Warner, 203

appearance improvements (products), 243
appraisals (performance), 58
area of responsibility, 20
ASEAN (Association of Southeastern Asian Nations), 68
assessing company resources, 320-321
assets, 142-143, 146
  accounts receivable, 147
  bad debt, 147
  cash, 146
  deferred charges, 149
  depreciation calculations, 192
    double declining balance, 193-194
    methods, selecting, 195-196
    productive life matching, 196-197
    straight-line, 193
    sum of years digits, 195
  fixed, 148
  intangibles, 150
  inventories, 148
  inventory calculations, 188-189
    FIFO, 189-190
    FIFO vs. LIFO, 191-192
    LIFO, 189-190
  land, 149
  liquidity, 145
  marketable securities, 147
  near-cash, 147
  prepayments, 149
  property/plant/equipment, 148-149
  ROA, 180
  turnover, 179-180
Association of Southeastern Asian Nations (ASEAN), 68

assurance (quality), 352, 356
    benchmarking, 358-359
    best practices, 358-359
    control charts, 357-358
    standards, 353-354
    supplier programs, 356-357
    zero defects, 353
Attention, capture Interest, create Desire, and request Action (AIDA), 278
audits, 187
authority, 20-21
averages (weighted), 117-118

B

back-office functions, 32
bad debt, 147
balance of trade, 67
balance sheets, 143-144
    assets, 142-143, 146-149
    example, 144-146
    formula, 143
    liabilities, 142-143, 150-152
    owner equity, 142-143, 152-154
Baldridge Award, 359
bankruptcy, 11, 379
banks (investment), 216
BCG (Boston Consulting Group), 318
bear markets, 219-220
benchmarking (quality), 358-359
benefits administrators, 53
best practices (quality), 358-359
beta sites, 304
beta tests, 304
bills (treasury), 229
board of directors, 37-39
bonds
    corporate, 227-228
    prices, 230-231
    treasury, 229
bookkeeping
    accountant opinion, 186-187
    double-entry system, 184-186
    financial statements, 186
    ledgers, 184
books, 142

booms (economy), 71-73
Boston Consulting Group (BCG), 318
bottom-feeder investors, 222
break-even points, 104
    finding, 105-106
    formula, 104
breakthroughs, 306
brokers, 217
bubbles (market), 219-220
budgets, 125-126
    advertising, 280-281
    budgeting process, 126
    capital, 126
    cost control, 133-134
    credit management, 135-137
    defined, 31
    expense variance reports, 129-131
    expenses, 127
    operating, 126
    sales, 127
    sales variance reports, 127-129
    types, 126-127
    variances, 131-133
bull markets, 219-220
bundling products, 132
businesses
    accounts payable, 31
    acquiring, 202-203
    administration, 4
    buying, 371-372
    community, 79-80
    corporations, 28
    customer-focused, 244
    cycles, 70-71
    defining, 313
    departments, 31-39. *See also* departments
    environments, 314
        assessing, 316-317
        competitors, monitoring, 314
        customers/prospects, 314
        economic trends, 315
        regulatory/social change, 315
        suppliers, 315

ethics, 383-385
    conflicts of interest, 386
    discrimination, 386
    fiduciary responsibilities, 386
    politics, 387
    privacy, 386
    sexual harassment, 386
    whistle-blowing, 385
    white collar crimes, 385
financing, finding, 367
general partners, 28
goals, 15, 312-313
growth
    financing, 370-371
    IPOs, 371
    managing, 368-370
law, 376
    antitrusts, 377
    bankruptcy, 379
    business organization, 379
    consumer-protection, 377-378
    contracts, 379
    discrimination, 386
    employment, 380
    insurance, 380
    intellectual properties, 380
    managers, 383
    politics, 387
    privacy, 386
    product liability, 378
    real estate, 380
    securities, 380-381
    sexual harassment, 386
    taxes, 382
    UCC, 381
    whistle-blowing, 385
    white collar crimes, 385
liquidation, 379
LLCs, 29
manufacturing, 32-33
market-driven, 243
organization, 28-30, 379
partnerships, 28
plans, 362
    business description, 363
    financial needs analysis, 366
    length, 366

management team, 365
market analysis, 364
marketing strategies, 364
operation description,
  365-366
outlines, 362-363
potential returns, 366
product description, 363
sales strategies, 364
service description, 363
principles
  competitive advantage,
    9-10
  controls, 10
  customer values, 8
  ethics, 11-12
  organization, 8-9
  profitability, 10-11
proprietorships, 28
reorganization, 379
regulations, 382
resources, 317, 320
  assessing, 320-321
  growth, 318-319
  humans, 319
  productive capacity, 320
  profitability, 318
sales-driven, 244
start-ups, 362
stock, selling, 217-218
busts (economy), 71, 73
buy-and-hold strategy, 222
buyer beware, 372
buying
  businesses, 371-372
  government securities, 79
  power, 84
  stock, 217

C

calculating
  cost of capital, 212-213
  depreciation, 192
    double declining balance,
      193-194
    methods, selecting,
      195-196

productive life matching,
  196-197
straight-line, 193
sum of years digits, 195
equity costs, 212
internal rate of return,
  207-208
inventory, 188-189
  FIFO, 189-190
  FIFO vs. LIFO, 191-192
  LIFO, 189-190
machine productivity, 345
NPV, 204-206
worker productivity, 344-345
calling (cold), 289
calls (option), 224-225
candidates, interviewing, 54-55
capital (working), 168-169
capital budgets, 126
capital stock. *See* stock
cash
  assets, 146
  flow, 163-165
Cash on Delivery (COD), 32
caveat emptor, 372
central tendencies, measuring,
  116
  mean, 117
  median, 119-120
  mode, 120
  weighted average, 117-118
centralization, 100-101
CEO (Chief Executive Officer),
  37-38
Certified Public Accountants
  (CPAs), 187
chain of command, 20
charts
  control, 357-358
  organization, 39-40
checking references, 55
Chief Executive Officer (CEO),
  37-38
Chief Operating Officer (COO),
  40
CIO (Chief Information Officer),
  338
circles (quality), 357
classes, frequency distributions,
  114

closed-end questions, 257
closing operations, 134
coaching, 49
COD (Cash on Delivery), 32
cold calling, 289
collaboration, 44
collections, 136-137
  agencies, 136
  attorney, 137
  period, 172
commercial papers, 147, 228
commercial sales, 237
commercials, 278
commission plans, 294
commodities, 252
commodities markets, 231
common stocks, 153
communication
  frame of reference, 24
  information sharing, 25
  listening skills, 23
  management skill, 23-25
  speaking directly, 24
companies. *See* businesses
compensation, 53
  analysts, 53
  sales force, 294-296
competencies (core), 46
competition
  advantages
    customer opinion, 331
    managers, 9-10
    money, 330
    corporate knowledge, 337
    global, 359-360
    monitoring, 314
    pricing, 268
concept testing (product development), 302-303
conflicts of interest, 386
Consumer Price Index (CPI), 84
consumers. *See also* customers
  confidence, 86
  protection, 377-378
  sales, 237
contests (sales), 295
contract manufacturers, 365
contracts, 379
control charts, 357-358
control limits, 357

controlling
   cost, 133-134
   quality, 352, 353-359
controlling to plan, 25
controls (managers), 10
COO (Chief Operating Officer), 40
cooling economy, 75
core competencies, 46
corporations, 28. *See also* businesses
   bonds, 227-228
   cash management, 77
   governing, 387-388
   knowledge
      competitors, 337
      exploiting, 335-337
      leverage, 336-337
      new products, 335
      processes, 335
      security, 333-335
      templates, 336
   start-ups, financing, 367
   ventures, 373-374
cost-plus pricing, 268
costs
   benefit analysis, 93-95
   capital
      calculating, 212-213
      investments, 210-212
   control, 133-134
   equity, 212
   fixed, 97-98
   goods sold, 157
      formula, 189
      income statements, 158
   opportunity, 210
   social, 94-95
   variable, 97-98
coverage (sales), 292
CPAs (certified public accountants), 187
CPI (Consumer Price Index), 84
CPM (Critical Path Method), 108-110
crashes (market), 219-220
creative messages, 277
credit, 31
   analysts, 135
   approval process, 135

departments, 31
   management, 135-137
      collections, 136-137
      credit-approval process, 135
Critical Path Method (CPM), 108
critical paths, 110
cross-functional teams, 60, 300
crossover analysis, 107-108
culture (quality), 355-356
current liabilities, 151
current portion of long-term debt, 151
current ratios, 169-170
customer service, 35, 297
customer-focused companies, 244
customers. *See also* consumers
   demographics, 282
   finding, 289
   market research, 250-261
   market segments, 250-251
   new, 240
   opinions, 331
   values, 8
cycles (business), 70-71

D

data (statistics), 113
   central tendency measures, 116-120
   frequency distributions, 114-115
   variability measures, 120-123
days sales on hand, 173
dealers, 217
debt
   long-term, 151
   ratio, 175
debt-to-equity ratio, 174
decentralization, 100
decision making
   analyzing information, 18
   information gathering, 18
   management skill, 17-19
   options, 18-19
   outcomes, 19

problems, defining, 18
   trees, 111-113
   support system, 18
dedication (managers), 4
deferred charges, 149
deficit spending, 76
delegation
   effective guidelines, 21-22
   management skill, 19-22
demands (economy), 70
demographics, 251
   advertising, 282
   segmentations, 250
departments
   accounting, 31-32
   accounts payable, 31
   accounts receivable, 31
   board of directors, 37-39
   credit, 31
   facilities, 37
   finance, 30-31
   human resources, 37
      benefits administrators, 53
      compensation analysts, 53
      firing employees, 58-59
      functions, 52-53
      general employee administrators, 53
      hiring, 53-56
      performance appraisals, 58
      problem employees, 56-57
      recruiters, 52
      training/development professionals, 53
   IS, 36
   legal, 36
   marketing, 33-34
   sales, 35
   support functions, 36-37
   tax, 32
depreciation, 149
   calculating, 192
      double declining balance, 193-194
      methods, selecting, 195-196
      productive life matching, 196-197
      straight-line, 193
      sum of years digits, 195

expenses, 159
straight-line, 193
descriptions (jobs), 53
designs (market research studies), 254-256
developing products, 34
competitors, watching, 302
concept testing, 302-303
cross-functional teams, 300
customers, listening to, 301
good ideas, 301
market test, 304-305
product launch, 305
product testing, 304
prototypes, 303
quality standards, 353-354
salespeople, asking, 301-302
zero defects, 353
development professionals, 53
differentiating products, 242-243, 252
diminishing returns (law of), 96-97
direct response selling, 271
direct sales force, 271
direct-to-customer (DTC) advertising, 277
directors (board), 37-38
discounts
rates, 78, 200
volume, 98
discrimination, 386
distributions
frequency, 114-115
normal, 122
products, 264, 271-273
double declining balance, 193-194
double-entry system (bookkeeping), 184-186
Dow Jones Industrial Average, 88
DRI/WEFA website, 82
DTC (direct-to-customer) advertising, 277
due diligence, 372

E

e-commerce, 339-341
earnings, 154
EBIT (Earnings Before Interest and Taxes), 176
economic growth rate, 83-84
economic indicators
buying power, 84
consumer confidence, 86
economic growth rate, 83-84
housing trends, 87
interest rates, 85
leading indicators index, 89
new car sales, 87
productivity growth, 88
retail sales, 87
stock market, 88
unemployment, 85-86
watching, 89-90
economic policy, 75
economic trends, 315
economies of scale, 98-99
economy. *See also* money
cooling, 75
deficit spending, 76
economic policy, 75
fiscal policy, 75-76
fiscal stimulus, 76
GDP, 70-73
government role, 73-75
growth, 69
indicators, 82
inflation, 73, 84
monetary policy, 75-77
business community relations, 79-80
Fed role, 77-78
government securities, 79
interest rates, 78
national, 66-68
overheating, 74
watching, 89-90
effective delegation, 21-22
efficiency experts, 6
efficient market theory, 221
employees
firing, 58-59
motivating, 346-347

net income per, 162
orientations, 56
performance appraisals, 58
problem
firing, 58-59
handling, 56-57
performance appraisals, 58
sales per, 162
skills, 346-347
supporting, 22-23
employment agencies, 54
employment laws, 380
engineering (reverse), 302
entrepreneurs, 374
businesses, buying, 371-372
business plan, 362
business description, 363
financial needs analysis, 366
length, 366
management team, 365
market analysis, 364
marketing strategies, 364
operation description, 365-366
outline, 362-363
potential returns, 366
product description, 363
sales strategies, 364
service description, 363
corporate ventures, 373-374
financing, finding, 367
growth
financing, 370-371
IPOs, 371
managing, 368-370
environments (companies), 314
assessing, 316-317
competitors, monitoring, 314
customers/prospects, 314
economic trends, 315
regulatory/social change, 315
suppliers, 315
equipment
assets, 148-149
improving, 348-349
investment, 202
equity, cost of, 212

ethics (business), 383-385
   conflicts of interest, 386
   discrimination, 386
   fiduciary responsibilities, 386
   managers, 11-12
   politics, 387
   privacy, 386
   sexual harassment, 386
   whistle-blowing, 385
   white collar crimes, 385
EU (European Union), 68
executive search firms, 54
expenses
   budgets, 127-131
   cost of goods sold, 157-158
   depreciation, 159
   income statements, 160
   interest, 160
   SG&A, 159
   variance reports, 129-131
exploiting corporate knowledge, 335-337
exports, 67-69
extending
   offers, 55
   product lines, 306-307
extraordinary income, 160-161

F

facilities department, 37
fact-finding teams, 60
factors (production), 344
failures (product), 247
Fed (Federal Reserve)
   business community relations, 79-80
   government securities, 79
   interest rates, 78
   monetary policy role, 77-78
Fed-watchers, 80
federal funds rate, 78, 85
federal income taxes, 151
Federal Reserve. *See* Fed
feedback, coaching, 49
fiduciary responsibilities, 386
FIFO (first in, first out), 189-190
finance departments, 30-31
financial goals, 15

financial leases, 213
financial markets
   bear market, 219-220
   bubbles, 219-220
   bull market, 219-220
   commercial papers, 228
   commodities, 231
   corporate bonds, 227-228
   crashes, 219-220
   efficient market theory, 221
   foreign exchanges, 232
   fundamental analysis, 226-227
   government securities, 229, 231
   information, 221-222
   investors, 222-223
   options, 223-224
      calls, 224-225
      puts, 225-226
   P/E ratio, 218-219
   precious metals, 232
   risks/returns, 231
   roles, 216-217
   technical analysis, 226-227
   traders, 222-223
   stock, 217-218
financial needs analysis, 366
financial ratios, 168
financial statement analysis
   accountant opinion, 186-187
   bookkeeping, 186
   calculations, 182
   financial ratios, 168
   goals, 197
   industry norms, 182
   liquidity ratios, 168
      accounts receivable turnover, 171-172
      collection period, 172
      current ratios, 169-170
      days sales on hand, 173
      inventory turnover, 173
      quick ratios, 170
      working capital, 168-169
   patterns, 182
   pro forma, 366
   profitability ratios, 177
      asset turnover, 179-180
      gross margin, 177
      net margin, 179

      operating margin, 178
      ROA, 180
      ROI, 181
   solvency ratios, 174
      debt ratios, 175
      debt-to-equity ratios, 174
      times interest earned ratios, 175-176
   source, 182
   tips, 181
   trends, 182
financial structure, 174
financing
   growth, 370-371
   new businesses, 367
finding
   break-even points, 105-106
   customers, 289
   financing, 367
firing employees, 58-59
first in, first out (FIFO), 189-190
fiscal policy, 75-76
fiscal stimulus, 76
fiscal years, 143
Five-P Rule (Proper Planning Prevents Poor Performance), 14, 264-265
fixed assets, 148
fixed costs, 97-98
flow (cash), 163-165
focusing people, 46
follow-up questions, 258
Ford Motor Company assembly line, 7
foreign exchange markets, 232
formulas
   accounts receivable turnover, 171
   asset turnover, 179
   balance sheets, 143
   break-even point, 104
   collection period, 172
   cost of goods sold, 189
   current ratios, 169-170
   days sales on hand, 173
   debt ratio, 175
   debt-to-equity ratio, 174
   GDP, 66
   gross margin, 177
   income statement, 156

inventory turnover, 173
net margin, 179
operating margin, 178
owner equity, 142
quick ratios, 170
ROI, 181
ROA, 180
times interest earned, 175
working capital, 168-169
frame of reference, 24
free trade, 68
frequency distributions, 114-115
fundamental analysis, 226-227

G

GAAP (Generally Accepted
Accounting Principles), 187
Garbage In, Garbage Out
(GIGO), 203
GDP (Gross Domestic Product),
66, 70
booms/busts, 71-73
business cycle, 70-71
demands, 70
formula, 66
general business partners, 28
general employee administrators,
53
Generally Accepted Accounting
Principles (GAAP), 187
geographic segmentations, 250
GIGO (Garbage In, Garbage
Out), 203
global competition, 359-360
GM product positioning, 274
goals
business, 15, 312-313
financial, 15
financial statements, 197
government economic, 73-74
individual, 15
marketing, 15, 254
measurable, 16, 313
setting, 15-17
specific, 16
time-limited, 16
websites, 16

good centralization, 101
governing corporations, 387-388
government
economy role, 73-75
securities, 79, 229, 231
greater good, 384
gross cash flow, 165
gross cash flow from operations,
165
Gross Domestic Product (GDP),
66
gross income, 158
gross margin, 177
growth
company resources, 318-319
economy, 69
financing, 370-371
IPOs, 371
managing, 368-370
growth-oriented investors, 222
growth-share matrixes, 319
guidelines
questionnaires, 258-259
strategic plans, 325-326

H

handling layoffs, 133
hard sells, 291
hiring, 53-54
candidates, 54-55
employee orientations, 56
offers, extending, 55
references, checking, 55
housing sales, 87
HR (Human Resources), 37, 52
benefits administrators, 53
compensation analysts, 53
firing employees, 58-59
functions, 52-53
general employee administrators, 53
hiring, 53-54
candidates, interviewing,
54-55
employee orientations, 56
offers, extending, 55
references, checking, 55

performance appraisals, 58
problem employees, 56-57
recruiters, 52
training/development professionals, 53

I

image advertising, 277
image improvements (products),
243
impact advertising, 284
implementing strategic plans,
324-325
imports, 67-68
improvements (products),
242-243
improving
equipment, 348-349
processes, 349-350
incentives (employees), 346
income
before taxes, 161
extraordinary, 160-161
gross, 158
net, 161-162
operating, 159
statements, 156, 162
cost of goods sold, 158
depreciation expenses, 159
example, 156-157
expenses, 160
extraordinary income,
160-161
formula, 156
gross income, 158
income before taxes, 161
interest expenses, 160
net income, 161-162
net income per employee,
162
operating income, 159
provision for income taxes,
161
sales, 158
sales per employee, 162
SG&A, 159
Incorporated (Inc.), 29

increasing
    productivity, 345-346
        employee skills, 346-347
        equipment improvements,
          348-349
        motivating employees,
          346-347
        process improvements,
          349-350
    sales, 239-241
independent sales reps, 271
indexes, 89
indicators (economic). *See* economic indicators
individual goals, 15
individual investors, 216
inflation, 73, 84
inflation-unemployment trade-off, 74-75
information (resource), 328-329
    competitive advantage,
      330-331
    flows, 331-333
    importance, 328
    Intelligence Pyramid, 329-330
Information Systems (IS), 36, 337-339
Information Technology (IT), 328
inside sales, 288
institutional investors, 216
insubordination, 56
insurance laws, 380
intangibles, 150
integrity, 388-389
intellectual property laws, 380
Intelligence Pyramid, 329-330
interest expenses, 160
interest rates
    bonds, 230
    discount rates, 200
    economic indicator, 85
    economy, 78
internal rate of returns, 206-208
international selling, 271
Internet e-commerce, 271, 339-341
interviewing candidates, 54-55

inventories
    assets, 148
    calculating, 188-189
      FIFO, 189-190
      FIFO vs. LIFO, 191-192
      LIFO, 189-190
    JIT, 339
    turnover, 173
investment banks, 216
investments
    analyzing, 204, 213
    buy-and-hold, 222
    company acquisitions,
      202-203
    cost of capital, 210-213
    equipment, 202
    equity costs, 212
    GIGO, 203
    internal rate of return,
      206-208
    NPV, 204-206
    opportunity cost, 210
    payback period, 208-209
    plants, 202
    present value table, 200-201
    rates, 209
    ROI, 181
    time value of money, 200
investors, 222-223
    bottom-feeder, 222
    growth-oriented, 222
    individual, 216
    institutional, 216
    short-term, 223
IPOs, 371
IS (Information Systems), 337-339
IT (Information Technology), 328

J

JIT (just-in-time), 339
job descriptions, 53
joint marketing agreements, 272
judgments, 137

K

Keynes, Maynard, 76
knowledge (corporate), 330
    competitors, 337
    exploiting, 335-337
    leverage, 336-337
    new products, 335
    processes, 335
    products, 293
    security, 333-335
    templates, 336

L

lagging, 89
land assets, 149
Last In, First Out (LIFO), 189-190
launching products, 305
law (business), 376
    antitrusts, 377
    bankruptcy, 379
    business organization, 379
    consumer-protection, 377-378
    contracts, 379
    discrimination, 386
    employment, 380
    insurance, 380
    intellectual properties, 380
    managers, 383
    politics, 387
    privacy, 386
    product liability, 378
    real estate, 380
    securities, 380-381
    sexual harassment, 386
    taxes, 382
    UCC, 381
    whistle-blowing, 385
    white collar crimes, 385
law of diminishing returns, 96-97
lax boards, 39
layoffs, 133
leaders, 42-43
    roles, 42
    skills, 43-49
    styles, 42

leadership skills, 43-49
leadership styles, 42
leads (sales), 289
leases, 213-214
ledgers, 184
legal departments, 36
liabilities, 142-143, 150
   accounts payable, 150
   accrued expenses, 151
   current, 151
   current portion of long-term
     debt, 151
   federal income taxes, 151
   limited, 29
   long-term debt, 152
   notes payable, 150
   products, 378
   taxes, 151
life cycles (products), 246-247
LIFO (Last In, First Out),
  189-190
Limited Liability Companies
  (LLCs), 29
line items (budgets), 128
liquidation, 379
liquidity ratios, 168
   assets, 145
   accounts receivable turnover,
     171-172
   collection period, 172
   current ratios, 169-170
   days sales on hand, 173
   inventory turnover, 173
   quick ratios, 170
   working capital, 168-169
listening skills, 23
LLCs (Limited Liability
  Companies), 29
long-term debt, 151-152
loss leaders, 267

M

machine productivity, 345
Malcolm Baldridge National
  Quality Award, 359
management
   business plan, 365
   defined, 3

scientific, 6
skills, 17-25
managers
   area of responsibility, 20
   business laws, 383
   competitive advantage, 9-10
   controls, 10
   customer value, 8
   dedication, 4
   defined, 3
   ethics, 11-12
   good qualities, 4-5
   integrity, 388-389
   organization, 8-9
   professional, 5-7
   profitability, 10-11
   responsibilities, 5
   roles, 5
manufacturing companies, 32-33
margins
   gross, 177
   net, 179
   operating, 178
market-driven companies, 243
marketable securities, 147
marketing
   competitive advantage, 331
   customer-focused companies,
     244
   departments, 33-34
   five Ps, 264-265
   goals, 15
   market-driven companies, 243
   mix, 263
   Product Adoption Curve,
     245-246
   product life cycle, 246-247
   products, 264-266
     benefits, 266
     distributing, 271-273
     features, 265
     packaging, 270-271
     planned obsolescence, 266
     positioning, 273-274
     pricing, 267-269
     promoting, 273
   sales, 236-237
   sales-driven companies, 244
   strategies, 238

markets
   analyzing, 364
   bear, 219-220
   bull, 219-220
   commodities, 231
   defined, 250
   demographic segmentations,
     250
   demographics, 251
   financial, 216
     bear market, 219-220
     bubbles, 219-220
     bull market, 219-220
     buying stock, 217
     commercial papers, 228
     commodities, 231
     corporate bonds, 227-228
     crashes, 219-220
     efficient market theory,
       221
     foreign exchanges, 232
     fundamental analysis,
       226-227
     government securities,
       229-231
     information, 221-222
     investors, 222-223
     options, 223-226
     P/E ratio, 218-219
     precious metals, 232
     risks/returns, 231
     roles, 216-217
     selling stock, 217-218
     technical analysis, 226-227
     traders, 222-223
   foreign exchange, 232
   geographic segmentations,
     250
   maturity, 241
   precious metals, 232
   product segmentations, 250
   researching, 34
     analysis, 260-261
     buying behavior, 251
     customer satisfaction, 251
     demographics, 251
     fielding questionnaires,
       259
     goals, defining, 254

needs, 252-253
presentations, 261
psychographics, 252
purpose, 251
questionnaire develop-
ment, 256-258
questionnaire guidelines,
258-259
studies, creating, 253-254
study design, 254-256
types, 253
sales-channel segmentations,
251
saturation, 241
segments, 250-251
strategies, 364
tests, 304-305
Master of Business
Administration (MBA), 4
matrixes (growth-share), 319
maturity (market), 241
Maynard Keynes, 76
MBA (Master of Business
Administration), 4
MBNA, 47
mean
central tendency measures,
117
standard deviation, 121-123
measurable goals, 16, 313
media
advertising, 281-282
buys, 280
planners, 281
median, 119-120
meetings (sales), 295
mentoring, 49
messages (advertising), 277-278
ad copy, 278-280
AIDA, 278
creative, 277
selling, 278
mode, 120
monetarists, 77
monetary policy, 75-77
business community relations,
79-80
Fed role, 77-78
government securities, 79

interest rates, 78
money. *See also* economy, 66
accounting departments,
31-32
accounts payable departments,
31
accounts receivable departments, 31
balance sheets, 143-144
accounts payable, 150
accounts receivable, 147
accrued expenses, 151
additional paid-in capital,
153
assets, 142-143, 146-147
common stocks, 153
current portion of long-
term debt, 151
deferred charges, 149
example, 144-146
federal income taxes, 151
formula, 143
intangibles, 150
inventories, 148
land, 149
liabilities, 142-143, 150
long-term debt, 152
marketable securities, 147
notes payable, 150
owner equity, 142-143,
152
preferred stocks, 153
prepayments, 149
property/plant/equipment,
148-149
retained earnings, 154
stock, 152-153
taxes, 151
budgets, 125-126
advertising, 280-281
budgeting process, 126
capital, 126
collections, 136-137
cost control, 133-134
credit management,
135-136
expense variance reports,
129-131
expenses, 127

operating, 126
sales, 127
sales variance reports,
127-129
types, 126-127
variances, 131-133
cash flow statements, 163
cash flow, 163-164
example, 164-165
reconciliation, 165-166
compensation, 53
competitive advantage, 330
corporate cash management,
77
credit departments, 31
finance departments, 30-31
income statements, 156, 162
cost of goods sold, 158
depreciation expenses, 159
example, 156-157
expenses, 160
extraordinary income,
160-161
formula, 156
gross income, 158
income before taxes, 161
interest expenses, 160
net income, 161-162
operating income, 159
provision for income taxes,
161
sales, 158
sales per employee, 162
SG&A, 159
present value, 200-201
severance pay, 59
tax departments, 32
time value, 200, 206
velocity, 77
moral suasion, 80
motivating
employees, 346-347
sales force, 294-296

N

NAFTA (North American Free
Trade Agreement), 68
national accounts, 35

national economy, 66-67
  balance of trade, 67
  exports, 67-69
  free trade, 68
  GDP, 66
  imports, 67-68
  protectionism, 68
  tariffs, 68
near-cash assets, 147
net benefit, 94
net exports, 67
net income, 161-162
net income per employee, 162
net margin, 179
Net Present Value (NPV), 204-206
new car sales, 87
nonrecurring income, 160-161
normal distribution, 122
North American Free Trade Agreement (NAFTA), 68
notes
  payable, 150
  treasury, 229
NPV (Net Present Value), 204-206

O

OEMs (Original Equipment Manufacturers), 271
off-balance-sheet financing, 198
offers, extending, 55
open-ended questions, 257
operating budgets, 126
operating income, 159
operating leases, 214
operating margin, 178
operations, 33
  back-office functions, 32
  closing, 134
opportunity costs, 210
order taking, 288
organization
  businesses, 28-30, 379
  charts, 39-40
  managers, 8-9
  service, 32-33

orientations (employee), 56
Original Equipment Manufacturers (OEMs), 271
outlines (business plan), 362-363
outside sales, 288
overheating economy, 74
owner equity, 142-143, 152
  formula, 142
  retained earnings, 154
  stocks, 152-153

P

P/E ratios (price/earnings), 218-219
packaging products, 270-271
paper (commercial), 147, 228
parity products, 302
partnerships, 28
paths, 110
payables, 31, 150
payback periods (investments), 208-209
people, focusing, 46
per value (stocks), 153
performance appraisals, 58
performance improvements (products), 242
periods (payback), 208-209
persuasion, 291
PERT (Program Evaluation and Review Technique), 110-111
placing products, 264
planned obsolescence, 266
planning
  business description, 363
  controlling to plan, 25
  financial needs analysis, 366
  Five-P Rule, 14
  length, 366
  management skill, 14-15
  management team, 365
  market analysis, 364
  marketing strategies, 364
  operation description, 365-366
  outline, 362-363
  potential returns, 366
  product description, 363

sales strategies, 364
service description, 363
strategic, 312
  actions, identifying, 323-324
  company environment, 314-317
  company goals, 312-313
  company resources, 317-321
  employee involvement, 325
  guidelines, 325-326
  implementing, 324-325
  needs, 326
  SWOT, 322
  time frames, 325
plants
  assets, 148-149
  investment, 202
policies
  economic, 75
  fiscal, 75-76
  monetary, 75-77
    business community relations, 79-80
    Fed role, 77-78
    government securities, 79
    interest rates, 78
politics, 387
poor references, 55
positioning products, 273-274
potential returns, 366
PPI (Producer Price Index), 84
PR programs, 285
precious metals, 232
preferred stocks, 153
prepayments, 149
present value (money), 200-201
presentations
  market research studies, 261
  sales, 290
price points, 267
price resistance, 239
price/earnings (P/E) ratio, 218
prices
  bonds, 230-231
  competitive, 268
  cost-plus, 268
  increasing, 239

products, 267-269
  value, 268
  Veblen Effect, 269
primary market research study,
  creating, 253-254
    analysis, 260-261
    design, 254-256
    fielding questionnaires, 259
    goals, defining, 254
    presentations, 261
    questionnaire
      development, 256-258
      guidelines, 258-259
prime rate, 85
privacy, 386
pro forma statements, 366
problem employees
  firing, 58-59
  handling, 56-57
  performance appraisals, 58
problem solving (sales), 290
processes
  corporate knowledge, apply-
    ing, 335
  improving, 349-350
  product development,
    301-305
Producer Price Index (PPI), 84
Product Adoption Curve,
  245-246
product-line extensions, 306-307
production factors, 344
productive capacity, 320
productive life (depreciation
  matching), 196-197
productivity, 344
  defined, 344
  growth, 88
  increasing, 345-350
  machine, 345
  measuring, 343-345
  worker, 344-346
products
  advertising, 276
    budget, 280-281
    demographics, 282
    DTC, 277
    frequency, 283
    image advertising, 277
    impact, 284

    media, selecting, 281-282
    messages, 277-280
    promotions, 284-285
    reach, 283
  benefits, 266
  breakthroughs, 306
  bundling, 132
  commodities, 252
  contract manufacturers, 365
  corporate knowledge, apply-
    ing, 335
  developing, 34
    competitors, watching, 302
    concept testing, 302-303
    cross-functional teams, 300
    customers, listening to,
      301
    good ideas, 301
    market test, 304-305
    product launch, 305
    product testing, 304
    prototypes, 303
    salespeople, asking,
      301-302
  differentiation, 242-243, 252
  distributing, 264, 271-273
  failures, 247
  features, 265
  knowledge, 293
  launching, 305
  liability, 378
  life cycle, 246-247
  loss leaders, 267
  marketing, 264-266
  new, 240
  packaging, 264, 270-271
  parity, 302
  placing, 264
  planned obsolescence, 266
  positioning, 273-274
  price points, 267
  pricing, 267
    competitive, 268
    cost-plus, 268
    strategies, 267-269
    value, 268
    Veblen Effect, 269
  product-line extensions,
    306-307
  promoting, 265, 273

  pushing, 240
  R&D, 307-308
  segmentations, 250
  stopping, 305
  testing, 304
professional managers, 5-7
professionals, 53
profitability
  company resources, 318
  managers, 10-11
  ratios, 177
    asset turnover, 179-180
    gross margin, 177
    net margin, 179
    operating margin, 178
    ROA, 180
    ROI, 181
Program Evaluation and Review
  Technique (PERT), 110-111
programs
  PR, 285
  supplier, 356
project management tools, 108
  CPM, 108-110
  critical paths, 110
  PERT, 110-111
promotability, 49
promoting products, 265, 273
promotional advertising, 284-285
Proper Planning Prevents Poor
  Performance (Five-P Rule),
  264-265
property, 148-149
proprietorships, 28
prospecting, 289
protecting consumers, 377-378
protectionism, 68
provision for income taxes, 161
public relations programs, 285
pushing products, 240
puts (option), 225-226

Q

QA (quality assurance), 339, 352,
  356
  benchmarking, 358-359
  best practices, 358-359
  control charts, 357-358

quality circles, 357
standards, 353-354
supplier programs, 356
zero defects, 353
qualifying questions, 258
quality, 351
assurance, 339, 352, 356
benchmarking, 358-359
best practices, 358-359
control charts, 357-358
quality circles, 357
standards, 353-354
supplier programs, 356
zero defects, 353
circles, 357
culture of, 355-356
defined, 351
global competition, 359-360
measuring, 343
standards, 353-354
zero defects, 353
quality assurance. *See* QA
quantitative information, 253
questionnaires
closed-end questions, 257
follow-up questions, 258
identifying questions, 257
market research studies,
256-259
open-ended questions, 257
qualifying questions, 258
quick ratios, 170
quotas (sales), 295

R

R&D (Research and
Development), 307-308
range, 120-121
rates
discount, 78, 200
economic growth, 83-84
federal funds, 78, 85
interest
bonds, 230
discount rates, 200
economic indicator, 85
economy, 78

internal rate of return,
206-208
prime, 85
selecting, 209
ratios
current, 169-170
debt, 175
debt-to-equity, 174
financial, 168
liquidity, 168
accounts receivable
turnover, 171-172
collection period, 172
current ratios, 169-170
days sales on hand, 173
inventory turnover, 173
quick ratios, 170
working capital, 168-169
P/E, 218-219
profitability, 177
asset turnover, 179-180
gross margin, 177
net margin, 179
operating margin, 178
ROA, 180
ROI, 181
quick, 170
solvency, 174
debt ratios, 175
debt-to-equity ratios, 174
times interest earned
ratios, 175-176
times interest, 175-176
real estate laws, 380
recessions, 70
reconciling accounts, 165-166
recoveries, 70
recruiters, 52
references, 55
referrals (sales), 289
regulations (business), 382
regulatory change, 315
reorganization, 379
reporting lines, 40
reports
expense variance, 129-131
sales variance, 127
example, 127-128
reading, 128-129
year-over-year, 129

Research and Development
(R&D), 307-308
researching markets
analysis, 260-261
buying behavior, 251
customer satisfaction, 251
demographics, 251
fielding questionnaires, 259
goals, defining, 254
needs, 252-253
presentations, 261
psychographics, 252
purpose, 251
questionnaires
development, 256-258
guidelines, 258-259
studies, creating, 253-254
study design, 254-256
types, 253
resistance
price, 239
sales, 288
resources
allocating, 92
company, 317, 320
assessing, 320-321
growth, 318-319
humans, 319
productive capacity, 320
profitability, 318
managing, 92-93
responsibility
area of responsibility, 20
defined, 20-21
managers, 5
retail sales, 87
retailers, 271
retained earnings, 154
Return On Assets (ROA), 180
Return On Investment (ROI),
181
reverse engineering, 302
risks (securities), 231
ROA (Return On Assets), 180
ROI (Return On Investment),
181

S

sales
    active selling, 288
    cold calling, 289
    commercial, 237
    consumer, 237
    contests, 295
    coverage, 292
    customer service, 35
    days sales on hand, 173
    departments, 35
    e-commerce, 339-341
    force
        alignment, 292-294
        commission plans, 294
        compensating, 294-296
        motivating, 294-296
        size, 292
        support, 296
    growth strategies, 313
    housing, 87
    income statements, 158
    increasing, 239-241
    inside, 288
    leads, 289
    manufacturing companies,
        32-33
    marketing departments, 33-34
    marketing, compared,
        236-237
    meetings, 295
    new car, 87
    order taking, 288
    outside, 288
    persuasion, 291
    presentations, 290
    problem solving, 290
    product differentiation,
        242-243
    prospecting, 289
    quotas, 295
    referrals, 289
    resistance, 288
    retail, 87
    sales departments, 35
    strategies, 364
    tactics, 238

    training, 297
    variance reports, 127
        example, 127-128
        reading, 128-129
        year-over-year, 129
sales per employee, 162
sales-channel segmentations, 251
sales-driven companies, 244
saturation, 241
SBA (Small Business
    Administration), 367
scientific management, 6
SEC (Securities and Exchange
    Commission), 221
securities
    government, 79, 229-231
    laws, 380-381
    marketable, 147
    risks/returns, 231
Securities and Exchange
    Commission (SEC), 221
segments (market), 250-251
selecting
    pricing strategies, 269
    rates, 209
selling. See sales
Selling, General, and
    Administrative Expense
    (SG&A), 159
service organizations, 32-33
severance pay, 59
sexual harassment, 386
SG&A (Selling, General, and
    Administrative Expense), 159
shares (stock), 152
sharing information (communi-
    cation), 25
sheets (balance), 143-144
    assets, 142-143, 146-150
    example, 144-146
    formula, 143
    liabilities, 142-143, 150-152
    owner equity, 142-143,
        152-154
short-term investors, 223
sites (beta), 304
skills
    employee, 346-347
    leadership, 43-49

    listening, 23
    management, 14-25
slice-of-life commercials, 278
Small Business Administration
    (SBA), 367
social change, 315
sole proprietorships, 28
solvency ratios, 174
    debt ratios, 175
    debt-to-equity ratios, 174
    times interest earned ratios,
        175-176
speaking directly (communica-
    tion), 24
stakeholders, 44
standard deviation from mean,
    121-123
standards (quality), 353-354
start-ups
    defined, 362
    financing, finding, 367
starts (housing), 87
statements
    cash flow, 163
        cash flow, 163-164
        example, 164-165
        reconciliation, 165-166
    financial. See financial state-
        ment analysis
    income, 156, 162
        cost of goods sold, 158
        depreciation expenses, 159
        example, 156-157
        expenses, 160
        extraordinary income,
            160-161
        formula, 156
        gross income, 158
        income before taxes, 161
        interest expenses, 160
        net income, 161-162
        net income per employee,
            162
        operating income, 159
        provision for income taxes,
            161
        sales, 158
        sales per employee, 162
        SG&A, 159
    pro forma, 366

statistics, 113
central tendency measures, 116-120
frequency distributions, 114-115
variability measures, 120-123
stocks. *See also* financial markets
additional paid-in capital, 153
buying, 217
common, 153
per value, 153
preferred, 153
selling, 217-218
shares of, 152
straight-line depreciation, 193
strategic initiatives, 236
strategic planning, 312
actions, identifying, 323-324
company environment
analyzing, 314
assessing, 316-317
customers/prospects, 314
economic trends, 315
regulatory/social change, 315
suppliers, 315
company goals, 312-313
company resources, 317-320
assessing, 320-321
growth, 318-319
humans, 319
productive capacity, 320
profitability, 318
competitors, monitoring, 314
employee involvement, 325
guidelines, 325-326
implementing, 324-325
needs, 326
SWOT, 322
time frames, 325
Strengths, Weaknesses, Opportunities, and Threats (SWOT), 322
structure, 8-9
studies (market-research)
analysis, 260-261
creating, 253-254
design, 254-256
goals, defining, 254

presentations, 261
questionnaires, 256-259
time-and-motion, 6
sum of years digits (depreciation), 195
supplier programs, 356
suppliers, 315, 367
support
departments, 36-37
employees, 22-23
management skill, 22-23
sales force, 296
SWOT (Strengths, Weaknesses, Opportunities, and Threats), 322

T

T-accounts, 185
tactical initiatives, 236
tactics (sales), 238
tamperproof packaging, 270
tariffs, 68
tax departments, 32
tax laws, 382
taxes, 151, 161
Taylor, Fredrick, 6
Taylorism, 6
teams, 59
advantages, 60
cross-functional, 60
disadvantages, 61
fact-finding, 60
managing, 61-62
technology, 339-341
Technology Adoption Curve, 245-246
telemarketing, 271
terminating
employees, 58-59
process, 57-59
wrongful, 56
testing products, 304
time value of money, 200, 206
time-and-motion studies, 6
time-limited goals, 16
times interest ratio, 175-176

tools
analytical, 104-108
decision making, 111-113
project management, 108
quality assurance, 356
tracking business cycles, 71
traders, 222-223
training
professionals, 53
sales, 297
treasury bills, 229
treasury bonds, 229
treasury notes, 229
trees (decision), 111-113
trust, 43-44
turnover
accounts receivable, 171-172
asset, 179-180
inventory, 173

U

UCC (Uniform Commercial Code), 381
unemployment, 85-86
unemployment-inflation trade-off, 74-75
Uniform Commercial Code (UCC), 381
unionized workers, 52

V

values
customers, 8
frequency distributions, 114
present, 200
pricing, 268
variability, measuring, 120-123
variable costs, 97-98
variance reports
expense, 129-131
sales, 127
example, 127-128
reading, 128-129
year-over-year, 129
VC (Venture Capital) firms, 367

Veblen Effect, 269
velocity (money), 77
ventures (corporate), 373-374
vision, 45-46
volume discounts, 98

W–X–Y–Z

Wal-Mart, 338
watching, economy, 89-90
websites
    DRI/WEFA, 82
    goals, 16
weighted averages, 117-118
whistle-blowing, 385
white collar crimes, 385
wholesalers, 271
wisdom, 330
workers
    productivity, 344-346
    unionized, 52
working capital, 168-169
writers options, 225
wrongful termination, 56

year-over-year variance reports,
  129
years (fiscal), 143

zero defects, 353